Routledge Revivals

THE LIFE OF
WILLIAM PITT
EARL OF CHATHAM

VOL. I.

THE LIFE OF
WILLIAM PITT

EARL OF CHATHAM

BY
BASIL WILLIAMS

IN TWO VOLUMES
VOL. I.

First published in 1913 by Longmans, Green, and Co.

This edition first published in 2018 by Routledge
2 Park Square, Milton Park, Abingdon, Oxon, OX14 4RN
and by Routledge
52 Vanderbilt Avenue, New York, NY 10017, USA

Routledge is an imprint of the Taylor & Francis Group, an informa business

© 1913 by Taylor and Francis

All rights reserved. No part of this book may be reprinted or reproduced or utilised in any form or by any electronic, mechanical, or other means, now known or hereafter invented, including photocopying and recording, or in any information storage or retrieval system, without permission in writing from the publishers.

Publisher's Note
The publisher has gone to great lengths to ensure the quality of this reprint but points out that some imperfections in the original copies may be apparent.

Disclaimer
The publisher has made every effort to trace copyright holders and welcomes correspondence from those they have been unable to contact.
A Library of Congress record exists under ISBN: 88007181

ISBN 13: 978-0-367-17545-0 (hbk)
ISBN 13: 978-0-367-17546-7 (pbk)
ISBN 13: 978-0-429-05737-3 (ebk)

THE LIFE OF
WILLIAM PITT
EARL OF CHATHAM

VOL. I.

STATUE OF WILLIAM PITT, EARL OF CHATHAM, IN CORK
By Joseph Wilton
(1766)

THE LIFE OF
WILLIAM PITT
EARL OF CHATHAM

BY

BASIL WILLIAMS

'Lord Chatham was a great, illustrious, faulty human being, whose character, like all the noblest works of human composition, should be determined by its excellences, not by its defects.'

IN TWO VOLUMES

VOL. I.

WITH PORTRAITS AND MAP

LONGMANS, GREEN, AND CO.
39 PATERNOSTER ROW, LONDON
NEW YORK, BOMBAY AND CALCUTTA
1913

[All rights reserved]

UXORI
AUXILIANTI
FILIIS
AUXILIO

PREFACE

THE Great Commoner's chief glory is not to have won an Empire, but to have united a people. He was understood and loved of Englishmen, Scotsmen, Irishmen, Americans of his day, because he had sympathy with them and called forth what was best in them for themselves and for those whom they were charged to rule. The object of this book is to give a picture of Pitt, true to life and 'captivating the people,' whom he served and loved. He has sometimes suffered in history because the people who appreciated him at his highest were inarticulate and have left the field to the surmises of courtiers, Whig magnates and gossips, whom he sought not to please. By his actions and his speeches, more truly, perhaps, than any other orator's, the mirror of his soul, he should principally be judged, if we would understand what he meant and still means for England. This I have attempted in all humility and in the spirit of Browning's traveller,

'Here and here did England help me : how can I help England ? '—
   say
Whoso turns as I, this evening, turn to God to praise and pray.

In preparing this biography I have read many books and manuscripts. In the text my references have been principally to unpublished authorities, but I have thought that it might be useful to others, anxious to pursue this or cognate subjects further, to have authorities for the speeches and a bibliography at the end of the book. I feel, however, that it is not merely from books and manuscripts that one can learn to appreciate Chatham. If this book has any merit, it is due less to them than to the example of my Father and Mother and to my good fortune in having had some experience of military and civil affairs.

The work required for the book has been lightened by many acts of kindness. To the Marquis of Lansdowne, the Earl of Egmont, Lord Lucas and Mr. Pretyman, I owe warm thanks for unrestricted permission to use their manuscripts; also to the owners of houses where Pitt lived for being allowed to roam through them. From those in charge of the London Library, the British Museum MSS. Department, the Record Office, and the Archives of the Ministère des Affaires Étrangères I have received that ungrudging help which it is the pride of those great institutions to afford to students.

To Mr. George Trevelyan I owe much for his inspiring encouragement and to Mr. Erskine Childers for his valuable suggestions. Mr. Denys Winstanley most generously read through and gave advice on the whole of the proof-sheets: it is difficult to thank him enough for the advantage I have derived from his accurate and extensive knowledge of Chatham and the period. Mrs. Hilary Jenkinson has stood by the book for over a year: for her scholarly researches and her unstinted help I am most deeply grateful.

BASIL WILLIAMS.

BANK FARM, HOLTYE, SUSSEX.
October 15, 1913.

CONTENTS

OF

THE FIRST VOLUME

CHAPTER		PAGES
I.	GOVERNOR PITT, 1653–1726	1–27
II.	PITT'S EARLY YEARS, 1708–1734	28–59
III.	PITT AND WALPOLE, 1734–1742	60–93
IV.	PITT AND CARTERET, 1742–1744	94–122
V.	PITT AND THE REBELLION, 1744–1746	123–150
VI.	PITT AS PAYMASTER	151–189
	I. IN WAR, 1746–1748	151–168
	II. IN PEACE, 1748–1754	168–189
VII.	PITT'S PRIVATE LIFE AND FRIENDSHIPS, 1735–1754	190–217
VIII.	GLOOM AND SUNSHINE, 1754	218–249
	I.	218–237
	II.	237–249
IX.	THE GREAT COMMONER, 1754–1756	250–286
X.	THE AWAKENING OF THE PEOPLE, 1756–1757	287–316

CHAPTER		PAGES
XI.	Mr. Secretary Pitt at Work, 1757 . . .	317–351
	I.	317–325
	II.	325–336
	III.	337–351
XII.	The Tide of Victory sets in, 1758 . . .	352–382
	I.	352–364
	II.	364–376
	III.	376–382
XIII.	Pitt and Choiseul, 1758–1759	383–408

ILLUSTRATIONS TO VOLUME I

PORTRAITS

STATUE OF WILLIAM PITT, EARL OF CHATHAM,
   IN CORK . . . . . . *Frontispiece*
      By *Joseph Wilton* (1766). *See vol. ii, p.* 121 *note.*

HESTER GRENVILLE, COUNTESS OF CHATHAM . *To face p.* 248
      From a painting in the possession of E. G. Pretyman, Esq.
      (*From Dr. Holland Rose's* 'William Pitt,' *by kind permission of Messrs. G. Bell & Sons, Ltd.*)

MAP AT END OF VOLUME

WESTERN AND CENTRAL EUROPE IN 1756

Note.—For Maps of

   (*a*) France and England in North America, 1756
      (with insets (i.) West Indies in 1756
           (ii.) Wolfe's Quebec Campaign)

   (*b*) India—Seven Years' War and Settlement of 1765

   (*c*) The World after Treaty of Paris in 1763 (with inset, West Indies in 1763)

                                          See Vol. II.

LIFE OF WILLIAM PITT

CHAPTER I

GOVERNOR PITT

> They well deserve to have,
> That know the strong'st and surest way to get.
> SHAKESPEARE, *Richard II*, iii, 3.

WHILE William Pitt was still a boy at Eton, it is recorded that his grandfather Thomas, the great Governor of Madras, used occasionally to fetch him over to his house at Swallowfield, and took favourable notice of the boy's capacity. In those days the old man was a gnarled and embittered person, wearied with a long life of toil, soured by the endless feuds of his quarrelsome family, and burdened with the care of his scattered properties. His portrait, which still hangs at Chevening, shows a short, thick-set, determined man, with the diamond—no doubt to his mind his greatest acquisition —shining gloriously in the hat by his side, and his left foot with the large heel, in which tradition says he carried it over to France, thrust prominently into the foreground. A mighty imperious man, unsparingly laborious in pursuit of his aims, and full of explosive energy, he was too shrewd a judge of men not to recognise the same strain in his grandson, a strain he had missed bitterly in his own sons. Melted by this sympathy of spirit, he must often have growled out to the boy stories of his own hard fights in youth, and of the stern task accomplished during his anxious years as Governor at Madras. And it must have been from him that William inherited his stern directness of vision, his love of England, and his peculiar insight into the minds of merchants and traders and sympathy with their aims, a sympathy which gained him the friendship of the Allens and Beckfords, and that great backing of City merchants who closed up round him and supported him whenever the Court or the great Whig families tried to crush him. He also, unfortunately, inherited from the old man that impatience of opposition, which often stood in his way, and that virulent form of gout, which, on one occasion at least, proved a dire calamity to himself and to the country.

Governor Pitt, the old buccaneer, is best known to history as the owner of the Pitt Diamond, which afterwards glittered in the sword of his great grandson's mighty foe. But he was remarkable for more than this. He broke the ground for the achievements of his descendants, and formed a link in their succession from the bygone Raleighs and Drakes. With all the Elizabethan sailors' audacious disregard for imposing appearances he attacked effete monopolies and helped the vigorous current of British commerce and energy to force a new channel to distant parts of the world: like Chatham and Pitt, he showed that the British adventurers who had insolently ravished an empire could hold and rule it. A sturdy adventurer was Governor Pitt, as ever set out from England, and yet with a deal of public spirit and love of country mixed with his passion for adventure. There is not one of his forbears that the great, dignified, yet fiery Earl of Chatham takes after so much as ' this desperate fellow, this roughling immoral man '; it is worth while, therefore, to know him, and through him to understand more of that lonely and mysterious grandson.

Thomas Pitt came of a Dorsetshire stock long established in the neighbourhood of Blandford, whence it had thrown out a vigorous offshoot to Hampshire. The Dorsetshire Pitts were of no special eminence in the county, but, to judge from indications in their wills and rent-rolls and in local records, for more than a century before Thomas's birth had been quietly taking their part as country gentlemen, mayors, parsons, doctors, or Government officials with profit to themselves and their fellow-citizens. Their industry helped by some judicious marriages, gradually added to their acres, and strong family feeling kept them knit together. The first member of the family of whom we find notice is Nicholas, of Blandford and Wimborne, who lived in the reign of Henry VIII. One of his grandsons, John, was a clerk of Queen Elizabeth's Exchequer; he died late in 1601, and appears to have been a man of substance, for besides legacies in money he left lands and houses at Blandford, Poole, Charleton, Preston, and Redcliff, and the Priory of Wareham. His eldest son, William, who inherited most of the property, like his father sought his fortune at Court, where he rose to be Comptroller of James I's Household, and principal officer of his Exchequer; he was knighted at Newmarket in 1618, and represented Wareham in several parliaments. But he is chiefly notable in the records of the Pitt family for buying Strathfieldsaye, in Hampshire, and settling the eldest and richest branch there. His descendants, however, still retained much property in Dorsetshire and never lost sight of their poorer Blandford cousins. George, Sir William's great-grandson, was looked up to as the head of the family by his contemporary the Governor, for whose children he acted as trustee and guardian; and George's second son, John of Encombe, was a good friend of William Pitt the elder. But though this branch added still further to their wealth by marriage, and in the eighteenth century gained the peerage of Rivers, it seems to have bred no men of marked ability after Sir William. Even financial success deserted them finally, for in Chatham's time they were compelled to sell most of their Dorsetshire property.

Thomas, a younger son of John, the clerk of the Exchequer, founded the branch with which English history is most concerned. He was left comfortably off by his father, with the property at Charleton, a house and 'shoppes' at Blandford, and £50. He confined his ambition to municipal politics. In James I's Charter of Incorporation to Blandford, dated 1606, he appears with his brother John as one of the seven 'capital burgesses,' and acted on several occasions as one of its bailiffs. His eldest son, William, became mayor of Dorchester; his second son, John, father of the Governor, took orders and became Rector of Blandford St. Mary's, of which he inherited the advowson from his father, with a stipend of £100 a year. He died in 1672, aged sixty-two, after a useful life passed, according to the monument set up many years later by the Governor, as ' a faithful shepherd of his flock, and a man worthy of respect for his integrity, his probity, and his simple faith.' Thomas Pitt, the third of the Rector's nine children by his wife Sara Jay, was born at his father's rectory, two miles outside Blandford, in 1653, the year when Cromwell was called upon to rule by the Instrument of Government.

Good sturdy citizens these early Pitts appear to have been during the century or more in which they were silently building up the fortunes and the character of the family, both in Dorsetshire and in London.[1] Characteristically English are their devotion to the public affairs suited to their station, and their solemn tenacity of family ties. English, too, the constant care shown by successive generations for parochial charities. Funds for a free school at Wareham were left by one Pitt, the alms-houses were rebuilt by another; sums of £500 were bequeathed by two of the family for charities at Blandford, and many smaller legacies by others. While these Dorsetshire Pitts had been gradually establishing a family tradition of public spirit and energy in local matters, and sharpening by constant practice their inborn practical temperament, they were also silently gathering strength for the great task of producing men, of the same strain as themselves, but with that added touch of genius needed to extend their sound principles of public life to the whole English commonwealth. For experience seems to show that genius is no mere *lusus naturæ*, but must spring from a land well tilled and cared for in previous generations; and, unless the land is exceptionally rich and prolific, the production of one genius apparently exhausts it. It is rare indeed to

---

[1] Robert, one of the Governor's cousins, attained eminence as a physician and a Fellow of the Royal Society, wrote some sensible tracts against quack medicines, and attracted Anthony Wood's favourable notice by a learned treatise on the weight of the land tortoise during and after hibernation.

find three great men of one stock succeeding one another so closely as Governor Pitt, Lord Chatham and his son. In Governor Pitt we seem to see the first riotous exuberance of a healthy but untutored growth; in Lord Chatham the glorious and ungrudging plenty of the fullest crop; and in his son still a fruitful return, but without that bounteous richness of savour that marks in men's memories the noblest years of the land's prosperity.

Thomas was only nineteen when the Rector died leaving his property in trust to his brothers William, the Mayor of Dorchester, and Robert, of Blandford, to be divided as they should determine among his children. Thomas, whose share could not have been large, determined on a life of adventure as a means of gaining a fortune. In the days of Charles II the East Indian trade offered one of the best openings for adventure and fortune-hunting. During the Commonwealth the monopoly of the East India Company, granted by charters of Elizabeth, James I and Charles I, but unsanctioned by Parliament, had been questioned by members of the trading community who were excluded from its benefits. In fact, until Cromwell granted a new charter in 1658, there had, after the rebellion began, been a general liberty of trade to the East Indies.[1] Charles II confirmed to the Company the privileges granted by Cromwell, but the taste of liberty enjoyed during the Commonwealth had whetted the private traders' appetite for a share in the rich Indian market. In spite of the reactionary fervour of loyalty during the early part of Charles II's reign, there was a growing disposition among commercial and other middle-class folk to question the King's right to grant exclusive trading privileges without the sanction of Parliament. For these reasons it became more and more the practice for private adventurers to charter ships and engage in the Indian trade, in spite of protests or even more drastic methods adopted by the Company, whose history during the reigns of the last two Stuarts is chiefly a record of their quarrels with these so-called interlopers.

[1] See Skinner's plea, which was not traversed by the Company, in the case of Skinner v. The East India Company.

In the fight between privilege and freedom of trade the odds were not so entirely on the side of the Company as may appear at first sight. They had, it is true, the advantages of an established position, of ships, factories and an organised staff of experienced agents in the East, of the King's favour, and of charters extending back for three-quarters of a century, which, though subject to some question, had never been declared illegal by any constituted authority. They had, too, the powerful support of the Privy Council and of judges such as Jeffreys, who lumped together in one condemnation ' the interlopers against the King's prerogative in this particular, and the horrid conspirators against the King's life in their last hellish conspiracy, who first appeared in Westminster Hall about the same time.' On the other hand the interlopers had the great advantage always enjoyed by freelances over more unwieldy bodies. They were difficult to reach, and had the sympathy of many Bristol and London merchants, and of many members of Parliament. Some of the East India shareholders themselves were inclined to allow greater liberty to private trade, and the Company had many local difficulties favourable to the interlopers' proceedings. The isolated positions of their Indian factories and their dependence on the goodwill of native princes were a considerable source of weakness. Surat and Bombay on the Malabar coast, Fort St. George, Masulipatam, and Vizagapatam on the Coromandel coast, Balasore, and Hugli, Kásimbázár and Patna in Bengal, and the factories at Bencoolen in Sumatra and Gombroon in the Persian Gulf, were so far apart and so much at the mercy of the native rulers that in moments of sudden danger they could not render one another much assistance. For the same reason the agents, factors and clerks of the Company were not very amenable to control from London, and their fidelity to the Company's interests depended almost entirely on their own good feeling. The scale of salaries was hardly calculated to ensure whole-hearted devotion. A writer began at £10, or even £5 a year, a factor earned £40, and an agent or president of one of the chief factories received no more than £200, with an allowance of £100 a year. To supplement these meagre salaries the Company's servants invariably engaged in private trade, and often actively assisted the interlopers competing with the Company. Even in cases of mutiny the proprietors were almost powerless against them. Thus in the early part of Charles II's reign Sir Edward Winter, a dismissed president of Fort St. George, clapped the man sent to supersede him into prison, and continued to carry on the government successfully for three years. All orders from the Company he treated as forgeries, and only submitted finally to two ships flying the King's flag on a guarantee of security for his person and property.

All these disadvantages might soon have proved fatal to the Company had they not possessed as chief guide in their councils one of the strongest and ablest commercial men in England. Sir Josiah Child, a victualler to the Navy under the Commonwealth, first became a director or 'committee' (to use the contemporary expression) of the East India Company in 1674, and thereafter with one exception was annually re-elected until his death in 1699. Thrice Governor and twice Deputy-Governor, he soon became the autocrat of the Company. By his influence at Court, once jeopardised in 1676, but recovered by a timely submission, his business capacity, his credit in the City, and his controversial vigour he overbore most men's opposition. He early recognised that merely defensive measures were unsuited to the Company's needs, and excused his aggressive policy by the observation that 'no great good was ever attained in this world without throes and convulsions.' For many years he succeeded in defeating all organised attempts by rival companies of merchants to obtain commercial privileges. He was also the private interlopers' implacable antagonist, finding a ready seconder in his brother, Sir John, the President of Surat, who marched several of them through the streets of his presidency with irons round their necks. Sir Josiah prevented many interlopers from ever leaving England—forty-eight it is said in one year alone—by means of Privy Council orders and prosecutions before Jeffreys and other amenable judges. But he was something more than a vigilant guardian of the Company's commercial interests: he looked forward to the time when the British government of India would be still more important than its trade. Under his rule a municipality was established in Madras, and a municipal rate levied for purposes of defence, since the natives 'do live easier under our government than under any government in Asia'; and he told the Council of Madras to 'establish such a Politie of civill and military power, and create and secure such a large Revenue as may bee the foundation of a large well-grounded sure English Dominion in India for all time to come'; nevertheless 'we would have you do no wrong or violence to any in amity with us. We would not wrong a worm. *Just and Stout* is the motto we hope to deserve and wear'—words which go far to explain the tribute paid to him by Thomas Pitt's grandson, Mr. Secretary Pitt, as 'not only a great mercantile writer, but fit to govern a great Empire or make a little kingdom a great one.'[1]

No man was a more determined and successful opponent of Child's attempts to preserve the monopoly of Indian trade than Thomas Pitt, son of the quiet country rector of Blandford St. Mary's. At what age he took to a life of adventure is not known; but his first recorded voyage to India was in 1674, two years after his father's death, when he was only twenty-one. He sailed either as a passenger or as a member of the crew in the *Lancaster*, one of the Company's ships. He must have started with some trading capital, for in the following year he was already established in trade at Balasore, and had become so notorious an interloper that orders came from Leadenhall Street for him to be confined and sent home by the next year's shipping. But Tom Pitt had already made powerful friends among the Company's servants in India. Edwards, chief of their Balasore factory, entertained the contumacious young interloper at his house; Matthias Vincent, their chief agent in Bengal, and Bugden, of the Hugli Council, were also his friends. So far from returning, therefore, Pitt carried on a lucrative business in alliance with some of the Company's agents. This alliance was further cemented about this time by his marriage with Vincent's and Edward's niece, Jane Innes, who belonged to an old Scottish family of that

[1] See below, vol. ii, pp. 53–4.

ilk, descended on the spindle side from a natural son of James V.[1]

Pitt was not slow in turning to account the advantage which his influential friends and connections gave him. ' 'Tis here as in all parts of the world—money begets money,' was a favourite expression of his in after life; and during his first seven years in the East, from 1674 to 1681, he fully justified his right to emphasise this maxim. Before he was twenty-five he had acquired an interest in several merchant ships and was engaged in trading concerns of some magnitude to Persia, to Achin and to the Malay Archipelago. In his business dealings he already showed signs of the arbitrary temper which characterised him as Governor of Madras and in his paternal relations. To the ' Worshipfull Matthias Vincent,' his uncle by marriage, he wrote with condescending frankness :

Sr,—I humbly beg your pardon for the freedom I take herein, which I thought better soe then doe as some endeavour to, hang men behind theire backs, butt speake faire to their faces, which are like Wolves in Sheepes Cloathing, whose ends I hope will bee irrecoverable miserable. I doubt not but in time you will finde them out. Heartily wishing you may . . . ;

and in spite of a promise, made in 1878 to the Council of Fort St. George, to be law-abiding, he was complained of in the following year as still ' huffing.'

Pitt returned to England in the *William and John* in 1681, at the very moment when specially determined efforts were being made to deprive the Company of its monopoly. Papillon, once Child's patron, was leading the party among the shareholders anxious to widen the Company's trading basis; but their efforts were frustrated by Child, and they themselves

---

[1] According to Collins's *Peerage* the Governor's wife was a daughter of James Innis, son of Adam Innis of Reid Hall in the shire of Murray in Scotland. Jane's great grandfather, Sir Robert Innis of that ilk, had married Lady Grisel Stewart, a daughter of the Earl of Murray and a granddaughter of Mary Queen of Scots' ' base-brother.'

A letter of November 1766 in the *Chatham MSS.* 46 from a James Innes settled in Jamaica, claiming kinship with Lord Chatham, gives a slightly different account of Jane's descent. The Governor's marriage seems to have taken place in India : see Yule, *Hedges's Diary*, iii, 27, 28. There is a portrait of Jane Pitt at Chevening.

driven out of the Company. The Levant Company was trying to secure a charter which would have admitted them to the Persian Gulf trade. They failed likewise. Many private adventurers were also foiled in attempts to outwit Child, but a few had better fortune. Among these was Pitt himself. He never showed fear in the course of his life, and was just the man for a daring enterprise, which promised annoyance to those opposed to him and profit to himself. Moreover, he was a sturdy Whig, all the more ready, therefore, to have his fling at privileges unsanctioned by Parliament and defended by questionable acts of prerogative. Materially he was well equipped for the adventure. Seven years in India had given him a good knowledge of Indian trade. The capital he himself could contribute must have been considerable, and he had gained the confidence of friends in the City, many of them old schoolfellows, who took a large share in his present venture.

By the beginning of 1682, less than a year after his return to England, Pitt had formed a small trading association and had collected a little fleet in the Thames. The Company, discovering its destination, succeeded in arresting some of the ships before they could cast off, and obtained a judgment against Pitt and another owner. But Pitt himself, in spite of the issue of a writ *ne exeat regnum*, escaped on February 20 on board the *Crown* (Captain Dorrell); while six other interloping ships, two at least of which belonged to his association, started about the same time. The Court of Directors then took all possible measures to forestall him in India. They wrote to their factories in Bengal, ordering his arrest, and 'when you have got him into your custody be sure to secure him, he being a desperate fellow and one that we fear will not stick at doing any mischief that lies in his power'; a warning was also sent to Fort St. George against this 'fellow of a haughty, huffying, daring temper.' Instructions were sent to the Company's fleet to make all haste away and arrive in the Bay of Bengal before him. But Pitt's ship was well chosen for speed, and not only outstripped the fleet, but also the ships conveying William Hedges, the new agent for Bengal, which had left

T. PITT'S SECOND VENTURE, 1682

the Downs a month before him. The *Crown* actually sighted Hedges's ship about three months out, but soon showed her a clean pair of heels, and dropped anchor at Balasore on July 6, 1682, just eleven days before her. Pitt did not waste those eleven days. He landed in state with guards and trumpets, gave out that the old Company was in a very low condition, and declared himself the agent of a new company. He hired a great house, brought several chests of treasure ashore, and at once began trading with the local merchants. He also raised an armed body of Portuguese and half-castes so formidable of aspect that, when Hedges arrived, he was forced to pay customs on goods landed in the Company's own factory. At Hugli it was just the same. Pitt arrived with three ships, 'lands in great state with four or five files of soldiers in red coats, well armed, and great attendance of Native Soldiers, with Trumpeters, and takes up his quarters with the Dutch, by the name of the New Company's Agent, bespattering the old Company.' With the help of his uncle Vincent, who had been dismissed the Company's service, he established a factory, and, after obtaining the necessary permit from the local nabob, carried on a thriving trade with the natives. Interlopers such as he had a great advantage over the Company in being willing to pay ready money for their goods; and, unhampered by scruples about creating precedents, they were lavish in their bribes to the Indian governors and officials. Thus, when Hedges had obtained an order for the arrest of Pitt and his associate by Bulchund, the native governor of Hugli, they 'compounded with Bulchund for a good sum of money and 5 per cent. paid by them for all their goods; with other great presents; though these men are so shameless as to deny it!' Seven months after landing at Balasore Pitt had finished his business and, after once more defying Hedges in an armed ship, sailed for England, where he arrived in June 1683. The Company immediately instituted an action for damages against him for 'crimes perpetrated in the Bay.' His wealth at this time may be inferred from his ability to give £40,000 security for his appearance in answer to the claim. The suit dragged on for three years, and resulted in a fine of £1,000 on Pitt. But in 1687 he persuaded the Company to rest content with a payment of £400. This was a cheap price for the seven months' trading, since the Company found that such interlopers, though they 'come to the Bay but for a short time and as it were by stealth, yet they bring home more in proportion of those new desireable goods by far than our ships.'

For some years after 1683 Thomas apparently remained in England, still keeping up his connection with the Indian trade.[1] He lived with some splendour in a house rented at £120, where he kept open table for his friends and relations and his growing family of children, and had a coach and horses and a due number of servants. He also bought for £1,500 from Lord Salisbury the Manor of Stratford-under-the-Castle, which carried with it the borough of Old Sarum. Though his Whig leanings were not to his advantage during James II's reign, they made him a person of some consequence at the sudden Revolution of 1688. The East India Company, under Child's influence, had so completely identified itself with James II, who was a shareholder, that his abdication threatened to leave it defenceless. But Child took early steps to gain friends at the new Court. It can hardly be mere coincidence that on November 23, 1688, less than a month after William's landing at Torbay, Thomas Pitt, the Whig and interloper, 'was admitted into the freedom of this Company gratis.' The reduction of his fine in the previous year indicated that some approaches had already been made to him by the Company, but it is unlikely that the reconciliation would have been so complete unless they had been anxious to secure for their interest so dangerous a member of the ruling party. Pitt was elected a member of the Convention Parliament for Old Sarum, but being unseated on petition, came in for Salisbury at a by-election in May 1689, and was re-elected there for William and Mary's first Parliament. He acted on a committee to consider the numerous cases of complaint against the East India Company, but was still chiefly occupied with commercial undertakings. He took shares in a scheme to render the Avon navigable

---

[1] This appears from Customs records in the Treasury and E. I. Co.'s books.

from Christchurch to Salisbury, no doubt with a view to securing a convenient wharf almost at his back door for loading ships engaged in his ventures. In partnership with eight other London merchants he fitted out the *Arcana* galley as a privateer in the French War at a cost of £8,000, and with a crew of 160.[1] He was also one of the founders of a company of merchant-adventurers trading to the north-west of America, established in 1691. Hitherto the Hudson Bay Company had enjoyed the monopoly of the fur and fish trade in Northern Canada under Charles II's charter of 1670. It is characteristic of the interloper Pitt to have helped on a project for trenching upon their privileged preserves. His company was granted the sole right of trading, fishing and mining over Labrador, the Davis and Frobisher Straits and Baffin's Bay, with permission to catch whale and sturgeon, and fit out men-of-war, also to buy land and raise joint-stock in consideration of occasional payments to the Manor of Greenwich of three elks and three black beavers. This North-West Company, as it was called, gave considerable trouble to the Hudson Bay Company, and was in rivalry with it until 1820, when the two united.

Elk-hunting and fishing for sturgeon in the snow-bound lands of North America offered little attraction to Pitt personally, whereas the East, with its promise of easily acquired wealth, still called to him. He resolved, therefore, in spite of his respectable position at home, and though actually a member of the East India Company, to venture on one more interloping expedition. He started in March 1693, with two ships, the *Edward*, armed with forty-four guns and commanded by Captain Gifford, and the *Seymore*, and took with him £60,000 in silver for purposes of trade. The Company, failing to obtain an Order in Council to stop him, wrote to their Bengal factory to warn them against Pitt's schemes. But Pitt and his associates ' who huff and bounce and give out Mountaines on their one side,' had all their old success, gaining over native

[1] This privateer was so large that the Admiralty agreed to send her out under the King's commission, while leaving to Pitt and his friends all prizes she might capture.

rulers and former friends in the Company's service, notably the trading chaplain Evans, who afterwards became Bishop of Bangor. At last the directors, moved partly by the outcry raised at their detention of the *Redbridge*, belonging to another interloper, and by their unpopularity in Parliament, announced early in January that they had come to terms with Pitt's partners at home, and directed that his stock was to be treated as their own, 'and that we hope is the end of all our long quarrels and contentions.' And so it proved, in spite of the fact that 'Captain Pitts to the last made a great bouncing and have carried himself very haughtily ever since his arrivall in these parts, and has not scrupled to speak very Disrespectfully and uncivilly of your Honours.'

On his return to England in 1695 he found that the Parliament of 1690 had been dissolved, and in the new House of Commons, which was much more Whig in colour than its predecessor, he appeared as member for his own borough of Old Sarum. His old adversaries of Leadenhall Street were now in great straits: although William III had renewed their charter in 1693, the House of Commons had resolved in January 1694 that 'all the subjects of England have equal right to trade to the East Indies unless prohibited by Act of Parliament,' and a rival Dowgate Association had sprung up; above all, Montague, First Lord of the Treasury and Chancellor of the Exchequer, was against them. The question was no longer one of stopping interlopers, but of maintaining their own existence. Concessions at home they felt to be indispensable; but they also had the wisdom to see that all was not lost if they could maintain and strengthen their position in India by appointing a representative at once above the temptation of truckling to their rivals for a share in the profits and masterful enough to inspire respect and exact obedience from subordinates. Pitt fulfilled all these requirements. That he had been an interloper and knew all the secrets of the trade, and that he was a Whig member of Parliament who might have done them considerable damage in the forthcoming struggle, were but additional reasons in his favour. Accordingly, on November 24, 1697, he was chosen President of the Company's settlements on the Coromandel coast, in Orissa, Gingee, and the Mahratta countries, and on the coast of Sumatra, and Commander-in-chief of Fort St. George and Fort St. David. Extraordinary powers of discipline over his own Council and the other servants of the Company were granted to him. 'For the defeating of interlopers,' the Court observed with some humour to their representative in Bengal, 'we think our President's advice may be helpful to you, he having engaged to Us to signalise himself therein.' That there was considerable opposition to his appointment is hardly surprising. The shareholders turned out eighteen of the directors responsible for it, and old Sir Josiah Child deplored, from his retirement at Wanstead, ' the sending of that roughling immoral man . . . which everybody knows I was always against.' Pitt himself made no bones about accepting the appointment. He was but forty years old, still in the prime of life, energy and high spirits. He had many interests in India which the Court could hardly expect him to neglect, since they offered him a salary of only £300 a year and specially sanctioned his eldest son Robert accompanying him as a free merchant. Moreover, the impending conflict between the old Company and the new, in which each would have to prove its capacity to hold the privileges entrusted to it, was one most likely to appeal to his quarrelsome and dictatorial nature.

Madras, where Pitt landed as President, or Governor, on July 7, 1698, was not the Madras of to-day. Fort St. George, the European quarter, was an oblong of 400 yards by 100, containing only twelve streets and alleys and 129 dwelling-houses, bringing in a yearly rental of under £60. On the whole Coromandel coast Pitt had under him only 119 Englishmen and 50 Englishwomen all told; the natives and half-castes were more numerous, but did not exceed 300,000 within the limits of the Presidency. Life at the fort was patriarchal. The President and all the Company's servants dined together at a common mess, off Pitt's service of silver plate, which he had sold to the Company for £765; and on Sunday mornings the Council would meet and accompany their chief to church. The President exercised a stern discipline over the morals and manners of his subordinates, but had cause to complain to the directors that 'here is an Imbibed Notion in some who ought to know better that noe Servant of yours Ought to have Corporall punishment, which has been the Ruine of many a Youth in this place.'

During his eleven years of office Pitt had to meet attacks from English and native adversaries, which called forth all his vigour. Shortly after his arrival, William III, empowered by an Act of 1698, gave a charter to the new 'English Company trading in the East Indies,' authorising them to establish their business in India and terminating the old Company's powers in 1701. The new Company forthwith sent out an ambassador accredited to the Great Mogul, and three Presidents armed with consular authority to Hugli, Surat, and Masulipatam. The three Presidents were all former servants of the old Company, and two of them—Sir Edward Littleton and John Pitt—had once been in association with Governor Pitt. John, the Governor's own cousin, was destined for Masulipatam, and became his chief adversary in the fight between the two Companies. He took up a false position at the outset, refusing to salute the Union Jack when he touched at Madras, and following this up by insolence to the Governor. Thomas paid him back with interest in his own coin.

> The fable of the froggs Suits your present temper [he wrote], and the Morall and reflexion I hope will make much impression on you soe as to prevent your having the fate of the froggs. I recommend to you allsoe the reading and practising the fables of the Lion and the Mouse and the Wolf and the Stork . . . If you passe by here you must behave your self very Civilly, noe Drums, fflags nor trumpets within our bounds, for here shall be but one Governor whilst I am here ; . . . I think I have now answer'd all your riff raff Stuff, which I hope will be as tiresome to you to read as 'tis to me to write.'

In the end John contented himself with strong language, which only brought him reproaches from his own directors. Not so Thomas. He forbade his subordinates to recognise or have any dealings with the new Company's officials ; and when he inadvertently sold a couple of his own horses to John he reflected with some satisfaction that he had obtained double their value, 'both being old and founder'd.' He hindered the new Company's trade, and threatened that if they touched 'a ship belonging to this Presidency we will certainly fit out a briske privateer to make reprisall.' Within the orbit of the Governor's influence the new Company was reduced to impotence. His cousin John died in 1703 and was curtly dismissed by Thomas as 'the ungratefullest wretch that ever was born. He is dead and there's an end.' In Bengal Sir Edward Littleton found his match in the local servants of the old Company, supported by Pitt from Madras, who told him that 'those whose ffronts are cased with Corinthian brass will stick at nothing.' Before John Pitt's death the victory had been won. In April 1702 the new Company agreed to union on terms favourable to the old Company. The defeat of the younger association's project of entirely superseding their rivals was undoubtedly a benefit to the English in India, for their own inexperience and their agents' folly were hampering trade and setting the natives against the English nation at a moment when the outbreak of war with France and Spain made it peculiarly necessary for all Anglo-Indians to show a united front under a strong government. The satisfactory union was largely the result of Thomas Pitt's vigorous defence of his masters' interest; and they had the grace to recognise this with unusual warmth. Not only the old Court, so a friend writes to him, 'were very hearty to your interest,' but 'most of the new spoke with great respect of you, soe by this I see you are safe with both sides.' His appointment was confirmed by the joint board, and Pitt thanked the new Company's directors in these dignified terms :

Whereas my gratitude as an Englishman obliges me to pay all Defference to the Blessed Memory of King William, So allso on this occasion I can't butt remember that great Saying of his to the French King's Plenipotentiarys att Ryswick upon concluding the Peace, which furnishes mee with apt words for this address to You.

'Twas my Fate and nott my choice that made mee Your Enemy,' and since You and my Masters are united, Itt shall bee my utmost Endeavours to purchase Your Good Opinion and deserve your Friendship.

Pitt also adopted a new tone towards the natives. ' When the Europeans first settled in India,' he wrote in one of his reports, ' they were mightily admired by the natives, believing that they were as innocent as themselves ; but since,' he added, ' by their example they are grown crafty and cautious . . . the more obliging your management the more jealous they are of you.' When he came to India, he found the Company regarded as a convenient milch cow by the natives. In 1690 the Great Mogul, Aurungzebe, had attacked several of the factories and imposed ignominious terms of peace upon them ; provincial nabobs likewise, and a whole chain of subordinate officials, besides wandering Mahratta raiders, used to exact toll on their trade. Pitt tried a less obliging management with the natives, and in his dealings with them showed signs of the same pride, untiring energy and stern consciousness of power so notable in his grandson. To a presuming local nabob he writes :

I received your impertinent and insolent letter. We all know your King to be great, wise and just . . . but most of his little Governors, amongst whom I reckon you, to be very corrupt and unjust. We would have you to know we are of a nation whose sovereign is great and powerful, able to protect his subjects in their just rights over all the world, and revenge whatever injustices shall be done them, of which there will be speedy instances given. I am not a little surprised at your saucy expressions, as well as actions in imprisoning my inhabitants, when you know that I can fetch you hither and correct you for both. This is an answer to your letter.

His chief adversary was Dúád Khan, Nabob of the Carnatic and the Gingee country, who in 1702, on Pitt's refusal to offer him the presents he expected, marched with an army to attack Madras. On this menace the Governor answered him firmly, ' We can put no other construction on this than declaring a war with all Europe nations, and accordingly we shall act.' The outlying factories of Fort St. David, Vizagapatam and Masulipatam were warned of the danger and their inhabitants ordered, if necessary, to retire on Madras. The neighbouring Danish, French, and Dutch factories were invited to send assistance, an invitation to which only the Danes, whom Pitt had previously helped, responded. The Fort St. George officials were encouraged to raise a troop of horse by allowances for horse-keep. Vigorous sorties were made to protect the Company's cloth-workers and convoys. The siege lasted four months, until Pitt bought off Dúád Khan by an offer of 20,000 rupees, a sum, as he shrewdly observes, 'which, considering the very long time they have been here, will be no inducement for him to come again, or any of his successors hereafter'; and even this amount was not to be paid until the damage to friendly villages and to the Company's trade had been made good. The Governor celebrated peace by a feast to all the troops in the fort, but abated none of his precautions. With that practical turn, which appears again in his grandson's arrangements for distant expeditions, he ordered a supply of 300 hogs, ready killed and salted, to be always on hand to prevent the recurrence of a scarcity of food, and was thus fully prepared, when war was declared against France and Spain, to give a good account of himself against any hostile fleet. Dúád Khan reappeared in 1705, and obtained nothing more from Pitt than cases of cordial waters and Pegu oranges, which he returned as fit only for children. When Aurungzebe died in 1707, Pitt from the outset gave his support to Shah Alam, who by killing all his rivals made good his claim to the empire. By this foresight Pitt obtained for the Company several desirable villages and valuable trading privileges, and greatly enhanced its influence.

During the intervals of peace he devoted himself energetically to developing the Company's resources. He had their possessions surveyed, and an exact plan drawn up of Madras and Fort St. George.[1] He encouraged the settlement of native painters and clothworkers, increased the revenue of the town, and farmed the taxes on betel-nuts, arrack and tobacco on advantageous terms. He even tried to raise silkworms, but the heat of Madras killed his mulberry trees. Like his grandson, he was an enthusiastic gardener. 'My leisure time,' he writes in 1703, 'I generally spend in gardening and planting and making such improvements which I hope will tend to the Company's advantage and

[1] This plan is reproduced in *Vestiges of Old Madras*, by H. D. Love.

the good of the whole place for that in a little time I hope the place will be able to subsist of itself without much dependence from the country for that in the late long siege we were not a little pinched for provisions.' He wound up the affairs of the new Company, left in great confusion by John Pitt, and helped the Bencoolen factory out of difficulties of their own making. He promoted an Anglican mission for half-castes and natives, but when the Roman Catholic bishop and his priests attempted to set up their authority against his, he took 'occasion to make those Churchmen know that they are under an English Government.' The native tax-collectors all over the country he found very insolent, 'only those within our reach I keep in pretty good order, by now and then giving 'em a pretty good banging.'[1] Even his manifold activities for the Company's interest did not absorb all his energy. His estates in England, the education of his children and the unsatisfactory conduct of his wife gave material for a vigorous correspondence. He also took endless trouble for his friends, collecting their debts and watching over the interests of their sons and relatives sent out to India to be under his protection. When the sons did well, he gladdened the fathers' hearts by his good reports, and even when one of them married—a grievous crime in his eyes after his own experience—he relented when he found the wife 'a vertuous, modest, good humour'd, comely young woman, and I don't doubt, but will make him a good Wife, since he was resolv'd to marry in these parts; for she justly deserves the character I give her.' A vast private trade also absorbed much of his energy. To forward this, directly he arrived in Madras he dispatched his eldest son, Robert, on the principle that 'a man's youth is the only time to drudge in busyness,' on an expedition of more than two years to China. Latterly, however, he confined his attention principally to diamonds, as the most portable and convenient form of merchandise. In the course of this business he came into possession of the famous Pitt Diamond, which gave him trouble and annoyance for fifteen years. After three months' haggling with Jamchund,

[1] It is recorded in the consultation book that the Governor himself 'twice or thrice thrashed' some native harbour official for neglecting his work.

the merchant who brought it from Golconda, he finally obtained it in March 1702 for £25,000—a quarter of the sum originally asked. It weighed 410 carats in the rough and 135 when cut as a brilliant.[1] In October 1702 he sent his son home in charge of the diamond with instructions to have it cut and sold ; and for the remaining seven years before his own return sent letters by every mail pestering him and the two or three friends in the secret with minute directions about ' the great concerne,' and violent upbraiding of their slackness in finding a purchaser at the price he expected. ' I will not part with it,' he told them, ' under £1500 a Carrat, which I am sure is as cheap as Neck-beef, and let any Potentate buy it, the next day 'tis worth a million of pounds sterling.'

Unfortunately Pitt's habit of ' banging ' grew with age and the nervous irritability caused by attacks of the family gout. Never of a placid disposition, he at times became outrageous. He mismanaged a serious dispute in the native quarters between the Right- and Left-hand castes and quarrelled with most of his council, putting one member in irons and threatening to whip and hang another. He himself became anxious to go home, and in September 1709 was recalled by the directors. But no disgrace was cast upon him, as upon some former governors after their discharge.

---

[1] Pope's lines are well known :
     ' Asleep and naked as an Indian lay,
     An *honest* factor stole a gem away :
     He pledged it to the knight ; the knight had wit,
     So kept the diamond, and the rogue was hit.'
—the last line of which originally ran :
     ' So robbed the robber and was rich as P——.'

The Governor, however, effectually disposed of the malevolent rumours current in England and India as to his method of obtaining the diamond, in a letter dated from Bergen in the year 1710 (*Hedges's Diary*, iii, 137). Many traditions were current at the time about the diamond. One was that it was stolen from the eye of the god Jagrenat at Chandernagor ; another that it was found near Golconda by a slave who concealed it in a gash in his leg, and that this slave was murdered by an English skipper, who sold the diamond to Jamchund for £1000. At Swallowfield (bought by the Governor on his return to England) there was recently a legend that ' a black man ' walked in Queen Anne's gallery still in search of the diamond, and Wilkie Collins derived his idea for *The Moonstone* from the stories he heard there. (See Lady Russell's *Swallowfield and its Owners*).

On the contrary, orders were sent that he should receive the 'Great Cabbin' on one of the Company's homeward-bound ships, and be treated with respect 'suitable to the character you have borne in our Service.' The respect of the directors for their old Governor increased with their experience of his successors' feebleness. Less than two years after his return to England two English officers were captured by a local rajah and ransomed at a cost of 200 pagodas; 'had the like case happen'd in the late President's time,' wrote the directors, 'he would have recover'd them both at a tenth part of the Money, or rather the Rajah would not have dared to attempt the Surprising of them.' Pitt himself thus summed up the results of his work in a letter to his son:

I delivered it [Madras] up in the most flourishing state that ever any place of the world was in, vastly rich notwithstanding our great losses, and famous throughout all those parts of the world for our honourable and just dealings; free from all manner of tyranny, extortion, oppression, or corruption as to mee (I wish I could averr the same of others), which I suppressed as far as it was in my power, and prevented its being very burthensome to the commonalty. I shall give but few instances here of the flourishing condition of Maderass. In May or June last there was at one time fifty sayle of ships in the roade, besides small craft at least 200; the revenues of last year amounting between 70 and 800,000! pagodas of which above 10,000 arises out of the Mint. The place, when I left it, was not onely admired but in favour of all the kings and princes in those parts; a regular and peaceable government within ourselves and continued friendship of all about us. I brought the trade of the King of Siam to our port . . . and the favours from the present Great Mogull are without a president. . . . And wee of all Europeans were the only favourites; the Dutch at the same time were put out of Golcunda.

When Pitt landed in England late in 1710 after more than a year's leisurely travelling by the Cape of Good Hope, and thence by a neutral ship round to the 'melancholy place of Bergen,' he was nearing sixty, and might well have earned a rest. But rest was the last thing he cared for, and he had become too great a personage to escape the attentions of politicians. The world of London was ringing with the achievements of the 'Great Pits' in Madras and with rumours of his 'dyomont . . . as big as a great egg.'¹ On his way from Bergen to England he was tracked out at Amsterdam by the banker Drummond, an agent of Harley, who was just forming his ministry. Drummond reports to Harley: 'I think I have made him yours, and have drunk your health heartily with him. He will have a powerful purse in England and be a thorn in the side of some great men now at the head of the Bank and the India Company if they should thwart you,' and advises that he should be brought into the House for Cornwall.² However, Pitt preferred the independence of Old Sarum, which he represented in the Parliament opened on November 25, 1710; and, whatever language he may have held under the genial influence of Dutch liquors, he remained firm to his Whig convictions, and expressed much indignation at his son Robert's lapse into Toryism. 'It is said,' he complained, 'you are taken up with factious caballs, and are contriving amongst you to put a French kickshaw upon the throne againe, for no true English heart as the present Queen has (and pursues no other interest than that of her own nation) can please your party. If I find or hear of any child of mine that herds with any to oppose her present Majesty's interest, I will renounce him for ever.'

Although he took no prominent part in the debates of the House, he never concealed his disapproval of the Tory ministry. In 1714 he opposed the expulsion of Steele for writing a Whig pamphlet, and spoke several times against the Treaty of Utrecht, once moving that 'an humble Address be presented to her Majesty that her present Ministry shou'd be sent to France to be his Ministry for three years.' On the accession of the Hanover dynasty he was received in audience by George I, in whom he tried to find a purchaser for his diamond, and secured a clerkship of the Green Cloth to the Prince of Wales for Robert. But he was more in his element when real danger threatened from the Pretender's invasion. He offered to appear with any number of horsemen that

---

[1] *Wentworth Papers* (Cartwright), p. 75.
[2] *Hist. MSS. Com.*, XV, iv (Portland), p. 594.

might be required and to equip and arm a company of foot at Blandford within ten days. He exulted that his second son Thomas was out with his regiment of horse, carrying as its motto *Amor regis et patriæ tantum valet*, and indulged in characteristically ferocious language about the rebels. But for this energy he had to pay : a few days later, for the first time probably in his life, he admits that ' desire of ease and retirement comes on with age, and it is as much as I can compass to write what is necessary for me.'

This, however, was but a passing feeling of lassitude. In the following year he accepted the governorship of Jamaica, an island troubled with a peculiarly unruly assembly, and before starting set himself with characteristic energy to master the subjects of dispute in the island and report on them; but at the last moment he threw up the appointment. The diamond, ' that great concern of Mine,' had at length found a purchaser. It had been hawked round to most of the rulers of Europe, before it was bought by the Regent of France in 1717 for the sum of £133,000. In the previous December he had told Robert that he was starting again on his travels in his sixty-fourth year to retrieve the losses due to his son's wasteful management of the estates and to the sums bestowed on his other children, amounting altogether to £90,000, while the capital of over £30,000 expended on the purchase and cutting of the diamond had for fifteen years brought him no return. But this windfall enabled him to realise his ambition to acquire ' such a competency . . . soe as that I should have been able to establish a family as considerable as any of the name except our kinsman,' George Pitt of Strathfieldsaye.

In his interloping days he had already acquired the Stratford-under-the-Castle estate, and on his return from India he bought several manors in his native county, including the Down House near Blandford and the parish where he was born. After the sale of the diamond he bought the Mohun estates, which included Boconnoc, then the finest house in Cornwall, for £53,000 from the widow of the Lord Mohun, killed in a duel by the Duke of Hamilton. From the Earl of Clarendon in 1719 he bought Swallowfield Place, near

Reading, which became his favourite abode; and in London he rented a house in Pall Mall to which was attached a close or field of forty-five acres. He was also fairly successful in establishing his family. His eldest son Robert married a granddaughter of the fourth Viscount Grandison, a member of the great Villiers family; Thomas married the heiress of the Earl of Londonderry and was himself raised to that title; the third surviving son married a daughter of Lord Fauconberg. Essex, the elder daughter, married a Cholmondeley, and her sister Lucy, whose gentleness is still a tradition at Chevening, Earl Stanhope, the soldier and statesman.

But all his property and his family's successful marriages brought the old Governor little peace. The furious energy, which in his younger days had found vent in his Indian adventures, under the influence of gout and a less active life was turned into an almost insane violence. He had always been a severe critic of his own family, had parted with his wife owing to some scandal connected with a 'scoundrell rascally villain,' and had consistently treated his eldest son as little better than a fool. He became 'extraordinary humorsome and testy' with his children and grandchildren, whom he alternately petted and chased out of the house. It was no joy for them to be living under his tyrannical eye: they could not, for example, go to the 'mascarade' without leave, for 'the keys were . . . carryed to the old gentleman's bedside at ten o'clock every night,' and they were constantly liable to outrageous abuse and insults from his ungovernable temper. Though very suspicious in money matters, and always on the look-out for robbery by his servants and agents, he was a bad husband of his wealth: he lost heavily by speculation at the time of the South Sea Bubble, and at his death his property was found to be worth much less than was expected. His sons were no comfort to him—Robert was weak and taken up with the 'hellish acquaintaince' of Tories; Thomas was little better than a scoundrel; and John, he declared, was good for nothing. In his old age this grandfather of Chatham and great-grandfather of Pitt is a pathetic figure. Throughout his long life he was a wild man; his hand against every man and every man's hand against him. At the end he became a tyrant, and terribly alone, as all tyrants must needs be. The habit of arbitrary command, fostered in him by his continual fights for wealth and superiority, is an evil pedagogue for character; and for this Governor Pitt suffered and made others to suffer. But, pathetic and savage as he was in his loneliness, he had accomplished much for his country and his family. Not the least memorable of the old man's traits was his affection for his grandson William, a lad of eighteen when Thomas died in 1726.

'He is a hopefull lad, and doubt not but he will answer yours and all his friends' expectations,' was the expression of his penetrating judgment. In William were reproduced that impetuous force of language, that directness of utterance, and that rich abundance in the English tongue, which are always apparent in the grandfather's letters. The Governor also kept before himself high ideals of conduct, even when his roughness and impetuous temper led him furthest astray from their dictates. Chatham's noble indignation at oppression and folly sometimes finds a parallel in the more untutored and ferocious expressions of the Governor's wrath against evil-doers. Mingled, too, with the violent diatribes to Chatham's father occur such passages as these—which seem to indicate one source of our great statesman's high purpose in public and private life :

Remember that wee are not borne only for ourselves, nor has God Almighty bestowed this plentifull fortune on me to give it only amongst my own children, but also necessitous relations and friends which I will not fail to doe for His glory and my own comfort and happiness. . . . If ever you intend to be great, you must be first good, and that will bring with it a lasting greatness, and without it, it will be but a bubble blown away with the least blast.

I would have your brothers get some insight into military affairs, not knowing what revolutions they may have to see, for I believe that trade will flourish rather than decay. Do you also follow the good advice I give you. Give good example to your family by your life and conversation ; avoid lending money or being surety for others ; be cautious what company you keep, and do not misspend your time. . . . If you are in Parliament, show yourself on all occasions a good Englishman, and a faithful servant to your country. If you aspire to fame in the House, you must make yourself master of its precedents and orders. Avoid faction and never enter the House prepossessed; but attend diligently to the debate, and vote according to your conscience and not for any sinister end whatever. I had rather see any child of mine want than have him get his bread by voting in the House of Commons.

Note.—The first writer to identify the interloper Thomas Pitt with Governor Pitt of Madras was Colonel Henry Yule, R.E., in his edition of *The Diary of William Hedges* (3 vols. 1887-9). This and other authorities for this chapter are referred to in Appendix B.

CHAPTER II

PITT'S EARLY YEARS

οὐκ . . . ἑορτὴν ἄλλο τι ἡγοῦνται ἢ τὸ τὰ δέοντα πρᾶξαι.—THUC. I, 70.[1]

WILLIAM, the fourth child of Robert and Harriet Pitt, was born at Golden Square in the parish of St. James's, Westminster, about eight o'clock on the morning of Monday, November 15, 1708. His birth was impetuous, like most of his life. Robert, in announcing it to the Governor on the same day, says that his wife intended to have written to him, but was suddenly prevented by the unexpected arrival of this son. He was christened in the parish church of St. James's, Piccadilly, where the entry in the register runs: '1708 December 13. William, of Robert Pitts, Esq., and Henrietta, born November 15; baptized.' His godfathers were George Pitt of Strathfieldsaye and his grandmother Grandison's second husband, General William Stewart, after whom he was named.

Through his grandfather, the Governor, Pitt was of English yeoman stock and belonged by right of conquest to the newly rising class of great City merchants. He was not, however, as Glover described him in after years, 'without the parade of birth.' On his mother's side he was of the great families of Villiers and Fitzgerald. His grandmother, Katharine Fitzgerald of Dromana, Lady of the Decies, handed down to him the hot rebellious blood of her Irish race. Married as a mere child by the Archbishop of Canterbury to her cousin of seven, son of the Earl of Tyrone, she soon repudiated this marriage, and three years later, in defiance of civil and spiritual authority,

---

[1] 'They look on duty as their only holiday.'

made a runaway match with the man of her choice, Brigadier Edward Villiers, son of Viscount Grandison. He was a dauntless soldier but, according to tradition, a man of wild and cruel humours, who had died fifteen years before Pitt's birth. His widow, created Viscountess Grandison in her own right, had married again and had many years yet to live, a notable woman in London. Though intensely proud of her own and her husband's families, she had a fellow-feeling with the masterful old adventurer, whose son had won her daughter's love. He also had respect for her and allowed himself sometimes to be softened by her pleadings for her extravagant son-in-law. The qualities and sympathies inherited by Pitt from his grandfather were none the worse for being tempered with old Lady Grandison's pride of race: and English, Scottish and Irish strains were happily blended in the first great statesman to recognise the claims of Scotland and Ireland to share equally in the liberties and responsibilities of Englishmen.[1]

William Pitt caught none of his fire and mastery from his father. Robert went through life oppressed by the Governor's dictatorial character and had no success either in business or as a politician. In 1715 he was employed by his brother-in-law, Lord Stanhope, to persuade the Duke of Ormond to leave the country to avoid impeachment[2]; but beyond that little is heard of him as a public character. The few letters of his extant give the impression that he had inherited all his father's querulousness without any of his vigour; he certainly inherited and transmitted to his children his father's gout. His persistent Toryism, which was original, was probably due more to social than to political considerations. For he was a handsome man, and popular in good society, where his marriage with Lady Harriet Villiers gave him an assured position. This marriage was his most fortunate venture. Pitt's mother was declared to be 'as beautiful, as sensible and as well-behaved as most I have seen in my life' by one of the Governor's cross-grained correspondents; and another

---

[1] For Lady Grandison's history and her correspondence with Governor Pitt see T. Muir Mackenzie, *Dromana*.
[2] *Egmont MSS.*, vol. 80, *sub* August 27, 1733.

could not make up his mind 'whether her beauty, understanding or good humour be the most captivating.' The report of her beauty and wisdom is confirmed by her portrait, and even the Governor, averse as he had been to the marriage, was won over by her charm and good sense.

Most of Pitt's early childhood was spent at Mawarden Court, given to his parents by the Governor in the year of his birth. Mawarden Court—*Parva sed Apta Domino*, says the inscription on the portal—is a substantially built house, now inhabited by the rector of Stratford-under-the-Castle; it lies a few yards back from the road to Salisbury, and faces towards the little church. Within a stone's throw of the nursery windows rose the grassy mounds and circles of Old Sarum, with their mysterious legends of buried treasure and fairy folk. Behind the house, at the end of the long garden, flowed sedately the river Avon. It was a quiet English spot, full of

> . . . the silence and the calm
> Of mute insensate things,

with a sweet and soothing influence for a nature fiery as Pitt's. Here he had a troop of brothers and sisters, all much of an age with himself, for happy play in grassy places. His eldest sister, Harriet, was four years older than he, Thomas and Catherine were separated from him by two or three years only, and within four years of his birth came two more sisters, Elizabeth and Ann. Every week their grandfather's dominant personality was obtruded on them by the pompous inscription, 'Thos. Pitt Esq. Benefactor,' in big letters right across the tower of the parish church, which he built in 1711; and occasionally the 'infantry,' as he called them, paid him a visit in Pall Mall, but not often, for he believed that 'all children are best under the eye of their parents.' Even before he went to school, young William must have been torn between the conflicting claims of Revolution Principles and the Jacobite Succession, for in 1715, when the children were staying with their grandfather, he and Robert had a violent explosion about the latter's 'cursed Tory principles,' and neither of them were men to hide their differences. There, too, he must

CHILDHOOD

have gained an unfortunate impression of family life, for the house in Pall Mall was used as a meeting-place by his brawling uncles and aunts to fight out their quarrels among themselves and with the Governor.

At the early age of ten or eleven [1] William was sent to Eton in company with his brother Thomas, no doubt on the advice of the Governor, who had sent his youngest son, John, there ten years before. At that time Eton shared with Westminster the almost exclusive privilege of educating those sons of peers and men of family who were not taught at home by private tutors. It was a school of politics, all the better for not being confined to one party. Dr. Godolphin, Provost of Eton from 1695 to 1732 and a munificent benefactor, was uncle of the powerful Whig minister, and in his own person well maintained the College's aristocratic dignity and connections. Eton also owed much to the energy of Andrew Snape, head master from 1711 to 1720, who by the time he left had brought the numbers up to the unprecedented figure of 399. He was a Tory and High Churchman, and his zeal for the school did not blunt his ardour as an ecclesiastical controversialist. But he loved and was beloved by his boys, and, in parting from them in 1720 to become Provost of King's, ' made a most affectionate speech to the scholars which drew tears from their eyes.' His successor, Henry Bland, head master during the greater part of Pitt's Eton career, was of the opposite school in religion and politics, but displayed the same unscholarly zeal in extraneous controversy. He was a great friend of Sir Robert Walpole, whom he brought to his house to meet the Dutch adventurer, Ripperda, exiled from Spain, and whose administration he supported by Whig pamphlets. The education then given at Eton was very much what it remained in Gladstone's days exactly a century later—severely classical from the lowest form, where only Latin grammar was taught, to the sixth, where only Latin and Greek authors were studied in school hours.

[1] The exact year is not known. He was certainly there in 1719, when he was eleven, since an Eton bill to his account is preserved for that year (Maxwell-Lyte, *History of Eton College*, p. 274). In Austen Leigh's *Eton College Lists* 1678–1790 two Pitts occur in 1718—one in ' Lower Greek,' the other in the ' First Form.' These were probably Robert Pitt's sons Thomas and William.

Spelling, mathematics, and geography were relegated to half-holidays, when they were taught by inferior masters. Nevertheless the intellectual discipline was thorough; and after allowance is made for the difference of fashions in teaching, the ideal of Eton education seems to have been then very much what it still remains—to give a minimum of sound groundwork and leave plenty of scope for the development of a boy's genius during his leisure hours and under his tutor's direction. As Gladstone said of his own day, a boy might learn nothing at Eton, but he could not learn anything inaccurately.

> While some on earnest Business bent;
> Their murmuring labours ply,

as Gray sang in his stately verse; others, to quote Walpole's no less enthusiastic prose, had full liberty to take a course of 'Jawing and Blackguard' from 'My Lord the Bargeman' or to loaf at 'The Christopher' and the coffee-houses.

At an early age William Pitt showed promise of ability. His uncle, Lord Stanhope, who died before he was thirteen, was impressed by his spirit and used to call him 'the young marshal,' and his school-fellows looked up to him and his contemporary Lyttelton as prodigies of genius. Starting in the lowest form but one, he followed the normal course of gaining a remove almost every half-year until he reached the sixth; in that respect he was a great contrast to his brother Thomas, who began four forms above him. In a letter to their father of February 1722-23 the two boys' tutor, Burchett, after lamenting Thomas's loss of time by negligence, especially in the study of Greek, and expressing a somewhat chastened hope of his ability to profit by a university course, concludes with this very different verdict on William:

> Your younger son has made a great progress since his coming hither, indeed I never was concerned with a young gentleman of so good abilities, and at the same time of so good a disposition, and there is no question to be made but he will answer all your hopes.

To the same year belongs the earliest extant letter of

William himself, interesting as a confirmation of Burchett's high opinion of his industry and capacity. It is docketed by his father 'From my son William, Sept. 29th, received Octr. 10th, 1728,' and runs as follows:

Eaton, September the 29th.

Hon^{ed} Sir,

I write this to pay my duty to you, and to lett you know that I am well. I hope you and my mama have found a great benefit from the Bath, and it would be a great satisfaction to me to hear how you do; I was in hopes of an answer to my last letter, to have heard how you both did, and how I should direct my letters to you; for not knowing how to direct my letters has hindered me writing to you, my time has been pretty much taken up this three weaks, in my trying for to gett into the fiveth form, and I am now removed into it; pray my duty to mama and service to my uncle and aunt Stuart if now att the Bath. I am with great respect;

Hon^{ed} Sir,
Your most dutiful son,
W. PITT.[1]

To Eton Pitt owed his first connection with many of those with whom he had lifelong dealings. At one period there were said to be four grandsons of Governor Pitt together at Eton—William and his brother Thomas, the young Lord Stanhope, and the fourth probably a son of Lord Londonderry. When he went to the school in 1718 he found there two of Sir Robert Walpole's sons and the two Foxes (afterwards Lord Ilchester and Lord Holland), a Hanbury, better known by his later name of Sir Charles Hanbury Williams, one of the St. Johns, and three sons of Lord Townshend, all Oppidans like himself. Henry Fielding, George Lyttelton, Wyndham, Richard Grenville (afterwards Lord Temple), and his brother George, Sir Francis Dashwood, a future president of the Hell-Fire Club and Chancellor of the Exchequer, and Pratt (who became Lord Camden and Lord Chancellor) were later contemporaries. Henry Fielding, George Lyttelton, Hanbury and Pratt are said to have been Pitt's special friends at Eton, and three of them remained so long afterwards.

Pitt left Eton in the middle of 1726. He kept no tender

---

[1] This and Burchett's letter are quoted by Maxwell-Lyte, *loc. cit.*

memories of the place in after life. None of his own three sons was sent there; they were all educated by a tutor under their father's eye. The reason of his antipathy to the school was given in later years to Lord Shelburne: 'that he scarcely observed a boy who was not cowed for life at Eton; that a public school might suit a boy of turbulent disposition but would not do where there was any gentleness.' This hatred of Eton may be partly accounted for by the tradition that even there he began to suffer from the family gout, which would prevent him from joining in school games and adventures. This alone would make him lonely and unpopular with the other boys. Moreover, though it is obviously untrue that he himself was cowed for life, he had a rare claim to speak for those of a gentle nature, for none was tenderer than his own. How tender appears from the extraordinary devotion he aroused among his early friends, from unguarded words of his sister Ann, from his perfect marriage, and from his own and his children's mutual love. Yet in later days, to those who knew him but slightly, he appeared a composition of unapproachable pride, affectation and parade; and no doubt natural pride and a tendency to cloak his dearest feelings and adopt an attitude of haughty reserve were encouraged by the rebuffs he endured at Eton. As Thomas Arnold said, 'The more we are destitute of opportunities for indulging our feelings, as is the case when we live in uncongenial society, the more we are apt to crisp and harden our outward manner to save our real feelings from exposure.'[1] Nevertheless, in spite of Pitt's own regrets, Eton gave him such a training in the classics as he would hardly have obtained elsewhere; it taught him method and industry, fostered his gift for politics and oratory, and, though it may have left him an unhappier man than he would otherwise have been, it did not injure the deep tenderness of his nature, which, for all his love of pomp and circumstance, left him to the end a more human person than his son.

About the time he left Eton Pitt was suddenly thrown almost entirely on his own resources by the early loss of most

[1] Stanley's *Life* (6th ed. 1846), p. 274.

of those to whom he would expect to look for loving counsel and guidance. In the two years 1726 and 1727, before he was nineteen, five deaths in his family occurred in rapid succession. First, in January 1726, came that of his grandmother, Viscountess Grandison, from whom, besides his love of the Irish, Pitt doubtless inherited his love of parade. The funeral was characteristic. Having married a Villiers she was entitled to rest in the great Duke of Buckingham's vault in Westminster Abbey, and thither her body was borne with all imaginable pomp after lying in state for three days in the back parlour hung with rusty velvet. Her coffin was covered with crimson velvet edged with gold lace; four dukes acted as pall-bearers, assisted by eight earls, all cloaked; sixteen mourning coaches and seventeen noblemen's and gentlemen's coaches, with a footman to every coach door and eight branches to every coach, besides forty men on horseback, each with a branch, came in the procession, which was duly marshalled by the heralds. Five months later came the death of her second husband, General Stewart, a sensible, kindly man, who had often been a good friend to Robert Pitt and his family when relations with the Governor were strained. But the greatest loss to William was the death of his grandfather, the Governor, on April 28 of the same year. The boy's visits with some of his ' comrogues ' to Swallowfield must have been welcome, if sometimes terrifying, alleviations of school trials. For the old man evidently loved this grandson, who had no one else of such ripe and varied experience to advise him, and no one of all his kindred with so much insight into his character and sympathy with his ideas. In the following January his other grandmother, the Governor's widow, also died. On the death of the grandfather the family dissensions burst out afresh. William's father, Robert, quarrelled with his brothers as to the division of the property and began an angry correspondence with his eldest son about his allowance. Then on May 20, 1727, shortly after William had gone to Oxford, Robert also died suddenly. William's mother, who died in Paris in October 1736, seems thereupon to have devoted herself almost exclusively to her youngest daughter, Mary, and came very little more into his life.

Before his father's death a suggestion had been made by some of his relations that Pitt should take Orders and settle down to the family living of Abbot's Anne. Fortunately nothing came of this idea, but in January 1727 he had been entered as a gentleman-commoner at Trinity College, Oxford.[1] Among his predecessors at the College were his uncle, Lord Stanhope, and the great Revolution lawyer, Lord Somers—as Pitt was reminded thirty years later in the dirge on the death of George II, addressed to him by Thomas Warton, fellow of Trinity and Poet Laureate. The poet begged him not to refuse

> This humble present of no partial Muse
> From that calm bower which nurs'd thy thoughtful youth
> In the pure precepts of Athenian truth;
> Where first the form of British Liberty
> Beam'd in full radiance on thy musing eye;
> That form whose mien sublime, with equal awe,
> In the same shade unblemish'd Somers saw.

Oxford in the early eighteenth century was hardly the place to choose for musing on the form of Liberty. At no time was our ancient University more stagnant and illiberal. Almost the only vestige of an idea left there was the obstinate Toryism of men like Hearne and Dr. King, and even their Toryism had perforce to content itself with such mild acts of insubordination as the setting of a penitential psalm in cathedral on George I's birthday or describing him in their private diaries as 'the Duke of Brunswick, commonly called King George.' The state of learning was lamentable, according to the uncontested testimony of such diverse men as Bishop Burnet in 1714, Amhurst (*Terræ Filius*) in 1720, Whitefield in 1732, Adam Smith in 1740, and Gibbon in 1754. But even in the degraded Oxford of those days there was some good stirring. At Christ Church, where Pitt's solemn and respectable friend George Lyttelton had

---

[1] His name appears on the Admission Register of Trinity College under date of January 10, 1726–7, with the following description in his own hand: ' Ego Guglielmus Pitt Filius Rob^{ti} Pitt armi: de Old Sarum in comitatu Wilts, natus Lond^{ini} in Par: Sancti Jacobi, annorum circiter octodecim admissus sum primi ordinis commensalis sub tutamine mag^{ri} Stockwell, J^{anrii} decimo die anno Domini 1726/7.' Some of Stockwell's letters to Robert Pitt about William's fees and rooms are quoted by Lord Rosebery.

preceded him by a year, the two Wesleys had already begun their life-work by taking spiritual and material consolation to the poor and the prisoners in Oxford, much to the scandal of the dons, who disliked any such exhibition of enthusiasm. They were even awakening religious feeling among a small band of undergraduates, whom, as we learn from Whitefield, they were taking to the weekly Sacrament at St. Mary's, the only place in High Church Oxford where it could then be received more than once a term. Samuel Johnson, also, who came up a year after Pitt, records that his thoughts were first turned seriously to religion at Oxford. Another Pembroke man, Richard Graves, afterwards Lady Chatham's chaplain, tells us that about this time there were four sets at the University— the sober little party of students who read Greek and drank water; the jolly west-country lads who drank ale, smoked tobacco, punned and sang catches; the gentleman-commoners, 'bucks of the first head,' who drank port wine and arrack and concluded with claret, a set appropriate to one of Pitt's Oxford contemporaries and future colleagues, Robert Henley, who is said to have laid the seeds of his gout by his excessive drinking at the University; and lastly 'the flying squadron of plain, sensible, matter-of-fact men, confined to no club, but associating occasionally with each party. They anxiously enquired after the news of the day and the politics of the time.'

Pitt, as a gentleman-commoner, was entitled to associate with the set of 'bucks of the first head,' and had the privilege of dining at high table and, if he chose, of taking wine with the Fellows and listening to their scandal and Tory politics. He is much more likely, however, to have attached himself to the flying squadron of anxious inquirers, both from taste, and because his means would hardly have permitted constant libations of port wine, arrack and claret. His university dues and other necessary expenses amounted to about £50 a term, which left him little to spare from his allowance of some £200 a year from his father. His health also inclined him to a studious life, for at Oxford, as at Eton, the gout tormented him—a calamity which, according to Lord Chesterfield, proved a blessing in disguise, since 'he employed the leisure which that tedious and painful distemper either procured or allowed him in acquiring a great fund of premature and useful knowledge,' while ' his constitution refused him the usual pleasures, and his genius forbade him the idle dissipations, of youth.'

Chesterfield's assertion about Pitt's studious habits is borne out by the comparatively large proportion accounted for in the term's expenses by his fees to tutors and his bookseller's bill.[1] His fidelity to his classical studies is attested by a Latin poem on the death of George I, sent up for the prize offered by the University during his first year. The hexameters of which it is composed do credit to Pitt's knowledge of the classical Pantheon and his familiarity with the Mantuan bard's language and sonorous rhythm, but they show no trace of genius. Still there is a touch of originality in his suggestion that

> Vel Berecynthia Mater
> Centum enixa Deos !

might envy the new King George II and his Queen Carolina their 'inclyta progenies,' and some precocious acumen in the courtly phrase hinting at the new King's dependence on his consort's judgment ; while it is characteristic that even in those early days he should have picked out ' Libertas atque Alma Themis ' from so many possible gods as ' præsentia numina Angliacæ gentis '—a belief which remained till the end the basis of his political system. Pitt did not win the prize, but was beaten by William Murray, a young B.A. of Christ Church, with whom this was not destined to be his last encounter.

Oxford appears not to have impressed Pitt more favourably than Eton. After a year's residence he was compelled by his persistent gout to leave without taking his degree, carrying away as his chief recollection of the University a deep conviction of its inveterate Toryism. Both his nephew, whose education he directed, and his son William were sent to Cambridge. In the following year he went to Utrecht, where he probably

---

[1] The account is quoted by Lord Rosebery (p. 37). It includes £5 to the bookseller, £4 4s. for courses in French and experimental philosophy, while the washing bill amounts to only £2 2s.

acquired the knowledge he afterwards displayed of Grotius and other writers on international law and diplomacy. How long he studied at Utrecht is not known; he was certainly there during the first quarter of 1728, in company with his cousin Lord Villiers and Lord Buchan and two other Erskines.[1]

Pitt had received help from his brother Thomas for his expenses at Utrecht,[2] and during the first year or two after his return to England lived chiefly at one of the family houses at Boconnoc, Blandford or Swallowfield. His personal income was very small. His grandfather had left him only £100 a year; his father had bequeathed to him and to each of his sisters a dividend on the estate amounting, perhaps, to another £100 a year, to be supplemented on their mother's death by a further share of his landed estate. The bulk both of the Governor's and Robert's properties in Cornwall, Dorsetshire, Hampshire and Berkshire went to Pitt's elder brother Thomas, who soon dissipated his fortune.[3] William Pitt was thus in the unfortunate position of a man brought up in circumstances of considerable wealth and lavish expenditure and then left with comparatively straitened means. But the way to advancement was opened by eager friends, whose admiration for him disposed them to do all they could to forward his plans. Lyttelton, above all, whose serious bent of mind, real scholarship, and turn for commonplace verse gave him a considerable reputation among the young men of wit and fashion in the political world, was enthusiastic in proclaiming his friend's capacity. In some trifling verses on Good Humour, composed at Eton, he noted that

> This magic power can make e'en folly please,
> This to Pitt's genius adds a brighter grace
> And sweetens every charm in Coelia's face.

[1] See the letters quoted by Lord Rosebery (pp. 40-6).
[2] *Ibid.* p. 42.
[3] The Governor's and Robert's wills are to be found in the Probate Registry at Somerset House (Plymouth, 88, and Farrant, 146). The abstract of the Governor's will in Yule, *Hedges*, iii, is not quite accurate in every particular: e.g. it is wrong in saying that the Governor left William Pitt £200 a year. Under the Governor's will William Pitt had certain reversionary claims on the estate which were never realised, as his elder brother's issue did not fail.

When Pitt was only twenty the bonds between the two had been drawn closer by the marriage of Christian, Lyttelton's eldest sister, to Pitt's brother, Thomas, on which Lyttelton writes to his father :

I heartily congratulate you upon my sister's marriage and wish you may dispose of all your children as much to your satisfaction and their own. Would to God Mr. P. had a fortune equal to his brother so that he might make a present of it to my pretty little M. ! but unhappily they have neither of them any portion but an uncommon share of merit which the world will not think them much the richer for.

George Lyttelton was instrumental in bringing Pitt to the notice of his uncle, Lord Cobham, whose family had a lasting influence on Pitt's career. Sir Richard Temple, created Lord Cobham at George I's coronation, with remainder to his sister Hester Grenville, had distinguished himself in the Queen's wars, notably when in command of the expedition which captured Vigo, and had all the coarse, roystering bluffness of the hardened old campaigners of that time. In addition to his real merits as a soldier he had political ambition and pretensions to literary and artistic taste. He patronised Congreve and Gay and was a friend of Pope's. In the grounds of his country seat of Stowe in Buckinghamshire he initiated the practice of building monuments to his dead friends, and temples to abstract virtues, pursued with so much zeal by his successor Lord Temple. He loved to think of himself as the patron of youthful merit, and to act as mentor to his clever nephews, the Grenvilles and Lyttelton, who, with their connection, Pitt, soon became known as the Cobham Cousinhood or Cobham's Cubs. Shelburne used to say of him that Cobham passed his time in clapping young men on the back, and in telling stories at table which nobody else would tell in private. At this time he was Governor of Jersey (an island which he is not known to have visited), and Colonel of the King's Own Regiment of Horse, then commonly known as Cobham's Horse, and after 1747 by its present title of 1st Dragoon Guards.

From an early age Pitt had a bent towards the profession

of arms; and the army seemed to offer the best field for his youthful energy. Moreover, it so happened that a commission in the regiment of his patron, Lord Cobham, provided an avenue to Court favour and was no obstacle to the political ambition he also cherished. At the age of twenty-two, therefore, he accepted a commission, dated February 9, 1730-1, as cornet in Cobham's Horse. The £1,000, being the cost of the commission according to the official scale, was probably waived in his case by Lord Cobham, since he could hardly have afforded it.

The regiment shared with the Life Guards the duty of providing travelling escorts for the royal family and was occasionally called upon to repress civil disturbance.[1] During his five years of service Pitt was quartered at Northampton, Newbury and Towcester. His pay was small, amounting to eight shillings a day, of which six shillings was devoted to the maintenance of two horses and a servant. On the other hand the duties were not exacting. From his letters to his sister it appears that the recognised method of passing the time for young officers of his station was in drinking bouts, lasting sixteen hours, or in flirtations with Dolly at the inn, 'who, young at the bar, is just learning to score.' When nominally quartered at Towcester he lived most of the time with his friends at Stowe, some ten miles distant, and he was even able to spend nearly a year away from his regiment in foreign travel. But, although little was expected from a cornet in Cobham's Horse beyond keeping up an agreeable appearance and waiting to get drunk until one o'clock in the afternoon—the hour after which, as Macaulay observes, court-martials were not allowed to continue—from the first Pitt took his military duties seriously and, like Wolfe, set himself, so he afterwards told Lord Shelburne, to read every military book on which he could lay his hands. The number of such books of any value was then not very great. There were of course many dissertations on the military art of the Greeks and Romans, and dry technical books, such as Turner's 'Pallas

---

[1] See *Historical Records of 1st D. G.*, 1836. Lord Rosebery quotes several of Pitt's letters preserved at Dropmore about his military career.

Armata or Military Instructions,' which were more concerned with the structure of an army and the mysteries of gabions, fascines, and counterscarps than with practical lessons of tactics and strategy. The numerous chronicles of William III's and Marlborough's campaigns, such as D'Auvergne's 'Relations' and Brodrick's 'Compleat History,' were more enlightening. Brodrick's work, published in 1713, must have been familiar to Pitt from his childhood, since both his father and grandfather subscribed for it and in return had the family arms engraved on one of the maps, where they are still to be seen. Two volumes of military memoirs by the foreign soldiers Montecucculi and Feuquières were on a higher plane. From Montecucculi, who was a general in the imperial service against Gustavur Adolphus and the Turks, Pitt possibly gained his first notions of the value in war of sudden raids and diversions, and of the use to which sea-power can be put; from Feuquières, one of Louis XIV's generals, whose book was long esteemed among the best on military art, he would learn to take account of the moral and political considerations which must weigh with a statesman directing hostilities. He also studied Vauban, and probably had useful hints in his reading from his own lieutenant-colonel, Bland, who afterwards published a 'Treatise on Military Discipline.'[1]

But books, even the best, are of slight value compared with the practical teaching of those who have actually borne a part in war; Pitt was fortunate in his opportunities for getting such teaching. In 1730 the countryside of England

[1] Wolfe, in a letter of July 18, 1756 (Beckles Wilson, *Wolfe*, p. 295), gives a list of the books which he recommends for a young officer. A great many of them were no doubt familiar to Pitt, and some were in his library. In 1773, for example, his son mentions that he found a treatise of Vauban's among his father's old books.—(*Lansd. Ho. MSS.*, P. 27; October 1773). Wolfe's list is: Turpin's *Essai sur l'art de la guerre*; K. *of Prussia's Regulations for his Horse and Foot*; *Memoirs of Marquis de Santa Cruz*; Feuquières; Montecucculi; Folard's *Commentaries upon Polybius*; *Projet de Tactique*; *L'Attaque et la Défense des Places* (by Vauban); *Memoires de Coulon*; *L'Ingénieur de Campagne*; *Le Sieur Renie on Artillery*: *Of the ancients*:—Vegetius, Cæsar, Thucydides, Xenophon, Polybius: *Of later days*:—Davila, Guicciardini, Strada, Sully's *Memoirs*: *Lives of* Gustavus Adolphus, Charles XII, Zisca the Bohemian, Scanderberg: *L'Art de la Guerre Pratique*; *Traité de la Petite Guerre*; Puységur; *Life of Suetonius*; Bland's *Treatise on Military Discipline* (1743).

was still full of the old soldiers who had fought under the Great Duke or even under the Great Deliverer; and Sterne's 'Tristram Shandy,' published thirty years later, shows how long-lived was the fascination of the camp stories and military jargon in which Uncle Toby and Corporal Trim luxuriated. The wars in the Netherlands and in Flanders were then something more than a glorious tradition—they were a personal and a living memory to half the population. On all sides Pitt would have heard every siege and battle of these wars fought over anew by veterans who had triumphed at Blenheim or lain before Lisle, and countless suggestions from them for mending our strategy and improving our victories. Such common talk would have given him the atmosphere of the camps and of war; from his own relations and friends would have come an insight into the considerations that move a great commander in the field or in council; from the Governor he would have gained some notion of the difficulties of Indian wars; and from Lord Stanhope, Lord Cobham, and above all from their friend Lord Peterborough, so apt a pupil would have caught the secret of the commander's flashing eye and lightning vision. At one time he had many talks with Lord Tyrawley who 'attended the Great Duke as his aid-de-camp at the battle of Malplaquet, when he gained the victory in his postchaise,'[1] and he was even admitted to the confidence of Marlborough's widow, the grim old Duchess Sarah, who was a friend of his grandmother Grandison and loved the young man for his spirit and his devotion to England.

His studies and his duties as cornet of horse left him ample leisure to gain the firm footing in that social and political world necessary for the development of his genius. In 1733 his military training was interrupted by a tour in France and Switzerland which lasted from May to the end of the year. After spending a few days in Paris and obtaining letters of introduction from the ambassador, Lord Waldegrave, he stayed at Besançon till August; thence he went through Marseilles, Montpelier, and Lyons to Geneva. From Geneva he travelled along the Rhine to Strasbourg and to Lunéville

[1] *Chatham MSS.* 64 (Lord Tyrawley to Chatham).

in Lorraine, where, following the example of his brother and his friend George Lyttelton a few years earlier, he spent the winter. Such a tour was usual with young men of family in the eighteenth century, and there was good reason for it in the case of those who intended to take a part in politics or cultivated society. Travelling was then so tedious and expensive that a young man's one Grand Tour often had to suffice for his life and afforded him his only chance of understanding anything of Continental conditions, manners and points of view. In the words of Mr. Nugent, the ingenious author of a guide to the Grand Tour through the Netherlands, Germany, Italy and France, this was a custom 'visibly tending to enrich the mind with knowledge, to rectify the judgement, to remove the prejudices of education, to compose the outward manners, and, in a word, to form the complete gentleman'; or, to quote George Lyttelton's experience,

> By foreign arts domestic faults to mend,
> Enlarge my notions and my views extend;
> The useful science of the world to know
> Which books can never teach, or pedants show.

One of Pitt's objects in travelling was evidently to improve his French, for most of his letters from abroad to his sister Ann are written in that language; and he succeeded so well that in later life a French ambassador declared that he spoke the language perfectly.[1] These letters to Ann give little information about his occupations except that at Besançon he fell in love with a French lady of whom all he tells is that 'quoique son cœur fût certainement neuf, son esprit ne l'etoit point . . . sa taille etoit grande et des plus parfaites, son air simple avec quelque chose de noble . . . suffit que vous sachiez que ce fut de ces beautés d'un grand effet, et que sa physionomie prononcât quelque chose des qualités d'une âme admirable'; but ' elle n'a point de titre ni de grand nom qui impose ; et c'est là le diable.' The affair cannot have been very serious, for even at the first pang of parting he says 'je n'en ai pas tout à travers le cœur, mais toutefois j'en ai';

[1] Guerchy to Choiseul, November 21, 1766, *Aff. Etr. Angl. Corr. Pol.* 471, f. 352.

and three months later he could write quite heart-free: 'c'etoit de ces flammes passagères, un eclair qui a passé si vîte qu'il n'en reste pas le moindre vestige.' The visit to Lyons is memorable for the use he made of it twenty years later, when he compared the meeting of the Rhone and Saône, which he saw below the town, to the alliance of Fox and Newcastle— 'the one a gentle, feeble, languid stream, and though feeble of no great depth, the other a boisterous and impetuous torrent.'[1]

During the later part of his sojourn abroad he had a good chance of studying French military methods and diplomacy, for on October 10 the war of the Polish Succession was declared; French troops were hurried into Italy, and Lunéville itself was destined by the peace of Vienna, which concluded the war, to fall into the hands of Stanislaus of Poland and, after his death, into the possession of France.

When Pitt returned from abroad, early in 1734, the political world was divided into two distinct camps, so opposed to one another that even social intercourse between them was almost impossible. On the one side was the Court of George II and Queen Caroline, of which the annals and the scandals are to be found at full length in the Memoirs of their Vice-Chamberlain, Lord Hervey. The great strength of this camp was that it represented the established government of the realm, and had on its side all the valuable patronage and most of the territorial influence of the great Whig landowners. Its mainstay in Parliament was the cunning and experienced old statesman at the head of the government, Sir Robert Walpole, who then bore the weight of office almost alone, for he had gradually lost or discarded all the men of ability who had once been his colleagues. Carteret, the most brilliant and ungovernable minister of the century, had been superseded in 1724; Pulteney, able and ambitious, but unstable, had left the ministry in the same year; Townshend, Walpole's loyal and capable brother-in-law, had been driven to resign in 1730 because Walpole feared that his mastery of foreign affairs might change the firm's name

[1] See below, pp. 270-1.

from 'Walpole and Townshend' to 'Townshend and Walpole.'
To replace these the minister had gathered to his cabinet men
of second-rate ability, who neither supported him efficiently
nor served him with that devotion which was the least that
might have been expected from their mediocrity. The secretaries of state were William Stanhope, Lord Harrington—a
cousin of Pitt's uncle, Lord Stanhope—a brave soldier and
a successful diplomatist, but as a minister 'absolutely nothing
—nobody's friend, nobody's foe, of use to nobody and of
prejudice to nobody,' and the Duke of Newcastle, whose
want of political sagacity was patent, but whose unrivalled
power of organising favourable elections made him of service
to the ministry he supported. Besides these were ill-natured
nonentities such as Lord Wilmington and the Duke of Dorset,
the Duke of Grafton—a vainglorious Lord Chamberlain, 'the
natural cloud of whose understanding, thickened by the
artificial cloud of his mistaken Court policy, made his meaning
always as unintelligible as his conversation was unentertaining,'
and the brilliant Vice-Chamberlain, who raised more difficulties
by his biting tongue than he allayed by his controversial
gifts, his political acumen, and his loyalty to Sir Robert. But
though Walpole found little support in his colleagues, in
the King and Queen he had allies who for many years enabled
him to snap his fingers at all the talents of the opposition.
Of the two, Queen Caroline was the master spirit. Fond of
power from a consciousness of her own capacity to exercise
it, she cared nothing for its show, and governed her husband
by an apparent submission to his authority. The old King
George I, who was shrewder than his son, recognising this
quality in her, used to speak of her as 'cette diablesse Madame
la Princesse.' With a woman's wit and sympathetic understanding she appreciated the conversation of men cleverer
than herself, especially divines of unorthodox tendencies.
Unfortunately for her husband and for Walpole, she died in
1737 of a cruel illness heroically endured. George II himself
had considerably greater merits as a king than are generally
credited to him. Like all the monarchs of his race, except
his eldest great-grandson, he had a strong sense of public

duty and, to a limited degree, a just idea of where that duty lay. He had proved his personal bravery in the War of the Spanish Succession and was to prove it again at the expense of his discretion at Dettingen; and he resembled all the other princes of his house in combining some discernment of his officers' military qualities with an exaggerated and meticulous attention to the uniforms and trappings of his soldiers. He had no subtlety of perception and no statesmanlike views, but he had a considerable share of that blunt common sense on which his adopted subjects pride themselves. He also possessed to the full that quality of dogged obstinacy, often degenerating into narrow prejudice, which is not alien to the English character and which in his case proved to have a serious influence on Pitt's career. To his obstinacy he added a choleric but not malevolent temper, characteristic of such short, strutting, self-satisfied men. He had little love for England or the English, and much preferred his native Hanover, with his obsequious little court at Herrenhausen, where every inch of his kingship was flattered and magnified. In his habits he was regular, in his expenses parsimonious, and in his pleasures no less dull and unromantic, if more discriminating than his father. At his levées he never shone in conversation and was rarely gracious; more often he cast a gloom on his courtiers by sulking over some tremendous trifle.

Few courts, indeed, have been more tedious and uninspiring than his. Even Lord Hervey's wit and the Queen's sprightly flow of talk could not dissipate the gloom which, after their death within six years of each other, must have been almost intolerable. This dreariness also had its pathetic side, especially during the last years of Walpole's ministry, when the Prince of Wales was in open rebellion against his parents, and the ablest men had fled to his camp, leaving the Court a solitude. Even the most respectable tastes of the King and Queen were turned to ridicule. Because they admired Handel the wits would only applaud Handel's rival Buononcini, and the royal pair were left to sit freezing in an empty opera house, whence my Lord Chesterfield once hastily withdrew, fearing to intrude upon their majesties' privacy. But for all his dulness George II did a good turn to the English nation in maintaining a standard of stolid solidity, vastly more effective against the designs of discontented Jacobites than would have been more brilliant gifts.

Pitt, as an officer in a favoured regiment, and from his family connections, could no doubt easily have acquired royal favour and political success through the dismal avenue of the Court. His father's service as Clerk of the Green Cloth would have made his name familiar to George II; the Stanhopes were his kin; his maternal uncle, Lord Grandison, had been raised to an earldom on account, says the Peerage, ' of his personal merits and noble descent '; and the only extant letters of his mother, asking for a lordship of the bedchamber for her brother, show that she was a person of some account in the circle of Queen Caroline when Princess of Wales. His sister Ann, who inherited her parents' good looks, and shared with William the legacy of passionate vigour, masterfulness, and a somewhat dour and disconcerting wit beqeathed to his family by the Governor, cast in her lot with the Court by accepting in the year 1733 the post of maid-of-honour to the Queen. Pitt, who was travelling abroad at the time, approved and sent her some sage advice, still in French, on the conduct she should hold in the slippery ways of a court. Difficulties he admitted there were, but for those one loves, he added, what better could be wished than that they should be forced to rely on their own prudence and good sense to deliver them from such perils; moreover, he characteristically refused to take the traditional view of the unrelieved evils of a court. This appointment no doubt helped Pitt to keep in touch with the ruling powers, for Ann was his favourite sister, and at this period their relations were particularly tender. Pitt's letters between 1730 and 1735 to his ' dearest Nanny ' are, save for a few written to his wife, the only intimate letters of his that have been preserved. ' Oh for the restless tongue of dear little Jug! ' he writes when bored with the dulness of country quarters, and he confides to her his hopes and troubles, rallies her on her admirers, and shows the tenderest brotherly feeling when she is in doubt or distress. To write to her he resists ' the gentle Impertinencies, the sportly solicitations, of two girls not quite despicable' who are 'thundering at the door' of George Lyttelton's room, into which he has locked himself, 'as if Heaven and Earth would come together.'[1] Ann seems to have followed his sage directions as to conduct at Court, for she is praised in some contemporary verses for her careful and circumspect behaviour:

> By Honour, Reason, and by Suffolk led.

These verses also allude to the deep affection she felt for her brother, concluding with the prophecy:

> Long shall he live and every Hour improve
> His fame and merit, our Esteem and Love,
> Live in the Senate or the Field to stand
> Firm and unshaken for his native land,
> Live to admit a Rival in your Heart
> To yield a Husband ev'n the warmer Part,
> To see the Wife and Mother's happier Fame
> Compleat whate'er adorns your Virgin Name.[2]

But in spite of some temptations to join the Court party Pitt chose the rougher path of Opposition. It was the natural course for a young man of spirit when he found that all the best brains of the country were on that side; and, as Lady Louisa Stuart observed, 'Opposition . . . is almost always a much more sociable body than the partisans of Government. The part of attacking raises people's spirits, gives them the spring of a vigorous courser on rising ground, makes them all hope and animation.' The Opposition centred round Frederick Prince of Wales, who ever since his belated arrival in England in 1729 had been discovering fresh causes of disaffection to his royal parents, not the least being the small allowance made to him by his father. Being supported in his complaints by the leading

---

[1] See Rosebery, p. 63. Chatham's daughter Harriot was writing under similar distractions fifty years later to her brother. 'You must not expect,' she writes in June 1783, ' a very correct performance from me at this moment, for the gentlemen are making such a noise in the next room and laughing so heartily that I really hardly know what I write.'

[2] The verses occur in B. M. Add. MSS. 22629. They must have been written in 1734, since in August of that year Lady Suffolk retired from Court. Pitt was not elected to Parliament until 1735.

Ann never yielded to a husband the warmer part.

members of the Opposition he gradually identified himself with all their measures. He found a grievance in his sister's marrying before himself in 1738, especially as he was not allowed to marry his lively cousin Wilhelmina of Prussia, with whom, though he had never seen her, he was madly in love. In revenge he encouraged his household to vote against Walpole's Excise Bill, and on all occasions showed distinctions to Lords Cobham, Stair and Chesterfield, some of its most violent opponents. But though able to inflict cruel wounds on his parents by his favour to the Opposition, the Prince personally gave little strength to his own side. He was weak and ill-educated, susceptible to the grossest flattery and quite unfit to deal with affairs of State.

The real organizer of the Opposition was Bolingbroke. In all English history there is hardly a figure more pathetic than that of Henry St. John, Viscount Bolingbroke, the clinging charm of whose name seems exactly fitted to his wonderful genius. Exuberant in all the outpourings of his nature, he had scandalised the town in King William's reign by his extravagant and dissolute life, as he had captured the imagination of his countrymen under Queen Anne by the brilliancy of his intellect, by his speeches—one of which Chatham's son would rather have recovered than the best compositions of antiquity—and by the audacity of his political career. When Pitt first came under his influence the blight of twenty years' exile and disgrace had settled upon him. Though he never seems to have become soured by misfortune or quite to have lost his buoyancy of nature, this leader once petted by Fortune and courted by his fellows was now reduced to courting those younger or inferior in attainments to himself. The spring of Bolingbroke's activity at this time was personal hatred of Walpole, to whom he owed the bitterness of a favour in his recall from exile and the lasting injury of exclusion from political life in Parliament. But, though personal in its origin and often factious in its manifestations, Bolingbroke's hatred was in the main turned to national ends.

While it is difficult to exaggerate Walpole's service to the country as an economist and in accustoming the people to a stable and quiet government, his system had a grave political defect in fostering the belief, sedulously encouraged by most governments that have held office long, that all opponents of the Ministry were enemies of the State. When Walpole came to power there was some ground for this belief, since there was a danger that the Opposition might become identified with rebels, whose main object was to restore the Roman Catholic dynasty, or with discontented Whig politicians, preoccupied with their own thwarted ambitions. Bolingbroke's merit was to attempt a fusion between these two classes on the ground of a common national policy in harmony with the existing institutions: the extreme Tories he taught to understand that a change of dynasty was no longer possible even if desirable, and individual malcontents among the Whigs that personal pique or a desire for office were not a sufficient basis for opposition. He thus completed Walpole's system of making the Administration national and constitutional by forming an Opposition equally national and constitutional in the aims it professed. However malevolent and shortsighted Bolingbroke's attacks in *The Craftsman* on Walpole's Excise Bill of 1733 may have been, they at any rate trained his Whig and Tory allies to treat politics from a practical standpoint and to formulate a broad and consistent policy. By a strange paradox the man who by his writings professed himself most anxious to abolish party government did as much as anybody to establish the English party system on a sure basis. Bolingbroke himself was pre-eminently fitted to inspire this new creed of opposition. Though wanting in stability and persistence and superficial in his writings he was an adroit politician, while his knowledge of domestic and foreign affairs was grounded on long practice and constant study of new circumstances. Of the elder men who helped him with their experience the most capable were Sir William Wyndham, William Pulteney and Lord Carteret. Wyndham was a Tory, but, as Bolingbroke told Lyttelton in later years, was the first of that party to cast off his feelings for the Pretender and to take up the idea of a coalition against what seemed to him a bad government for England. He was respected on both sides of the

House for his honesty and his judgment; 'he was,' said Speaker Onslow, 'the most made for a great man of any one that I have known in this age. Everything about him seemed great.' Of Pulteney, more infirm of purpose and less public-spirited, it was said that his speeches began like Demosthenes and ended with Billingsgate: he was nevertheless the ablest debater in the House, and, as a pamphleteer and writer on *The Craftsman*, second only to Bolingbroke. But Carteret was the finest genius of them all as a scholar, a man of the world, and a diplomatist. When Pitt first came into Bolingbroke's circle Carteret was in the full vigour of his powers, and willingly imparted some of his own political lore to the young cornet, in whom he must have recognised a kindred fire. The two afterwards parted company, but forty years later Chatham still recalled what he owed to Carteret in noble words of gratitude: 'In the upper departments of government Lord Granville had not his equal; and I feel a pride in declaring that to his patronage, to his friendship and instruction, I owe whatever I am.'

The Excise Bill of 1733 enabled Bolingbroke and his three chief adherents to create the formidable party against Walpole which finally compassed his downfall. The Bill was nowhere popular, but it was finally killed by *The Craftsman*. This was Bolingbroke's first triumph, and Walpole proceeded to play into his hands by the savage revenge he took upon all his own supporters who had expressed disapproval of the measure, thus driving them into Bolingbroke's and Pulteney's camp. The dangerously witty Chesterfield had to yield up his staff as Steward of the Household, dukes and earls lost their places, and Pitt's patron, Lord Cobham, was even deprived of his regiment. Walpole's very success in the following general election of 1734, when his henchman, the Duke of Newcastle, first displayed his unrivalled skill as a political manager, only confirmed the growing impression that Walpole's sole art in government lay not in representing the popular opinion but in securing personal pre-eminence by all the arts of corruption and the unscrupulous abuse of political pressure. Outwardly the Government was strong as ever. Walpole still affected to laugh at his enemies' attacks, and sneered at the young 'Patriots,' as they were called, telling them they 'would soon come off that and grow wiser.' But his task was done; his policy, 'quieta non movere,' had acted as a sorely needed sedative to a nation wrought up by all the changes of the Stuart Period and had given the comfortable House of Hanover time to take firm root. England had now recovered her balance and was beginning to suffer from lethargy.

Bolingbroke, Pulteney, Wyndham and Carteret on the other hand opened out a field of inquiry and discontent which implied some life and energy. They began to ask the reason for institutions and lines of policy which the Government treated as accepted facts. What, for example, was the good of a standing army at the very time when the fixed principle of government appeared to be peace at any price, if not to bolster up an arbitrary power by 'those casuists in red who, having swords by their sides, are able at once to cut those Gordian knots which others must untie by degrees?' The outcry against an excise and excisemen gained much plausibility when it was seen what a powerful instrument for electoral corruption was provided by places in the Customs: the numerous tales of unredressed wrongs from Spain and the apathy of the Government during the war of the Polish Succession; the King's manifest preference for Hanover and Hanoverian interests, and his contemptuous treatment of the Prince of Wales, all lent weight to the Opposition clamours against the Government. Then the grinding dulness of the Court and ministerial circles, their gross and stupid pleasures, and their soulless indifference to all the nobler intellectual and spiritual cravings of the country drove all the young men of promise and ambition into the ranks led by Bolingbroke. Pope, the poet of the age and the high priest of taste, writing to Swift, shows the spirit which animated the men with whom his friend Bolingbroke had brought him into touch:

> I have acquired without my seeking a few chance acquaintances of young men, who look rather to the past age than the present, and therefore the future may have some hopes of them. If I love them, it is because they honour some of those whom I and the world

have lost or are losing. Two or three of them have distinguished themselves in Parliament, and you will own in a very uncommon manner, when I tell you it is by their asserting of independency and contempt of corruption.

Rarely indeed in our history has such a galaxy of eager and public-spirited young men been gathered together for a common object as the Boy Patriots who learned their politics from Bolingbroke and his friends. The oldest of them was Chesterfield, just forty when dismissed by Walpole in 1734, and already experienced in the mysteries of Court etiquette and diplomacy. His wit and his cynicism in private life have often obscured to later generations his sound political sense and the important part he took in bringing to an end Walpole's ministry. The first two letters printed in the Chatham Correspondence show that he could inspire younger men with a conviction of his patriotism and statesmanship, and that Pitt himself turned for guidance to one who afterwards partly justified this confidence by his enlightened toleration and the wisdom of his government in Ireland. Among the younger men one of the ablest was Murray, whose success at the bar soon fulfilled the promise of his Oxford days, and who was made famous when barely thirty by Mr. Pope's dedication to him of an 'Imitation of Horace.' Quarendon, whom Lady Louisa Stuart remembered as Lord Lichfield, 'a red-faced old gentleman . . . who had almost drunk away his senses,' was then 'a bud of genius fostered by the opposition chiefs as likely to prove the future pride of their garland.' Polwarth, Marchmont's son, noted for his impetuous honesty and independence and for the affection of Pope and Bolingbroke, was also of the band; and Cornbury, to whom Bolingbroke addressed his 'Letters on the Study of History,' a great-grandson of the Chancellor Clarendon and grandson of Dryden's Hushai. With them Cobham, after his dismissal, finally cast in his lot, bringing with him his 'cubs,' Lyttelton, the Grenvilles, Robert and George, and William Pitt. The extraordinary regard in which the last was held by his fellows in this company is shown by the opinion frequently expressed of him by Lyttelton, Chesterfield and the Grenvilles, and such testimony as this from Lord Cornbury: 'For the good of others I form many wishes about you; for your own I can wish you nothing but to continue the same man; whether Happyness or Vanity be your aim, that will secure either';[1] while his patron, Cobham, could hardly put his 'talent of insinuation' too high: 'in a very short quarter of an hour,' he said, 'Mr. Pitt can persuade a man of anything.'

Nor was the band composed solely of men whose primary interest was political ambition. At times of political ferment such as occurred during the concluding years of Walpole's administration and such as exists to-day, a wave of political feeling seems to carry along all that is best in the youth of the nation to think and talk of little but the urgent evils of our state and how to remedy them. The great Mr. Pope himself set the fashion in literary circles by entering whole-heartedly into the political schemes of his friend Bolingbroke. Largely by his influence Burlington, famed for his building and his gardens, Cobham, Marchmont and Chesterfield were first attracted to the movement, and his own loyalty to it was confirmed by the Prince of Wales's judicious visit to Twickenham in 1735. Later he made a meeting-place for the conciliabula of the Opposition at his own villa, in that

> Egerian grot
> Where nobly pensive St. John sate and thought;
> Where *British* sighs for dying Wyndham stole,
> And the bright flame was shot from Marchmont's soul;

and he expressed in the 'Epistle to Augustus' and the 'Epilogue to the Satires' all that the most polished invective and irony in our literature could convey of the feelings of the Opposition. All the great stars of the literary world were on the same side: Swift of course sympathised; and Gay had suffered persecution for the political innuendoes in his 'Beggar's Opera' and its unacted sequel 'Polly.' Thomson, a frequent visitor at Stowe, to comply with the spirit of his surroundings wrote a poem on Liberty, of which Johnson unkindly said 'no man felt the want.' However, its dedication to the Prince of

---

[1] *Chatham MSS.* 27 (Cornbury to Pitt, November 3, 1736).

Wales earned him a pension and the commission to compose with Mallet the masque 'Alfred,' which was performed at Clifden and is notable for its ode 'Rule Britannia.' Pitt had 'a sincere value for the amiable author,' and in later years busied himself with Lyttelton in getting his 'Tancred and Sigismunda' produced by Garrick at Drury Lane. Another, greater than Thomson, took a more active part in attacking Walpole. Henry Fielding, who in early youth had with Pitt worshipped learning 'in her favourite fields, where the limpid, gently-rolling Thames washed her Etonian banks,' had come back from Leyden with no less ardour for the political fray than for the joys of conviviality. In 1735 he took the small theatre in the Haymarket and produced 'Pasquin,' which earned a great success and amused the town by its attacks on Walpole and 'Lord Fanny.' In 1737 another attack on Walpole in 'The Register' led to the establishment of the censorship, which put an end to the attempts of Fielding and others to ridicule the Ministry on the stage. Thereupon Fielding turned to journalism, and, as 'Captain Hercules Vinegar' in his paper *The Champion*, continued his anti-ministerial campaign. Of minor poets there was no dearth among the members of the Prince of Wales's Court. One of his equerries, James Hammond, as a man of pleasure was 'the joy and dread of Bath,' and as a poet sang the charms of Kitty Dashwood the Oxfordshire toast. Another 'whiffler in poetry,' David Mallet, 'alias Malloch,' is better remembered in connection with a contemptuous phrase of Dr. Johnson about Bolingbroke's unbelief. He and Brooke, a friend of Pitt's, served the cause by writing plays which earned the censor's condemnation. Better remembered is Glover for the name of his play 'Leonidas' and for his ballad on 'Admiral Hosier's Ghost'; he afterwards made a mark in politics and in commerce.

Three women, as different from one another as possible, were peculiarly identified with the Patriots. The terrible old Duchess Sarah sought their aid to satisfy a personal pique, and signalled out two of them, Chesterfield and Pitt, to benefit under her will. Her arrogance made her a bad counsellor, but in her grim way she showed shrewdness as a judge of character. Lady Suffolk was gentle as Atossa was savage, and, in her pleasant home at Marble Hill, Twickenham, adorned for her by poets and statesmen, she made welcome Pope and all his friends, charming them with her amiability and her accurate, if lengthy, stories of events at Court.[1] The third was Prior's and Gay's Kitty, Duchess of Queensberry, Cornbury's sister, and the most impertinent and daintiest of rogues. 'Whenever vexation is in question,' she once wrote petulantly to Pitt, 'I hardly met with anybody who could outdo me.'[2] She it was who had sent the saucy answer to the King, when he forbade her the Court for collecting subscriptions in his own palace on behalf of Gay's 'Polly.' Later she attacked the second estate of the realm, when peeresses were excluded from their debates, spending half a day with the Duchess of Ancaster and other sprightly dames knocking at the doors of the House, into which they finally gained admittance by a ruse. Used from her childhood to the compliments and pettings of all the wits and poets, she was unspoiled by their incense, and returned them the greatest benefit that can befall such high mortals by frankly teasing and rallying them and teaching them that a pretty woman has no respect for outward dignities. She even exchanged banter with the great Dr. Swift. She was an intimate friend of Ann Pitt and especially distinguished William by her friendship.

I do think [she wrote to him, when he was obliged to forgo a promised visit to Amesbury] Mr. Pitt should come at some other time, and that because he may be morally sure to be wellcome . . . I too am extreamly in character, for I am not certain whether I am most angry or sorry for being disappointed. I pout extreamly and have not got to the top of the hill yet. This man and this

---

[1] To the end Lady Suffolk remained Pitt's faithful friend. There are two charming letters written some thirty years later, when she was old and blind, to Lady Chatham about her and her husband (*Chatham MSS.* 60). The scandal about Lady Suffolk's relations with George II is based on very slender evidence and is probably untrue. Lord Egmont said that her reputation was very unjustly aspersed, the whole fact being that the King, like many of his subjects, enjoyed her conversation (*Egmont MSS.* vol. 82); this view is also confirmed by the Suffolk Papers (*Hist. MSS. Com.*).

[2] To Pitt in 1742 (*Chatham MSS.* 54).

woman I find agree extreamly in their very sincere regard for Mr. Pitt, for itt has not yett been a matter of dispute the which of them has the greatest regard. . . . I fancy the Duke will not give it up and I am very sure I will not.

This light and easy wit of the Duchess, joined to her sincerity and hearty loyalty to those she cared for, made her just the friend needed by Pitt at this stage of his life to drive out of him some of the stiffness and coldness due to his early training.

Such were the influences that had helped to form Pitt when, at the age of twenty-seven, he took the plunge into full political life. His own disposition, his ailments, and his education at Eton, Oxford and Utrecht encouraged in him a studious disposition; his early losses forced upon him habits of self-dependence. While still a child his kinship with Stanhope had made him familiar with men versed in affairs of State and accustomed to command, and his grandfather had shown him an example of ruthless energy and uncompromising plainness. His military training, though not put to the test of practice, also helped to fit him for his future task. In politics, with a Tory father and a grandfather who was a furious Whig, he had a training in both schools; and this training, with the doctrines he imbibed from Bolingbroke and Wyndham, disposed him throughout life to think far less of the ordinary party distinctions than most of his contemporaries. But, though he never became a strong party man, he always regarded the glorious Revolution as a fundamental fact of the British constitution. This could not well be otherwise, since from his Oxford days he had formed his guiding principles on Locke's philosophy and politics. One of his notebooks contains an elaborate analysis of the reasoning of the ' Essay concerning the Human Understanding.' In moral philosophy Locke's great service to the men of the eighteenth century was to create a confidence in their own understanding and their ability to judge of facts; to use Pitt's own words, he taught us that we must ' use our own reason and not that of another, if we would deal fairly by ourselves and hope to enjoy a peaceful and contented conscience.' For constitutional questions

Locke's treatises on Government and on Toleration were the political bible of the eighteenth century, and as such were pondered over deeply by Pitt. Locke's theory of the perfect balance of the English constitution, with distinct functions for the three constituent members of the Legislature—King, Lords and Commons—his triumphant defence of our polity on utilitarian grounds, and his vindication of religious tolerance, are apparent by their fruits in almost every speech and action of the Great Commoner.[1]

In spite of cricket matches that we hear of at Stowe, of rollicking games in camp or at Lyttelton's, and of the society of his 'dearest Nanny,' the sprightly Duchess of Queensberry, and the restful Countess of Suffolk, Pitt's was a grave upbringing. In after years he quoted as a guide to his nephew the text, 'Remember now thy Creator in the days of thy youth,' giving it the most ascetic interpretation, and in his own early years there are few signs of that careless rapture in the passing hour which gives to youth its happiest moments and its greatest charm. Such moments have their uses in forming a man's character : they make him more supple and give him tact in dealing with individuals, which Pitt never possessed. He was brave and steadfast in upholding before his countrymen what seemed to him noblest, and he could impose his will by the force of his character, but he sometimes failed from lack of buoyancy and ability to give and take with men inferior to himself. But with all its limitations there was nothing mean or paltry in his education. 'Guided by faith and matchless fortitude,' he schooled himself to fine ideals ; he disciplined himself to an intense, almost passionate, belief in England's greatness, to a knowledge and love of her ancient traditions and her happy constitution, and to that overmastering sense of duty which ranks him with Cromwell alone among our statesmen.

[1] Even in details Pitt showed his intimate acquaintance with Locke: witness his letter to Warburton re-echoing Locke's exception of Roman Catholicism from general toleration Acts as 'a subversion of all civil as well as religious liberty,' and his quotation of the first paragraph of the chapter 'Of Prerogative' in his speech defending the embargo on the export of corn. (See vol. ii, p. 228.)

CHAPTER III

PITT AND WALPOLE

Ehrgeiz ist die Leuchte die allen grossen Handlungen voraufgeht.
WALLENSTEIN.

ON Pitt's return from abroad at the beginning of 1734 England was on the eve of a general election. Walpole had wisely not dissolved upon the defeat of his excise scheme in April 1733. After punishing insubordinate followers he had allowed the excitement in the country to cool down during a quiet session and had called in the Duke of Newcastle to prepare the ground by a judicious dressing of gold and beer. The result of the elections in May 1734 justified this caution. When Newcastle began operations in the previous August he found the irritation against the ministry's excise scheme almost universal. It was acute in Sussex, Newcastle's own county, which then returned twenty-eight members to Parliament. Here grossly exaggerated rumours were afloat. Voters were convinced that their bread and meal would cost them more, and that their pork would have to be accounted for to the Treasury. The country grocer was seriously alarmed at the trouble he foresaw in weighing out tobacco under the scheme, and truculent shopkeepers vowed they would kill any exciseman that offered to come into their houses. Ministerialists going to church or to race meetings were greeted with cries of 'No excise, no dragoons!' and the slumber of honest citizens was disturbed by vulgar fellows beating drums and hoarsely shouting 'No excise!' at dead of night. The methods of dealing with these prejudices were nicely calculated to meet the special circumstances of each case. The influence exercised by the bishops on their clergy, and by the great landowners on their tenants and dependents was called into play by Newcastle, who had created half the bishops and was connected with a considerable proportion of the nobility. The patronage of the Crown and even its prerogative of mercy to prisoners condemned to death for smuggling were employed to influence votes, and at need the voters' roll was manipulated by obsequious officials. But the most effective appeal was to the stomach. A typical letter from one of the Duke's agents gives an insight into this method. Twenty-six freeholders of Worth in Sussex, accompanied by their wives, were invited to a dinner succeeded by punch-drinking. ' By nine in the evening they were all fully convinc'd y^t ye clamour of a gen^l Excise was false and scandalous, and were perfectly satisfied of the ability, honour, and honesty of their present members, and express'd their indignation and concern y^t any credit had been given to the many misrepresentations y^t had lately been so industriously spread about ye country.' At a later stage they all adjourned ' to the most Eminent place on the hill, where with loud huzzas and in full glasses ' they proclaimed their conversion to the Government's policy ' in the most Publick manner they then could.'

By such means the Duke of Newcastle was directly responsible for the return of sixty or seventy members favourable to the Government's interest from counties where his influence was either paramount or one of the forces to be reckoned with ; and in other places where he did not employ his own personal agents his part in tuning the voice of the constituencies to a favourable key must have been considerable, owing to his extensive patronage and his unfailing energy as an electioneer.[1] Even in the election of Scottish

[1] Newcastle's love of electioneering cost him dear. Though his estates brought in originally £32,000 a year and from various official sources he had an income of £19,000 in addition, he was deeply in debt in 1741-2 from his profusion in granting pensions to J.P.'s and others, and electoral bribery. (See *Egmont MSS.* vol. 88, *sub* January 18, 1741-2.) Nor were his lavish methods always appreciated. According to d'Éon he once regaled some voters with champagne, at which they complained that his cider was sour. (*Aff. Etr. Angl. Corr. Pol.* 454.)

representative peers, the Duke of Newcastle helped Lord Isla to secure the nomination of sixteen men favourable to Sir Robert. The result of the elections was an ample reward for all these exertions. Some disappointments there were, such as the loss of Walpole's own county of Norfolk by a few votes, and the more natural triumph of the Opposition in Somersetshire, a stronghold of Pulteney and Sir William Wyndham. But, though his majority was reduced, on the whole Sir Robert found the new Parliament as docile as he could have expected, or indeed required.[1] At any rate, Bolingbroke, who had inspired the determined attack on him, and had once seemed within grasp of victory, was so disgusted at the result that he abandoned politics for the time being, and in January 1735 retired to France.

Throughout Pitt's life elections were conducted on the same lines as in 1734, the only change being that after 1760 the King took Newcastle's place as chief organizer of victory. It would not indeed be true to say that public opinion had no weight in the composition of the House of Commons or in directing its action. Walpole's refusal to proceed with the excise scheme, though it was still undefeated in the House of Commons, and the extraordinary precautions taken at this election show that the people was to be feared when its interest was aroused; and, in spite of the preponderance of rotten boroughs, the counties and a few boroughs, where the judgment of the freeholders was comparatively unfettered, were important enough to secure the expression in the House of Commons of any violent outburst of popular feeling. But Newcastle's resources for working on the self-interest of an electorate were manifold; and, given ample time, such as he had before the election of 1734, it would have been a serious excitement indeed which he could not have quelled. It is significant that before the next election, in 1741, the Duke had already begun intriguing against Sir Robert, and that the new Parliament soon reflected this archplotter's change of view. In later years even Pitt

---

[1] Walpole reposed such confidence in Newcastle that, acording to Hervey, he troubled himself not at all about the election, but spent the time in dalliance with his mistress, Mrs. Skerrit.

was constrained to admit that with Newcastle against him little was to be done either in or out of Parliament.

Pitt has left it on record in one of the characteristically frank admissions of his later speeches that, though he afterwards came to see the merit of Walpole's excise scheme, had he been in Parliament at the time, ' he would probably have been induced by the general and groundless clamour to have joined with those that opposed it.' Already his abilities were so marked, and his opposition to the Government so notorious, that Walpole himself thought it worth making an effort to silence him. First he attempted to bribe him with the offer of the troop afterwards given to Conway. When that method failed, he tried to keep him out of Parliament. At the general election Pitt's brother, Thomas, had been elected for Okehampton as well as for Old Sarum, and, choosing to sit for the former, he had the seat at Old Sarum to give away. He had apparently promised it to William, but Walpole, anxious to keep out William Pitt as a dangerous young man, put forward the claims of a certain T. Harrison, who had sat for it in the last Parliament.[1] The suggestion now made to Thomas through his sister Harriet, and at first favourably regarded by him, was that Harrison should be again elected on condition that he paid William a sum of money in compensation for his disappointment. Pitt was indignant at the proposal. From his quarters at Newbury he wrote to Ann of his ' thorough contempt of the . . . ridiculous offer ' made by their sister Harriet. It was not even to Thomas's advantage, he pointed out, for if he let the seat go out of the family he might at least have expected to recover from his nominee the £2000 he had spent on the Okehampton election, whereas he was personally to obtain nothing.[2] This consideration perhaps weighed with Thomas, who ignored Walpole's appeal and fulfilled his promise of the seat to William. On February 18, 1735, therefore, William was duly chosen member for Old Sarum. His election did not then involve loss of active

[1] He had been elected at a bye caused by Lord Londonderry's resignation in 1728, probably because there was no Pitt in want of a seat.
[2] Pitt's letters on the subject are quoted in Rosebery, pp. 74–7. For Walpole's part in the business Lord Camelford is the authority. (See *ibid.* p. 159.)

service with his regiment, and for another year he performed such military duties as were incumbent upon him. He found many friends and relations in the new Parliament: his brother Thomas, John Pitt of Encombe, Lord Cobham's nephew Richard Grenville, and Lord Marchmont's twin sons, Polwarth and Hume Campbell. His future opponents, Lord Egmont and Henry Fox, also took their seats for the first time, and two months later George Lyttelton came as Thomas Pitt's colleague for Okehampton. All these, save Fox, were then united against Walpole under the banner of the Prince of Wales, who had recently dismissed the time-serving Dodington and taken Pitt's friend Lyttelton in his stead. Bolingbroke, had he known, need not have despaired of the prospects of the Opposition with such an infusion of young blood, led by Pulteney and Wyndham in the Commons, and by Bedford, Carteret, Chesterfield, Cobham, Gower and Bathurst in the Lords.

Walpole had already marked him down, but few others in the House that February afternoon of 1735 could have guessed that the tall, slim young cornet, with the long neck and the great nose, going up to shake hands with Speaker Onslow, was to hold them all by his voice in a few years and that he would rule every succeeding House for the next twenty-five years by his voice, his flashing glance and his very presence. Without title or fortune with which to open the charmed circle of the Whig governing class, with no traditions of soldier or statesmen ancestors to arouse curiosity and interest, he could only boast the name of old Diamond Pitt, the eccentric, coarse-mannered adventurer, of whom strange stories were put about, and who had cut no figure in Parliament or polite society. In his first session Pitt kept silence and was content to learn the traditions, customs and procedure of an assembly where, for the next thirty years, the chief part of his life was to be spent. But he took an early opportunity of showing that he meant to enrol himself with the Opposition, by acting as teller for the minority on the navy estimates. No very important debates occurred to tempt him to break silence, for, as often happens at the beginning of a new Parliament, the minister had no formidable attacks to meet from an Opposition which had not yet come to feel its strength.

An unexpected opening for a speech occurred to Pitt on April 29, 1736, towards the end of his second session. For many years his patron, the Prince of Wales, had been restive under the parsimonious tutelage imposed upon him by his father and mother. At length, in June 1734, he had demanded an interview with the King, and submitted three requests: to serve under the Emperor in the war of the Polish Succession; to have a fixed allowance; and, lastly, to be permitted to marry. After more than a year, the King had complied with the last demand, but gave his son no voice in the choice of his bride. She was a Princess Augusta of Saxe-Gotha, whom the King had noticed with favour on one of his Hanoverian journeys, and whom the Prince saw for the first time only a few days before his marriage. On April 27, 1736, the marriage took place with scant ceremony. No courtier dared even allude to the event in Parliament, for the King and Queen had intimated that any show of respect to the Prince would be taken as an act of disrespect to themselves. It was left to Pulteney to move a dutiful address to the King, expressing the congratulations of the House, mingled with some unseasonable allusions to the liberties of this nation: Lyttelton supported it. Then came Pitt.

The chief points in Pitt's maiden speech, as reported by Guthrie, are the satirical allusions to royal dissensions, clothed in language of almost oriental submission; the hints at the King's delay in satisfying the Prince's reiterated wishes for marriage—'this so desirable and long-desired measure . . . which the nation thought could never come too soon'; and the grim observation that, however great may be the nation's joy, 'it must be inferior to that high satisfaction which His Majesty himself enjoys in bestowing it :—and, if I may be allowed to suppose that to a royal mind anything can transcend the pleasure of gratifying the impatient wishes of a loyal people, it can only be the parental delight of tenderly indulging the most dutiful application, and most humble request of a submissive indulgent son.' This is followed by a delicate

April 29, 1736.

insinuation that the merit of the son, who asked for a means of continuing the succession, was greater than that of the father who granted it so reluctantly. The prince's domestic life he only lightly touches upon for fear of ' offending the delicacy of the virtue he so ardently desires to do justice to. . . . But, Sir, filial duty to his Royal parents, a generous love of liberty, and a just reverence for the British constitution—these are public virtues, and cannot escape the applause and benedictions of the public: they are virtues, Sir, which render His Royal Highness not only a noble ornament, but a firm support, if any could possibly be necessary, of that throne so greatly filled by his Royal father.' He then significantly reminds the King and ministers that the spirit of liberty dictated the Hanover succession, and concludes with the prayer that this marriage 'may afford the comfort of seeing the Royal Family (numerous as I thank God it is) still growing and rising up in a third generation: a family, Sir, which I most sincerely wish may be as immortal as those liberties and that constitution it came to maintain.'

The covert irony of Pitt's allusion to King George's domestic and patriotic virtues, and to the Prince of Wales's dutiful behaviour, seem sufficient in the circumstances to account for the delight with which this speech was received by the Opposition. But that it should have been compared favourably with the best orations of Cicero and Demosthenes is obviously the result of political partiality and the fame which its punishment brought, unless Guthrie grievously misrepresented his words. Lyttelton's speech, which was on the same lines as Pitt's, seems at first to have attracted more attention;[1] but Lyttelton was beyond the reach of Walpole's vengeance, while Pitt was not. He was already a marked man for his constant support of Opposition measures, and for the favour he enjoyed from the Prince of Wales; by this display of oratorical capacity and cool impertinence he had shown that he might be dangerous. 'We must muzzle,' said Walpole, ' this terrible cornet of horse,' and forthwith dismissed him

[1] For example, the French envoy in London sent to Paris a full account of Lyttelton's speech, but did not mention Pitt. (*Aff. Etr. Angl. Corr. Pol.* 393, f. 379.)

from the army. No more effective way of unmuzzling the cornet, and giving him the prominence his ambition sought, could have been devised by Pitt's greatest friend. The army, already alarmed at the removal of Lords Stair and Cobham, saw in this vengeance on a mere subaltern a blow struck at all liberty of opinion in the commissioned ranks, and warmly took up Pitt's cause. The Opposition naturally made the most of it. Lyttelton celebrated his friend's honourable disgrace in his usual vapid verses;[1] Lord Cornbury wrote an ode on the same subject, enclosing it in a letter expressing the confidence felt by the young Patriots in Pitt's extraordinary merit;[2] Lord Cobham showed increased favour to the young man; Lady Suffolk's husband, George Berkeley, wrote him a warm letter of sympathy; and the Prince of Wales countenanced him with the most gracious and flattering marks of distinction. Nor was the incident allowed to rest in the House of Commons. In the following session a member, alluding to Pitt's punishment, said: 'I know the danger I am in by appearing in favour of this motion [against the ministry]. I may, perhaps, have a message sent me, I may lose the command I have in the army, as other gentlemen have done for the same reason before me.' Pulteney and Lyttelton attacked Walpole for his action, and especially for descending so low in his vengeance as to cashier a cornet of horse for his vote. But Walpole was quite unabashed and cynically avowed that 'if an officer, of whatever rank or merit, wished to meddle with affairs of State . . . which were outside his sphere, or even show aversion to a minister, that minister would be the most wretched of creatures if he did not cashier him, and he left the practice as a legacy to his successors.'[3]

[1] Long had thy virtues marked thee out for fame
Far, far superior to a Cornet's name;
This generous Walpole saw, and grieved to find
So mean a post disgrace that noble mind.
The servile standard from the free-born hand
He took, and bade thee lead the patriot band.

[2] See above, p. 55.

[3] This debate was on February 18–March 1, 1736–7, when the Opposition moved to reduce the army from 17,000 to 12,000. Pitt made his second speech on this occasion; but no record of it remains. (*Egmont MSS.* vol. 84; and *Aff. Etr. Angl. Corr. Pol.* 394, f. 109.)

February 4, 1738.

Pitt himself showed a becoming spirit. Two years later in the House of Commons he emphasised the dangerous effect of Walpole's doctrine on any freedom of opinion in Parliament. 'As the laws now stand,' he said, 'an old officer . . . may be dismissed and reduced, perhaps, to a starving condition, at the arbitrary will and pleasure, perhaps at the whim of a minister; so that by the present establishment of the army the reward of a soldier seems not to depend upon the services done to his country, but upon the service he does to those who happen to be ministers at the time.' He was evidently touched by the tokens of affection lavished on him by his friends, and answers Berkeley, 'from the abundance of a heart full of gratitude for the kind concern you take in my situation,' that he and Lady Suffolk 'think a great deal too highly of my talents'—their friendship 'is the surest means for me to acquire . . . and deserve the esteem of the world, and attain in any degree the worth or talents you are willing to suppose in me . . . though I should not be a little vain to be the object of the hatred of a minister, hated even by those who call themselves his friends.' He made no concealment of this form of vanity. During the summer of 1736 he travelled about the country in a one-horse chaise without a servant, as if to emphasise the narrow straits to which he had been reduced, and to appeal from a corrupt ministry to a generous people. Wherever he went, it is related, he was received with acclamation, partly no doubt due to the general discontent with the ministry, which in some places manifested itself in riotous outbreaks. Such an appeal to popular sentiment was then almost unprecedented; with Pitt it soon became a settled principle to look beyond the House of Commons to the people of England, not only for personal support but as the true source of a national policy.

On his return in the autumn of 1736 he entered with zest into the Prince's continued campaign of annoyance against his parents. While the King was in Hanover, Frederick quarrelled with his mother, because he was required to take up his abode with her in the damp palace of Kensington. He yielded finally with some grace in a letter, which, on account

FREDERICK'S ALLOWANCE, 1737

of its terse vigour, Lord Hervey suspected to have been Pitt's composition. Next year a more serious question arose. The fixed allowance which the Prince had demanded in 1734 had never been granted, nor had any jointure been paid to the Princess; they both depended on the King's bounty for an income of £50,000 a year, which might be withdrawn at any time. On the advice of Pitt and his other young men, Frederick determined that a motion for a fixed allowance of £100,000 out of the Civil List should be suddenly brought forward in Parliament. The scheme was elaborated with great secrecy. Almost every member of the Opposition, and even shifty members of the ministerial party, like Dodington, were sounded, before a hint was allowed to reach the ear of Walpole, or of the King and Queen. So admirably was the secret kept that the Ministry heard of the plan only a few days before the motion was to be sprung upon the House. An attempt at compromise made at the eleventh hour failed, and on February 22 Pulteney proposed the humble address to the King. The Prince of Wales's friends had a strong argument in the facts that the King had a larger Civil List than his father, but allowed his son only half what he had himself received as Prince of Wales; and that Frederick's expenditure, including an ostentatiously large allowance for charity, exceeded his income by £21,000. Walpole escaped defeat by a majority of only thirty, which would have been a minority had not Wyndham and forty-four Tories abstained from voting. In this engagement Pitt had his first practical lesson in political organisation; he also made another speech, not reported, which added to his growing reputation and to his friends' enthusiasm for his abilities. [February 23, 1737.] So unmeasured were they in their praises, and in their comparisons of him to the greatest orators of antiquity, that *The Gazetteer*, a ministerial paper, attacked him as a young man of little consequence, who 'has the vanity to put himself in the place of Tully,' and warned him that, though he might have Tully's natural imperfections, a long neck and a slender body, he had not his advantages of a sonorous voice and just action. *The Craftsman*, in prophetic vein, retorted to this attack by comparing him with Demosthenes:

Let us consider the great Demosthenes returning from the bar, discontented at his own performances, meeting such an adviser as this, persuading him, already too much prejudiced against his own imperfections, not to attempt to establish his reputation as an orator, for which he was no way designed by nature. Such advice, in the situation he was in, might perhaps have had its fatal effect; but what, O Athenians, would you have lost in this case? Not only the reputation of producing one of the brightest orators that ever lived, but the boldest defender of your liberties, and the greatest check to the Macedonian monarch: a man of whom Philip, by his own confession, stood more in awe than of all the Grecian states he fought to oppress.

Such newspaper controversies increased Pitt's importance, and the Prince of Wales shortly afterwards found room in his household for so rising a politician. In the summer of 1737, after his act of insolence and folly in withdrawing his wife from his parents' roof on the eve of her delivery, Frederick had been forbidden the Court; and several of his household resigned. He immediately appointed Lyttelton his private secretary and Pitt a groom of the bedchamber. The French ambassador thought Pitt prominent enough to inform his Court of the appointment and to regard it as an indication that no reconciliation between the Prince and his father was likely.[1] Pitt's salary was £400 a year—no doubt a welcome addition to his small private income of about £300, and his duties about the Prince's person were light. Attendances at Clifden were the most onerous, and it is recorded that he accompanied the Prince on a state visit to Bath in November, 1738, and was himself admitted to the freedom of the town he was afterwards to represent. But the office was useful to him in other ways: it secured him a recognised position in the ranks of the Opposition and gave him a voice in their plans against the Government, which were generally concocted under the Prince's eye. In accepting the post he had no intention of surrendering his independence. In a speech made soon afterwards in answer to a colleague in the Prince's household, 'I think it my honour to be a "placeman,"' he boasted; 'but,' he added, 'I should not think it, if I were not as free to give

February 4, 1738.

[1] *Aff. Etr. Angl. Corr. Pol.* 397, f. 138.

IN FREDERICK'S SERVICE, 1737

my opinion upon any question that happens in this House, as I was before I had any such place.'

The Queen's death in November 1737 removed the Prince's bitterest critic from his father's Court and produced a lull in the domestic squabbles, and Pitt was not again called upon to bring forward in Parliament his master's sordid disputes with the King. Foreign policy, a subject more worthy of his genius, once more forced itself upon public attention. The war of the Polish Succession, of which Pitt had seen the beginning at Lunéville, had come to an end in October 1735. Walpole boasted that although 50,000 men had fallen in battle during a single year of that war, not one of these was an Englishman. Nevertheless the death-blow had been given to his constant policy of alliance with the two branches of the House of Bourbon. In 1733 the first Family Compact, with provisions directed against England, had been signed by the Kings of France and Spain, and by the Treaty of Vienna in 1735 the allied Bourbon Powers had gained the lion's share of advantage. To France had fallen the reversion of Lorraine; to Don Carlos, the King of Spain's son, the kingdom of Naples and Sicily; while the Emperor, England's traditional ally, had to rest content with empty promises to observe the Pragmatic Sanction. Since that time the enmity of Spain, only held in check by the Spanish Queen's hope of English assistance in carving out appanages in Italy for her sons, had shown itself more openly and found a ready excuse in the chronic disputes about trade with the English merchants. These disputes arose from the English attempts to poach on the preserve of Spain's vast American possessions. The Spanish monarchy had always claimed the right of excluding foreign traders from her colonies in the West Indies and South America, but in 1713 had granted two privileges for the benefit of the English South Sea Company, (1) trafficking in slaves and (2) sending an annual ship with merchandise for sale in the Spanish colonies. The Company derived little satisfaction from these concessions, which on various pretexts were being constantly interfered with. On the other hand the English freebooters of commerce refused to respect the Spanish attempts at exclusion. They carried on their contraband trade with the Spanish Main, principally from Jamaica, a veritable smugglers' nest, underselling the legitimate Spanish traders as well as the South Sea Company and bringing much wealth to their English ports of origin, Bristol and London. In reprisal the Spanish governors gave licences indiscriminately to Spanish privateers to act as *guarda-costas*— licences interpreted with the utmost latitude by the privateering captains. They claimed a right of search, even on the high seas, over all vessels anywhere within reach of Spanish possessions, and carried them off to the nearest Spanish port. A few Spanish coins or products of South America in the cargo, which might well have been brought from the English islands, were there treated as sufficient justification by the prize courts for the adjudication of such vessels to the captor. Nor were trade losses the worst grievance. Reports of English sailors being loaded with chains and cast into filthy Spanish dungeons recalled tales of the Inquisition in Elizabeth's time. The most notorious story of outrage was that of Robert Jenkins, master of the sloop *Rebecca*, who declared that his ship was attacked by Spanish *guarda-costas*, that his ear was cut off, and that he was told to carry it to his King George.

In spite of these difficulties the South Sea trade, both above-board and illegitimate, went on merrily—proof enough for Walpole of its value; and he made a cardinal point in his foreign policy of maintaining it at all costs. For this trade he had always been willing to go great lengths in humouring Spain and the Spanish Queen's Italian ambitions, and regarded the close alliance with France from 1717 to 1733 as chiefly valuable for the hold it gave us on Spain. But the Family Compact and the Treaty of Vienna had taught France and Spain they could obtain all they needed without England. Spain no longer feared offending her commercial rival, and the French traders were becoming restive under England's commercial superiority. Though both Fleury and Walpole grew more and more peace-loving with age, they found it more and more difficult to curb three exasperated nations. And as the arrogance of Spain grew, so did the indignation of the English merchants. Petitions from London,

Bristol, Liverpool, Lancaster, Aberdeen, Edinburgh, Dunfermline, Dundee, Montrose, Stirling, Lauder, Cupar, and Kinghorn, even from Kingston in Jamaica and from the trustees for the new settlement of Georgia, came pouring in to swell the clamour against Spain. The great days of Elizabeth and Cromwell were recalled in countless broadsheets and newspapers to stir up a languid generation against the hereditary foe. Johnson himself added fuel to the flame of resentment against 'Oppression's insolence' when, in his poem 'London,' he sought for some 'peaceful desert yet unclaimed by Spain.'

In this dispute the English with their smuggling propensities were technically as much, if not more, to blame than the Spaniards. But it was something more than a technical dispute about treaty rights. Spain claimed more territory in South America and the West Indies than she could really control or supply with European goods, and, ever since the days of Queen Elizabeth, English seafaring men had been protesting against this dog-in-the-manger policy and fighting for the privilege of doing what Spain could not. Treaty concessions had been gradually wrung from Spain, principally in Charles II's and Queen Anne's reigns, but she always attempted to compensate herself for concessions by exacting exaggerated penalties for every small infraction of a treaty and by winking at the excesses of *guarda-costas*, whom the Madrid government was neither able nor willing to control. For nearly twenty years Walpole had been attempting to arrive at a satisfactory settlement, but always in vain. Spain had become a nuisance in the West Indies from her weakness and inability to maintain her rights by direct methods; and the merchants of London and Bristol, who had long been piling up grievances against her, were now set on obtaining more satisfactory conditions, and the abolition of the vexatious right of search, if need be by force of arms. The Opposition certainly encouraged the popular indignation against Walpole for what seemed to be dilatory methods, but they did not manufacture it; and Pitt, who now for the first time took a leading part on a great question, was naturally moved to adopt their view not only by his hatred of Walpole and his methods, but also by his hereditary associations with the mercantile classes.¹

Before taking in hand the serious business of the session of 1738 the Opposition had their usual fling at the standing army, which they moved to reduce from 17,704 to 12,000. A proposal to weaken the army on the eve of a war which they were themselves urging on the nation seemed inconsistent, but they defended their action on the ground that the struggle with Spain would be purely naval, and that a standing army was likely to become an engine of domestic despotism. The days of the Stuarts were recalled, and the House was reminded that some special emergency was the sole justification for its existence. Even Walpole had to defend the demand for the larger number of troops by having recourse to the danger from 'his old friend, the Pretender,' and by pointing to the unsettled state of the country. This argument only confirmed his opponents in their belief that Walpole wanted the army for purposes of oppression. When Sir Thomas Saunderson compared the Opposition to the fat man in the crowd, who muttered at the pressure caused chiefly by his own bulk, Pitt rose to administer a solemn reproof to those who made merry on a subject ' of so much importance with respect to our constitution and the happiness of our country,' and turned the laugh against Sir Thomas by retorting that the army, or rather those who kept it up, should more properly be compared to the fat man, since its size was the principal cause of muttering and discontent. 'Remove the army or but a considerable part of it, and the discontents complained of will cease . . . the loading of our people with an additional expense of £200,000 or £300,000 is in my opinion an affair of too affecting a nature to be treated in a ludicrous manner.'

February 4, 1738.

Next month the petitions against Spanish outrages came pouring in. The House spent several days in Committee hearing evidence from aggrieved merchants and sea-captains. Among others Robert Jenkins came up, and after displaying

¹ For the disputes with Spain, see H. W. Temperley on 'The War of Jenkins's Ear' in *R. Hist. Soc. Trans.* 3rd Ser. vol. iii; Hertz, *British Imperialism in 18th Century*, and articles on 'The Foreign Policy of Walpole' in *Engl. Hist. Rev.* vols. xv, xvi.

the famous ear,[1] carefully preserved in a bottle since 1731, he declared that at the time of the outrage he had 'committed his soul to his God, and his cause to his country'—words which, as Pulteney said, would raise volunteers at the mere name of Jenkins. On March 28, in a House of 468 (stated to have been the largest attendance since the Union), the evidence was concluded and summed up for the petitioners by Murray, then one of the leading counsel below the bar. Pulteney thereupon rose, and in one of his best speeches proposed six resolutions declaring our complaints and our rights. Walpole, on the ground that too much particularity might hinder further negotiation, proposed to substitute one resolution declaring our right of navigating unhindered to our own colonies, and requiring redress of outrages inflicted by Spain. Pitt, speaking late in the debate after Pulteney and Wyndham, pointed out that a similar proposal had been made eight years before and had produced nothing but a series of useless solicitations for eight years: doubtless Walpole's resolution would have exactly the same effect—solicitations for eight more years equally without result.[2] Nevertheless, Walpole carried his proposal by a majority of forty-seven. *March 28, 1738.*

This debate in the House encouraged the warlike party in the Cabinet, represented by Newcastle, who had accurately gauged public opinion in England. In May Admiral Haddock was sent with a squadron to cruise in the Mediterranean, a regiment was shipped to Georgia, where there was a boundary dispute with Spain, and peremptory despatches were presented by Keene to the Spanish Court. The Spaniards began feverish preparations, repairing their fortifications and overhauling their ships. War seemed inevitable. But Haddock's fleet was more imposing than the Spanish defences, and Spain offered a financial accommodation, which Walpole welcomed eagerly. During the autumn negotiations were carried on between the two Courts, resulting in the Convention of the

---

[1] His own ear or somebody else's. Doubt has been cast on Jenkins's story, and it was asserted that, if his wig had been removed, both his ears would have been found intact.

[2] The only account of Pitt's speech is in *Aff. Etr. Angl. Corr. Pol.* 398, f. 23.

Pardo on January 3–14, 1739, which Walpole boasted was one of his greatest services to the State, and Haddock was recalled. But on examination the merits of the Convention were not so apparent to the country. Spain promised to pay a sum of £95,000 in satisfaction of claims for outrages on British shipping, an amount ludicrously inadequate to the estimate of over £340,000 made of British losses; and even that £95,000, it was soon discovered, was to be whittled down to £27,000 on account of a claim against the South Sea Company, which they did not admit. The separate disputes between the King of Spain and the South Sea Company were left undetermined, while the root of all the mercantile community's grievances—the Spanish claim to an unrestricted right of search even on the high seas—was left to stand over to a further treaty. As soon as these terms were made known they were received with mingled protest and derision. The agitation throughout the country was redoubled: caricatures and satires against Walpole and his Convention stirred the people to fury; and the West India merchants and the City of London again presented petitions to Parliament, denouncing the sacrifice of national interest and honour.

Pitt now for the first time learned his power of giving voice to the people. In the memorable debate of March 8, 1739, in which twenty-five speakers discussed the Convention till one o'clock in the morning, he made his first great speech under the eyes of his master, the Prince of Wales, who remained through the whole sitting. Old Horace Walpole, Sir Robert's brother, had moved an address to the King, thanking him for the Convention, and in the course of his speech had dwelt on the weakness of England, unbefriended abroad, and oppressed by excessive taxation at home.

Here [cried Pitt] is all the confidence, here is the conscious sense of the greatest service that ever was done to this country:—to be complicating questions; to be lumping sanction and approbation like a commisary's accompt; to be covering and taking sanctuary in the Royal name, instead of meeting openly and standing fairly the direct judgment and sentence of Parliament upon this Convention. . . . We are told of our low, unallied condition abroad: to what is

CONVENTION OF PARDO, 1739

that condition due if not to your policy of giving kingdoms to Spain, and all to bring her back again to that great branch of the House of Bourbon, which is now thrown out to you with so much terror. . . . Is this any longer a nation ? or what is an English Parliament if, with more ships in your harbours than in all the navies of Europe, with above two millions of people in your American colonies, you will bear to hear of the expediency of receiving from Spain an insecure, unsatisfactory, dishonourable Convention ? You tell us that our right of sailing unmolested by Spanish searchers will be submitted to plenipotentiaries : the mere submission of such a right is an indignity. . . . Does a man in Spain reason that those pretensions must be regulated to the satisfaction and honour of England ? No, Sir ; they conclude, and with reason, from the high spirit of their administration, from the superiority with which they have so long treated you, that this reference must end, as it has begun, to their honour and advantage. . . . This Convention, Sir, I think from my soul, is nothing but a stipulation for national ignominy ; an illusory expedient, to baffle the resentment of the nation ; a truce without a suspension of hostilities on the part of Spain ; on the part of England a suspension : . . . a surrender of the rights and trade of England to the mercy of plenipotentiaries, and, in this infinitely highest and sacred point—future security, not only inadequate, but directly repugnant to the resolutions of Parliament and the gracious promise from the Throne. The complaints of your despairing merchants—the voice of England—has condemned it. Be the guilt of it upon the head of the adviser. God forbid that this Committee should share the guilt by approving it ![1]

This speech, as may well be believed, created a great stir in the ministerial camp. Of the twenty-five speeches delivered in the debate Sir Robert took notes of only three, of which this was one ; and two of his young men, Fox and Liddell, made a special attack upon Pitt for his abuse of the Ministry ; Winnington, a Lord of the Treasury, remarked that Pitt's were 'the prettyest words and the worst language he had ever heard.' The Opposition were correspondingly delighted, and

---

[1] The general accuracy of this report from *Chandler's Debates* is confirmed by the notes of the speech taken by Sir Robert Walpole during the debate. John Selwyn wrote that ' Mr. Pitt spoke very well, but very abusively, and provoked Mr. Henry Fox and Sir Henry Liddell both to answer him.' Pitt's abuse—no doubt in the passage contrasting Spain's Ministry with our own—is confirmed by Orlebar.

the Prince of Wales kissed Pitt in the House.[1] The importance of the speech lies in its direct appeal to the people from the Ministry and the House of Commons—a new note in parliamentary debates, and the most insistent in all Pitt's oratory and statesmanship. Hardly less important and characteristic is the recollection that there were men in America ready to help us fight our battles. In the division the Ministry carried their address by 260 to 232, and after an almost equally long debate on Report next day by 244 to 214. Thereupon Wyndham declared his intention of seceding from Parliament with most of the minority. He accused the House of being a faction uninfluenced by the universal opinion outside against the Convention, an opinion much strengthened by the calculations made at the time that no less than 234 members had places under the Court, with salaries amounting in the aggregate to over £200,000. But secession was no more help to a cause then than it has ever been, and Walpole openly rejoiced at the ease with which he carried his measures for the rest of the session.

Neither the Convention nor Walpole's success in Parliament were of any avail in averting war. The people of England were set upon it; in the Ministry Newcastle was almost as bellicose from fear of losing his place; and the King of Spain made matters no easier for Walpole by refusing all accommodation with the South Sea Company. Finally, on October 19, 1739, the heralds solemnly proclaimed war at Temple Bar and the Mansion House, amidst the frantic applause of the citizens and the ringing of church bells. The Prince of Wales himself joined the procession and testified to his share in the enthusiasm by stopping outside the Rose Tavern and drinking to the

---

[1] These details are to be found in another letter of J. Selwyn printed in Coxe's *Sir R. Walpole*, iii, 607, printed as of March 17, 1739-40. This letter has hitherto been taken to refer to the debate on Wager's first bill for manning the fleet, introduced in 1739-40, but it obviously refers to 1738-9 and to the debate of March 8, 1738-9. Mention is made in the letter of the secession of the Opposition (see text above), and a call of the House ordered for March 19, which was avoided by an adjournment from March 10 to the 20th. From the Journals it appears that these events happened in March 1738-9, not in 1739-40. Selwyn probably wrote the date 1739 (in the New Style), and Coxe must have thought this was intended for the Old Style, 1739-40.

success of the British arms. No war was ever entered upon so light-heartedly by the people of this country.

The most leading politicians [in Burke's words], the finest orators, and the greatest poets of the time were for it. . . . For that war Pope sang his dying notes. For that war Johnson, in more energetic strains, employed the voice of his early genius. For that war Glover distinguished himself in the way in which his merit was the most natural and happy. The crowd readily followed the politicians in the cry for a war which threatened little bloodshed, and which promised victories that were attended with something more solid than glory.

But though the war was in a sense, as Burke said, one of plunder, it also touched deeper issues in the half-conscious striving of the nation to free its trade from the foreign obstruction which was strangling it. And in perceiving this truth Pitt and his friends saw deeper at the time than Burke half a century later.

When Parliament met in November 1739 the Opposition returned to their duty somewhat shamefacedly. But if they had lost some credit by their secession, Walpole had lost more by continuing in office to carry on a war of which he thoroughly disapproved. The Opposition granted the supplies without difficulty, but showed their distrust of Walpole as a war minister by various motions directed against him. They proposed an address, which was supported by Pitt, that no peace should be made with Spain unless the right of search were entirely abandoned. They picked holes in his warlike measures so effectively that in several respects he was constrained to modify or abandon them. An attempt was made to weaken his majority by reducing the scandalous number of placemen in the House of Commons, to which attention had been pointedly drawn after the division on the Spanish Convention, and was only defeated by a majority of sixteen, in spite of a vigorous speech against it by Walpole himself. From the reports of the debate it does not appear whether Pitt spoke; probably he did, for among his papers is a draft of a speech obviously intended for this occasion. In it he meets the objection, that a Place Bill had often before been brought in unsuccessfully, by recalling Livy's phrase about the Samnites : ' adeo ne infeliciter quidem defensæ libertatis taedebat, et vinci quam non tentare victoriam malebant ' ; and he has this striking phrase about corruption : ' it must cut up Liberty by the root and poison the Fountain of Publick security ; and who that has an English heart can ever be weary of asserting Liberty ? '[1]

Meanwhile the war went but ill for England. After twenty years of peace the fleet, though imposing numerically, was lamentably unready. The ships were undermanned, and a large part of the time of Cabinet councils was devoted to discussing methods of scraping together their proper complements. Pressing, laying an embargo on merchant ships, drafting regiments of foot into the sea-service, were each rejected in turn. The garrison of Minorca, too, was far below its proper strength, and half the officers were on leave in England for over a year after war had begun.[2] The plans of attack on Spain were equally futile. The only success attained during the first year of the war was the easy capture of Porto Bello by Admiral Vernon in December 1739, and that was regarded almost as a rebuff to Walpole, since Vernon was a prominent member of the Opposition.

You do me justice [writes Gower to Pitt] in thinking that no one feels a more sincere joy than I do upon our honest Admiral's glorious triumph over Sir Robert and Spain; I most heartily wish he may continue to persecute them with victories until he has completely revenged all the injuries they have both done this most abused, insulted Nation.[3]

The coast of Spain was supposed to be watched by Admirals Haddock and Balchen ; but so ill equipped were their ships and so contradictory their orders from home that the Spaniards were able to sail without hindrance. In the second half of 1740 two grand expeditions were projected against the Spanish possessions in the West Indies. Vernon, to whom large reinforcements in ships and men were dispatched, was to

---

[1] *Chatham MSS.* 74.   [2] *Add. MSS.* 37934 (Windham Papers).
[3] *Chatham MSS.* 33.

attack Cartagena on the eastern coast of Central America, and Anson was sent with a small squadron to round Cape Horn and co-operate from the western side of the Isthmus of Panama. Anson's ships had to be manned partly by Chelsea pensioners; but in spite of all difficulties he circumnavigated the globe, an achievement which ranks among the proudest annals of the navy, though it had no serious effect on the war. Vernon's attempt was more disastrous. He was a vain blusterer, and quarrelled with General Wentworth, the commander of the troops, like 'Cæsar with Pompey,' says Smollett. His fleet was ill-found, many of his captains were ignorant of their business, and the dissensions of the commanders took the heart out of all ranks. The attack on Cartagena failed miserably, and the subsequent miseries of the wounded and plague-stricken crews have been made notorious by Smollett in 'Roderick Random.' Pitt, whose notes show that he studied carefully the details of this expedition, no doubt learned from them what to avoid when planning expeditions for himself.

The Opposition had justification enough for attempting to turn out so incompetent a government. But when the attempt seemed most promising they received a heavy blow. The death of Wyndham in June 1740 deprived them of their best and most uncompromising leader, and left them a divided party. Carteret, Pulteney and Sandys were becoming lukewarm in Opposition, as Walpole's weakness seemed to offer the prospect of an invitation to join the Ministry; Carteret at any rate was known to be in close communication with Newcastle and Hardwicke.[1] On the other hand Bolingbroke from his French retreat, and the old Duchess Sarah of Marlborough, stimulated the young men of the party to an increasingly active policy. The leader of this section in Parliament was Chesterfield, who saw clearly the need of a thorough change of men and measures and of a new spirit in the councils of the nation. The Duke of Argyll, Cobham, Lord Marchmont, Pope and Lyttelton were all of the same mind, and Pitt, who was then much in Chesterfield's confidence, was one of the foremost on this side.

[1] *Aff. Etr. Angl. Corr. Pol.* 408, f. 254 (Bussy to Fleury, November 1740).

Whatever may have been Walpole's merits in the past, Chesterfield and his friends were right in thinking the time had come, for the good of the country, to drive him out of office, for he had entirely lost control of his own Ministry and as a war minister showed none of the aptitude which had made his long career as a peace-maker illustrious. 'We ought to be very sorry to see him defeated,' wrote the French envoy, ' for no minister could suit us better. He makes war on his enemies at enormous cost without hurting them, and is prodigal to his friends without doing them any benefit.'[1]

The forward party of the Opposition had their way in the session which began in November 1740. On the Address Pitt and Lyttelton were ' very warm,' and Walpole answered them with equal warmth. In January, a motion that the instructions to Haddock should be produced, together with any other papers that might throw light on the mismanagement in the Mediterranean command and the escape of the Spanish fleet, was opposed by Sir Robert on the ground that it would be a mere waste of time.

November 18, 1740.
January 26, 1741.

On the contrary, [retorted Pitt] our time cannot be more usefully employed, during a war, than in examining how it has been conducted, and settling the degree of confidence that may be reposed in those to whose care are entrusted our reputations, our fortunes, and our lives. . . . We are now to examine whether it is probable that we shall preserve our commerce and our independence, or whether we are sinking into subjection to a foreign power.

The Opposition's transient victory in obtaining Haddock's instructions was soon thrown into the shade by their overwhelming defeat in both Houses on the motion made on February 13, 1741, for an address to the King to remove Sir Robert Walpole from his presence and councils for ever.[2] The attack, which appears to have been instigated by Bolingbroke, was feebly supported. Many of the Tories and some of the Prince's household did not vote, and the want of vigour noted in Carteret and Pulteney's

---

[1] *Aff. Etr. Angl. Corr. Pol.* 414, f. 21.
[2] The celebrated bet between Walpole and Pulteney as to the line

$$\text{Nil conscire sibi } \begin{Bmatrix} \text{nulla} \\ \text{nulli} \end{Bmatrix} \text{ pallescere} \begin{Bmatrix} \text{culpa} \\ \text{culpæ} \end{Bmatrix}$$

was made when Sandys gave notice of this motion.

speeches seems to have communicated itself to most of the Opposition speakers in both Houses. Although Walpole again paid him the compliment of taking a note of his speech, Pitt was not at his best. According to Sir Robert,

February 13, 1741.

Pitt observed in his emphatic language that during the administration that was the object of censure, at home debts were increased and taxes multiplied and the sinking fund alienated; abroad the system of Europe was totally subverted, and at this awful moment, when the greatest scene was opening to Europe that has ever occurred, he who had lost the confidence of all mankind should not be permitted to continue at the head of the King's government.

According to the more detailed account in Cobbett, he made a sweeping attack on Walpole's past policy of alliance with the Bourbon Powers, and made great play with the sacrifice of Admiral Hosier's fleet to the worms in 1727 and of the admiral himself and a large part of his crews to the poisonous climate of Porto Bello, then fresh in his hearers' minds through the recent publication of Glover's ballad. The speech contained too a curious anticipation of his future change of attitude to the minister he was then attacking. 'I shall be ready,' he said, ' to declare my approbation of integrity and wisdom, though they should be found where I have long suspected ignorance and corruption.' According to all accounts the honours, not only of the majority but of eloquence, rested with Walpole. As usual when he was at his best, his tone was frankly cynical. One characteristic gibe at Pitt and his young friends is recorded: 'A patriot, Sir! Why, patriots spring up like mushrooms! I could raise fifty of them within the four-and-twenty hours. I have raised many of them in one night. It is but refusing to gratify an unreasonable or insolent demand, and up starts a patriot.'[1]

[1] Pitt's rough notes of this debate are preserved in *Chatham MSS.* 74, of which here are a few extracts : ' What has been the conduct of the war, &c. . . . To what but to the exorbitance of one man. . . . If gentlemen are convinced upon this experience of things that measures have been wise and able, that the Plan, &c. But, Sir, if they think a load of debt perpetuated by destructive schemes, a subversion. . . . What is the voice of the People ? is a lye that travels. Abhor Patriotism as long as he lives.' A curious confirmation of one of these phrases occurs in Bussy's report of the debate (*Aff. Etr.*

Walpole might raise patriots, but he could not suppress this one by flouts or gibes. A few weeks later Pitt was once more in his most fiery mood, re-echoing the popular indignation at an outrageous bill of the Government to secure the men who were not forthcoming for the fleet, and calling the extraordinary powers of inquisition and of pressing, which were to be given to magistrates and constables, ' cruelties . . . as are yet unknown among the most savage nations ; such as slavery has not yet borne, or tyranny invented ; such as cannot be heard without resentment, nor thought of without horror.' To prevent competition with the Royal Navy a clause was proposed restricting the pay that might be offered in the merchant service. This clause, Pitt remarked contemptuously,

March 10, 1741.

may be considered with less ardour and resentment, and fewer emotions of zeal ; because, though not perhaps equally iniquitous, it will do no harm ; for a law that can never be executed can never be felt. That it will consume the manufacture of paper and swell the Book of Statutes is all the good or hurt that can be hoped or feared from a law like this : a law which fixes what is in its own nature mutable, which prescribes rules to the seasons and limits to the wind ;

but he warned Walpole and his brother that even ' those who have only their own interest in view, will be afraid of adhering to those leaders, however old and practised in expedients, however strengthened by corruption, or elated with power, who have no reason to hope for success from either virtue or abilities.' Thereupon old Horace Walpole rose to reprove him for ' formidable sounds and furious declamation, confident assertions and lofty periods,' suggesting that his vehemence of

Angl. Corr. Pol. 411, f. 151). Lyttelton had said that public rumour was a sufficient ground for accusation, to which one of the Court party replied : ' You are yet young and don't know that public rumour is a wandering lie, born in London, sent to the provinces, and thence returned to London as an instruction.' Pitt seems to have been taken by the phrase. In his second speech for an inquiry on Sir Robert Walpole's administration he used the phrase ' Common fame is a sufficient ground for an inquisition at common law, and for the same reason the general voice of England ought always to be looked on as a sufficient ground for a parliamentary inquiry.'

The fiasco of the Opposition was satirised in a popular caricature of the time entitled ' The Motion.'

gesture, theatrical emotion and exaggerated expressions might have been corrected had he conversed with ' such as have had more opportunities of acquiring knowledge and more successful methods of communicating their sentiments.'

The atrocious crime of being a young man—which the hon. gentleman has with such spirit and decency charged upon me [retorts Pitt with ready impertinence] I shall neither attempt to palliate nor deny, but content myself with wishing that I may be one of those whose follies may cease with their youth, and not of that number who are ignorant in spite of experience. Whether youth can be imputed to any man as a reproach I will not assume the province of determining. . . . Much more is he to be abhorred who, as he has advanced in age, has receded from virtue and becomes more wicked with less temptation; who prostitutes himself for money which he cannot enjoy, and spends the remains of his life in the ruin of his country.

The charge of acting a theatrical part he answered more seriously, with a recollection, perhaps, of Sir Robert's sneer:

I am at liberty, like every other man, to use my own language; and though I may, perhaps, have some ambition, yet . . . if any man shall, by charging me with theatrical behaviour, imply that I utter any sentiments but my own, I shall treat him as a calumniator and a villain. . . . I shall, on such an occasion, without scruple trample upon all those forms with which wealth and dignity entrench themselves; nor shall anything but age restrain my resentment; age which always brings one privilege, that of being insolent and supercilious without punishment. But with regard to those whom I have offended . . . the heat that offended them is the ardour of conviction, and that zeal for the service of my country which neither hope nor fear shall influence me to suppress. I will not sit unconcerned while my liberty is invaded nor look in silence upon public robbery.

As he was expatiating on this topic, Winnington rose and called him to order in violent terms. Pitt turned in a flash on the new aggressor:

If this be to preserve order, there is no danger of indecency from the most licentious tongue. . . . Order may sometimes be broken by passion or inadvertency, but will hardly be re-established by a monitor like this, who cannot govern his own passion whilst he is restraining the impetuosity of others. . . .

This spirited bout gives the first taste on record of Pitt's quality in the rapier play of quick retort and passionate invective. There is a touch of cruelty, perhaps, in this picture of the splendid young man with his proud mien and his rush of eloquence thus confounding the pompous old diplomatist. But, to do Pitt justice, it must be remembered that his adversary was buttressed with all those forms with which wealth and dignity entrench themselves and seemed fair game after his stinging sneers at himself, unconnected and fighting desperately for what he believed to be justice and liberty. After this fling at one of its most influential members, the House soon came to recognise in Pitt the master who could silence his opponents with a word or scorch them with a look.[1]

This is Pitt's last recorded speech in his first Parliament. In six years he had become, if not the leader, at any rate the most pertinacious and most dangerous of the Walpole-baiters in the House of Commons. But eloquence and invective made no impression on the minister's docile band of placemen, and Pitt took a sombre view of the state of England:

The scene abroad is most gloomy [he wrote to Chesterfield in August 1741]; whether day is ever to break forth again or destruction and darkness is finally to cover all—*impiaque æternam meruerunt sæcula noctem*—must soon be determined. . . . I only wish, in this great crisis, every man in England may awake.

France, then as powerful to appearance as at any previous period, especially alarmed him, and he believed that 'by her influence and her arms she means, to be sure, to undo all Europe.' Yet, when he wrote these words, Walpole, the chief obstacle to a vigorous policy, was doomed. The general election of May had been a great triumph for the Opposition. Cornwall with its forty-four members had been won over by the Prince of Wales, assisted by Pitt and his brother,[2] and

---

[1] The actual words of Pitt's retort may have been adjusted by Johnson, as he claimed, in his garret, but the dignity of his self-defence rings true, and the sarcastic invective is in keeping with all his known speeches.

[2] In *Chatham MSS.* 83 is a bundle of papers referring to the two brothers' help in the Cornish elections.

through the apathy of the Duke of Newcastle, as well as by the exertions of the other side, Walpole's majority had almost vanished. In the new Parliament Pitt himself was again nominated for Old Sarum and had as his fellow-member one of his friends the Grenvilles, four of whom altogether found seats. For two months of the session of 1742 Walpole, game to the last, clung to office in spite of dwindling support or even defeat. In a great debate on the Spanish war on January 21 he saved himself by a majority of only three votes,[1] and a week later, being beaten on the Chippenham election petition, he resigned.

The victory was more apparent than real, and the dreams of the young men, Pitt, Lyttelton and Chesterfield, that with Walpole's fall corruption and oppression would cease and the arch-criminal be signally punished, were speedily dispelled. The new Earl of Orford's influence was almost as great as Sir Robert Walpole's; he became reconciled with the Prince of Wales, had secret interviews with Carteret and Pulteney within a few days of his resignation, and arranged the new Ministry to suit his wishes. Pulteney called a great meeting of the Opposition at the Fountain Tavern to talk over the disposal of offices, but it was merely to throw dust in their eyes, for everything had been settled behind their backs. Wilmington, a nonentity, took the Treasury; Pulteney committed political suicide by accepting a peerage and declining office; Carteret, the new Secretary of State, had no desire to take vindictive measures against the late Prime Minister; Sandys, the maker of motions, was silenced by the Exchequer; and the Prince of Wales was gratified by the offer of Court appointments to two of his household. An attempt was even made to secure Waller, the nominal leader of the Young

---

[1] It is not recorded whether Pitt spoke in this debate, but it is clear that he intended to, from notes for a speech to be found among his papers (*Chatham MSS.* 74). These notes, after 'Thanks for his Royal care in the prosecution of the war agst. Spain' and his 'Paternal concern for the affairs of Europe,' dwell on the complaints of the merchants, on the vast consequence of Leghorn to us, of our unallied condition, and of ministers 'talking big when the fate of Europe and [. . . ?] of other countries are in suspense.'

Patriots in the Commons,[1] but he refused to join without knowing what the measures of the new Ministry were to be. Walpole's chief object was to retain sufficient interest in the Government to prevent the same fate being meted out to him which he had contrived for Oxford and Bolingbroke. The only men he feared and excluded were those who by their energy and determination within the last few years had most contributed to his fall—Argyll,[2] Cobham and all the Grenvilles, Chesterfield, Lyttelton and Pitt.

The country was barely considered in these arrangements. The stories, largely exaggerated, of Walpole's methods of corruption, retailed week by week in *The Craftsman*, the attacks on his foreign policy, and the obvious failure of the Spanish war, had produced their effect on the nation. Petitions flowed into the House of Commons for inquiry into the charges so freely made against him, and the politicians who formerly had never ceased abusing him as a rogue and traitor were called upon by their constituents to make good their statements and arraign him for his misdemeanours. No less than eighteen counties and twenty-seven cities and boroughs sent up instructions to their members, calling upon them to restore triennial parliaments, limit placemen, and 'strictly inquire into the conduct of those who have insulted the merchants, sacrificed the trade, and prostituted the honour of Great Britain, that their punishment upon due conviction may be as exemplary as their crimes are notorious.' But Walpole's friends in the new Ministry were too numerous and under too much obligation to him to contemplate taking serious notice of these complaints of the people. It was left to the outcasts to press for the inquiry demanded by the nation. Pitt and Lyttelton at any rate were determined, in the words of one of Walpole's

---

[1] *Egmont MSS.* 88 (February 12, 1742). There appears no solid ground for the story told by Glover, and repeated on his authority by Coxe and Macaulay, that Lyttelton, Pitt and the Grenvilles offered terms to Walpole. Glover is not very trustworthy, and the Prince of Wales, whom he quotes as his authority, still less so. The *Hagley MSS.* are silent on the subject, and all the evidence tends to disprove it.

[2] Argyll at first accepted the Board of Ordnance at the request of his party, but, on finding the hollowness of the reconstruction, rejoined his old friends.

supporters, 'to blow up Carlton House, rather than not have a chance to do more mischief.'

When, on March 9, 1742, Lord Limerick, one of the Young Patriots, moved for an inquiry into Sir Robert's administration during the last twenty years, it was noticed that both Pulteney and Sandys were absent, and that Sir John Barnard, who had been a prominent antagonist of the late minister, did not speak. Pulteney had a good reason for absence in the illness of his daughter, but a hint was given to his friends by Carteret that their absence would not be taken amiss. Nevertheless the debate called forth some vigorous speeches, of which the ablest and the most eloquent was Pitt's. Nettled by a request of Pelham for no long harangues or flowers of rhetoric, he retorted that

<small>March 9, 1742.</small>

a man who speaks from his heart and is sincerely affected with the subject he speaks on, as every honest man must be who speaks in the cause of his country—such a man, I say, falls naturally into expressions which may be called flowers of rhetoric, and therefore deserves as little to be charged with affectation as the most stupid serjeant-at-law that ever spoke for half a guinea a fee.

A large portion of the speech was naturally taken up with a criticism of Walpole's home and foreign policy. He passed in review his tenderness to the South Sea directors in 1721, the lavish and secret expenditure from the Civil List, the excise scheme, encroachments on the sinking fund, and the large army maintained in time of peace. He attacked his foreign policy, especially his alienation from the Emperor since the Treaty of Hanover of 1727, and his constant subservience to the Bourbon Powers, Pitt's bugbear on the Continent. Commenting on Walpole's complacency at steering the country clear through the war of the Polish Succession, 'It was not our preparation,' he declared, 'that set bounds to the ambition of France, but her getting all she wanted at that time for herself, and all she desired for her allies.' The principle, too, which he always upheld, of Parliament's unfettered right of advice and inquiry, already found clear expression in his answer to the objection that the proposed inquiry should not be instituted, since no definite charges had been formulated:

Sir, the very name given to this House of Parliament shows the contrary! We are called the Grand Inquest of the Nation, and as such it is our duty to inquire into every step of public management, either abroad or at home, in order to see that nothing has been done amiss.

To another objection that an inquiry was inopportune at a time of distress at home and abroad Pitt also had his answer:

According to this way of arguing, a minister that has plundered and betrayed his country, and fears being called to an account in Parliament, has nothing to do but to involve his country in a dangerous war or some other distress, in order to prevent an inquiry into his conduct. . . . Thus, like the most villainous of all thieves, after he has plundered the house, he has nothing to do but to set it in a flame that he may escape in the confusion. . . . But, say these gentlemen, if you found yourself upon a precipice, would you stand to inquire how you was led there, before you considered how to get off? No, Sir; but if a guide had led me there, I should very probably be provoked to throw him over, before I thought of anything else; at least, I am sure I should not trust to the same guide for bringing me off.

Even Parliament was not the ultimate tribunal, unless it was a true mirror of the nation; and, because he believed it was not, Pitt pleaded even then for a more representative system in words that find an echo in some of his latest speeches:

The murmurs of the people against the conduct of the Administration are now as general and as loud as ever they were upon any occasion; but . . . gentlemen who are in Administration or in any office under it, can rarely know the voice of the people. The voice of this House was formerly, I shall grant, and always ought to be, the voice of the people. If new parliaments were more frequent, and few placemen and no pensioners admitted, it would be so still; but if long parliaments should prevail, not only at elections, but in this House, the voice of this House will generally be very different from—nay, often directly contrary to—the voice of the people.

A consciousness that he was himself the mouthpiece of this voice of the people gave him the right to demand Walpole's punishment in stern and uncompromising language:

Let it be ever so severe, it will be but a small atonement to his country for what is past. But his impunity will be the source of many future miseries to Europe, as well as his native country. Let us be as merciful as we will, as any man can reasonably desire, when we come to pronounce sentence; but sentence we must pronounce, and for this purpose we must inquire, unless we are resolved to sacrifice our own liberties and the liberties of Europe to the preservation of one guilty man.

On the division, the motion was defeated by only two votes. A fortnight later Pulteney, aware that his credit would be ruined for ever if he failed to avert the suspicion that he was privy to this miscarriage, encouraged Lord Limerick to renew his motion, confining the examination to ten years instead of twenty. In this debate Pulteney himself made a hard-hitting speech, and young Horace Walpole defended his father with skill and modesty, drawing from Pitt the artful compliment that 'his speech must have made an impression on the House. March 23, But if it is becoming in him to remember that he is the child 1742. of the accused, it also behoves the House to remember that we are the children of our country.' Otherwise Pitt's speech was little more than a re-capitulation of the arguments he had used on March 9.

On this occasion Walpole's adversaries carried the motion for inquiry by a majority of seven. The House immediately proceeded to elect the secret committee of twenty-one, each member handing in his own list of names. The work of scrutinising these lists occupied a committee uninterruptedly from 5 p.m. on March 26 to 4 p.m. on March 27. At the head of the list came Sir John St. Aubyn with 518 votes; the most notable among the other members were Sandys, Lord Quarendon, Sir John Barnard, Lord Limerick and Lord Cornbury: Pitt came almost last of those elected, with 259 votes. For the last two places four tied at 258, of whom the Speaker selected two members stated to be Walpole's only friends among the twenty-one. The committee set to work without delay, and continued their labours during April and May. These were much impeded by the steady refusal of the Treasury officials to answer questions which might incriminate themselves or the minister. Scrope, Secretary of the

Treasury, a testy old gentleman who had fought in Monmouth's Rebellion, so highly resented a peremptory inquiry from Pitt that he was hardly restrained from challenging him to a duel. Finally, the committee asked the House to pass a Bill of Indemnity covering witnesses who should incriminate themselves. It passed the Commons, but, largely by Carteret's influence, was rejected in the Lords. The committee did, however, elicit the total amounts of Secret Service money issued during the last ten years of Walpole's Administration. These were so high as to go far to justify the accusations of corruption. The average amount expended had risen from £45,900 a year between 1707 and 1720 to £145,390 between 1730 and 1740, and during the year of the Excise Bill, as Pitt specially noted,[1] it had stood at the large sum of £165,112. But the committee was cut short by the prorogation before it could investigate fully the purposes to which these amounts were devoted, and although Waller, supported by Pitt, pressed for its revival in the next session, the motion was rejected by a large majority.

Pitt was highly indignant at the way in which the inquiry was shelved, recurring to it several times in succeeding sessions; but he made no more attacks on his first great adversary. Some things about Walpole's administration he never forgave, and thirteen years later recalled that during this period 'this nation was brought to its distressed condition by the French being allowed to make their establishments on the Mississippi and the Great Lakes, to acquire Lorraine, and to found two Bourbon lines in Italy.' Nor did he ever withdraw his criticisms on Walpole's use of corruption, his cynical disregard of public opinion, and his contempt of patriotic sentiment, so alien to his own generous belief in the ready response his countrymen would make to an appeal for union and public spirit. But as years went by the feelings of the two men softened to one another. In 1743 Orford wrote to his disciple Pelham, 'Pitt is thought able and formidable; try him or show him.' Pitt came to see that in many respects

December 2, 1755.

[1] *Chatham MSS.* 81, which contains notes taken by Pitt during the proceedings of the committee.

the cautious old statesman had been in the right, and avowed his changes of opinion with his accustomed frankness, thereby exposing himself to the absurd charge of insincerity and faction in his former attacks. Speaking of the claim, declared by Walpole to be impracticable, to abolish the Spaniards' right of search even on their own coasts, he said: *January 17, 1751.*

> I once was an advocate for that claim; it was when I was very young and sanguine. But now I am ten years older; I have considered public affairs more coolly and am convinced that the claim of *no search* respecting British vessels near the coast of Spanish America can never be obtained, unless Spain were so reduced as to consent to any terms her conqueror might think proper to impose.

His quixotic confession about his change of view on the excise scheme has already been noted. Little wonder that at first the zealous young patriot could see only the obvious faults of a system which was outworn and resting mainly on corruption; as he grew older he was better able to appreciate the great work of Walpole's first ten years in the consolidation of the Protestant dynasty. No doubt the troubled days of 1744, when he, Orford and the King kept their heads better than anyone in England, brought him to see that Walpole's fear of the Pretender was not imaginary, and that for all his cynicism he had a true love of his country. By 1755 he was able to glory in the reflection that Walpole, 'a truly English minister, thought well of me and died at peace with me,' and on another occasion he boasted: *December 2; 1755.*

> I constantly opposed him as a minister and yet after he resigned I always spoke well of him as a man. Gentlemen may laugh if they please, but I can perceive no joke in what I have said. It is only a proof that my opposition did not proceed from any personal resentment, nor my praise from any desire to flatter.

CHAPTER IV

PITT AND CARTERET

Βροντᾶν μὲν αὐτὸν καὶ ἀστράπτειν ὅτε δημηγορείη, δεινὸν δὲ κεραυνὸν ἐν γλώσσῃ φέρειν.—PLUTARCH, *Pericles*.[1]

AFTER the Queen's death in 1737 Pitt's sister Ann had lost her employment at Court, and the two had kept house together while he was in London for the session. She soon, however, showed symptoms of the restless disposition which became more marked with age. In 1741 she went off to Spa and settled for some time in France with friends recommended by Lady Suffolk. William not only approved, but expressed strong resentment to Lady Suffolk against a meddlesome lady who ventured to question the wisdom of his sister's conduct. To Lord Chesterfield he also wrote approving of this expedition, though the whimsical artificiality of his comparison between her journey and current political topics suggests that he may have felt her loss more than he cared to say.

I am extremely obliged to your Lordship [he writes on August 6, 1741] for the account you are so good as to give me of my sister's journey to France. I am perfectly satisfied with this measure which as her minister you transmit to me. . . . I like the state y^r Lordship gives me of her foreign affairs as much as I dislike that of another great Power; first she knows where she is going and what she is going about, the recovery of what is essentially necessary to her, her health : in the next place she is in good company strengthened

---

[1] 'He thundered and lightened as he spoke, and his tongue was armed with the thunderbolt.'—(This is quoted of Pitt in *The English Pericles*, a pamphlet of 1759.)

with proper alliances which will be both agreeable and usefull to her in her designs; and lastly, far from burdening her People with extraordinary votes for credit she will be able to live very well within her Civil list. . . . I wish half so much could be said for all foreign journeys.[1]

But when, in the following year, Ann conceived the idea of setting up for herself alone in Paris, he objected strongly. To Lady Suffolk, who was consulted by both of them on the proposal, he writes that he told Ann,

that I could not see the scheme proposed to her in any light that let me think it fit for her; that I thought Paris the most improper place for a single woman to live at, nor could I like her settling abroad anywhere, if her health did not make it necessary; that I made no doubt but the society my lady Bolingbroke's protection (which was the best in France [2]) must place her in, would be, to all the world on that side the water, the most reputable advantageous thing imaginable; but that the world here would not know (and perhaps part of it not choose to know) anything more of her situation than that she was living at Paris, a single woman.

Although Ann gave up the idea of a solitary establishment in Paris, Pitt must have felt deeply the separation from his dearest Nanny, a separation which seems to have permanently weakened the tenderness of their early relations. This

---

[1] *Chatham MSS.* 6. It is interesting to trace the development of this stilted language—still more characteristic of Pitt's later correspondence. A draft of another letter to Chesterfield of the same year (1741) shows by its erasures and corrections the extraordinary care with which Pitt would sometimes elaborate even the most unimportant letters. The draft runs as follows: 'Your lordship will have performed your revolutions round the Provinces and {visible} that you are now {seen} again at Paris and {will-be-in-your-meridian-of-pleasure-at} {Versailles} -again where we hear {they} {are-as-much-struck} {be-with} {you-are-really-look'd-at} as astronomers would -do- of } a -new of uncommon magnitude } {appeared} Star not-known that had } just {discovered} in that hemisphere. . . . {not to descend} {of-the-celestial-bodies} My Lord {I will not make} from this high-flown {metaphor -any-further . . . ' Even for relatively trifling affairs Pitt took infinite pains.

[2] Lady Bolingbroke was a Frenchwoman.

interruption of their happy union was a serious loss to him at a time of special strain, when a man stands most in need of something more than political friendships.

Pitt himself had now taken lodgings in Cork Street, Burlington Gardens, but as usual spent most of the summer and autumn visiting friends in the country. He had his turn of attendance on the Prince of Wales at Clifden, but found a coolness there owing to his opposition to Carteret, still a favourite with the Prince. He was invited to the Queensberrys at Amesbury, and stayed with Lord Cobham at Stowe, with Lady Suffolk at Marble Hill, with Lord Cornbury, and at Hagley to meet Lyttelton and his newly wedded bride, Lucy Fortescue. At several of these houses he found William Murray, with whom he had his last intimate talks; soon afterwards their ways parted, for Murray joined the Ministry and began his life-long antagonism to Pitt.

Meanwhile the Spanish war had sunk into the background, partly owing to the half-hearted way in which it was waged, partly owing to the more exciting scene unrolled upon the Continent since the death of Frederick William of Prussia in May and of the Emperor Charles VI in October 1740. Charles, foreseeing the troubles which would befall his daughter and heir, Maria Theresa, had spent a considerable proportion of his long reign in obtaining the adhesion of the Powers to the Pragmatic Sanction, which guaranteed her the succession to the hereditary dominions of the Hapsburgs, Austria, the Tyrol, Silesia, Transylvania, Bohemia, Hungary, the Milanese in the north of Italy, and the Low Countries. All the Powers, by solemn treaties,[1] adhered to the Pragmatic Sanction; but the breath had hardly left Charles's body before the emptiness of most of these promises was manifest. Frederic II, within two months of the Emperor's death, invaded and occupied Silesia, to part of which his house had ancient claims. Belle-

---

[1] Spain in April 1725; Russia in August 1726; Prussia in December 1728; England in March 1731; the Empire (including Hanover) in February 1732; Holland in February 1732; Denmark in May 1732; France in November 1738.

isle and other hot-heads at the French Court brushed aside old Cardinal Fleury's feeble scruples about breaking a solemn engagement, and persuaded Louis XV that a suitable method of reviving the glories of the Grand Siècle would be to attack the young princess while she was still weak and unsupported. Louis came to an understanding with Frederic; the Elector of Bavaria was encouraged by the promise of French aid to assert his claims to parts of Bohemia and Austria; and Bellisle was sent on a gorgeous embassy to impress the German princelings with French magnificence and persuade them to choose the Elector of Bavaria as Emperor, instead of Maria Theresa's husband. The Queen of Spain was not one to neglect so favourable an opportunity of providing for her own brood. Don Carlos, her eldest son, was already established in the two Sicilies, but the second, Don Philip, was without an appanage. A claim was accordingly made on part of the unlucky Hapsburgs' dominions in North Italy and a Spanish army dispatched to enforce it. Maria Theresa, attacked by hungry freebooters on all sides, appealed with success to the chivalry of her discontented Hungarian subjects and called for aid from Holland, Russia and England. Holland, though sympathetic, would not budge. Russia was willing enough to help but was crippled for the first years of the struggle by a Swedish war and the dynastic troubles, which followed the death of the Empress Anne.

England alone remained true to her engagements. The hard fate of the young Queen of Hungary aroused a chivalrous feeling in the people, and the aggressive spirit of the Bourbon Powers confirmed the politicians' affection for the 'Old System' of alliance with the Hapsburgs. Unfortunately, these right inclinations were not guided by any clear perception of our proper function in a continental war or by any consistent policy. Old Horace Walpole's criticism on his brother's system at the beginning of the war applies to English policy throughout: 'We have no great plan in view, or *système suivi*; we act by fits and starts; we will have this and that; another shall not have anything without giving us what does not belong to us; . . . there are no two powers of a mind, about measures to be taken to save England.'[1] Instead of carrying on a vigorous campaign against France and Spain at sea, where we were strong, and encouraging the Queen of Hungary by timely concessions to create a powerful confederacy in Germany against France, we frittered away our resources, sending useless little armies of our own to the Continent and paying large subsidies to hire half-hearted mercenaries. Walpole began this system in 1741 by a subsidy of £300,000 to Maria Theresa, and a promise to hire 12,000 Danes and Hessians for her, while he encouraged her to resist Frederic of Prussia to the utmost. Then, as soon as France became menacing, he persuaded her, too late, to make a temporary truce with Frederic.

The French had already captured Prague and were threatening Vienna when Carteret took over the direction of foreign affairs. Among the statesmen of the eighteenth century Carteret's personality is one of the most engaging. Frank and jovial, he never showed a trace of vindictiveness even to his bitterest opponents. From Oxford, according to his friend Swift, 'with a singularity scarce to be justified, he carried away more Greek, Latin, and philosophy than properly became a person of his rank.' This love of the classics he kept to the last, and solaced his dying moments by quoting to an under-secretary, who brought him the Treaty of Paris to sign, the rolling lines of Sarpedon's speech in the 'Iliad.' He had a greater knowledge of continental politics than any Englishman of his time; he could express himself in most foreign languages, and in his own was an accomplished orator. He was also an eminently courageous man. 'As

---

[1] The same sentiment was more flippantly expressed by Hanbury Williams in his ballad on the year 1743:

> 'Who is there but the Lord above
> That knoweth what this nation's doing;
> Whether the war goes on with Spain,
> In which so many Britons fell;
> And what our fleets do on the main,
> The Lord, and only he, can tell.
>
>   .   .   .   .   .
>
> The Lord knows how our army'll fare,
> We're governed by the Lord knows who;
> Our King is gone the Lord knows where,
> And the Lord knows what we shall do.'

I have courage enough,' he thanked God, ' to risque in a good cause my natural life; I am much less solicitous about my political life, which is all my enemies can take from me'; but he would have done better for himself and his country had he taken more thought of his political life, if by that he meant the confidence of his countrymen. ' What is it to me,' he once said, ' who is a judge or a bishop ? It is my business to make kings and emperors, and to maintain the balance of Europe.' This spirit would, as Chesterfield said, have enabled him to become a Richelieu in France, but with a parliamentary government would not do. Twenty years earlier his bad judgment in paying court to the younger instead of the older mistress of George I had lost him his post of Secretary of State. And age had not improved his judgment. Secure in the favour of George II, who was pleased and flattered by his knowledge of German politics and the German language, Carteret now made the mistake of despising his fellow-ministers, to whom he displayed ' an obstinate and offensive silence,' often leaving them ' in entire ignorance . . . both with respect to the operations of the war, and the sources from whence they arose ; and to any negotiations that may have been carrying either for peace or war.'[1] Vigorous he undoubtedly was, but with little method in his vigour, making treaties or conducting warlike operations without any clear plan of action or consideration of details. His main idea, like Pitt's, was aversion to France. In words reproducing the very spirit of the younger man's letter to Chesterfield in 1741,[2] he declared in 1743 that the sole issue in foreign affairs was, ' Will you submit to France or not ? I will always traverse the views of France in place and out of place ; for France will ruin this nation if it can.' But these words, unlike Pitt's, were not fruitful in action, for his success in humbling France was slight. Again like Pitt he rejected the word ' impossible ' from his vocabulary, but was less fortunate in excluding it from his practice.

---

[1] He was reported to have said of Pelham: ' he was only chief clerk to Sir Robert Walpole. Why should he expect to be more under me . . . he did his drudgery and he shall do mine.' (*Egmont MSS.* vol. 88 ; January 6, 1743–4.)

[2] See above, p. 86.

In spite, therefore, of all his charm and accomplishments he remained to the end little more than a type of the dilettante statesman so common in our history. Such men try many methods of attaining the desired results without any certainty of the goal to which these methods will lead them. They often succeed after a fashion if they are given time. Carteret was unlucky in never having had enough time. At this crisis his very understanding of German politics proved his undoing, for instead of simplifying the issue it encouraged him to plunge the country irrevocably into the mazes of continental complications.

In the course of 1742 Carteret displayed vigour and resource in marked contrast to Walpole's lethargic methods. He promptly raised the Queen of Hungary's subsidy from £300,000 to £500,000, told the French ambassador the King would allow no diminution of the Hapsburg dominions, and tried to form a great German confederacy to expel the French from the Empire. He even went over to Holland himself for a week to arouse the Dutch to action. At first all seemed to promise well. In June, after Frederic's victory at Chotusitz in Bohemia, Maria Theresa was induced, chiefly by Carteret's mediation, to sign the Treaty of Breslau with Prussia. The French were hard pressed in Prague, and Bavaria was invaded by the Austrian armies. In Italy Maria Theresa was temporarily relieved of one enemy by an English squadron under Martin, who in August appeared in the Bay of Naples and, watch in hand, gave Don Carlos half an hour to decide whether he would withdraw his troops from North Italy or have his capital bombarded. Don Carlos yielded, but never forgave England, as Pitt had cause to know eighteen years later, when Carlos succeeded to the throne of Spain. But, so far as England was concerned, Carteret's measures were a failure. He planned a great campaign in the Low Countries against France, and sent over 16,000 English troops to join with 6000 Hessians and 16,000 Hanoverians. These he hired from George II as Elector without the consent of Parliament. Lord Stair, the fiery veteran of seventy placed in command, proposed to march on Dunkirk or even Paris, but was held back for want of the

Dutch troops, which, though promised to Carteret, were never dispatched. The army consequently spent the autumn in Ghent, 'idle, unemployed, and quarrelling with the inhabitants,' the Hanoverians on English pay and doing nothing.

The hiring of these Hanoverian troops, far more than the idleness of the army during the campaign of 1742, brought on Carteret unmeasured obloquy. 'The Ministry,' wrote Edward Montagu, 'have got themselves more enemies in the short time they have been in, than Lord Orford in his long reign, for they are ruining the country faster than ever he did, and this infamous job of the Hanoverian troops, it's thought was what he never would give way to.' The English of the eighteenth century had a tendency to savage national antipathies far more marked than to-day, when the population of this kingdom has vastly increased and the bounds of the Empire embrace almost every quarter of the globe. These antipathies were manifested at different times against the French, the Scots, and the Jews, but never perhaps more strongly than against Hanover during the reigns of the first two Hanoverian kings. This prejudice, however unreasonable, is intelligible. Neither George I nor his son concealed their dislike of a kingdom where they were ridiculed or at best tolerated, and their devotion to an electorate where they were understood and venerated. 'There are kings enough in England,' fretfully exclaimed George II; 'I am nothing there; I am old and want rest, and should only be plagued and teased there about that d——d House of Commons.'[1] Accordingly they went to Hanover as often as possible, regardless of the state of business in England, and at great inconvenience to the English ministers. This inconvenience might have been borne had it not been suspected that English interests abroad were habitually sacrificed to those of Hanover, and at no time more so than when the King was in his own electorate away from the control of the aforesaid House of Commons. The very general belief in England that our national interests had been subordinated to those of Hanover found utterance at this time in a celebrated pamphlet, 'The case of the Hanover Forces in the pay of Great Britain,' which

[1] *Add. MSS.* 32857, f. 553.

was probably written by Chesterfield and Waller, but is sometimes attributed to Pitt, and certainly represents his views. In this pamphlet the superiority of France, the Hapsburgs' weakness and our own impotence were all ascribed to Walpole's system of alliance with the Bourbons, of which the chief motive was found in the quarrels of the electorate with the Emperor. In the present conjuncture the writers admitted our obligation to support the Queen of Hungary with subsidies and auxiliary troops, but protested against our taking a direct part in the continental war that did not concern us; the Low Countries, in which alone our merchants and our allies the Dutch were vitally interested, were not threatened by French operations in Bohemia. Least of all should we hire Hanoverian troops. In the previous year Hanover had shuffled off her own obligations to Maria Theresa by signing a treaty of neutrality with France. If Hanover desired to fulfil her engagement to guarantee the Pragmatic Sanction, let her do so at her own expense, not at ours.[1] On Walpole's policy Pitt and his friends were unjust. The acquisition of Bremen and Verden by the electorate and some obscure quarrels with the Emperor about Mecklenburg were not the reason of Walpole's devotion to the French alliance, but a well-founded belief that England needed rest for the consolidation of the Protestant dynasty. Against Carteret the charges had more substance. Being anxious to secure the favour of a sovereign who looked on the affairs of the Empire as the only subject of serious interest to mankind, he forgot that England was primarily a maritime, not a continental, power. In the war of the Austrian Succession he lost all interest in the national war with Spain and plunged lightheartedly into the European struggles.

Pitt had not reached the clear conception of British policy that he afterwards attained: he was still in the critical rather than the constructive stage. But his criticisms touched vital issues. He was constantly asking himself and his countrymen what they were aiming at; what they were fighting for; and

[1] Hanbury Williams's profane wit once more supplies an indication of the popular feeling. A sufficient taste of his *Old England's Te Deum* may be given by the line: 'Vouchsafe, O King, to keep us this year without thy Hanoverians.'

refused to take jargon about the 'old system' for an answer. On one conclusion he was clear—that if we were to fight, we should fight with all our might for ourselves instead of trusting to Hanoverian or other mercenaries. When a minister of the Chancellor's eminence defended the employment of Hanoverians on the ground that 'to hire foreigners of whatever country, only to save the blood of Englishmen, is in my opinion an instance of preference which ought to produce rather acknowledgments of gratitude than sallies of indignation,'[1] it was indeed high time for a Pitt to raise his voice in protest. While groping for the light he uttered many sentiments in his impulsive way which his maturer judgment did not confirm; but he never cared greatly for verbal consistency and never hesitated afterwards to admit his errors. Later he frankly stated his early obligations to Carteret's knowledge of statecraft, but never recanted the savage philippics he gave vent to at this time against the 'desperate rhodomontading minister.' He objected to Carteret's absorption in purely continental policy, to his ill-digested schemes, to the narrow basis of his administration, and to his want of confidence in the English people, who were dragged blindly behind his car instead of marching joyfully at the call of a trusting and trusted leader. Ever since Carteret's first parleyings with Walpole's Ministry in 1738 Pitt had mistrusted him. In a letter of advice to the Prince of Wales, written when there was some talk of reconciliation with the King, Pitt had told him 'to resolve to set quite still,' and above all not to trust himself to Carteret, who was always chopping and changing to suit his own interest and passion.[2] This advice had not been taken, consequently Pitt, in his growing opposition to Carteret, found himself as much at variance with the Prince of Wales as with the King. But thanks to the reputation he had acquired by his attacks on Walpole he was now strong enough to stand by himself. In the session which opened in November 1742, the Boy Patriots were nominally under Waller, but 'Pitt,' says Glover, 'the most distinguished among the younger sort, and by

[1] Harris, *Hardwicke*, ii, 38.
[2] The draft of this letter is in *Chatham MSS*. 74.

his pompous and sarcastical oratory reputed an excellent orator, took the lead'; Philip Yorke, too, the Chancellor's son, calls him 'the most popular speaker in the House of Commons and at the head of his party.' This impression was confirmed by his speech on the Address, which his friend Grenville likened to that of ten thousand angels, and the cooler French agent declared to be distinguished by eloquence and knowledge in a debate otherwise tumultuous and ill informed.¹

A few days later he had the first of many encounters with 'the English Cicero,' Murray, who had disowned all his old connections with Pitt, Lyttelton, and the Grenvilles and had accepted from Carteret the post of Solicitor-General for the express purpose of standing up to Pitt.² On December 7, on the motion for maintaining the English army in Flanders, Murray made his maiden speech both as minister and as member, and gained great applause by his attack on what he called the factious inconsistency of the Opposition in demanding a vigorous policy and then turning on the minister who gave it. Pitt, 'the new Demosthenes, rose to reply amid the hushed expectation of the House of Commons, then as now delighted at the prospect of a personal encounter. The House was not disappointed. Pitt spoke in his best manner. He used all Murray's arguments and turned them against him. The inconsistency, he retorted, was not in the Opposition but in ministers who were now engaged on an aggressive policy on their own account, whereas in the previous session all they had asked for was a provision to support the Queen of Hungary with money and auxiliary troops. Pitt's triumph was immediate.

The one [said a fellow-member] spoke like a pleader, and could not divest himself of a certain appearance of having been employed by

¹ *Aff. Etr. Angl. Corr. Pol.* 416, f. 60.
² Murray had married in 1738 Lady Elizabeth Finch, daughter of Lord Winchilsea, who was one of Carteret's few personal supporters in the Ministry, and he was probably chosen by Carteret for this reason as well as for his ability. He proved disloyal to his patron as he had been to his friends, an in the following year made several revelations of Cabinet secrets to the leaders of the Opposition.

others. The other spoke like a gentleman, like a statesman, who felt what he said, and possessed the strongest desire of conveying that feeling to others, for their own interest and that of their country. Murray *gains* your attention by the perspicuity of his arguments and the elegance of his diction. Pitt *commands* your attention and respect by the nobleness, the greatness of his sentiments, the strength and energy of his expression, and the certainty you are in of his always rising to a greater elevation both of thought and style. For this talent he possesses beyond any speaker I ever heard—of never falling from the beginning to the end of his speech, either in thought or in expression. And, as in this session he has begun to speak like a man of business, as well as an orator. he will in all probability be, or rather at present is, allowed to make as great an appearance as ever man did in that House. . . . I think him sincerely the most finished character I ever knew.

Oswald, the writer of this passage, adds that Murray, after this first defeat by Pitt, never opened his lips on the same subject for the rest of the year. Murray was always a timorous creature.

During the rest of the session 1742–3 Pitt thundered against the useless army in Flanders and the Hanoverian troops. He had another bout with old Horace Walpole, who accused him of 'inciting the dregs of society to insult their superiors,' and he made a telling point against Carteret's ill-considered policy by producing a letter of Frederic II to show that any army we sent into the Empire would have to reckon with him as well as with France. He even attacked the King in a great speech of December 10 on the pay of the Hanover troops.

_{February 24, 1743.}

_{December 10, 1742.}

* Neither justice nor policy [he began] required us to engage in the quarrels of the Continent : . . . the confidence of the people is abused by making unnecessary alliances, they are then pillaged to provide the subsidies. Let us be better husbands of the people's money and then show our gratitude for the confidence they repose in us. . . . We are already tired of seeing a large idle army here. Will it profit us more that it is doing nothing on the Continent ? We are told the Dutch would join us, but they say that was never their intention. Now to remedy this deficiency we have taken Hanoverian troops.* [1]

[1] In the *Magazin des Nouvelles Anglaises* of December 29, 1742, published at the Hague, this speech of Pitt's is given at length and no other speech in the debate is reported. The reports in this sheet are interesting as they profess to be sent direct from London and indeed are the only reports published at the

How will it help us to hire these troops to eat and sleep ? I will readily allow that we should inviolably observe our treaties and observe them though every other nation should disregard them; that we should show an example of fidelity to mankind and stand firm though we should stand alone in the practice; yet is Hanover to be prevented from sending her quota to the Queen of Hungary because we hire all her available troops ? For it is not to be imagined that his Majesty has more or less regard to justice as King of Great Britain than as Elector of Hanover; or that he would not have sent his proportion of troops to an Austrian army, had not the temptation of greater profit been industriously laid before him. . . . But why should the Elector of Hanover exert his liberality at the expense of Great Britain ? It is now too apparent that this great, this powerful, this formidable kingdom is considered only as a province to a despicable electorate. . . . We need only look at the instances of partiality which have been shown; the yearly visits that have been made to that delightful country . . . all the sums that have been spent to aggrandize and enrich it.

He concluded with a solemn adjuration to the House to remember ' the duty of the representatives of the people . . . and to show that, however the interest of Hanover has been preferred by the ministers, the Parliament pays no regard but to that of Great Britain.'

This speech and others like it in succeeding years were little calculated to allay George II's growing aversion to Pitt. Nor for the moment did they avail to shake the position of Carteret, who, strong in his master's confidence, was still able to impose his will on his colleagues. In the House of Lords he defended his policy with vigour, and, contrary to expectation, had open support even from the Duke of Newcastle for his Hanoverian measures. In the ensuing campaign a transient success seemed for a while to justify his policy.

In the spring of 1743 the allied army under Stair was at last put in motion. One French army under the Duc de Broglie was in great straits in Bavaria, and another of 60,000 under the Duc de Noailles was ordered to cross the

time. The reports in the London and Gentleman's Magazines were generally published over a year after the speeches were delivered. A few copies of the Magazin are in Aff. Etr. Paris. The passage within the marks * . . . * is taken from the Magazin.

Rhine and go to his assistance. Stair's plan was to cut off
Noailles and then close in on Broglie. Leaving his winter
quarters at Ghent he marched up the Rhine to Coblenz,
where he crossed over to the right bank and took up a position
at Aschaffenburg on the Main, opposite Noailles. The state
of his army was not satisfactory. The English troops had
constant bickerings with the Hanoverians; the Hessians
refused to fight on the side opposed to the Bavarian Emperor;
and the Dutch had not sent their promised contingent. In
June the King, his second son, the Duke of Cumberland, and
Carteret joined the army at Aschaffenburg; but, though
the King was able to restore some measure of discipline and
harmony between the English and Hanoverians, a lack of
supplies forced him to retreat to the magazines at Hanau,
sixteen miles north of Aschaffenburg. On June 27, 1743, at
Dettingen, midway on his march, the King found a strongly
posted detachment under Grammont sent round by Noailles to
waylay him. The allied army would infallibly have been destroyed had Grammont trusted to the strength of his position,
but he advanced too soon on to ground favourable to his adversaries.[1] On seeing the advance of the French, George II,
the last King of England to appear in the fighting line, had all
his martial instincts aroused. When the Duc d'Arenberg begged
him not to expose himself to danger, he replied, ' What do
you think I came here for ? To be a poltroon ? ' Discarding
his horse, which had become unmanageable, he stepped forward
at the head of the English and Hanoverian foot and, sword
in hand, met the onslaught of the French cavalry. Some of
the English cavalry, including Pitt's old dragoon regiment,
did not show to great advantage on this day, but the English
and Austrian infantry and some Hanoverian regiments of
foot behaved with the utmost gallantry. After a short engagement the French were routed and driven headlong into the
river with the loss of over five thousand men. Carteret, who

[1] The French dispositions at Dettingen may be compared with those of the
Boers at Sanna's Post in the South African War. De Wet in his donga corresponds to Grammont, and the Boers at Thabanchu to Noailles at Aschaffenburg,
and Broadwood's force, taken between the two forces to George II's. But De
Wet had more patience than Grammont.

had been sitting in his coach and six by the roadside, immediately scribbled off a triumphant note announcing the victory to his colleagues. But it was not followed up.

December 1, 1743.
'Instead of pursuing the enemy,' said Pitt in the following session, 'we ourselves ran away in the night time, and in such haste that we left all our wounded to the care of the enemy, who had likewise the honour of burying our dead as well as their own.'

Dettingen, though it increased the King's popularity, gave point to all Pitt's and his friends' criticisms of the war. For what national purpose was an English army wandering about the Spessart Wald and fighting two French armies in the centre of Germany when we were nominally at peace with France? After this quixotic adventure Carteret, in spite of Stair's protests, kept the army idle at Hanau for the rest of the campaign, while he contrived fantastic schemes of alliance against France, accompanied with promises of English subsidies. By the convention of Hanau he offered the Bavarian Emperor the restoration of his dominions and a subsidy on condition he abandoned the French alliance; but this agreement was never ratified, because Maria Theresa was not inclined to give up her conquests, and Carteret's colleagues refused to pay the subsidy.[1] By the Treaty of Worms he gained the King of Sardinia as an ally for Maria Theresa in North Italy at a cost to England of a £200,000 subsidy and the promise of the English fleet's support in the Mediterranean; as a result Frederic of Prussia at once took alarm, and began fresh intrigues against Maria Theresa, while the Bourbon Powers cemented their alliance more closely in the second Family Compact of October 1743. Carteret rarely condescended to explain the reasons for his intricate negotiations, but his idea in the treaties of Hanau and Worms appears to have been to secure peace in Ger-

---

[1] Pitt and his friends thought favourably of this treaty, which seemed to promise a relief to Maria Theresa, and they poured much unmerited obloquy on Carteret for its breakdown. It appears from Marchmont's diary that it became known only a year later in England that Carteret's colleagues—not Carteret himself—had refused to ratify the treaty. It was characteristic of Carteret that he was either too proud or too careless to trouble himself about setting the facts in their true light.

many and concentrate the efforts of the maritime powers on France and Spain. Unfortunately he took too little account of Frederic, who was the real arbiter of peace in Germany, and had failed to secure the co-operation of the Dutch, then regarded as necessary allies against France.

In the meantime, while he was breezily negotiating treaties on the Continent, of which he deigned to inform his colleagues only after they had been signed, a formidable opposition was springing up against him in England. The national exultation at the first news of Dettingen and of the King's personal bravery was soon tempered by later intelligence from English officers at headquarters. It was reported with truth that on the day of the battle the English Guards had been put under the command of the Hanoverian general, Ilten, who had kept them with the Hanoverian Guards on a wooded hill safe out of reach of the fighting ; that the advice of English generals was put aside for that of Hanoverians ; and that the King had gone into action wearing the Hanoverian colours. The army's long inaction and the neglect of Stair's proposal to strike a blow, which might have annihilated Noailles's retreating army, added fuel to the discontent against the King and Carteret. The first serious check to the masterful Secretary came in July 1743, on the death of Wilmington, the nonentity at the head of the Treasury. Carteret was anxious for his old friend Pulteney, now Lord Bath, to succeed him ; but Lord Orford, still keenly observant of politics from his retreat at Houghton, advised the King to choose Henry Pelham, the Duke of Newcastle's brother ; and his advice was followed. Pelham, described as 'a moderate man, who pleased by assuming no airs of superiority,' was an able financier and one eminently qualified to conciliate opposition. Without Carteret's brilliance, of which the country was already surfeited, he could be trusted to conduct affairs with safety. He remains a shadowy figure in our history, yet deserves some remembrance as the first minister to appreciate and have dealings with the terrible Mr. Pitt.

On the advice of his mentor, Lord Orford, who urged him

to gain strength by obtaining recruits from the Cobham squadron, Pelham entered into communication with the Opposition. Cobham and Waller would have no dealings with a ministry containing Carteret, but Pitt, Lyttelton, Bedford, Chesterfield, and even Cobham's nephew, George Grenville, were less uncompromising. One of their grievances against Carteret was the restriction of government to a narrow clique, the same clique in fact as Walpole's, as if all other sections were unworthy of confidence. Already Pitt, inspired no doubt by Bolingbroke's teaching, had adopted the maxim measures not men' as his criterion of governments; and in this year, 1743, Chesterfield had started *Old England, or the Constitutional Journal*, in which 'Jeffrey Broadbottom' advocated an administration embracing all parties.[1] Pelham was quite prepared for a 'Broadbottom' administration, and as apprehensive of Carteret's impetuosity and secret methods as any Patriot. He was anxious, says Chesterfield, 'to soften people and save himself from Pitt in the House of Commons,' and saw the danger of continuing to ignore the nation's wishes in foreign politics. He hoped by a treaty with the young men to find a method of reconciling 'the minds of men to the management of the war and making it in some degree popular. This could not possibly be done without taking the nation to a certain degree along with them.' Although this guarded expression of Pelham's ally, Hardwicke, fell considerably short of Pitt's new and audacious claims for the people, it was a great advance on Carteret's system. On the strength of it Pitt and the majority of the Patriots made an informal alliance with Pelham on his promotion to the Treasury in July 1743. Neither side was committed to definite engagements. Pelham would not oppose his colleagues publicly, whatever might happen in the Cabinet; and the Patriots retained full liberty to attack

---

[1] In a caricature of March 1, 1743, probably the first in which Pitt figures, the 'Claims of the Broadbottom Administration' are satirised. Pitt and Lyttelton appear very thin and gaunt and afraid they will not find a place, Pitt saying, 'Who knows but I may be puffed into something by and bye. . . . Am not I an Orator? Make me Secretary at War. Murray is a fool to me.' The idea of a Broadbottom Administration was in the air at the time of Walpole's fall. (See *Egmont MSS.* vol. 88, *sub* March 8, 1741–2.)

measures of the Government, of which they disapproved. Concessions, however, were made on both sides. Pelham convinced Pitt of the necessity for an English army in the Low Countries to protect our interests in that vital corner of Europe against France. Pitt indeed hardly needed convincing on this point. His objection had been to English troops aimlessly wandering over Germany; as soon as the French under Maurice de Saxe seriously threatened the Low Countries he recognised that we should, in conjunction with the Dutch, defend a point of access to the Continent so essential to our commerce and our navy.[1] On the other hand he was unyielding about taking the Hanoverians into English pay and finally brought Pelham over to his view. He also insisted that in any future engagements with foreign princes no subsidies should be paid unless we retained a controlling voice in the conduct of operations.

Carteret, against whom this formidable alliance had been concerted, was never so magnificent as in the session of 1743–4, fighting with his back to the wall. With hardly a follower left in the Ministry he was more contemptuous of his colleagues than ever, more full of resource and more brilliant in the House of Lords. His troubles seemed to make him younger and more reckless. In the thick of the struggle, less than a year after his first wife's death, he found time to woo and win Lady Sophia Fermor, one of the beauties of the Court, for whom young Horace Walpole and Lord Lincoln, the Duke of Newcastle's heir, had sighed in vain. That he and Pitt never met in debate is one of the great losses in our history, for they were worthy antagonists. Pitt himself felt the loss, if we may judge from the exclamation with which he concluded one of his invectives: 'But I have done: if he were present I would say ten times more.'

On the first day of the session Pitt renewed his attack. He began quietly by a criticism of Walpole for not having at the outset of the war urged the Queen of Hungary to buy off her most redoubtable opponent, Frederic of Prussia,

December 1, 1743.

---

[1] It is sometimes forgotten that even to-day we guarantee the neutrality of the Low Countries (Belgium).

'both because his claim was the smallest and because he was one of the most neutral, as well as one of the most powerful allies we could treat with'—a sentiment which was reported to Frederic and not lost on him. Instead we encouraged her to fight, and then, 'having led that Princess upon the ice, . . . we left her there to shift for herself' directly France began to bluster against Hanover. But if Walpole 'betrayed the interest of his country by his pusillanimity, our present minister sacrifices it by his quixotism,' running all over Europe for allies who do little for us beyond taking our subsidies, and thinking of

nothing but war, or at least the resemblance of it; . . . for we have no reason to hope for success, if war be not prosecuted with more vigour than it was during the last campaign. . . . Nay, I doubt much if any action would have happened . . . if the French had not by the misconduct of some one or other of our generals caught our army in a hose net, from which it could not have escaped if the French generals had all observed the directions of their commander-in-chief; . . . a lucky escape you may call that action, but I shall never give my consent to call it by the name of a victory.

Even the King's personal courage did not escape a somewhat unworthy sneer:

Suppose it should appear that his Majesty was exposed to few or no dangers abroad but what he is daily exposed to at home, such as the overturning of his coach or the stumbling of his horse—would not the address proposed be an affront and an insult upon our Sovereign instead of being a compliment ? . . . What then should be our policy ? Everything with the Dutch and nothing without them, and no more war of equivalent and acquisition, for which we pay nearly a million in subsidies and are heading straight for bankruptcy.[1] If the present system is continued our credit will be ruined, our troops will be obliged to live upon free quarters, the farmer will no longer sow nor reap, to have the produce seized by the starving soldiers, the Pretender will land and will be joined by a despairing people as a last hope against an execrable, a sole minister, who had renounced the British nation and seemed to have drunk of the

---

[1] This was in the day of ten-million budgets.

potion described in poetic fictions, which made men forget their country.[1]

Five days later Waller formally proposed that the King should be asked to dismiss the Hanoverians at the end of the year. 'Disaffection to His Majesty's person and Government is at the root of this indecent proposal,' said a speaker for the Court.

I have always looked upon it as a principle of the British con- December stitution [retorted Pitt] that the King can no more do wrong in 6, 1743. camp than in the Cabinet; that, whatsoever is done in either, his advisers are accountable for it. But, unhappily for his Majesty, unhappily for Great Britain, while he was at the army he was hemmed in by Hanoverian generals and one infamous English minister, who seems to have renounced the name of an Englishman. With regard to the decency of this address, I say that the people of Britain are discontented but not yet disaffected. What the continuance of such measures might produce, I tremble to think of. His Majesty is now situated upon the brink of a precipice. At such a time at least it little becomes his faithful Commons to be strewing flowers of flattery and panegyric under his feet. They should rather, with a rough but friendly hand, snatch him from the abyss he is ready to fall into, and with their timely aid place him again upon the secure basis of the affections of his people.[2]

On January 18 and 19 Pitt made his last onslaughts on January the Hanoverians, speaking three times in the discussions on 18 and 19, 1744.

---

[1] Philip Yorke, Horace Walpole, and Edward Montagu all allude to this final phrase. Montagu's version differs slightly: 'Pitt said what he meant was not against the Ministry but against one who was a minister and had renounced Great Britain, who had eat of a certain tree that the poet tells us makes people forget everything, even their own country, but he hoped the people would never taste of the same tree, nor after his example forget their country.' (Climenson, *Montagu*, i, 171.) The *London Magazine* has yet another version: 'They will dream on till they have dreamed Europe and their country, as well as themselves, into perdition.'

A rough note for this speech is to be found in *Chatham MSS.* 74.

[2] The general authenticity of this passage is also well attested: Philip Yorke gives an almost similar version; instead of 'who seems . . . name of Englishman' he reports 'one English minister without an English heart.' The version in the text is from a letter of R. Mure in *Caldwell Papers*, ii, 55. It explains the context rather better than Yorke's.

their pay. Knowing that Pelham and his friends in the Ministry had no love for these mercenaries, he opened with a cunning appeal to 'the amiable part of the Administration to give up so odious a point, which, if carried, will do them no service with the nation and only tend to advance another's power in the Closet.' He then turned to the more congenial task of abusing Carteret: 'a Hanover troop minister, a flagitious taskmaster, whose only party are the sixteen thousand Hanoverians, the placemen by whose means he has conquered the Cabinet, . . . the source whence these waters of bitterness flow.' Why, it had been asked, should not the King follow the timid advice of his German velt-marshal as well as Lord Stair's?—

a monstrous and unconstitutional doctrine [thundered Pitt] for it takes away the control and inquiry of parliament, and justifies the Austrian general's sneer that a bold course 'n'est pas du gout de votre cour'. . . . I have a contempt for the abilities as well as the honesty of any minister in this country who will not endeavour to gain the confidence of the people. Their sense about any point was never more strongly or universally declared than against taking these troops. . . . The passing the question will be to erect a triumphal arch to Hanover over the military honour and independence of Great Britain.[1]

Pitt's speeches, and still more the feeling in the country, to which he appealed, were beginning to tell. In December the address to dismiss the Hanoverians was defeated by only fifty; in January, although Lord Orford came up specially to talk over the waverers, the Government majority sank to forty-five. In the following year the pay of the Hanoverians no longer appeared on the estimates. In judging the part played by Pitt's violent, often outrageous, tirades towards this result, it is fair to distinguish between his methods of controversy and the principles inspiring him. Some of his methods are indefensible. To attain his object he made himself a party to the ignorant and panic-stricken clamour of the day—that we

[1] This account combines the main points of Pitt's speech on the 18th, and his two speeches on the 19th, as given by Philip Yorke and Walpole.

were being constantly betrayed for the electorate; he condescended to most unjust sneers at the King's personal courage; and repeated unfounded stories of the Hanoverians' cowardice. His willingness to employ such arguments shows little statesmanship, and he soon had bitter cause to regret it. But in principle his objection to hiring Hanoverians was sound. The violent opposition of the English people, who were called upon to pay for these troops, was in itself a mighty argument against it. Still more justified was Pitt's courageous expression of his view that England must learn to fight her battles for herself and determine her own foreign policy without regard to the separate interests either of Hanover or of any other continental state. However questionable his methods, his aim was a noble one—to arouse a sense of national unity and self dependence.

Pitt was not always so successful as he was in his fight against the Hanoverians. He then belonged to what Yorke calls an anti-ministerial cabinet, with Lyttelton, Chesterfield, Waller and Dodington. Their first attempt to 'regulate the Opposition in Parliament' was a failure. On December 15, 1743, they put up George Grenville to move a wordy address praying the King '. . . in consideration of the exhausted and impoverished state of this kingdom . . . not to engage this nation any further . . . without first entering into an alliance with the States-General'—which, during the debate, Pitt himself admitted to be so undignified that he tried to amend it. Even with his own party he did not always have his way. At a meeting held at the Fountain Tavern in January 1744 he could not convert the Opposition to the necessity of an English army in the Low Countries, of which Pelham had convinced him, and in order not to break with his friends, agreed to vote but not speak with them on the motion.[1] But these minor disappointments did not affect his growing position in the House and the country. The French agents

December 15, 1743.

---

[1] The speech in this debate, attributed by Almon and Thackeray to Pitt, was really George Grenville's, who on this occasion followed the lead of his uncle, Lord Cobham. Thackeray also post-dates the debate from January 11 to January 17.

speak of him as 'the famous Mr. William Pitt, so well known for his patriotic zeal.'[1] One member's opinion of his oratory has already been quoted; another, the husband of his friend Mrs. Montagu, wrote of him after the Hanoverian debates that 'none has [distinguished himself] so eminently as Mr. Pit, who in the opinion of several, as well as me, is a greater man than ever I have sat with, and if he preserves his integrity, will be transmitted to posterity in the most illustrious of characters.' Even the Speaker's fulminations began to have no terrors for him. On one occasion he had alluded to the 'hand of power' over the officers in the House, and on being called to order explained that he alluded to ministerial, not royal, power. This brought up the Speaker who ruled it out of order to speak of the King and mean to insinuate that ministers had such power. Pitt, unabashed, lamented that 'his train of thought was disordered by the interruption,' and proceeded to give further instances of a great person's partiality to the Hanoverians and of the delinquencies of the minister 'who seemed to have renounced the name of an Englishman.'

December 6, 1743.

But Pitt's power had soon to be turned to a better use than invective, and his constant appeals for vigour and unity in the national councils were justified. Even our navy felt the need of a new spirit. In February 1744 Admiral Mathews's fleet met a combined French and Spanish fleet off Toulon in an engagement which showed a lamentable want of discipline and even courage among the senior officers. Lestock, Mathews's second-in-command, made no attempt to assist his chief; several of his captains hesitated to bring their ships alongside the enemy; Mathews himself abandoned a promising chase and even allowed the enemy to recover one of the English prizes. Almost the only redeeming feature of the battle was the courage displayed by Captain Cornwall of the *Marlborough* and by Captain Hawke of the *Berwick*, whose valour was afterwards put to good use by Pitt. A few days before this battle Captain Brodrick, cruising in the Channel, had sent the alarming news to London that, although England and

[1] *Aff. Etr. Angl. Corr. Pol.* 418, f. 472, &c.

France were still nominally at peace,[1] a French fleet of twenty-one sail was on its way from Brest to the English coast, and that a flotilla with the Pretender and an army under Maurice de Saxe were making ready at Dunkirk. This news found the Ministry totally unprepared. The garrison of London was barely 3000 strong, and, if all available troops were called in, 9000 was the most we could muster to meet the force of 10,000 expected from France. So out of touch were those in authority with the feeling in the country that fears were freely expressed lest, when the troops were concentrated about London, ' the people might rise in Devonshire, Cornwall, Somerset, Dorset, Lancashire, Cheshire, Denbigh, North Wales, Scotland, not to say Ireland.' There was panic in political circles. The safety of England seemed to hang on the quarter from which the wind blew. Would it enable the Channel fleet under Admiral Norris to come up with the Brest fleet in time ? At White's the members sat up till the early hours of the morning noting and betting on the quarter of the wind. The House of Commons met in permanent session. Happily the wind, once again in our history, saved us. Norris came upon the Brest fleet off Dungeness on February 17–28; the English shore was lined with spectators, and one enthusiastic member of Parliament climbed the steeple of Hythe to see the expected battle. But Norris postponed the attack and next morning woke to find the French fleet in full flight under a strong north-easterly gale. The same gale destroyed a large part of the Dunkirk flotilla and put an end to Maurice de Saxe's plans. The panic-stricken Londoners were further comforted by the landing of Dutch soldiers at Sheerness to defend them.[2]

While the evidence of the ministers' unreadiness and incompetence was alarming, the national peril proved how sound at heart were the people, who had so little voice in government. The merchants of London came to St. James's in a procession of ninety coaches to proffer a loan of £6,000,000 to the King.

[1] War between England and France was not formally declared until the following month.

[2] Interesting details of the panic aroused by this fear of invasion, some of which are quoted in the text, are to be seen in *Egmont Papers*, vols. 88 and 212.

Loyal addresses were sent up from all parts of the kingdom, and so unfounded were the apprehensions of a rising among the humbler sort, that the regiments marching to London were everywhere received with enthusiasm and treated at the public-houses along the road, because, they were told, ' you are going to defend us against the French.' Pitt on this occasion did not belie his growing reputation as the representative of the people's true feelings. On February 15, when a message came from the King, announcing the plan of an invasion by the Pretender ' in concert with disaffected persons in England,' Pitt, while supporting a proposal by Waller to inquire into naval mismanagement, did so

February 15, 1744.

not with any view of damping the zeal and loyalty of gentlemen at this dangerous crisis ; for even were the amendment thrown out he should concur most heartily in the address and take that and every other occasion of expressing the most disinterested duty to the present royal family ; . . . but, since we are involved in these difficulties by the neglect of our natural strength at sea it is incumbent on Parliament to intimate their opinion to the Crown, and seek out the remedy as soon as possible.

He also protested against the suggestion of disaffection to the dynasty :

If there are any grounds for asserting it, what could be more impolitic than to animate the French with such an encouragement to prosecute their design ? If there are none, as I am inclined to believe, how monstrous is it in any minister to poison the fountains of truth, and fill the nation with mutual jealousies and distrust ?

With the nearer approach of danger, and while the issue of Norris's encounter with the French was still uncertain, he ostentatiously separated himself from the factious opposition of some of his friends, supported a temporary suspension of the Habeas Corpus Act on evidence of treasonable practices by Lord Barrymore and other Jacobites,[1] and declared ' if ever confidence should be reposed in ministers, it was at this time ; and as they were accountable to Parliament for the use

February 28 and 29, 1744.

---

[1] When Lord Barrington from the Opposition benches was speaking against this suspension, Pitt marked his disapproval by walking contemptuously out of the House.

they made of it, he was for agreeing with their proposals.'
He deprecated panic in words that drew a high compliment February
from Pelham: 24, 1744.

It is a time to be alarmed, to be on our guard [he said] . . . but not
to be terrified as if the danger was of the extremest sort. Our fleet is
out and may intercept the embarkation. But suppose the worst—
that troops were landed (which God forbid) ; . . . surely no military
man could in this situation be uneasy about the event. . . . My
hope is that good may be drawn out of evil by this event, as it will
tend to unite the nation ; for I cannot think any so desperate or so
mad as to think of joining in the attempt.[1]

This confidence in the soundness of the nation made him
resist the pusillanimous idea of bringing over Dutch soldiers
to defend our shores. He refused, too, to be led away by May 3,
panic to sanction vindictive measures of repression proposed 1744.
not only against those guilty of correspondence with the
Pretender but against their children also. When the immediate danger was past he returned with undiminished zest April 3,
to his attacks on Carteret—' whom perdition would infallibly 1744.
attend as the rash author of those measures which had produced
this disastrous impracticable war,' and whose Treaty of Worms January
he had already denounced as containing sufficient matter for 25, 1744.
an impeachment, demanding to see an unratified clause ' which
that audacious hand had signed, but to which the noble lord
who had the custody of the seal refused to set it, as knowing
he should be called to account by Parliament if he did it.' On
a particularly glaring instance of irregular payments to a April 10,
foreign general, sanctioned not only by Carteret but even 1744.
by Pelham, he denounced the

prerogative administration . . . In cases of extreme necessity extraordinary measures might be resorted to, and the utmost stretch of
prerogative is then constitutional ; [2] but there is no such extremity

[1] On February 24, the same evening that Pitt made this speech, Lord
Orford broke his silence for the first and last time in the House of Lords, adopting much the same line as his former adversary in the House of Commons.
He attacked the Ministry for their unreadiness and apathy in presence of a
national danger, to avert which he had devoted his whole life.

[2] This doctrine was called upon by Chatham in 1766 to defend one of his
own acts of prerogative (see vol. ii, p. 228).

here. . . . If this method of conducting business goes on, a seat in the House will not be the way to power or favour, and I hope that for their own sakes, if not for that of the public, gentlemen will concur in putting a timely stop to it.

He even found time in the last months of this laborious session to take a leading part in debates on commercial subjects. There is a story that Pitt once expressed an ambition to be Chancellor of the Exchequer, but this may be doubted, for he never showed a special turn for finance. On commercial regulations, however, particularly in their political effect, he always showed great interest. To provide the interest for a new loan Pelham proposed an additional duty on West Indian sugar. But it was pointed out by Pitt and his friends that the Molasses Act of 1733 had already hampered West Indian trade to such an extent that many sugar-planters from Jamaica had emigrated to the Dutch islands; and they proposed a tax on foreign linens exported to the Plantations instead of the new sugar tax, partly as an encouragement to English and Scottish linens. Finally, Pelham adopted a spirit tax as a compromise and agreed to a committee to consider the question of protection for linens. Pitt also, recalling perhaps his grandfather's early struggles with the East India Company's monopoly of trade, supported a proposal to extend the privileges of the Levant Company's close corporation to all merchants willing to pay £20 and observe the Company's rules. During this session Pitt showed a more versatile activity than at any other time of his life except one, when he was again fighting an incompetent minister at a time of danger.[1] But it nearly killed him. Immediately after the session he was seized with violent gout in the stomach, and was obliged to spend the summer and autumn at Bath. The waters did him so little good that in October his friend Grenville almost despaired of his life.

When Pitt first retired to Bath, ill and exhausted, his efforts seemed to have little prospect of success. Carteret, secure of the King's favour, was cheerful as ever. Every

February 13, 20; 22, 1744.

April 24, 1744.

---

[1] Pitt's speeches during this session are well reported by Philip Yorke, whose verbal accuracy is often confirmed by Walpole and other writers.

one else had the gloomiest anticipations for the future of the country. Even the courtiers, who knew the want of any connected plan abroad, had little hope from the next campaign of any victory likely to infuse a better spirit into the services. Events thoroughly justified this pessimism. The navy, instead of attacking the enemy's fleet, was chiefly employed in convoy duty; and the Admiralty had so poor an opinion of the chief flag officers that when a fleet was sent to convoy ships to the Mediterranean, the admirals on the active list were passed over in favour of Sir John Balchen, a retired veteran of William III's days. There were stories of captains coming into action drunk, and of ships needlessly surrendered, or capsizing owing to faulty construction in the dockyards. The state of the army was no better. The command in Flanders was given to General Wade, a superannuated invalid of seventy-three, who required two days to recover from the fatigue of four hours on horseback. Artillery needed for the army was allowed to remain three months on the quays at Antwerp and Ostend. In the campaign of 1744 the allied army, though at last reinforced by a Dutch contingent, was so torn with hesitations and dissensions that it hardly attempted anything against Maurice de Saxe, who, in a brilliant campaign of six weeks, captured the chief fortresses in the Low Countries. The French and Spaniards were equally successful in Italy in spite of Carteret's £200,000 to the King of Sardinia; and Frederic of Prussia once more joined Maria Theresa's enemies. The only glad sight to English eyes this year was the return of Anson in June from his three years' circumnavigation of the globe and his triumphal procession from Portsmouth to London with wagons drawing the treasure of the Acapulco galleon. But for this little credit was due to the Ministry.

Instead of attempting to impart some of his own vigour to the national services, Carteret was meditating fresh subsidies and planning another great alliance with Russia, Saxony and Poland. He had a wild idea of sending the Hanover troops in English pay to defend their own country at our expense, if France invaded Westphalia.[1] But the bankruptcy of his

[1] *Aff. Etr. Angl. Corr. Pol.* 418, f. 400.

policy was becoming evident; all his expensive allies were found to be broken reeds, and Frederic, the only prince worth securing in Germany, was hopelessly alienated. His haughtiness and reputation for insincerity with his colleagues had left him with hardly a friend; the other ministers, timorous as they were, at last rose in open revolt. In October Carteret, with the King's sanction, made one last despairing effort to retain power by an offer of places to Pitt and his friends. The offer was contemptuously rejected, 'for fear of losing the people,' it was reported, 'and above all from distrust of him.'[1] On November 1, 1744, the Duke of Newcastle presented to the King a long memorial drawn up by Lord Hardwicke, recapitulating the grievances against Carteret felt by most of his colleagues, and stating the policy they recommended. This document admitted almost everything for which Pitt had been contending: a formal treaty of alliance with the Dutch, a concerted plan of operations, and the employment of Great Britain's strength and resources to the best advantage of the country. The King put off a decision for three weeks and asked Lord Orford for his advice, in the hope that it would be favourable to his chosen minister. Orford, though at the point of death, set out at once for London and sent a message urging the King to yield to the Pelhams. The King sorrowfully acquiesced, and on November 23, 1744, four days before the meeting of Parliament, took back the seals from Carteret. For the second time within three years Pitt's attacks had been a principal cause of a great minister's fall. Pitt had shown the King and the Whig clique that when he represented the people he could make a ministry impossible; he had still to prove that, strong as he was as the people's mouthpiece in opposition, he could be equally strong as their minister.

[1] *Egmont Papers*, vol. 212. See also *Aff. Etr. Angl. Corr. Pol.* 418, f. 442: Intelligence from London.

CHAPTER V

PITT AND THE REBELLION

Εἷs οἰωνὸs ἄριστοs ἀμύνεσθαι περὶ πάτρηs.
HOMER, *Iliad* xii. 243.
Nature, Sir, is the best teacher: she will teach us to be men.
WILLIAM PITT.

PITT's long illness at Bath, which lasted during most of the year 1744, was the first of a series of attacks which prostrated him at ever shorter intervals and returned with increasing severity throughout his life. In the succeeding ten years before his marriage his state of health was so serious that he was obliged to make an annual pilgrimage to Bath or Tunbridge to drink the waters and dose himself with Raleigh's cordial and other fashionable specifics. These attacks took various forms, affecting his bowels, his arms, and his legs; during one of them 'my sleep continues very broken,' he complains, 'and the irritation not yet off my nerves and out of my blood.' A temporary cure was sometimes effected by a sharp attack of gout, which the doctors' treatment aimed at inducing; but his friends became alarmed at his condition. In May 1744 he went to Bath, and in October of that year George Grenville writes to his brother that

Pitt is still at Bath and . . . in a very bad way, having never been able to get rid of the gout in his bowels ever since it first seized him before you left London, in the spring. The Bath waters have done him no good. This is a grievous misfortune to him, since, if it does not affect his life, it may perhaps disable him, and make a cripple of him for ever; though for my own part I cannot help thinking that his youth and ease are most likely to get the better of it in a great degree.

Even as late as the following January the French secret agent, who saw him carried to the House of Commons, spoke of him as ' the great patriot, who, though young, seems almost dying'; and twice within the next ten years he was reported to be in the utmost danger.

His enemies, on the other hand, saw nothing but parade and hypocrisy in these illnesses, and insinuated that on occasion he and his hereditary enemy, the gout, understood each other. The accepted view has been taken chiefly from the pages of one of the bitterest of his detractors, Horace Walpole, from whose sneers none of his contemporaries save his own father and his worthy friend Conway was sacred. He accounts for Pitt's silence during 1753, a year of almost constant suffering, by the insinuation that it was ' a year of sullen illness,' and is never tired of finding some deep purpose in Pitt's long absences and sudden returns. No doubt his frequent appearances in the House with all the trappings of the gout—a flannelled foot, a monstrous boot, crutches—and a face drawn with pain, lent themselves to the ridicule of those unable to believe in the genuine patriotism which drew Pitt from his sick bed on momentous occasions. In their view the sufferer's gout was not so bad as it was made to seem, and his pathetic appeals to the sympathy of his audience were merely the stratagems of the practised orator. Pitt may have made little effort to conceal his sufferings at such times, and have had no objection to enforcing his arguments by personal touches likely to produce an effect. But there can be little question of the serious nature of his affliction, and it is evident from the correspondence of his closest friends that his gout was a very real torment and often barely allowed him to crawl to the House. As to his diplomatic absences, as they were called, if they were really prompted by sinister motives of intrigue, it must be allowed Pitt was singularly ill-judged from his own point of view in some of the occasions he chose to absent himself.

During his retirement at Bath in 1744 his old friend,

Sarah, Duchess of Marlborough, died, and her will brought him one of his first pieces of good fortune. For some years she seems to have been meditating a provision for him, for in 1740 Chesterfield, writing to one of her executors, Lord Marchmont, urged him to ' encourage her Grace in so right and generous a resolution,' since ' I share the marks of your friendship to Mr. Pitt, looking upon everything that concerns him as personal to myself.' He added, ' I have not yet had an opportunity of speaking to him on that subject, and when I have, shall break it gently, knowing his delicacy.' The Duchess's resolution did not, however, take effect until four years later, for her last will and the codicil benefiting Pitt were dated August 1744, only two months before her death on October 18. In this codicil £20,000 was left to Lord Chesterfield, and £10,000 to ' William Pitt of the Parish of St. James, within the Liberty of Westminster, Esq., . . . upon account of his merit in the noble defence he has made of the laws of England, and to prevent the ruin of his country.' In addition to this she made him co-heir presumptive to part of her estates. Her daughter Anna, Countess of Sunderland and Duchess of Marlborough, had two sons—Charles, third Duke of Marlborough, and John Spencer. To the latter, her favourite grandson, and after him to his son John, she left all the residue of her unsettled estates, with a proviso that on the failure of this line Chesterfield should inherit her Wimbledon property and Pitt her property in Buckinghamshire, Staffordshire and Northamptonshire, formerly the estates of Richard Hampden, Lord Fauconberg and Nathaniel Lord Crewe respectively : she also persuaded John Spencer to make a will leaving all his Sunderland estates to Pitt in case his own son died without issue. Pitt seemed at first to have a good chance of succeeding to this noble inheritance. Within two years John Spencer died of self-indulgence, leaving only an infant between Pitt and the succession, which was taken seriously into account when his marriage settlement was drawn up some years later. The infant, however, survived and Pitt never succeeded to the Marlborough and Sunderland estates. Nevertheless, the provisions of this will gave him added consideration and brought him nearer the charmed circle of aristocratic Whig families who treated the government of England as their peculiar appanage. At one stroke, also, he was released from the comparative poverty, galling to a man of his tastes and ambition, of a younger son's portion of just £300 a year, and put into possession of an assured income of £700 or £800 a year. Either as part of this income or in addition to it he received an annuity of £300 from the Duke of Bedford under a deed executed in March 1745.[1] The Duke of Bedford's first wife was Lady Diana, sister of John Spencer; and this arrangement may have been made in view of Pitt's prospective claims to the estate.

The will containing this and other characteristic exhibitions of the old Duchess's prejudices was immediately published, with appropriate comments, and became the talk of the town. Pitt's stroke of good fortune was welcomed with joy by old friends like the Grenvilles, Chesterfield and Marchmont, but it gave occasion for cavilling to the less well-disposed. His alliance with the Pelhams, entered into a year previously, but only recently made public, was seized upon as a proof that his attacks on Walpole and Carteret and his philippics against the Hanoverians were made simply in order to curry favour with the Duchess. That the Pelhams had virtually yielded to all Pitt's demands on policy was ignored by Pitt's enemies. A characteristic expression of their views is to be found in a letter, written in her bad French, by Lady Bolingbroke to Lady Denbigh: ' Voila, ma chère comtesse, les jeux de la fortune et le comble de liniquité de cette vieille Malborough ... Le patriotisme est une belle chose quand il rend bien, car on peut quitter ensuite quand on veut pour quelque autre recolte.' It so happened that at this very time Pitt was

---

[1] See *Bedford Correspondence*, i, 34, and a letter to Chatham's banker, Coutts, of June 30, 1778, in *Chatham MSS.* 28:

' Mr. Palmer presents his compliments to Mr. Coutts, acquaints him that the annuity granted by the late Duke of Bedford to the late Earl of Chatham was made payable at the four usual quarter days. . . . The security . . . is dated 23rd March, 1744 [probably O.S.].' The librarian of the present Duke of Bedford kindly made a search in the *Woburn Papers,* but found no further information about this annuity.

feeling sore with the Pelhams, suspecting them of weakness to Carteret, and quite ignorant of the memorial they had presented to the King. Bolingbroke, who saw Pitt on November 6, was angry with him for his suspicion of the Pelhams and found him 'extremely supercilious'; he complained that, when he himself was a young man, 'Sir Edward Seymour and Musgrave and such heard him with more deference than Pitt had done'; and he attributed his arrogance to the legacy. Cobham re-echoed this charge of arrogance on the same occasion. 'Mr. Pitt is a young man of fine parts,' he confided to Chesterfield, 'but he is narrow, does not know much of the world, and is a little too dogmatical.' Pitt may well have ruffled the dignity of Cobham and Bolingbroke, who were accustomed to unmeasured adulation,[1] but that the legacy had anything to do with this exhibition of independence or with his alliance with Pelham is out of the question. He was never of an accommodating temper, and, like most men of genius, was inclined to be dogmatical and pertinacious in having his own way. At a time when Carteret's fall was impending, and Bolingbroke and Cobham may have hoped for a considerable voice in the new arrangements, they probably became especially sensitive to the independent spirit of their young ally: hence their anxiety to account for it by a discreditable motive.

At the close of 1744 Bolingbroke's pet project of a non-party government, or a Broadbottom administration, as Chesterfield called it, was at last accomplished. In those days the party system, as we understand it, was not developed. Nominally there was a broad division between Whigs and Tories, which Walpole had accentuated for his own purposes, calling all who did not support the Ministry by the invidious name of Tories. But, except for those Tories who were

[1] Cobham's conceit was well known. Lord Granville once gave as an instance of it that 'when he was speaking in the House of Lords (as he thought very well) he overheard Lord Cobham whispering his neighbour, "Very well, but why does he not say so and so?" Upon which Lord Granville, at the end of the speech, produced Lord Cobham's argument (a mighty absurd one), who thereupon cried out, "What an incomparable speaker Lord Granville is!"' (*Wrest Park MSS.*; Hon. T. Robinson's memoranda.)

Jacobites and had hardly any representation in Parliament, there was little real difference of principle between the two parties. Pitt and Chesterfield were among the few Whigs who admitted this frankly.

The distinction between the Court and Country of Great Britain [says their mouthpiece, Jeffrey Broadbottom,] does not subsist in the nature of things, but in the mismanagement of persons and therefore may be done away by a virtuous ministry or an uncorrupted people. . . . As to Whig and Tory I know no real distinction between 'em; I look upon them as two brothers, who in truth mean the same thing tho' they pursue it differently.

On the other hand the various cliques, to which most members of the House were attached, were of great importance. Each clique followed some great personage, who owed his position chiefly to his command of influence in parliamentary boroughs and to the number of votes he could in consequence muster in the House of Commons. The Prince of Wales, strong in Cornwall, had his personal following, and his brother the Duke of Cumberland already had a section attached to him. Granville (as Carteret had recently become through his mother's death) commanded a small group consisting chiefly of Pulteney, Earl of Bath, Lord Winchilsea and his tribe of ' black funereal Finches.' Another important group was the Duke of Bedford's, which included his father-in-law Lord Gower, once a notorious Jacobite, Lord Sandwich, the cricketer and the godfather of 'sandwiches,' and Rigby, prototype of all the Tadpoles. Cobham's set comprised the Grenvilles, Lytteltons and Pitt, with Chesterfield as a free-lance. Bubb Dodington, who had some dozen seats at his disposal, prowled about from set to set like a jackal on the look-out for pickings. Last and chief of all were the Pelhams, who reckoned as their foremost supporters the Lord Chancellor Hardwicke, Harrington and Murray: they were indispensable as a basis for any ministry, partly owing to the enormous parliamentary interest possessed by the Duke of Newcastle, partly owing to their strict alliance with Archibald, Duke of Argyll, formerly Lord Isla, who was practically king of Scotland, and returned all the sixteen Scottish peers and a very large number of the Scottish members.

PARTIES IN 1744

These subdivisions had not been so clearly marked until Walpole's fall. The Pelhams had formed the mainstay of his power in Parliament: the other groups had been held together by Bolingbroke under the nominal leadership of the Prince of Wales. On the break-up of Walpole's Ministry, the Prince of Wales still adhered to Carteret, while most of the other groups separated under their respective leaders, who roamed about the political world, like *condottieri* bent on securing the largest spoils for themselves and their followers. On Granville's fall, Pelham, left undisputed head of the Ministry, contrived another way of uniting them. Walpole had brought them together against him by the open contempt he showed to any man who dared oppose him ; Pelham, conciliatory by temperament, secured their almost united support by a judicious distribution of favours to all the groups. What Pelham did—principally, it may be suspected, from love of ease—happened to coincide exactly with Pitt's conviction that government should not be the business of one clique, but representative of all those who were faithful to Revolution principles.

In the Broadbottom Administration formed by the Pelhams in November 1744, the Bedford group was represented by the Duke himself, as First Lord of the Admiralty, by Gower, as Lord Privy Seal, and by Sandwich, who was given a place at the Admiralty. Lord Chesterfield, in spite of the King's dislike of him, was made Lord-Lieutenant of Ireland ; Cobham was restored to the command of a regiment ; while his 'cubs,' George Lyttelton and George Grenville, joined the Treasury and Admiralty Boards respectively. The Prince's friend, Lord Middlesex, got a household appointment ; Sir J. Hynde Cotton, a notorious old Jacobite, became Treasurer of the Chambers ; and Bubb Dodington was appeased with the lucrative post of Treasurer of the Navy. The nominal leader of the Opposition, Edmund Waller, became Cofferer, and one man of pre-eminent merit, Admiral Anson, was put in his right place at the Navy Board. Walpole's Secretary of State, Lord Harrington, resumed the seals laid down by Granville, and he, with Pelham, the Duke of Newcastle and Hardwicke, represented the 'old corps' of Walpole's era. Thus the only man of importance left out was Pitt himself. In the negotiations for forming the new Ministry carried on between the Pelhams and Lords Chesterfield, Gower and Cobham, Pitt was proposed as Secretary at War, the post which he had long marked out for himself.[1] But the King, who had already made a difficulty about admitting Chesterfield, absolutely refused to have Pitt in an office requiring frequent attendance on himself. Considering Pitt's attacks on the beloved electorate and his sneers at George II's behaviour at Dettingen, this veto is hardly surprising and seems to have been regarded as natural by Pitt himself. At any rate he contented himself with a promise from the Pelhams that the King's prejudices should be overcome and agreed at once to support the Ministry; he even persuaded his friend George Grenville, who had qualms about taking office while Pitt had nothing, to accept the post offered him at the Admiralty. In April 1745 he gave a final mark of his adherence to the Ministry by resigning his appointment in the Prince of Wales's household. Friendly relations between himself and the Prince were never entirely broken off, but his master's continued favour to Carteret had for some time caused a coolness between them.

On measures as well as men the Pelhams showed a conciliatory spirit. Two of Pitt's chief charges against Carteret were his failure to secure the vigorous co-operation of the Dutch and his employment of Hanover troops. The Pelhams did their utmost to meet his views on both these points. One of their first acts was to send over Lord Chesterfield to The Hague in the hope that a man of his rank, who had previously been ambassador there, might wake the Dutch out of their torpor. The Dutch, however, said—and there was some force in the contention—that so long as George II persisted in maintaining the neutrality of Hanover they saw no reason for declaring war in a cause which affected them but slightly. George II was persuaded to abandon this neutrality in the autumn of 1745, whereupon the Dutch came forward as belligerents. Meanwhile Chesterfield had obtained from them pro-

---

[1] In the caricature of March 1, 1743, mentioned above (p. 110, *note*), Pitt is represented saying, 'Make me Secretary at War.'

mises of fixed quotas of troops and ships ; and they agreed to contribute part of the subsidy payable to the Elector of Saxony as his price for joining a quadruple alliance signed in January 1745 between England, Holland, Saxony and the Queen of Hungary. The Pelhams also, after a fashion, got rid of the Hanover troops. In deference to the popular agitation they obtained the King's permission not to take these troops directly into the pay of Great Britain for the year 1745 ; but recognising that without them it would be difficult to find enough men for the allies, they agreed to increase the Queen of Hungary's subsidy by £200,000, on the understanding that she should engage them. By this subterfuge England, while really paying for Hanoverians as before, would not have them on her pay-sheets. It was not an heroic method of dealing with the difficulty, but it removed a great cause of unpopularity from the dynasty, while not impairing the strength of the continental coalition against France.

Parliament met for a month on November 27, 1744, but Pitt, still taking the waters at Bath, was too ill to attend. On January 23, a fortnight after the Christmas recess, he suddenly appeared, 'with the mien and apparatus of an invalid,' to speak in committee on the vote of 28,000 men for Flanders. It was a critical moment for the ministers. In spite of their apparent success in bringing the chief members of the Opposition within their fold, they were almost on the verge of disruption, for ' there is not a half-witted prater in the House,' wrote Horace Walpole, ' but can divide with every new minister on his side, . . . and on the first tinkling of the brass, all the new bees swarm back to the Tory side of the House' ; while Bath, Granville and the King himself were eagerly on the look-out for any false step they might take. Maurice de Saxe's overwhelming success in last year's campaign in the Low Countries had made it essential to resist his further progress, and a defeat on the question of voting the necessary force would be the signal for the Pelhams' downfall and the triumphant return of Granville.

Yonge, the Secretary at War, opened the debate, and

Pelham supported the motion with unusual force and earnestness. Two speakers opposed the Government: one of them, Sir Roger Newdigate, taunted ministers with pursuing the same policy as their predecessors, and described it as a series of 'old measures by a new ministry.' Before any further criticisms could be offered, Pitt rose in his most majestic mood to crush opposition. Alluding to his illness, he declared that if this was to be the last day of his life he would spend it in the House of Commons, since he judged the condition of his country to be worse than his own. Pleading his weakness as an excuse for not entering into details, he expressed a hope that Pelham would already not only have persuaded but awed the House into an approbation of the measure. Taking up Sir Roger Newdigate's objection he showed that the whole question had changed from the last year, when

a certain fatal influence prevailed in His Majesty's councils. Then the object seemed the multiplying of war upon war, expense upon expense, and the abetting the House of Austria in romantic schemes of acquisition such as the recovery of the *avulsa imperii*, without regard to the interest of Great Britain. Now the object is, by connecting ourselves closely with Holland, to arrive at a situation which might enable us to hold out fair and reasonable terms of peace both to our friends and enemies and not to pursue the war a moment longer than we could obtain an equitable and sufficient security for our rights and those of our allies pursuant to public treaties. Already there are symptoms of a better disposition in the States, and if they complete their last augmentation of twelve thousand men, they will have a more numerous army on foot than they kept up during King William's war.

As he brought out each point of his version of a changed policy he faced round on Sir Roger and demanded with an air of disdain, 'Can this be called an old measure for a new ministry?' Then, contrasting Lord Granville's policy with that of the present ministers, he described him as one who flattered the King's dominant passions and fed him with false hopes of aggrandizing non-English States at the expense of national objects, supporting himself in the closet on that broken reed, an opinion of his credit with foreign princes; one who kept

January 23, 1745.

the people in misery by heaping up crushing debts and charges and had not ten men in the nation to follow him : the present Ministry, on the other hand, were devoted to the King's and the country's interests. He paid a marked compliment to Pelham for his just and reasonable measures of finance :

He and those acting with him are to be commended for pursuing moderate and healing measures and such as tend to set the King at the head of his people. I believe a dawn of salvation has broken forth : I shall follow it as far as it will lead me. If those now at the helm do not mean the honour of their master and the good of the nation I am the greatest dupe in the world. If I find myself deceived, nothing will be left but an honest despair.[1]

The fulminating eloquence of Pitt's attack on Granville and his sarcasms on poor Sir Roger silenced all opposition. But the speech, delivered throughout, says Philip Yorke, with much grace of action and elocution, was something more than a debating triumph. Even Horace Walpole declared it to be ' a very strong but much-admired speech for coalition.' By his allusions to the country's danger, by his earnest pleading for national unity and his high hopes of the Ministry's capacity and success, he raised the tone of the proceedings above the petty personal issues which had long been so prominent, and produced, it was said, such unanimity as had not been seen in Parliament for a century. By this speech Pitt, the most prominent member of the old Opposition, who alone had been passed over, gained for the Administration a victory such as they had not dared to expect, and in it gave a foretaste of that constructive genius to which within twelve years the harmonious action of a united nation so gloriously responded.

A better opening for damaging the Ministry occurred on February 18, when Pelham proposed an increased grant to

---

[1] In *Chatham MSS.* 74 are undated notes in Pitt's handwriting for a speech which appears to be this one. Some of these notes are : ' My confidence . . . change in the administration now wrought ? upon measures . . . abandoning the allies ruin and infamy . . . hazard of the experiment in popularity ; honest hazard uncertainty this way, sure inevitable ruin the other. . . .'

the Queen of Hungary, defending it on the ground that, 'out of the King's paternal regard to the jealousies and heart-burnings' in the nation, the Hanover troops would no longer be paid by England. Lord Granville's friends had little difficulty in exposing the subterfuge whereby the Queen was to be paid to hire the same troops. But once more Pitt, with almost quixotic courage, went out of his way to defend the Ministry and awed the House into submission: the withdrawal of the Hanover troops was a meritorious and popular measure, which did honour to the minister who advised it and the prince who so graciously vouchsafed to follow it, a measure which must give pleasure to every honest heart. It had been thrown out that the Queen might take them into her pay when they were dismissed from ours, but who could object to that? The Queen, he supposed, was at liberty to take them or refuse them:

February 18, 1745.

God forbid that they should be forced on the one hand, or on the other that those unfortunate troops should by our votes be proscribed at every court in Europe. It is sufficient for us that the ill consequences which were apprehended from the voting them year by year as part of our own army . . . have been removed by His Majesty's wisdom and goodness.

In his zeal for unity Pitt, contrary to his habit, refused to be drawn into a personal altercation with a member who had warmly attacked him for his depreciation of the Hanoverians and for suggesting that they were unworthy to be on the roll with English troops.

Pitt in his reply [says Yorke] carried himself with all the art and temper imaginable; he soothed and complimented Sir H. Liddell and at the same time put the question in a more just and acceptable light. The honourable gentleman had quoted his words exactly, but mistook his meaning, which was not to give offence to a heart so honourable and honest as his. He considered the question as an expedient for unanimity, without making any invidious retrospect to what had passed in former debates; and he heartily wished all the differences they had occasioned might be buried in oblivion and not revived again to the reproach of any gentleman whatever.

The irate member was so impressed by this mild answer that

he rose to apologise and thanked Pitt for telling him of his warmth; the House again passed the Government's proposal almost unanimously.

The King's Government needed all the support they could obtain, for this was a year of nearly uninterrupted disaster. On the Continent, in spite of English subsidies amounting to over a million sterling, England and her allies could not muster an army of half the number of men poured into Flanders by France, and their generals were no match for Marshal Saxe, the military genius of the age. At Fontenoy in May 1745 the allies attempted to cover the important fortress of Tournai but were defeated, not ingloriously, by the French, led by Saxe and encouraged by the presence of their 'well-beloved' monarch. Tournai fell in June, Ghent and Oudenarde in July, and, at the end of August, Ostend, the port of approach to the Netherlands from England, was surrendered by the Austrian commandant. In Italy the allies fared no better: the English fleet won a few slight successes over the Genoese allies of France, but on land the French, Spanish and Neapolitan forces carried all before them in North Italy. In Germany alone France gained nothing, but then neither did Maria Theresa. Her one gleam of comfort was the death of the Bavarian Emperor in January, when her husband was allowed to succeed him without objection from Frederic or France; but her attempts to recover Silesia were ignominiously defeated. Frederic played his usual game of keeping in with both sides. In June he signed a new treaty with France, but in August was so alarmed at the French successes in the Low Countries, that the Pelhams induced him to enter into an alliance with England, after overcoming their own King's aversion to his nephew.

Our only military success during 1745 was the capture of Louisburg, 'the Dunkirk of North America,' and even that was due chiefly to the enterprise of the New England colonists in raising a land force of four thousand men under Pepperell to co-operate with a small fleet under Commodore Warren. To the Duke of Newcastle and other timorous spirits in the Ministry this solitary conquest seemed a source of embarrassment rather than congratulation.¹ With little appreciation of its importance their first thought was to hand it back to France as a set-off to her Flemish conquests. The nation, with surer judgment, had acclaimed the capture of the fortress as the greatest triumph of the war; 'it is become,' says Chesterfield, ' the darling object of the whole nation; it is ten times more so than ever Gibraltar was.' Pitt also saw its importance from the first: 'I heartily wish your Grace joy of Cape Breton,' he wrote to Bedford at the Admiralty; 'I know you feel national success.' Thirty years later he still recalled the impression made on him by the colonists' brave dash under Pepperell, and answered the question, ' What have these rebels done heretofore ? ' by the retort : ' I remember when they raised four regiments on their own bottom and took Louisburg from the veteran troops of France.'

<small>May 30, 1777.</small>

The final calamity in this unfortunate year was the Jacobite rising, which Walpole had always dreaded. Happily that great statesman did not live to see it: he was laid to rest five months before July 26, when the young Pretender landed on the west coast of Scotland with the ' seven men of Moidart.' In less than a month Charles Edward rallied 2,000 Highlanders to his standard; by the middle of September he had entered Perth and Edinburgh and put to flight two English cavalry regiments at ' the Canter o' Colt Brig.' On September 21 at Prestonpans he defeated the only troops in Scotland under Sir John Cope. The Rebellion found the Government as unprepared as it was to meet a French invasion in the preceding year. The King was away in Hanover and did not return until August 31; there were scarcely any regular troops in the country, and even ministers had the gloomiest apprehensions. The Paymaster thought the Pretender would be successful, and Pelham did not find the zeal to venture purses and lives he had expected.² It was fortunate that the French, being unprepared for the Rebellion, did not attempt another invasion. ' Had 5,000 landed a week ago in any

---

¹ Even Pelham thought it would be ' a stumbling-block to negotiation.' (Coxe, *Pelham Administration*, i, 282 : Pelham to Trevor.)

² See *Historical MSS. Commission*, xiv, 9 (Pelham to Trevor), and *Egmont MSS.* 277 (for Winnington the Paymaster's views).

part of this island,' wrote Henry Fox in September, ' I verily believe the entire conquest would not have cost them a battle.' Prompt measures, however, were taken to restore confidence. Most of the English troops in Flanders were recalled, the Dutch were asked to send an auxiliary force, and 6,000 Hessians were landed in the country. A camp of the Guards with militia and trained bands was formed at Finchley, and by the end of October Wade had an army of 10,000 men at Newcastle and Ligonier another at Lichfield. Chesterfield sent over two regiments from Dublin, and on his own authority called out the Irish militia and issued beating orders in Ulster. The London bar offered to enrol themselves as a body-guard to the King, and the Duke of Bedford, with thirteen other noblemen, volunteered to raise regiments for the defence of the Protestant succession. Parliament was summoned early—on October 17— when the Pretender had most of Scotland at his mercy, and England lay well-nigh undefended before him. In such a crisis character tells more than eloquence. Men began to feel that in Pitt was something greater than his words, and instinctively turned for the word of command—not to the Treasury bench but to this young, untried man. On the first day of the session Sir Francis Dashwood, with misplaced zeal, had chosen the moment to move an amendment to the Address, praying for purer elections, shorter parliaments, and the prevention of undue influence on members. His motion was shortly disposed of by Pitt: *October 17, 1745.*

> I shall always be a real friend to any regulation which may appear to me to be effectual for preventing the fatal effects of corruption; but at a time when our all is at stake, whatever opinion we may have of our ministers for the time being, surely it is unseasonable to attempt anything that may raise discontents among the people, or lessen their confidence in those who are placed in authority over them. Whilst the nation is engaged in a most dangerous and expensive foreign war, a rebellion breaks out at home. Those rebels have already gained a victory over the King's troops, which has made them almost wholly masters of one part of the United Kingdom. . . . In such circumstances shall we amuse ourselves with contriving methods to prevent the effects of corruption? Shall we spend our time in projects for guarding our liberties against

corruption when they are in such immediate danger of being trampled under foot by force of arms?

The people without doors, he reminded the House, were not troubling themselves about corruption then, or sending up letters, instructions, and remonstrances in favour of shorter parliaments; all they were thinking of was 'how to defend their sovereign and themselves against those who have traitorously conspired to rob him of their crown and them of their liberties, properties and religion.' Such a people, he believed, could well be trusted to defend themselves. Instead, therefore, of relying on the Dutchmen and Hessians brought over by the Government, he moved on October 23 to recall the English troops still remaining in Flanders as 'the most proper and surest means to suppress and entirely to extinguish this detestable rebellion, effectually to discourage any foreign power from assisting the rebels, and to restore the peace of the kingdom'; and the House was so much impressed by his eloquent pleading and the respect he showed the King that Pelham only averted defeat by a majority of twelve on the 'previous question.'[1]

October 23, 1745

The most remarkable sign of confidence in Pitt came from the Scottish peers and members of Parliament. They were having an unhappy time, with rebellion aflame in their own country and black looks directed against them from all quarters in England. They were anxious to demonstrate the real loyalty of Scotland by a parliamentary inquiry, which would make it appear 'that the country was zealously affected to the present Government'; to prove their own attachment to the Throne by being allowed to raise similar volunteer regiments to those sanctioned in England; and to air their grievances against the Duke of Argyll, and Lord Tweeddale, the Secretary for Scotland, for the inefficiency of their measures against the rebels. But they had no fixed plan of action; conferences of their chief men, Lords Stair and Marchmont, the Dukes of Queensberry and Montrose, and Oswald and Hume Campbell, resulted in nothing. In their despair they turned to Pitt, one of the few men in England

[1] Malmesbury, *Letters*, i, 7, and *Commons Journal*.

who never countenanced the popular prejudice against Scotsmen. 'I would walk barefooted from one end of the town to the other to gain Mr. Pitt,' said Lord Marchmont, whose appeal to him was not in vain. Pitt first proposed meeting them with Barrington and Lyttelton, but this, they said, would be 'only multiplying himself,' as his two friends were sure to agree with him: so Pitt came alone. He made the Scotch peers and members first define clearly what they wanted, asked them pertinent questions about the evidence they expected to produce at an inquiry, and finally agreed to support their demand for a committee, on condition it were open and not secret, and that they entertained no idea of embarrassing the Government. But after Pitt had talked to his friends and induced Pelham to agree to the committee, Oswald broke the understanding by a violent attack on the Government in seconding the motion for a committee on October 28. Pitt accordingly withheld his support, and the motion was rejected by a large majority.[1]

Three days after this incident the young Pretender began his march on Carlisle, which he captured on November 17 with the loss of one man killed and one wounded. Wade's army at Newcastle could not reach him, as there were no roads from the east to the west of that part of England; it was, therefore, not a time to discourage those who were attempting to raise fresh men to meet the emergency. But Hume Campbell, embittered perhaps by the failure of his motion on October 28, thought otherwise, and on November 4 made an attack on the fourteen regiments that were being raised by the Dukes of Bedford and Rutland and other patriotic noblemen, under cover of a motion not to grant army rank to the officers. He found some sympathy in the House owing to a prevalent

In the *Marchmont Memoirs* there is an unfortunate gap between October 24 and November 6, 1745. On the 24th Pitt is said to have agreed to support the motion of the 28th. All that is recorded of the debate is to be found in *Parl. Hist.* xiii. No speech of Pitt's is there given, and it appears just to assume that he did not speak owing to Oswald's attack on the Government, contrary to the agreement. On November 4 Pitt was on bad terms with Hume Campbell, who moved for the committee of inquiry on October 28, and with whom Pitt had previously discussed the matter.

suspicion that these noblemen made their offer from sordid views and had no intention of raising the men, when they had drawn the pay and levy-money. Horace Walpole even went so far as to assert that not six of the regiments were ever raised.[1] This suspicion was afterwards proved to have no foundation whatever; a Committee of the House investigated the charge and reported that none of the regiments fell below 100 of their proper effectives.[2] Pitt at least, who knew the zeal of his friends the Duke of Bedford and Lord Granby, was not going to allow loyalty to be damped down at such a conjuncture. Hume Campbell's proposal he condemned as

November 4, 1745.

unequitable, because it would injure those who have engaged, at this time of danger and distress, in the service of their country; and imprudent because it would discourage them from offering to serve it, if the same danger should at any time return. The noble Peers, who have undertaken to raise regiments for the public service at this time, have signalized themselves by a very laudable and eminent degree of zeal, and such zeal deserves to be rewarded. They have stood like men of fortitude and integrity in the gap at which war and confusion were breaking in upon us, and have by their influence and example raised the same spirit in others, who, had they not been thus animated to resistance and resolution, would inevitably have sunk under their fears, and suffered all the calamities of an invasion without daring to attempt the means of opposing or preventing them. . . . I cannot but think such a spirit of more importance on the present occasion than the pomp of alliances and the prospect of succours, and it may with justice be concluded that such men contribute more to the public security than so many battalions in the service of his Majesty.

He treated with scorn Hume Campbell's unconstitutional

---

[1] His friend Hanbury Williams expressed the same view in his ballad, *The Heroes*, which opens in this strain:

> Of all the jobs that e'er had past
> Our house, since times of jobbing:
> Sure none was ever like the last,
> Ev'n in the days of Robin.

See *Gentleman's Magazine*, xvi, p. 403, quoted in Manners, *Lord Granby*, p. 25.

PITT ON NATIONAL UNITY

argument that the regular army might object to these new commissions:

The right of inquiring what measures may conduce to the advantage and security of the Public belongs not to the army, but to this House; to this House belongs the power of constituting the army, or of advising his Majesty with regard to its constitution; our armies have no better right to determine for themselves than any other body of men; nor are we to suffer them to prescribe laws to the Legislature, or to govern those by whose authority they subsist. . . . And to set aside the King's promise of these commissions as of no value would be to weaken him at a time when he wants an addition of strength, and to show our enemies that he is at variance with his Parliament, when we should endeavour to exalt him by new acts of confidence and regard.

With the Pretender advancing almost unopposed through Lancashire and the King in constant ill-humour and as eager as ever for an excuse to replace them by Granville, the Pelhams were casting about for support to their tottering Administration. The Prince of Wales offered to support them on the scarcely alluring condition that they turned out all their own friends to make room for Granville's. But the Pelhams' object was 'to fix a solid scheme with those they had always wanted to unite with'; in other words, they came cap in hand to the great orator, who had shown more capacity than any man to rouse the country to a sense of its danger and its duty, and had more than once saved the administration. This was the first but not the only occasion of national danger on which Pitt, unconnected and comparatively poor and with no boroughs to sell, saw himself approached as the saviour of his country. He himself had shown his willingness to support the Pelhams in necessary measures of defence, but he was not so eager for office as to join the Ministry without conditions. Newcastle, in a letter to Chesterfield,[1] gives a detailed account of the Government's attempt to secure Pitt, and of Pitt's own conception of a national policy.

First Pelham had an interview alone with Pitt, who stated the following to be his conditions for joining the Ministry:

[1] November 20, 1745. (*Add. MSS.* 32705, f. 318.)

(1) a Place Bill to be introduced, excluding all officers under the rank of lieutenant-colonel or captain in the navy from the House of Commons ; (2) the removal of all Granville's remaining friends, notably the Finches, from their places at Court ; (3) a total alteration of the foreign system : while we had the Rebellion on our hands our part in the continental war was to be confined to sending an auxiliary force of not more than 10,000 troops to the support of the Dutch ; on the other hand no efforts were to be spared in carrying on the naval war with France and Spain ; and peace with France, of which there had been rumours, was not to be thought of.

After some further conferences between Pitt and the Duke of Newcastle, a formal meeting was arranged at Lord Gower's house on the night of Saturday, November 16, at which the Lord Chancellor, Lord Harrington, Pelham and the Duke of Newcastle represented the Pelham interest, Lord Gower, the Duke of Bedford, Lord Cobham (though all three already in the Ministry), together with Pitt, represented the former Opposition. The Pelhams opened with an appeal for union, declaring that they would never have been instrumental in removing Granville had they not relied on the support of Pitt and his friends. On Pitt's two first demands they made no difficulty. All agreed with Chesterfield that the House could well spare the ' puppey subalterns '[1] who used their votes to obtain promotion—some, perhaps, with a lively recollection of the trouble a certain ' puppey cornet ' had once given them ; the only objection to removing the Finches seemed to be the fear of still further irritating the King. The chief difference appeared on the third point—of foreign policy.

All present were pleased at the recently concluded Prussian treaty and determined to support it ; and all were equally agreed that the Queen of Hungary, by her obstinacy in refusing to come into that treaty, had lost all claim to English subsidies or troops. So far so good ; but Pitt was supported by Cobham alone in his proposal to abandon the continental war. The arguments put forward by the Duke of Newcastle on behalf of the others were that Holland would never support the war

[1] *Add. MSS.* 32705, f. 379.

in Flanders with a paltry auxiliary force of 10,000 men, but would at once make peace with France and leave us without a friend in Europe : France and Spain would then be able to concentrate their energy on their fleets and beat us even at sea, especially if the Duke of Bedford was right in asserting that our fleet could not be augmented or improved. Pitt, supported by Cobham, took a bolder view of what England could do : a defensive war in Flanders would never, he said, bring the French to their knees ; but if, without distractions on the Continent, we took a vigorous offensive at sea, our proper element, France and Spain would soon be brought to reason. In our present circumstances 10,000 men seemed to him 'a generous and noble succour' to the Dutch ; anything more would simply tempt them to leave all the fighting to us, and commit us to a war as expensive as that of helping the Queen of Hungary. From this stalwart attitude Pitt and Cobham would not budge ; Newcastle recognised that 'to bring in Mr. Pitt against his own will is impossible' ; accordingly the conference broke up without result, though 'with much civility and apparent friendship.' But Pitt would not give up his point about the navy. Failing to impress the Cabinet by his arguments, he attempted to convince the House of Commons. On November 21 he brought forward a motion to increase our fleet, arguing that, even to suppress the Rebellion, we must depend on our strength at sea. The argument seemed paradoxical, but Pitt was clearly referring to the prospect of assistance from France, which could alone give the rebels any chance of ultimate success. Old Horace Walpole once more ventured to sneer at the wisdom of the modern young man, and suggested sarcastically that his own son of twenty-two was young enough to give even better advice. Pitt was annoyed and retorted on his grey-headed experience, but joined heartily in the laugh when Walpole lifted up his wig to prove the literal justice of the retort. He found, however, only thirty-six to join him in the lobby, being left, as young Horace Walpole contemptuously observed, to 'his words, his haughtiness, his Lytteltons, and his Grenvilles.' *[marginal note: November 21, 1745.]*

Meanwhile events were driving the Pelhams to gain Pitt

by accepting his views. The young Pretender reached Derby on December 4, and the Duke of Cumberland, who had succeeded Ligonier in command at Lichfield, left him a clear road to the capital. When the news reached London on December 6, there was 'a terror scarce to be credited,' says Fielding; there was a run on the Bank of England, which saved itself only by paying all demands in sixpences[1]; and a wild rumour was afloat that the King's yacht was in the Thames ready to carry him back to Hanover. Even Pitt, courageous as he was, confessed in a speech to the House of Commons four years later that though

April 21, 1749.

> convinced that the spirit of England was sincere and true, yet I am afraid if the rebel leader could have persuaded his people to have ventured a battle against the Duke in Staffordshire, or to have given him the slip, marched towards London, and fought a battle near this city, the fate of England would have depended on the issue of that battle; for if they had obtained a victory, and made themselves masters of London, I question if the spirit of the populace would not have taken a very different turn.

But Charles Edward, sorely against his will, was persuaded to advance no farther than Derby, whence he began his retreat to Scotland, closely pressed by the Duke of Cumberland. He had one more victory over Hawley at Falkirk on January 17, 1746, but was finally routed by the Duke of Cumberland at Culloden on April 16.

'Black Friday,' December 6, appears to have convinced Pelham that Pitt's views on the continental war, at any rate, were sound. 'Whatever puts a speedy end to the Rebellion,' he wrote a few days later to the English minister at the Hague, 'is the best measure for our allies as well as ourselves. Till that is done, we are not a nation: and whatever good words we might send you, I am sure it would not be in our power to keep them.'[2] Accordingly the Dutch were to be told that, as Pitt had required, only a limited auxiliary force would be sent

---

[1] Egmont in his diary states that there was a similar run on the Bank on September 25, after the news of Prestonpans (*Egmont MSS.* 277).

[2] Coxe, *Pelham Administration*, i, 282: Pelham to Trevor, December 11, 1745.

END OF REBELLION, 1746

them—a measure which was made easier by the accession of Maria Theresa to the Anglo-Prussian alliance in December, enabling her to direct all her forces against France. Under these altered conditions Pitt went in January to see the Duke of Bedford, and on receiving a satisfactory explanation of the minister's plans, agreed to support them if he could obtain the consent of his ally Lord Cobham. To this Cobham made no objection, provided posts were given to two more of the 'cubs' and Pitt made Secretary at War. Pelham was delighted, but the next stage was not so easy. George II was already deeply annoyed with his ministers for curtailing England's part in the continental war, and was being secretly encouraged by Lords Granville and Bath to adopt William III's Grand Alliance as the model for a more ambitious policy. His indignation knew no bounds when, on February 6, Pelham again suggested that a man he regarded with so much aversion as Pitt should be made Secretary at War. He refused point-blank to have him in an office requiring constant access to his person. He did not know the man by sight, he said, and only knew of him by his insolence and impudence : if he were forced to submit, he promised Pelham he would use Pitt ill nor ever transact business with him: nay, he would publish in every market town in England how he was used by his minister, and was sure his people would stand by him.[1] Arguments were of no avail with the choleric old gentleman. Sir Robert's brother, Horace Walpole, had been brought to see that the young orator of 'the formidable sounds and furious declamation' had become the indispensable statesman, and told the King so in a long epistle.

Should his majesty, [he wrote] although unwillingly, condescend (and a very great condescension it would indeed be) to take a certain person into a certain place, it seems to be the only probable measure to carry on his business effectually in parliament, especially in regard to foreign affairs. Should his majesty, as is now currently reported, absolutely refuse to come into this measure, it is to be apprehended that things would run into confusion in parliament, as the House is now constituted.[2]

[1] *Egmont MSS.* 277 and *Aff. Etr. Angl. Corr. Pol.* 422, f. 56.
[2] Coxe, *Memoirs of Lord Walpole*, ii, 138.

The Pelhams, who, according to Marchmont, thought Mr. Pitt the only man they need fear, threatened to resign, and the King told them they might for all he cared. Pitt, with the Pretender still unbeaten in the kingdom, was too patriotic to desire the fall of the Ministry, and immediately offered to resign all pretension to the post of Secretary at War; but the ministers were on their mettle, and demanded a signal mark of royal confidence. Instead, the King met them with violent reproaches, whereupon they resigned on February 10. Bath and Granville, who had promised that 'a party behind the curtain' would support the King, were called on to fulfil their promises. After four days of futile attempts to form a party or even to find enough supporters to fill the public offices, they ignominiously abandoned the task and were thenceforward known as the heroes of the shortest Administration.[1]

The Pelhams returned to power and were able to dictate terms. Granville's remaining friends were turned out and two more of Cobham's 'cubs' admitted. Pitt still declined to insist against the King's wish on the office he coveted, and on February 22 accepted the sinecure of Vice-Treasurer of Ireland, in the belief that this would soon lead to a post more worthy of his capacity. One of his first duties as a minister was anything but agreeable. Since no English troops could then be spared for the auxiliary force promised to the Dutch, the Ministry had decided to hire 18,000 Hanoverians to make up the numbers. On April 10 the vote for these Hanoverians was proposed, and Pitt was called upon to support it. Circumstances had materially altered since he had thundered so eloquently and so successfully against a similar vote. Hanover had now entered the war as a principal and could no longer be said to be fulfilling her obligations solely at our expense; the Dutch were in such imminent danger from Maurice de Saxe that even in our own interest it was imperative to help them; and, since no English troops could be spared from the Rebellion, foreign troops, of which the Hanoverians were the best avail-

---

[1] See allusion to this Ministry in Pitt's speech of November 13, 1755 (below, pp. 269–70).

able, had to take their place. Nevertheless Pitt's former opposition to the Hanoverians had been uncompromising and unconditional: he had declared, or was said to have declared, in an extravagant outburst that he would consent to be branded on the forehead as a traitor if he ever consented to pay Hanoverian troops; and the numerous enemies his eminence and haughtiness had raised did not allow him to forget it. All his old speeches were brought up against him in the debate: he was racked, it was said, with the question both ordinary and extraordinary. According to all accounts Pitt felt these attacks acutely;[1] but he was not the man to give a silent vote on such an occasion, as did the Grenvilles and Lyttelton, who had been equally violent in the past. His speech was differently regarded according to his critics' point of view: it cannot have been unduly humble, for Walpole says it added impudence to profligacy. On the other hand Pelham said that he showed 'the dignity of Sir William Wyndham, the wit of Mr. Pulteney and the knowledge and judgment of Sir Robert Walpole.' 'In short,' adds Newcastle, 'he said all that was right for the King, kind and respectful to the old corps, and resolute and contemptuous for the Tory Opposition.' It pleased the King so much that he suggested Pitt for the honour of proposing the parliamentary grant to the Duke of Cumberland in acknowledgment of the victory at Culloden,[2] and a fortnight later allowed him to succeed Winnington as Paymaster of the forces and to be sworn of the Privy Council.[3] But he still maintained his veto on the Secretaryship at War, which was given to Pitt's future rival, Henry Fox.

April 8, 1746.

Pitt had to suffer far more obloquy for accepting a post under Government than for his support of the Hanover troops. Five days later a caricature was published with the legend, 'A ghost of a D—h—s to W——m P—— Esq.,' in which

[1] The French agent's account states that 'on l'emporta de la Chambre plus mort que vif,' which, however, is an obvious exaggeration in view of what Pelham and Newcastle said of his speech.

[2] At the Duke's express request, however, the motion was proposed by Pelham.

[3] Pitt was appointed Paymaster-General on May 6, and sworn of the Privy Council on May 28, 1746.

Pitt appears with 'Hanover T——s' branded on his brow.[1] His friend Lyttelton did not mend matters by addressing him as 'Blest Genius' in a laudatory poem, which declared,

> To prove your justice you must greatness bear
> And suffer honours you are doomed to wear.

This poem was the signal for a host of ribald parodies, of which the most famous was Hanbury Williams's 'Unembarrassed Countenance,' containing the lines,

> When from an old woman, by standing his ground,
> He had got the possession of ten thousand pound,
> He said he car'd not for what others might call him,
> He would show himself now the true son of Sir Balaam.
>   Derry Down, &c.
>
> . . . .
>
> Whilst Balaam was poor, he was full of renown;
> But now that he's rich, he's the jest of the town.
> Then let all men learn by his present disgrace,
> That honesty's better by far than a place.
>   Derry Down, &c.[2]

On the other hand, the greatest living statesman outside England was glad to recognise a kindred spirit in Pitt and welcomed his accession to the Ministry. Frederic the Great's envoy in London had spoken of Pitt as 'the greatest orator in the House of Commons . . . a man universally beloved by the nation'; whereupon his master replied : 'From your report I can see that Mr. Pitt has the feelings of a true Englishman, you are therefore to compliment him from me and inform him that I wish his views were generally held : England and Prussia would then be closely united, a thing impossible as long as England is directed according to the special interests of Hanover.'[3] Pitt himself took care that

---

[1] Pitt's reputation at this time may be estimated from the fact that the French secret agent in London procured a copy of this print to send to the French Foreign Office (*Aff. Etr. Angl. Corr. Pol.* 422, f. 182).

[2] Hanbury Williams's poem suggested a caricature of Pitt's 'Unembarrassed Countenance' depicted in a style uncongenial to modern taste. Hanbury Williams also wrote *A Duchess's Ghost to Orator Hanover Pitt*, and *Short Verses in Imitation of Long Verses in an Epistle to William Pitt Esq.* (a parody of Lyttelton's poem).

[3] *Pol. Corr.* v, 45.

attacks to his face were not repeated in the House of Commons. In the following November George Selwyn's father attempted it, but it resulted in 'the great mirth of the whole House and the mortification of the major's oratorship.'[1]

The violent attacks on Pitt are intelligible at a time when a post in the Government was more commonly regarded as the price of silence than as a means of advancing the national interests. Inconsistency, too, has always been a popular cause of reproach to politicians, whether the inconsistency applies to details or to fundamentals; and Pitt undoubtedly laid himself open to the charge of inconsistency. He had used the Hanoverians as a whip wherewith to chastise Carteret for his un-English schemes of continental adventure, and, though the circumstances had changed since Hanover had taken an active part in the war and England needed allies for her own protection, Pitt's attacks had been too sweeping to be reconciled with his present attitude. To do him justice, he did not attempt to reconcile them. Throughout life he looked on charges of inconsistency with Olympian indifference, and often suffered from his impetuous habit of using any arguments that came to hand to drive home his point, however dangerous they might prove afterwards. But on the fundamental issue of husbanding the national resources for national objects and not wasting them on objects which did not concern England he was always consistent. Although the Pelhams were not very courageous men, he felt that on the whole they represented this view better than any other school of politicians. He realised, too, that at this crisis, when England was smarting from the disgrace of the Jacobite rebellion and France was carrying her victorious arms all over Flanders, a ministry founded on a broad basis and disinclined to a policy of adventure deserved the support of every patriotic man. As a member of such a government he would have more chance of influencing their decisions than in opposition. He had already succeeded in limiting the continental war to the single object of turning the French out of Flanders, and his vigorous

[1] *Chatham MSS.* 34: Elizabeth Wyndham to Hester Grenville (Pitt's future wife), November 1746.

naval policy had some chance of fulfilment under Bedford, who had the good sense to rely on Anson's advice. In accepting office at this time his anxiety for the country may best be told in his own words in answer to Trevor's congratulations from The Hague :

I heartily wish I had as much reason to be contented with the state of the Public, as I have to be with my own. . . . I will not trouble you with anything more than a wish in return for yours : may our good friends where you are, learn of you to feel for us, for Europe, and for themselves.[1]

[1] *Historical MSS. Commission*, XIV, ix, 146.

CHAPTER VI

PITT AS PAYMASTER

πειθαρχία γάρ ἐστι τῆς εὐπραξίας
μήτηρ, γυνὴ σωτῆρος.
 ÆSCHYLUS, *S. c. Thebas*, 224.[1]

I—IN WAR

PITT was Paymaster of the Forces for over nine years, eight of which were the most peaceful in his stormy life. Pelham's bland sway allayed the discontents which Walpole and Carteret's forcible personalities had aroused, and at few periods in our history were politics so dull or so harmonious. Pitt, himself in the Government but outside the Cabinet, had no temptation to oppose, no counterbalancing responsibility to absorb his energies. In contrast to the notoriety his philippics against Walpole and the 'Hanover troop-minister' had brought him and the glory he afterwards attained, this intervening period was one of obscurity. The lampoons and caricatures and the public eulogies alike died down.

But these years of obscurity were not wasted. Even in his own office he learned something of the business of administration, and, from the confidence reposed in him by the Pelhams, gained an insight into affairs of State that years of zealous industry in opposition could never have supplied. Convinced after twelve years in politics that, though much could be said, little could be done for the public good by a man labouring under the royal displeasure, he put a curb on

---

[1] 'Obedience breeds success and is mated to safety.'

his impetuosity, and in spite of occasional lapses conscientiously set himself to gain the royal favour and thereby earn the right to serve his country fully. His efforts were poorly rewarded at first, but they strengthened his character. And in this period he had the leisure, rarely granted him, to enjoy a private life of his own, to have long spells with his friends, to read copiously, plan gardens, and talk at large—humanities all good for the growth of a man's soul, which is apt to languish if confined to a single sphere, even so full of human interest as politics.

The Paymaster-General of the Guards, Garrisons and Marching Forces was in Pitt's time a minister with little business but large opportunities of profit. The work of his office, little more than routine, was to issue regimental pay and the half-pay of the pensioners connected with Chelsea Hospital, and to settle the bills of army contractors. The Paymaster also had some patronage as *ex officio* Treasurer of Chelsea Hospital and paid over to their London agents subsidies voted by Parliament to foreign princes. One means of irregular emolument to the Paymaster was the commission of one-fourth per cent. which it was the custom to exact on all these subsidies, a considerable perquisite in such a year as 1745, when over £1,250,000 was paid to secure allies abroad. But the chief opportunity for profit arose from the Treasury practice of issuing to the Paymaster the money voted by Parliament in lump sums, irrespective of the calls on him for payment.[1] Under this system the Paymaster's office was one of the 'subordinate treasuries,' as Burke called them in his speech on Economical Reform of 1780, and not merely an

[1] For example, in the year 1755 a King's Warrant of January 24 directed the Treasury to pay over to Pitt £300,000 'by way of imprest and upon account for the service of our said guards, garrisons and land forces or any other publick services under his care of payment for the year 1755 according to such establishments and pursuant to such warrants and orders as are or shall be signed by Us on that behalf'; while on February 21 a King's Warrant ordered 'the clerk of the Signet attending' to 'prepare a bill to pass under Privy Seal,' granting Pitt £839,548. Thus within one month the whole of the £1,139,548 granted by Parliament for guards, garrisons, and marching forces for the current year was issued. (See Record Office, *King's Warrant Book* 47.) Thanks are due to Dr. W. A. Shaw for his kindness in giving references to documents in the Record Office relating to Pitt's accounts.

PAY OFFICE SYSTEM 153

accounting department, as the corresponding office now is and as Burke wished to make it by his Establishment Bill. 'The great and invidious profits of the Pay Office,' he declared in the same speech, 'are from the bank that is held in it.' It often happened that the amount voted largely exceeded the actual payments made in one year, with the result that large balances remained in the Paymaster's hands. The amounts he received from the Treasury at the beginning of the year he could put out to interest for his own account until payments fell due, as well as all the unexpended balances of previous years, which were never returned to the Exchequer until his accounts had been finally audited, long after he had left office.[1] As examples of the large amount of these balances, it is related that the Duke of Chandos built Canons from his emoluments as Paymaster in Queen Anne's war; and that in 1760, when the Government found a difficulty in raising a loan, Fox, then Paymaster, was able to start the subscription with £80,000 out of his balances.[2] Undoubtedly also Fox, from his profits in the office, secured comfort for his old age and the means of starting his sons generously on their career of dissipation. For the time being all issues to the Paymaster, as well as all the office books and papers, were treated as his personal property.[3] These abuses lasted until 1782, when Rigby's balances were the subject of a series of debates.[4] Rigby and others openly admitted the practice of using these balances for private profit and defended it strenuously; but the House of Commons thought otherwise, and resolved 'that from henceforward the Paymaster-General of His Majesty's land forces and the Treasurer of the Navy for the time being shall

---

[1] In Record Office, *King's Warrant Book* 48 (December 20, 1756), a retiring Paymaster is ordered to pay over part of his balance to his successor, with the express proviso, however, that in the following year, when the financial strain is relaxed, he is to be repaid.

[2] See Torrens, ii, 539, and *Add. MSS.* 32907 (January 1760). Fox's reputation in these loan transactions was not savoury (see *Add. MSS.* 32998, f. 290, and his own account in *Life and Letters of Lady Sarah Lennox*, 72).

[3] Burke incidentally mentioned in a speech of 1783 that Pitt's Pay Office books were still in the hands of his executors. They are not, however, among the *Chatham MSS.* at the Record Office.

[4] *Parl. Hist.* xxiii, pp. 115 *sqq.*, 127 *sqq.*

not apply any sum or sums of money imprested to them or either of them to any purpose of advantage or interest to themselves either directly or indirectly.'

Such was the system when Pitt took office, such the facilities for making private profit out of public funds. Pitt resolutely set his face against these practices, though they were sanctioned by long custom. When the Sardinian envoy offered him the usual commission on the subsidy of £200,000, Pitt refused to touch it, and he also declined a large present, which the King of Sardinia, marvelling at his disinterested conduct, pressed upon him.[1] So with his balances. All sums issued to him from the Treasury he lodged in the Bank of England at call for the public service, and never touched a penny of interest from them. When his accounts were audited in 1767—twelve years after he had left the Pay Office, according to the lax system of the time—it was discovered that he had a balance of £90,000, which he had never made the least use of, 'though it might have been worth,' it was surmised, 'in interest to him £30,000 to £40,000 since that time.'[2] To-day Pitt's conduct in refusing to make personal profit from public money entrusted to him would seem the most natural thing in the world; it was far from obvious in an age when such perquisites were regarded as a politician's right. Only a man great enough to neglect conventional rules of conduct and apply his own canons of

---

[1] Almon (6th ed.) i, 121. See also *The Test* for January 8, 1757. 'He is greatly admired by the King of Sardinia, at whose courts the doctor [Dr. Guliemo Bombasto de Podagra] performed wonders and afterwards refused to take his fees, which was thought an extraordinary thing in a physician.'

[2] *Historical MSS. Commission* (Weston Underwood), p. 405. See also J. Nicoll's letter to Lord Chatham of January 15, 1767, on the subject of his balance (*Chatham MSS.* 51).

The warrant directing Chatham to remit his balance to the Joint Paymasters at the time is dated April 7, 1767, and states that 'out of the monies which from time to time have been issued to you for the service of our Forces and other services relative thereto in former years the sum of £90,000 remains in your hands over and above such sums of money as were found necessary to be applied for defraying the expenses of the services within the said years.' (Record Office, *King's Warrant Book* 58). Even then the account was not closed, for it appears that some of the imprests to sub-accountants were not finally cleared till 1791 (Record Office, *Declared Accounts*; Audit Office Bundle 70, Roll 91).

right and wrong could have done this in the face of his contemporaries' examples and conventions. This attitude soon became known and enhanced his reputation with the people, who were accustomed to regard politicians as chartered libertines fattening on money from the public purse ; even in the height of Pitt's fame as a war minister it was counted to him as an added glory.[1] His example had, it is true, no immediate effect on his successors, men like Fox and Rigby, but it set up a standard which was recalled in the better days when Burke dealt the first serious blows at organised political corruption.[2]

Those less scrupulous than Pitt had not the excuse that the salary attached to the office of Paymaster was meagre. Nominally £3,000, it was reckoned, with the legitimate allowances, to amount to over £4,000.[3] The work required to earn this salary need have consisted in nothing more on Pitt's part than taking responsibility for the labours of the Deputy Pay-

---

See, for example, the eulogy on Pitt in *The English Pericles*, a pamphlet published in 1759.

[2] Lord Rosebery, on Camelford's authority, states (*Chatham*, p. 256) that Pitt consulted Pelham on the question of giving up the percentages on foreign subsidies and that Pelham told him he had never claimed them. From this Camelford's deduction is that Pitt's refusal had no special merit. Camelford's testimony, as Lord Rosebery admits, is not very trustworthy whenever it tends to detract from the merit of the uncle who was his benefactor. Besides, it is remarkable that, if Pelham, who was Paymaster for thirteen years (1730-43), never followed the practice of his predecessors, nothing should ever have been heard of his self-restraint, and that Pitt's action should have caused so much surprise and admiration. Even Camelford apparently makes no suggestion that Pitt's refusal to make a profit on his balances was not his own idea.

[3] From papers in *Chatham MSS.* 76 it appears that—

The payments to the Paymaster were :	£	Less deductions :	£
Salary	3,000	For fees	165
For clerks, etc.	1,500	For clerks and messengers	1,571
Contingencies	600		
As Treasurer of Chelsea Hospital	365		
£1 a day on the establishment of a general	365		
	£5,830		£1,736

This left a net income of over £4000.

master, James Grenville, and a staff of about a dozen clerks,[1] with a few sub-accountants attached to the headquarters of the army in time of war. But the new Paymaster took an active interest in his duties, and infused some of his own energy into subordinates accustomed to take things easily. One of them, Peregrine Furze, wrote barely two months after Pitt's appointment that he already felt better for the increase of work, for ' the pleasure of obeying your commands gave me spirit that I have at other times wanted ' ; on another occasion he told Pitt ' no Paymaster-General has ever made a payment to the Reduced officers with that promptness as you did that to the 24th December last, and you have had, tho' I forgot to tell it to you, the Praises and Thanks of them all upon that account.' [2] Thomas Orby Hunter, the Paymaster's agent at Rotterdam during the war, showed the same zeal in his

---

[1] The personnel of Pitt's staff is set out in a King's Warrant of April 16, 1767 (Record Office; *King's Warrant Book* 58), granting Lord Chatham's petition for a sum of £11,151 to pay the extra services of his staff ' for their diligence and application ' in accounting for £20,328,320 (the gross total of his audited accounts) ' without any expense to the public for additional assistance or allowance.' This sum was allocated as follows :

	£
Deputy Paymaster, J. Grenville	1,950
Cashier, Anthony Sawyer	1,880
Accountant-General, J. L. Nicoll	1,560
Ledger Keeper, J. Powell	800
Keeper of Off reckonings, J. F. A. Hesse	500
Half Pay Cashier, R. Randell	500
Accountant's Clerk	480
5 Under Clerks	550
Housekeeper	60
Office Keeper	50
Messenger	25
Treasurer of Chelsea	200
	8,555
Incidental charges, expenses and allowances to clerks and officers at the offices through which the accounts pass	2,596
	£11,151

A study of the audit rolls in question, from June 1746 to December 1755, shows that the sum, though large, was not excessive for the extra labour involved in drawing them up.

[2] *Chatham MSS.* 32 ; see also *ibid.* 51 and 55 for letters on Pay Office business from J. Nicoll and A. Sawyer.

chief's service. Though at first surprised at Pitt's unusual request that he should correspond directly with him, he thenceforth sent him full accounts of his own proceedings and early information of the movements of troops, which was no doubt as interesting to his correspondent as the purely financial side of the department. Nicoll, Hunter's successor at Rotterdam, showed his appreciation of the new Paymaster's disposition by refusing to take orders even from the Duke of Newcastle at the Treasury, unless they were confirmed by Pitt. Evidence shows that Pitt kept a sharp look-out for waste in the expenditure of public money. He ruthlessly cut down unwarrantable claims made by one of his agents, and, on the more important matter of Lord Loudoun's army accounts, made 'strong and reasonable objections,' it is said, to certain irregular items. He introduced a much needed reform in the administration of the pension branch. He found that the Chelsea out-pensioners had to wait a twelvemonth before receiving the first instalment of their pensions, and were generally tided over that period by money-lenders, who charged exorbitant interest and took a mortgage on their pensions. The commissions charged by the Pay-Office clerks also made a serious inroad on their allowances. Pitt for some time 'had it much at heart,' he says, ' to redeem these helpless, unthinking creatures from their harpies,' but found great difficulty in devising any practicable and effectual scheme for their relief. Encouraged, however, by a personal appeal from the Duke of Cumberland, he at last contrived a method to which there was no objection. His Bill, providing that six months' pension should be paid in advance, that all future mortgages on pensions should be void, and that commissions should no longer be exacted by pension officers, was presented to the House on November 14, 1754, two days before his wedding, and passed with uncommon expedition.

In 1747, the year after Pitt accepted office, the Pelhams suddenly dissolved,[1] in order to secure a majority more agreeable to their views. The Prince of Wales's party, which

[1] This was the first and for a long time the only instance under the Septennial Act of a dissolution before the seven years of a parliament had elapsed.

had made so brave a show at the elections six years earlier, was reduced to a mere rump. Instead of having William Pitt, Lyttelton, and Sarah, Duchess of Marlborough, besides the older Patriots to manage his electoral business, the Prince had to entrust it to the Rev. Dr. Ayscough, and to Pitt's incapable elder brother, Thomas.[1] In spite of alluring promises to the electors—whereby he engaged to abolish all party distinctions and widen the qualifications for justices of the peace; to establish a militia; to exclude all officers of the lower ranks in the army and navy from the House of Commons; to inquire into departmental abuses; and to content himself with a Civil List of £800,000—thunder, most of it, stolen from Pitt's own armoury—in spite, too, of an election fund of £200,000, which, as Walpole remarked, he had much better have saved to buy Parliament after it was chosen, the results were most disappointing. Partly owing to the fact that Newcastle was once more heart and soul in the work of increasing the Government majority, partly because the country, tired of the last few years' confusion, really wished for the healing measures expected from the Pelhams, the Government increased its following in the House and won seats never before carried by the Whigs, among others Westminster and the City and Middlesex; while Okehampton, one of Thomas Pitt's own boroughs, rebelled against him and elected Lyttelton.[2]

The most remarkable of the new members in this Parliament was William Beckford, elected for the City. Descended from a line of Jamaica planters, by the death of two brothers he inherited a fortune, chiefly derived from sugar and said to have been worth over a million pounds. He soon became the chief representative of the West Indian interest in the House of Commons, where, in spite of an uncouth address, he was regarded as an authority on commercial subjects; in the City,

---

[1] Thomas seems to have sadly mismanaged the elections in Cornwall and had much trouble with the Prince in consequence. He had the gift of forcible language in common with his namesake the Governor. Talking of the electors at Grampound he says that 'The villains have got ahead to a degree, and rise in their demands so extravagantly that I have been very near damning them and kicking them to the devil at once.'

[2] See Phillimore's *Lyttelton*, i, 256.

then the home of democratic principles, he was twice Lord Mayor, and all-powerful. He attached himself to Pitt from the outset and became his most devoted follower. Pitt's sympathy with the mercantile community and his understanding of the colonies were kept constantly fresh by his intercourse with Beckford, whom he could always count upon to bring him the support of the City, and to undertake preliminary skirmishes on his behalf or lead a forlorn hope in the House of Commons. In return, though sometimes allowing himself to poke gentle fun at his friend, Pitt was always ready to defend him against the supercilious adversaries, who ridiculed the alderman's rough manners and downright sentiments; he also stood godfather to Beckford's son, and, when he was left an orphan, cared for the boy's education.

For Pitt himself Old Sarum was no longer available, since it belonged to his brother, now on the opposite side. He therefore accepted the Duke of Newcastle's offer of Seaford. This borough, with all the Cinque Ports to which it belonged, was a close Treasury preserve. The right of election had been declared in 1670 to be 'in the populacy,' but this was interpreted to mean householders paying scot and lot, and good care was taken that only revenue officers and dependents on the patron should appear as such in the rate book. Really the Duke of Newcastle's word, as in most parts of Sussex, was supreme. At a by-election in the year 1733 the electors wrote to assure him that their representative should be 'who your Grace shall be pleased to recommend'; and for the modest price of 'a dinner to the Gentlemen, a double fee to the Ringers, and a double portion of Beer to the Populace' they obeyed his *congé d'élire* in favour of his connection, William Hay.[1] On June 20, 1747, the Duke wrote a letter to the 'Bailiff and the Jurats, Freemen and Inhabitants of the Corporation of Seaford,' recommending to their

[1] *Add. MSS.* 32688, and article in *English Historical Review*, July 1897, on 'The Duke of Newcastle and the Elections of 1734.' Hay, Pitt's colleague in one Parliament, was a minor poet, an agricultural reformer, and the writer of a eulogy on deformity, he being deformed himself. Pitt, no doubt in compliment to his colleague, bought a copy of Hay's *Essay on Deformity* in 1753 (see *Chatham MSS.* 74).

Favor at the ensuing election Mr. Pitt, Paymaster-General of H.M. Forces, and your late member Mr. Hay. . . . Mr. Pitt's zeal for H.M.'s service and for the Interest of His country and his known ability and inclination to promote them are such qualifications as I doubt not but will make him as agreeable to you, as the choice of him will be serviceable to the Publick. Mr. Pitt intends to be with me at Bishopstone the end of the week where he will have an opportunity of being personally known to you, and as no man is better able to serve you I am sure nobody will be more willing. Your favor to Mr. Pitt and Mr. Hay upon this occasion will ever be gratefully acknowledged by . . . Holles Newcastle.[1]

This decently veiled command was accompanied by instructions to an agent addressed as 'Sam,' whom the Duke sent to the bailiff with orders to read out his letter to the corporation, treat them and the freemen to a bowl of punch, and fix the election for June 29. Sam was also to go round the town informing people 'how considerable a man Mr. Pitt is and how able he will be to serve them.' But opposition 'unexpected and unaccountable' to the Duke appeared. Lord Gage, his former ally, came to Seaford on the 24th with his son, who had been Hay's colleague in the last Parliament, and announced that if he obtained the promise of only one vote he would send him to the poll. Newcastle's agents reported to him that Lord Gage had little support and was obliged to entertain his friends in a barn, as the innkeeper would not serve him; and Henry Pelham bade him not fret at Lord Gage's 'impertinence; it is what might happen in your own or any nobleman's family in case such a fellow could get admittance to it.' But the Duke, who was easily upset, took the incident seriously to heart. He assured Pitt that if that nobleman's money 'should have an effect in a place where it was never before offered, it shall in no way affect you, for Mr. Hay will not be thought of.' In the same letter he gave fussy directions for their journey to Bishopstone :

Lord Lincoln and Lord Ashburnham, two very well-disposed young

---

[1] This and other details of the election are to be found in *Add. MSS.* 32711, and the Duke of Newcastle's letter to Pitt in *Chatham MSS.* 51. See also an account of this election in *A History of the Boroughs of Great Britain* (3 vols. 1792) by T. H. B. Oldfield.

gentlemen, are my Sussex companions. We go to Godstone, about twenty miles off, in Lord Ashburnham's coach, there take my coach to East Grinstead and then ride to my house about nineteen miles. . . . If you would be so good as to be at my lodgings at Kensington in your riding dress at one o'clock I hope we may get away soon after and then we shall be in time. . . . I hope you have sent your horses to East Grinstead.

Pitt next day gravely returns

ten thousand thanks for the honour of your letter and for the trouble you are so good to give yourself in informing me of this unexpected attack at Seaford. I never can enough express the high sense I have of the honour of your Grace's friendship and goodness to me: whatever the event prove, . . . I shall with great pride meet any persecution in which I have the honour to be joined with your Grace and Mr. Pelham. I have sent on horses to East Grinstead and a post chaise, in case of rain, which I am too infirm to venture to stand. I will be sure to attend your Grace at the time appointed.

When these strange travelling companions arrived on the Saturday night, they found yet another opponent in Lord Middlesex, who had recently resigned his place in the Treasury and returned to the Prince's service as Master of the Horse. But the Duke showed himself equal to the occasion. On Sunday night he invited the whole corporation to dinner at Bishopstone, and talked to most of the voters one by one. Next day, the 29th, he went over with Pitt to the hustings at Seaford, in spite of protests, sat by the returning officer all day to overawe supporters of Lords Gage and Middlesex, and gave 'the usual entertainments' to the electors. On the following day Pitt returned to London as member for Seaford.

Though the Duke's hospitable exertions had assured Pitt's and Hay's success at the polls, an election petition was in consequence brought against their return in the following session. In the debate Pitt treated the petition in cavalier fashion, passing it off as a jest; but he was soundly rebuked for this levity by Potter, a young follower of the Prince of Wales. Pitt had asked what was the object of the petition, and Potter told him that it was for 'the security, the freedom of parliaments and protecting the privileges of the Commons of Great Britain'; he

November 20, 1747

also reminded him that while ' a dependence upon the Crown would in the end prove fatal to our liberties, a dependence upon the minister, as it is infinitely more dishonourable, is infinitely more dangerous. . . . I can suppose too, Sir, that in some future time a minister may arise profligate enough to carry his views so high as to attempt to make both king and people subservient to his own ambition.' Pitt made no reply at the time ; but the spirit and even the words of the reproof seem to have sunk into his mind, for within seven years he was adopting the same tone and using almost the same language against the very man by whose unconstitutional action he was on this occasion profiting.[1] Does such a change of attitude go to prove that Pitt was inconsistent and animated merely by motives of self-interest ? Inconsistent, perhaps, but with the inconsistency of the man who casts off the evil trappings of the past as he advances. One of the chief lessons to be gained from Pitt's life is that of a man who never ceased learning from his own experience and the teaching of others, and therefore never ceased growing in moral stature. But it would be an unworthy defence of Pitt's conduct in this instance to dismiss it as venial, because he was following the bad traditions of his contemporaries, which, in regard to the Pay Office, he had shown himself strong enough to disregard.

Later Pitt himself recognised the scandal of the methods then used to decide on contested elections. The cases were heard by the whole House and voted on as a trial of party strength, and hardly a pretence was made to judge them on their merits. Walpole indeed had made an adverse vote on the Chippenham election a reason for resigning. At the beginning of the 1747 parliament there were, as usual, many such cases, in several of which Pitt spoke. On the Wareham petition, in which his cousin, John Pitt, was involved, he made a lasting enemy of the future judge, Wilmot,

January 26, 1748.

who [says Walpole] had been an admired pleader before the House of Commons, but being reprimanded . . . with great haughtiness by Pitt, who told him he had brought thither the pertness of his profession, and being prohibited by the Speaker from making a

[1] See below, p. 256 (speech of November 25, 1754).

reply, he flung down his brief in a passion and never would return to plead there any more.[1]

A more noted case was that of the Westminster by-election in 1751, on which also Pitt spoke at length, hinting dire penalties against Crowle and Murray, two supporters of the Prince's candidate, who had insulted the High Bailiff and defied the House of Commons. Crowle was constrained to kneel to receive the Speaker's reprimand, but, on rising, ostentatiously dusted his knees and remarked that it was the dirtiest house he had ever been in, an incident which, for the first time, brought home to members how lowering such farcical travesties of justice were to their dignity. [February 6, 1750.]

By the time the new Parliament met in November 1747 Pitt and nearly everybody else in England were heartily anxious for peace. During 1746 the French had carried all before them on the Continent, completing their conquest of the Low Countries and beating the English and their allies in the battle of Roucoux. In India the East India Company had been unable to make headway against the enterprise of Dupleix and Labourdonnais, and had lost Madras, which Pitt's grandfather once held so masterfully against all comers. In the same year Bedford, encouraged by the colonial success at Louisburg in 1745, had collected a fleet and army with the design of attacking Quebec and driving the French out of Canada, but had the support of Pitt alone in the Ministry. He, indeed, entered heartily into a plan so congenial to his own spirit, and wrote urging Bedford ' to pursue firmly those great and practicable views in America, which so far as they have gone or are to go, we owe to your Grace alone. . . . The nation is certainly with you ; with such a second, your Grace can surmount all obstacles.' But Pelham and the Duke of Newcastle had no stomach for such an adventure. They threw obstacles in the way until the season for an American expedi-

[1] Walpole, *George II*, ii, 273. Pitt appears to have studied the brief for this election petition, which is preserved in *Chatham MSS*. 83. Oswald (p. 69) states that it was at Pelham's urgent request that he spoke for John and William Augustus Pitt, the members returned, against the Prince's friends, Henry and Thomas Drax, petitioning. Pitt again spoke on a Wareham election petition on December 19, 1754.

tion had passed, then, thinking it necessary 'to save appearances, that the vast charges of our naval armament this year may not seem to have been flung away,'[1] they sent the expedition under Admiral Lestock and General St. Clair on a roving mission to the coast of France, leaving it open to them to attack L'Orient, La Rochelle, Rochefort, or Bordeaux at their discretion. L'Orient was decided upon, but the operations were conducted in a slovenly manner; guns were landed without ammunition and the troops were re-embarked, having inflicted no more damage than the destruction of some trifling forts.[2] 'A gloomy scene,' wrote Pitt dolefully, 'is, I fear, opening in public affairs for this disgraced country.'[3]

Peace would have been too dearly bought by England at the end of 1746, but the re-conquest of her position on her own element in 1747 made it possible for her to negotiate on more equal terms. Anson's work at the Admiralty had at last begun to tell. Better methods of naval construction, a more just system of promotion, and stricter discipline had been introduced.[4] Admirals of the stamp of Vernon, Lestock and Mathews were being gradually superseded by Anson's own lieutenants, who had caught some of his energetic spirit. A promise to carry out the more vigorous naval policy, which Pitt had insisted upon as a condition of taking office,[5] was conveyed in the King's Speech of November 1746, declaring that it would be his 'particular care to exert our strength at sea in the most effectual manner, for the defence of my kingdoms and possessions, the protection of the trade of my subjects, and the annoyance of our enemies.' This promise was amply fulfilled. On May 3, 1747, Anson, by his victory off Finisterre, captured six ships of the line and four Indiamen, 'the best

[1] So wrote old Horace Walpole, then in Pelham's confidence.
[2] Among the *Chatham MSS.* is an account of this expedition, one of the many indications of the attention bestowed by Pitt on military and naval affairs. David Hume, philosopher and historian, went on this expedition as St. Clair's military secretary.
[3] *Grenville Papers*, i, 52, October 1746.
[4] Bedford supported Anson manfully in his fight against favouritism and sharply reprimanded George Grenville, who was on the Board of Admiralty; for an attempt to favour his brother, Captain Thomas Grenville.
[5] See above, p. 142.

stroke,' he boasted, 'that has been made upon the French since La Hogue.' On October 14 his old shipmate, Hawke, captured six more French men-of-war off Belleisle, remarking in his laconic despatch that ' as the enemy's ships were large they took a great deal of drubbing.' These and other successes at sea reduced the French navy to impotence for the rest of the war and thereby turned the tables on Dupleix in India, who, for want of reinforcement, was himself besieged by Boscawen with ten sail at Pondichery. But on the Continent the French were still uniformly successful. Maurice de Saxe defeated Cumberland and the allies at Lauffeldt, began the invasion of Holland with the capture of Bergen-op-Zoom, and laid his plans for besieging the important Dutch fortress of Maestricht early in 1748.

The loss to their commerce from the destruction of their fleets had by this time inclined the French to peace, the death of Philip V of Spain—a ' great event,' Pitt called it—had destroyed the bellicose influence of his turbulent consort, Elizabeth Farnese, and the danger to England from the French occupation of the Low Countries had convinced most English statesmen of the futility of continuing the war. ' We fight all and pay all, it is true,' grumbled Pelham to old Horace Walpole, ' but we are beaten and shall be broke.' In Pitt he found a sympathizer : ' Mr. Pitt and I seem entirely to agree in opinion,' he wrote to Lyttelton, ' which is a melancholy truth, because we both see our condition so bad that nothing can be thought of but to take the lesser evil.' In a speech two years later Pitt explained the reason for his apprehensions at this period : [February 5, 1750.]

I must confess [he said] that when the French laid siege to Maestricht in the beginning of 1748, I had such a gloomy prospect of affairs that I thought it next to impossible to preserve our friends the Dutch from the imminent ruin they were then threatened with, or to maintain the present Emperor on the imperial throne ; and if the Dutch had been ruined, and the Emperor dispossessed, this nation would have been so far from being in a condition to insist upon what it had a right to demand that we must have yielded to every demand our enemies might have been pleased to make upon us.

With these good dispositions to peace on all sides the

belligerents agreed to a congress at Aix-la-Chapelle in March 1748, and peace was signed there in November. The inconclusive character of the war was reflected in this treaty. France gave up all her conquests, Madras, the Low Countries, and the Barrier fortresses, and agreed once more to demolish the fortifications of Dunkirk. England restored Cape Breton with Louisburg. Between these two Powers the peace hardly brought a truce except in Europe. In America France persisted in her design of linking up her possessions of Canada in the north and Louisiana, on the Gulf of Mexico, by a chain of forts, which would exclude the English seaboard colonists from the interior; in India the French and English companies carried on hostilities with unabated ardour. Between England and Spain the question of the right of search, the original cause of the war, was left unsettled; but Spain was a decaying power, and during Ferdinand's reign did not embarrass England. Frederic the Great had gained most by the war, but even though the treaty confirmed him in the possession of Silesia he had to fight for it once more. Italy alone, long the happy hunting ground of Bourbon, Hapsburg and Sardinian freebooters, secured by the treaty a settlement which gave her fifty years of comparative peace. But a truce in Europe was necessary to England and the other Powers to recover from a war lasting nearly ten years. 'We have fought it to the stumps,' said Pelham, and if that was true of England it was still more the case with France: Louis XV had little to show for his successes in the Low Countries, after a treaty which originated the saying, '*bête comme la paix*,' beyond a crippled navy and finances in disorder. England, while securing no material advantages from the peace, had regained her supremacy at sea and increased her commercial wealth, benefits which stood her in good stead in the coming struggle for India and America.

Pitt rejoiced in 'the happy event of the Preliminaries— happy, I call it, because absolutely necessary to our very being,' not because he despaired of his country, but from the conviction that a continental war against France under such conditions as we had hitherto waged it was disastrous. He had no illusions as to the necessity of renewing the struggle with France, but he saw plainly who ought to be our ally in that struggle. Our foreign policy was on wrong lines in clinging to the traditional system of alliance with the Austrians and ignoring Prussia's rising power; without peace he was convinced we should never shake ourselves free of the old system. Frederic of Prussia had the best army in Europe, which his undiminished fears of Maria Theresa and his new alarm at Russia, 'that great cloud of power in the north,'[1] obliged him to keep in a perfect state of efficiency. England needed an ally on the Continent with such an army. Frederic desired to be on good terms with England: 'then I should have nothing to fear from Russia,' he wrote in 1748.[2] Religion also, which still counted in European statecraft, was a bond between England and Prussia such as did not exist between England and the bigots at Vienna. One of Pitt's great arguments for peace had been that it would give an opportunity to carry out this change in our system. In a letter of December 17, 1747, on 'the melancholy scene of public affairs,' he put this view before the Duke of Newcastle, the most determined supporter of the 'old system':

I will not teaze your Grace [he wrote] with the repetition of things which don't meet with your approbation, nor agree with your view of publick affairs. I will sum up my whole political creed in two propositions: this country and Europe are undone without a secure, lasting peace; the alliance as it now stands has not the force ever to obtain it without the interposition of Prussia. The umbrage of that Prince, justly taken at the language of the court of Vienna ever since the cession of Silesia, once effectually removed, it is his interest and therefore his inclination to see Europe pacified and France contained within some bounds. I am not sanguine enough to imagine he would on any account engage in the war, but I must believe, if the proper steps were taken and taken in earnest, he might be brought to care for such a peace as we ought to think ourselves happy to obtain.[3]

Frederic at heart had almost as ingrained a distrust of France as Pitt himself, and, only a year after Pitt was writing

---

[1] A phrase of Chatham's. [2] *Pol. Corr.* vi, 122.
[3] *Add. MSS.* 32713, f. 517.

these lines to Newcastle, uttered almost corresponding sentiments : ' The system of Europe has changed so entirely that I should find myself soon on a good footing with Great Britain, for there is great divergence of interests between England and the Queen of Hungary.'[1] England all but missed the opportunity of this alliance, for few could see its advantage so clearly as Pitt, whose only avowed supporter on this matter was his old antagonist, Horace Walpole : and Pitt himself for many years could only offer counsel ; he had no power to act.

II—In Peace

During the six years following the peace of Aix-la-Chapelle Pelham's conciliatory methods of government, the harmony he restored to the nation, and his wise measures of reform in finance and administration met with Pitt's approval and gave him little scope for active exertion in his subordinate department. He was on the whole content to be a benevolent spectator of the minister who in spirit followed out Walpole's maxim, *quieta non movere*, and was patiently preparing the country for the coming struggle.

Pelham's chief service to the nation was his reorganization of its finances. England was then poor, compared not only with her present condition but with other nations of the time. Her population barely exceeded 6,000,000 ; her main industry, agriculture, was backward ; her coal and iron were almost neglected ; there were no cotton mills ; and the state of the roads and other means of internal transport was a great hindrance to trade. The only growing sources of wealth were the carrying trade and commerce to India and America, which the naval successes in the late war had much encouraged. The national income was wastefully raised by innumerable customs and excise taxes, by a land tax of 4s. in the pound in wartime and by loans at a high rate of interest. The budget of

[1] *Pol. Corr.* vi, 126.

£13,000,000 [1] for the last year of the war and the national debt of £78,000,000 were regarded as intolerable burdens. Pelham ruthlessly cut down expenditure as soon as the war was over. Deaf alike to appeals from the Duke of Cumberland to preserve useless regiments on the establishment and to unfounded claims of the Empress Queen to arrears of subsidy, by these and other economies in the first year he reduced the budget to £9,000,000 [1] and gradually to £5,000,000.[1] He also considerably simplified the debt service, by consolidating a number of separate funds, besides reducing the interest on the whole from 4 per cent. by successive stages to $3\frac{1}{2}$ and finally 3 per cent. By this means he saved the nation £500,000 annually. Within a few years Pitt had cause to be grateful to Pelham for the increased elasticity these measures brought to the national revenue, and at the time paid a glowing tribute to his consummate wisdom 'in increasing the sinking fund by this saving of interest. By means of that fund, by economy in our domestic affairs, and by making the most of our public revenue, we shall be able to pay off a very large sum yearly; and our ability to do so will increase yearly in proportion, especially if we take proper methods to put an end to all smuggling.' *February 22, 1751.*

In one instance only Pitt opposed Pelham's zeal for economy, when in 1751 he proposed to reduce the naval establishment to 8,000 men. It had stood at 40,000 in the last year of the war, next year was brought down to 17,000, and in 1750 to the normal peace establishment of 10,000. The further reduction to 8,000 left barely enough men to provide full complements for thirteen 74-gun men-of-war. Even Walpole only twice, in a time of profound peace, 1732 and 1733, proposed so low a number; in 1751 the chances of war were much greater. Both in Committee and on Report Pitt spoke against the reduction and carried with him into the lobby his colleagues Lyttelton and the Grenvilles.[2] He was much pained, he said, at differing *January 22 and 29, 1751.*

---

[1] These figures are exclusive of the Civil List of £800,000 which was granted for the King's reign.

[2] It will be remembered that Pitt's first recorded act in the House of Commons was as teller for the minority who desired to reduce Walpole's figure of 30,000 men for the navy (see above, p. 64). But that was a time of peace, when Walpole was asking for an establishment on a war figure.

from Pelham and his friends, with whom he was determined to remain united, but could not compromise on 'our standing army,' as he called the navy, especially when Jacobitism was still alive; and he expressed the conviction that the majority of the House agreed with him in preferring 10,000 men to 8,000. In this debate he was drawn into an altercation with one of the chartered buffoons of the House, Hampden, who, according to Walpole, possessed none of the qualifications of his renowned ancestor save courage. 'He drew a burlesque picture of Pitt and Lyttelton under the titles of "Oratory" and "Solemnity" and painted in the most comic colours what mischiefs rhetoric had brought to the nation and what emoluments to Pitt.' 'Pitt'—to continue Walpole's account—'flamed into a rage, and nodded menaces of highest import to Hampden, who retorted them, undaunted, with a droll voice that was naturally hoarse and inarticulate.' Pelham thereupon interposed in defence of Pitt, and the Speaker had to insist that the matter should go no further, with which 'Punch first and then Alexander the Great complied.' Pitt was beaten by a majority of over 180; but Pelham had learned a lesson, and in the succeeding years complied with Pitt's demand for a minimum establishment of 10,000 men.

Economies led also to an improved administration of the army and navy. Anson reformed many hoary abuses in the dockyards and passed a revised navy discipline Act with a clause about cowardice and desertion, memorable thereafter to Pitt and others in the Byng affair. He was supported by Pitt in a proposal to make half-pay officers amenable to martial law, but was forced to drop it before the storm of indignation from the senior officers, a fate which also befel a serious attempt to abolish the evils of impressment by forming a reserve of sailors. Pitt, owing to his official position, was more prominent in debates on the army. Then, as in more recent days, a war which had revealed defects in our military system stimulated the imagination of our army reformers, without much success. On the other hand, after the recent experience of the Rebellion and the French invasion of the Low Countries, little more was heard of the constitutional objection to a standing army, with which Pitt himself and every Opposition since William III's day had played on the fears of quiet citizens. The prolonged army debates during the years 1749, 1750 and 1751 turned chiefly on questions of discipline. which the Duke of Cumberland, now Captain-General, had found in a lax condition. To remedy this he entirely recast the Mutiny Bill, introducing into it a German standard of severity. In 1749 and the succeeding years the opposition to these innovations was led by Lord Egmont, an old fellow-conspirator of Pitt's. Egmont now acted as spokesman of the Prince of Wales's party, and was chiefly influenced by the jealousy with which the Prince viewed any accession of power to his brother. He was especially severe on a clause giving the Captain-General the right to order successive revisions of a court-martial's sentence, until he was satisfied with it—a monstrous proposal, which the Grenvilles and Lyttelton joined him in resisting. In the second year that this clause was debated the Government gave way to the extent of limiting this power of revision to one occasion, but in both years Pitt took a high line in defence of the original clause and cast a temporary cloud on his relations with the Cousinhood by his slighting references to their opposition. In spite of his democratic views he had a curious leaning to prerogative in certain departments, especially in regard to the discipline of the army :

February 7, 1749.

February 7, 1750.

The only danger of oppression under martial law [he said in one of these debates] is when the direction of the army becomes wicked or the army itself loses its virtue . . . and without this virtue should the Lords, the Commons, and the people of England entrench themselves behind parchment up to the teeth, the sword will find a passage to the vitals of the constitution.

In another debate of the same session of 1750 he laid down clearly his view of the respective functions of the House of Commons and of military commanders. Some soldiers had been reduced in rank for cheering one of the candidates at the Westminster election when on duty, and a proposal had been made to call the officers responsible to account for their conduct at the bar of the House.

January 23, 1750.

What ! [cried Pitt] would you call officers and soldiers to traduce and impeach one another at your bar ? This, Sir, might be of the most dangerous consequence to the very existence of this august assembly. I hope neither will ever learn the way to this House. If they should once learn the way of coming here with their complaints we may expect that they will soon learn the way of coming here with their petitions and remonstrances, as they did about a century ago ; and the consequence at that time I need not desire gentlemen to recollect. Our business, Sir, is to consider what number of regular forces may be necessary for the defence of the nation, and to grant money for maintaining that number ; but we have no business with the conduct of the army, or with their complaints against one another, which belongs to the King alone or such as shall be commissioned by him. If we ever give ear to any such complaints it will certainly produce one of these two consequences : it will either destroy all manner of discipline and subordination in the army, or it will render this House despised by the officers and detested by the common soldiers of the army ; and either of these consequences will be fatal to the nation. . . . I believe that as a colonel's life as well as character very often in time of war depends upon the behaviour of his regiment, every colonel will choose to have a regiment of brave and well-disciplined soldiers, rather than a regiment of voters at an election.

Once, however, Pitt was moved by passionate indignation at a flagrant abuse of military power to insist on a parliamentary inquiry. In the debates on the Mutiny Bill of 1751 complaints were brought against General Anstruther for tampering with court-martials and other acts of oppression when Governor of Minorca. Pelham wished to hush it up, but Pitt insisted on dragging it into the light. Even then, however, he carefully guarded against any attempt to erect the House into a judicial tribunal and denied that his purpose was to found a criminal prosecution, ' since the business of the House was not to hear causes that are without their jurisdiction, but to find deficiencies in our laws and remedies for them,' which might be incorporated in the Mutiny Bill then under review.[1] This system of entrusting wide powers to military

April 18, 1751.

---

[1] In the course of the debates arising out of Anstruther's case Pitt espoused with some violence the cause of an unfortunate Minorchese, Don Compagni, who had been ruined by Anstruther, and to whom Pelham had refused a Treasury grant to enable him to prosecute his claims. According to

ARMY AND SOCIAL REFORM, 1751

officers without interference from Parliament seems to have answered. The want of discipline in the rank and file and the lack of zeal among the officers had been notorious in the previous war; but already in 1751 Pitt asserted that the army, 'though small, had military spirit and had then been much improved by discipline, itself equal to five thousand men'; and when he came to put it to the test a few years later, he found a very different spirit in all but the highest ranks, which Cumberland unfortunately filled with men only fit to be sergeants and corporals, 'who were dreadfully frightened when they came to think of a chief command.' March 5, 1751. February 19 and 26, 1751.

Active measures to improve the lot of the poorer classes were rare in the aristocratic parliaments of the eighteenth century. To defend the people's liberties, to resist oppression of the humblest, and to encourage tolerance of religious and racial differences seemed the highest flight of altruism to which the most enlightened statesmen attained, and for these things Pitt fought with all his might. The Chelsea pensioner cheated of his pension, the citizen unjustly pressed, or the prisoner defrauded of his full right of trial by jury looked to him for redress and did not look in vain. But, although the younger Beckford speaks of 'the true patriotic spirit which he breathed for the poor—the ever-wretched poor,' he never showed much interest in social questions except in times of acute distress and on the one occasion when all London was stirred by the misery and crime revealed in his friend Fielding's 'Inquiry into the Increase of Robberies' and Hogarth's companion caricature of 'Gin Lane.' Pitt sat on the committee which was appointed as a result of the 'Inquiry,' and which proposed, among other remedies, to restrain the excessive harshness of the law, remove some of the worst abuses of prisons, and exact contributions from the richer for the poorer parishes. But he is not known to have taken a prominent part in its proceedings. On the

Walpole, Pitt incurred much ridicule by his extravagance in declaring that he would support such a cause to the last drop of his blood, and by the unexpected knowledge he showed of Minorchese history and genealogies. For Pitt's part in these debates, see *Historical MSS. Commission* XI, ix, 313.

other hand he was always ready to do good service in denouncing abuses in the law or in the Church. Like his rival Fox, he had a peculiar hatred of lawyers as a class, and is once reported to have said, 'The constitution may be shaken to its centre and the lawyer will sit calm in his cabinet. But let a cobweb be disturbed in Westminster Hall, and out the bloated spider will crawl in its defence.'[1] He also set his face against the bitter anti-Scottish feeling in England. So bitter was this feeling after the Rebellion that it must have required some courage, even in Pitt, to defend, as he did in 1749, the grant of £10,000 to recoup Glasgow for the fine exacted by the young Pretender.

April 21, 1749.

Without derogating [he went so far as to say] from the merit of anyone, I may say that there are not many cities in the United Kingdom that have so often and so remarkably distinguished themselves in the cause of liberty. . . . It was the whole tenour of this city's conduct from the time of the Reformation that drew the resentment of the rebels upon it.

February-April, 1751.

He showed the same broad-mindedness in supporting Pelham's attempts to promote new forms of industry by offering naturalization to foreign Protestants. One of the most thriving manufactures of the country was already due to the Huguenot refugees at Spitalfields; others might, it was hoped, be induced to follow. But popular prejudice against the foreigner, advocated with cynical effrontery in the House by Henry Fox, proved too strong for even Pitt's eloquence to resist. 'Cæsar and Pompey squabbling,' Walpole described the prolonged debates between the two, at the end of which Fox admitted that 'Pitt is better speaker than I am; but thank God I have more judgment.' Pitt's judgment of his own self-interest could certainly not stand beside Fox's; but the foreseeing judgment of the statesman was not of much concern to that gifted politician.

Pitt also took up the unpopular cause in support of Pelham's

---

[1] Communicated by Mr. G. M. Trevelyan from John Bright's *Diary* of February 14, 1850. Sheil told Bright of the phrase, which he had received on Butler's first-hand authority.

Jews Naturalization Bill of 1753. Pelham's aim was to encourage public-spirited Jews like Sampson Gideon, who had given him much assistance in floating public loans, to settle permanently in the country and also to reward the London Jews for their patriotism in volunteering for service in 1745. This harmless proposal, though unpopular with merchants and manufacturers, who feared that the Jews might interfere with their business, was passed by a small majority in a thin House. But its passage aroused a storm of indignant fanaticism. Although the bishops had made no objection to the Act, the country clergy led the hue and cry against it. Pamphlets denouncing the blow against Christianity rained from the Press; old wives' tales were revived about secret and nefarious practices of the Jews; bishops and members of Parliament known to have voted for the Act were mobbed wherever they appeared, and assailed with the popular cry, 'No Jews, no wooden shoes.'[1] The Pelhams might have waited for the storm to blow over, had not an election been due in 1754 and Newcastle reported that the Jews Act might seriously menace their majority. Its repeal was therefore proposed in November 1753, in a bill of which the preamble ran: '... Whereas occasion has been taken from the said act to raise discontents and disquiets in the minds of many of His Majesty's subjects.' The only discussion was on this preamble, which the religious fanatics opposed as a reflection on themselves. Pitt, back in the House after a year of illness, flamed up at this, and lashed out at our ridiculous laws against aliens and our persecuting unchristian laws relating to religion:[2]

November 27, 1753.

With this dispute, religion has really nothing to do; but the people without doors have been made to believe it has; and upon this the old High Church persecuting spirit has begun to take hold of them. . . . It is wise not to dispute with them, but we ought to let them know that . . . the spirit they are at present possessed with is not a true Christian spirit.

[1] 'Wooden shoes' referred to the Huguenots, who were almost as unpopular as the Jews, as the rejection of the Foreign Protestants Bill had shown. A good account of this *Judenhetze* is to be found in Hertz; *British Imperialism in the Eighteenth Century.*
[2] See Sanderson Miller, p. 200.

When he came to defend the repeal his argument was halting. He suggested as a parallel case that of a peevish and perverse boy asking for something which was not quite right but would be attended with no very bad consequence : an indulgent father might humour him, but in doing so would let him know that he did so out of complaisance, not because he approved of what the child insisted on—a view of parental duty which Pitt would certainly not have endorsed when he had children of his own.

I must still think [he concluded] that the law passed last session in favour of the Jews was in itself right, and I shall now agree to the repeal of it, merely out of complaisance to that enthusiastic spirit that has taken hold of the people ; but then I am for letting them know why I do so.

But when the religious bigots wished to follow up this victory by repealing an act of 1740, which permitted Jewish settlers in the plantations to become naturalized, Pitt lost all patience with them :

December 4, 1753.

Is this [he asked] to be the first return to Parliament for its condescension in repealing the last act ? Here the stand must be made, or *venit summa dies !* we shall have a Church spirit revived. The late clamour, I believe, was only a little election art, which had been given way to genteelly. . . . My maxim is never to do more for the Church than it now enjoys ; it is the Jew to-day, it will be the Presbyterian to-morrow ; and we shall be sure to have a septennial Church clamour.

Fortunately the House had the strength of mind to follow this plain-spoken advice and reject the proposed repeal by a large majority.

In foreign politics Pitt was less in sympathy with the Duke of Newcastle, who had charge of them, than with his brother in domestic affairs. Newcastle's chief task during the last six years of his brother's administration was to keep the peace abroad. In this he succeeded, because no nation was yet anxious for war ; but he showed little of his brother's statesmanship in making preparation for the future. Wedded to the Old System of foreign politics he continued bidding for the support of the Emperor and the electors as if our interests were the same as they had been in the reign of William III. In his efforts for peace Pitt supported him without hesitation, and, in his zeal for the stability of the Pelham Ministry, carried complaisance so far as to support some of his German bargains. Peace at home and abroad was at this time with him the paramount consideration.

This desire for peace made him most anxious not to revive questions temporarily settled by the treaties of 1748. In February 1750 Egmont and some other old allies of his at the Prince of Wales's Court, undeterred by Dodington's judicious advice to be certain of their facts before stating a case, complained that France had not fulfilled her promise of destroying the harbour and fortifications of Dunkirk. It was an old grievance brought up almost annually against Walpole. In the debate Pelham bluntly told the House that the country was not in a state to contend with her enemies, and for that reason deprecated raising the question. Lord Strange made a spirited speech in reply, and was answered by Pitt that 'no man in his senses would provoke a combat, when he is but just recovered from a violent fever, and his adversary is full of strength and vigour.' But while agreeing with Pelham that England in her present weak unallied state was unable to cope with the whole House of Bourbon, and that the motion seemed to him both wicked, as tending to inflame the minds of the people, and absurd from our want of strength to back any complaints, he added with robuster confidence that a few years would remedy this condition. Egmont retorted that it ill became Pitt to support a position which he had formerly attacked with violence, and apply so malignant and opprobrious an epithet as 'wicked' to his motion. Pitt felt the justice of the reproach, and gave back a soft answer to his old friend. 'I must confess that upon some former occasions I have been hurried by the heat of youth, and the warmth of debate, into expressions which, upon cool recollection, I have deeply regretted; and I believe the same thing has happened to many gentlemen in this House, and especially to the noble lord.' After qualifying his epithet 'wicked,' he

February 5, 1750.

asked for the evidence that the French were fortifying Dunkirk. Even if they were,

> Nations, as well as individuals, must sometimes forbear from the rigorous exaction of what is due to them. Prudence may require them to tolerate a delay, or even a refusal of justice, especially when their right can no way suffer by such acquiescence; and that this is our case at present there are abundant proofs. . . . I think that no gentleman, after due consideration of the question whether it would be prudent in us to declare war against France, in case she should not, on the first demand, instantly begin to demolish the port of Dunkirk, can agree to this motion.

Astonishment at this new tone from a much chastened Pitt may have held the House silent. No one ventured a reply, and the motion was rejected by 242 to 115.

Next year Pitt again came forward in repentant mood to defend a supplementary treaty concluded with Spain in October 1750. By this agreement certain causes of difference still left open between the two nations at Aix-la-Chapelle were finally removed, with the result that good relations between England and Spain were restored, and our trade obtained better security than it had enjoyed since Charles II's reign. But the Spanish claims to a right of search, which had been one of the chief causes of the war, were still not explicitly surrendered, an omission which Egmont, Dodington, Potter and Lee indignantly criticised in the debate on January 17, 1751. In his speech Pitt, after his manner when he had changed his mind, plainly told the House so. He admitted that in the debates of 1739 he had been foremost in demanding that the right of search should be absolutely surrendered by Spain: but now, in a passage already quoted,[1] recognised that this was an impossible demand, unless Spain should be brought so low as to give us *carte blanche*, which neither our own interest nor the claims of other Powers would suffer. He also recanted his error in voting, early in the war,[2] for an address to the Crown prescribing the terms on which alone peace would be acceptable. This he now recognised to be unduly trenching upon the royal prerogative:

January 17, 1751.

[1] See above, p. 93. [2] See above, p. 79.

None can foresee the sudden turns and chances of war . . . and, as the Crown has the sole power of making peace or war, every such address must certainly be an encroachment on the King's prerogative, which has always hitherto proved to be unlucky. For these reasons I believe I shall never hereafter concur in any such address, unless made so conditional as to leave the Crown at full liberty to agree to such terms of peace as may at the time be thought proper.

Having cleared the ground of past mistakes he made out a strong case for the treaty, because of the favourable terms granted to British trade, and still more because it enabled Spain to shake herself free from French influence and assert her intention of taking a stand on the side of England.

The Spanish ambassador, Wall, was so well pleased with this speech, which even the carping Walpole calls remarkable, that he sent a special report to his Court of the ' great orator Pitt's ' words. It is a remarkable example of Pitt's essential consistency on broad lines of policy and his carelessness about consistency in details. Throughout his life the danger to England of the Bourbon power dominated his mind. He hated the Bourbons because they represented to him all the intolerance and arbitrary rule which his soul most abhorred. United he dreaded their strength for evil against the land of liberty he loved, and he spent a large part of his life in attempts to keep them apart, or in raising a counterpoise to their union. During the period that Spain kept France at arm's length by a reconciliation with us, he was all for humouring her, a policy which he consistently followed until Spain returned to the French alliance in 1761. This intense hatred of the Bourbons and of the spirit they represented was one great source of Pitt's power with his countrymen. It was a simple idea which they could easily grasp ; it was one they shared and in which Pitt never failed them. Another great source of his power was the perfect frankness of his public utterances. When Pitt changed his mind he never concealed the fact : on the contrary, he seemed to glory in it and took the whole world into his confidence. Mysterious and difficult as he often was in his private relations and correspondence, when he was speaking to the House of Commons, and through it to England, he thought aloud and spoke out more of his real self than he revealed even to those dearest to him. 'When I am on my feet,' he once said of himself, 'I speak everything that is in my mind.'

Pitt had more occasion to complain of Newcastle's German policy. The hopes he and Frederic II had entertained of an understanding between England and Prussia soon evaporated before George II's openly expressed dislike of his nephew. 'The King of Prussia,' he told the French ambassador, 'is a mischievous rascal, a bad friend, a bad ally, a bad relation and a bad neighbour, in fact the most dangerous and evil-disposed prince in Europe.'[1] Newcastle was well pleased to adopt his master's prejudices and turned with relief to the Old System. Not content with this outworn alliance, he and the King, when left to themselves at Hanover, attempted to revive in a new form the Emperor Charles VI's Pragmatic Sanction policy, a bubble long ago pricked. To avoid disputes on the death of Maria Theresa's husband, they conceived the ingenious idea of assuring beforehand in the electoral college a majority for his son; as if it could matter to England who became emperor. The persons principally interested, Maria Theresa and her husband, threw cold water on the scheme, but most of the electors were willing enough to promise votes for England's money. In October 1750, after laborious negotiations about the price, Newcastle secured the Bavarian vote for a subsidy of £20,000 a year, with a further proviso that the Elector should hold a force of 6,000 men at England's disposal. Newcastle could hardly contain himself for joy at the result of his diplomacy. The treaty 'lays a foundation of a solid system for the preservation of the peace,' he wrote to Pitt, 'and, though full of business, I am full of joy upon public transactions, full of the goodness of my friends and, if I hear a good account of my dear friend the Duke of Richmond, full of joy upon all accounts.' His good friends were not so enthusiastic. Pelham grumbled at the expense but agreed to it on condition it should be the last demand of the kind. Pitt made the same stipulation, in the spirit of his 'indulgent father who humoured a peevish

[1] *Aff. Etr. Angl. Corr. Pol.* 431, f. 385.

and perverse boy,' and guardedly replied to the Duke's self-congratulations that if this treaty really secured his object of peace it was cheap. In the House of Commons, when it was attacked by Egmont in 1751, Pitt defended it in perfunctory fashion, chiefly on the ground that, while 'the preservation of peace is our maxim,' we should be prepared for the possibility of war. This treaty, unlike the more aggressive treaties of France, was solely, he said, directed to preserving peace and the existing rights of European nations; the alternative to the force to be provided by Bavaria would be a large addition to our own standing army, 'which might be of the most dangerous consequence to our constitution.' *February 22, 1751.*

But Newcastle was incorrigible. Taking no warning from this chilling advocacy, in the autumn he concluded another treaty, this time with the Elector of Saxony, whereby England was to pay him an annual subsidy of £32,000. No one was more disgusted at this fresh expense than Newcastle's brother. Talking in confidence to Dodington, Pelham said 'he was against these subsidies . . . to be buying one elector after another was what he abhorred and could not approve of. It must have an end . . . he had declared so in Parliament.' Indeed, in his first outburst of anger he threatened to lead the opposition to it in Parliament himself, but, thinking better of it, made the best defence he could when the charge came up for sanction in 1752. Pitt was not so accommodating. In a conference with Newcastle he told him plainly that he engaged for subsidies without knowing the extent of the sums and for alliances without knowing the terms, and his language was so contemptuous that Newcastle would have dismissed him from office had he dared. Though unable from his position to lead the opposition to the treaty himself, Pitt was ostentatiously absent from the debate, and allowed his ally, the eldest Grenville, to speak against it. Old Horace Walpole, who made the best speech against the treaty and for an alliance with Prussia, afterwards had it printed and sent a copy to Pitt, now entirely reconciled to him. Pitt was delighted with it:

Your speech [he wrote] from beginning to end breathes the spirit of a man who loves his country. If your endeavours contribute to the honest end you aim at, namely to check foreign expenses and prevent entanglements abroad, under a situation burdened and exhausted at present and liable to many alarming apprehensions in futurity, you deserve the thanks of this generation and will have those of the next.

Pitt and old Horace Walpole almost alone in the House of Commons interpreted the country's growing antipathy to the traditional alliance with the house of Hapsburg. While George II and Newcastle were running about the German courts to secure votes for Maria Theresa's son, she was constantly ruffling English susceptibilities.[1] In disregard of treaties she attempted to revive the Ostend trade, an old bugbear to English merchants, and to oust our allies the Dutch from the Barrier fortresses which defended the Low Countries from France. The only real obstacle, apart from Newcastle's blindness and George II's prejudices, to the Anglo-Prussian alliance desired by Pitt was the mutual jealousy between Prussia and Russia, which Newcastle accentuated by promoting another treaty of subsidy between England, Russia and the Emperor. The need of strong alliances was becoming daily more apparent to Pitt. In the summer of 1750, while the Duke of Newcastle was chattering in his letters to him about Bavaria and the King of the Romans, Pitt was keeping his eye on the first signs of danger in America. The colonists of Nova Scotia were being enticed away to the French islands under instruction from the French Government, and an English fort had been attacked by Frenchmen from across the border. Pitt had vainly tried to arouse Newcastle to these ominous proceedings:

Very alarming I confess it is to me [he writes]; your Grace will soon see (perhaps you already do) if France be in earnest to maintain this violence; if she be, I can't figure to myself a more unhappy event: for his Majesty's right to the country in question and the infinite importance to all North America of asserting that right I find are equally undeniable.[2]

[1] A few years later Hardwicke, Newcastle's confidant, had to admit that the money spent on buying Electors was 'all entirely thrown away.' (*Add. MSS.* 32921, f. 340.)

[2] *Add. MSS.* 32721, f. 129.

Newcastle passed it off as a trifling affair and, in spite of a further note of warning from Pitt, returned to his congenial topics of self-praise and complaints of his colleagues. Pitt saw that a treaty for 6,000 men from Bavaria hardly met the case; on the contrary, it distracted attention from the real seat of danger. But without sowing dissension in a ministry, for which no better could then be substituted, he could not enforce his convictions; for the Pelhams never thought of offering him the post of real responsibility, for which he craved, during all these eight years, when, as he afterwards wrote to the Duke of Newcastle.

I have never been wanting in my most zealous endeavours in Parliament, on the points that laboured the most—those of military discipline and of foreign affairs; nor have I differed on any whatever but the crying complaint against General Anstruther and the too small number of seamen one year, which was admitted to be such the next.[1]

The brothers certainly appreciated his value to them. They consulted him on all the treaties they made and placed the utmost confidence in his advice and support. 'Go on in your correspondence with him,' wrote Pelham to his brother in 1750, 'with all the frankness and cordiality you can; I do so in all my conversations with him. I think him besides the most able and useful man we have amongst us; truly honourable and strictly honest.' He sometimes acted the part of peacemaker between them in the quarrels provoked by Newcastle's fits of jealousy, and even escaped the usual fate of peacemakers by earning the gratitude of both parties. After one such incident Newcastle says, ' Pitt wrote in the handsomest and most friendly manner imaginable, and took notice of my brother's satisfaction with me.' Pitt himself modestly disclaimed any merit for the reconciliation :

You are both [he said] too good to mention, as you are pleased to do, my poor little part between you. My good wishes were sincere, and wishing well was all I could possibly have to do. I should be

[1] *Add. MSS.* 32734, f. 322.

foolishly vain with a witness, if I ascribed the least part of the perfect union between you to anything but your own good hearts and understandings. . . . Whatever determination you come to, I heartily wish it may more and more secure and strengthen power and authority in your hands.

On one of the two occasions when Pitt opposed the Government, Newcastle gave him a remarkable testimony in a circular letter to his supporters :

> As you can be no stranger [he wrote] (if you attended the late debate) to the able and affectionate manner in which Mr. Pitt took upon himself to defend me and the measures which have been solely carried on by me, when both have been openly attacked with violence and when no other person in the House opened his lips in defence of either but Mr. Pitt, I think myself bound, in honour and gratitude, to shew my sense of it in the best manner I am able. I must therefore desire that neither you nor any of my friends would give into any clamour or run, that may be made against him from any of the party, on account of his differing as to the number of seamen. For after the kind part he has acted to me, and (as far as I am allowed to be a part of it) the meritorious one to the administration, I cannot think any man my friend who shall join in any such clamour and who does not do all in his power to discourage it.

But, though quite willing to pay for Pitt's services by flattering words, the Pelhams probably thought his good inclinations towards them and the smallness of the party of Grenvilles and Lyttelton which would follow him into Opposition, if disappointed, made it needless to attach him by greater rewards. It was not for want of opportunities that they gave him no better post. No less than four Secretaries of State successively became Newcastle's colleagues during the eight years from 1746 to 1754. In October 1746 Chesterfield succeeded Harrington. Chesterfield had once given promise of becoming one of our greatest statesmen ; he had much of Pitt's grasp of foreign politics, and, as he showed when Lord Lieutenant of Ireland, was a good administrator, with broad and sympathetic views. But he had no staying power. Unlike Pitt, with all his brilliant ability he was easily tired of contending against such difficulties as his jealous colleague

Newcastle was careful to put in his path, and had too much wit to be a strenuous fighter.[1] Weary of contending for peace he resigned in February 1748 ; two months later he would have seen his policy triumph. On his resignation Fox's claims to the post were actively canvassed, and none were louder in his favour than Pitt and his friends.[2] The rivalry between Fox and Pitt had not then become pronounced, and, until their final breach in 1755, Pitt had the highest esteem for Fox's ability as a politician : moreover, his promotion might have given Pitt the chance of stepping into his shoes as Secretary-at-War. But at that time Bedford was in high favour with Newcastle, and was chosen for the post. Bedford's vigour as First Lord of the Admiralty disappeared entirely when he became Secretary of State. The King said he ' did nothing but ride post from Woburn once a week and fancied he performed the duties of his office when he did little or nothing.' But he came under Newcastle's suspicion for actively espousing the party of the Duke of Cumberland, who was considered dangerous by the Pelhams, and after a year of intrigues he also was dismissed in 1751. Pitt, who was constantly consulted by the brothers while they were intriguing against Bedford, had advised caution. ' Pitt has been with me,' wrote Pelham to the Duke, ' and he seems of my opinion, mighty desirous that you should be made easy, but very doubtful whether any violent stroke will produce that good result.' [3] The list of possible Secretaries of State had now become almost exhausted, but Newcastle discovered one to his mind in Lord Holderness, ' so good-natured you may tell him his faults and he will mend them, and no pride in him though a d'Arcy.' At the same time Anson succeeded Sandwich at the head of the Admiralty, and Granville, who had lost all his fire and

---

[1] It was well said of him by the French envoy, Bussy, that he was too much inclined to make epigrams of the most serious business and never touched men's souls, only their minds.

[2] Coxe, *Pelham*, i, 391 : Fox to Hanbury Williams.

[3] Pitt probably knew that the King would object, as he did, to dismissing his favourite son's ally. When Bedford resigned the seals the King hoped that the ' happy hour was not far off ' when he would be taking them from Newcastle and restoring them to Bedford. (*Egmont MSS.* 76.)

become dead to ambition, was reconciled to Pelham and entered the Ministry as Lord President of the Council.

There was something almost contemptuous in the way Pelham and Newcastle discussed with Pitt other candidates for important posts as if he had no possible claim himself. They could always, when Pitt showed ill-humour at this neglect, entrench themselves behind the King's dislike of him. George II, after his momentary attention to Pitt, in 1746,[1] relapsed into his old attitude of distrust. All Pitt's confessions of error in the past, his defence of the prerogative in army matters, and his loyal support of the Government were wasted on him. After Pitt's signal service in reconciling the Pelhams in 1750 Newcastle told him he had 'acquainted the King with that proper zeal, satisfaction and regard for his Majesty's honour and Service which is shown in your letter, and, I may say, it was not thrown away.' Pitt thanked him warmly for his 'good office in that Place, where I deservedly stand in need of it so much, and where I have it so much at heart to efface the pass'd by every action of my life.'[2] Nevertheless the King could hardly be persuaded to address one gracious word to Pitt, and in the following year was so indignant at his opposing the reduction of the navy that he ignored him entirely at the levée. It is very doubtful if the Pelhams took much trouble to overcome this ill-feeling. They thought themselves secure of Pitt, or they might have been more successful: for the King's obstinacy could always, if necessary, be overcome. The Princess of Wales once said to Dodington: 'If they talked of the King she was out of patience; it was as if they should tell her that her little Harry below would not do what was proper for him; that just so the King would splutter and make a bustle, but when they told him it must be done from the necessity of his service, he must do it, as little Harry must when she came down.'

These continual disappointments disposed Pitt in 1751 to welcome a suggestion from Newcastle, who of the two brothers had always spoken him more fairly, to renew his intercourse with the Prince of Wales's Court. Newcastle was seriously

[1] See above, p. 147.   [2] *Add. MSS.* 32723, f. 44.

alarmed at the opposition of the Duke of Cumberland's party, which included Fox and the Bedfords, and wished to secure the favour of the heir to the throne, and Pitt had found himself in agreement with the Prince's followers on the navy and General Anstruther's case. His maxim was to serve whoever was King of England, and he may have hoped, since George II gave him no opening, to obtain better employment on his successor's accession. The Prince had since 1746 become estranged from Pitt, and in the various plans he amused himself by drawing up with Egmont and Dodington for the reconstitution of the House of Commons and the Ministry on his accession had always marked Pitt down for exclusion from both.[1] But a common fear of the Duke of Cumberland seemed to open a promising negotiation between the Prince, Newcastle and Pitt and the Grenvilles,[2] when the whole situation was altered by the sudden death of the Prince on March 22, 1751. His Court was temporarily broken up and the Princess ostentatiously abandoned politics to devote herself to the education of her sons. Since George, the new Prince of Wales, was under age, a Regency Bill was necessary, the debates on which revealed the growing antagonism between the Pelhams, with Pitt on their side, and the Duke of Cumberland's party, headed by Fox. Under the provisions of the Bill the Princess Dowager was to be Regent, in case of a minority, aided by a council presided over by the Duke of Cumberland. Every proposal of Fox to increase the council's power Pitt warmly resisted, indicating with his usual frankness the apprehensions that he shared with many others, of a military dictatorship, unless Cumberland's powers were limited. He also expressed his devotion to the Princess of Wales, promising to remove any restrictions on the Regent, which might prove irksome to her, and praising her husband in language of hyperbole hardly justified even by his death, as

May 16, 17, and 20, 1751.

---

[1] Several of these plans, drawn up in 1749 and 1750 and annotated by Frederick himself, are preserved in *Egmont MSS*. 277. In one of them is a note against Pitt's name : 'To have likewise some profitable employment and inconsistent with a seat in Parliament' ; in another the embassy at Turin is assigned to him. See Vol. II. p. 59.

[2] See Coxe, *Lord Walpole*, ii, 288 *sqq.*; Dodington, *Diary*, 181 *sqq.*; Coxe, *Pelham*, ii, 164 *sqq.*; and Walpole, *Memoirs*.

'the most patriot prince that ever lived, to whom I had such infinite obligations and such early attachments, which I am proud to transfer to his family.' Then a touch of the old Adam peeped out at the recollection of those early days of light-hearted opposition, and he added in his former vein of sarcasm : 'I wonder at His Majesty exerting a fortitude at this calamity which Edward III was not master of when he lost the Black Prince.'

After this momentary ebullition Pitt once more resigned himself to a secondary position for the rest of Pelham's life. He remained, with the brothers' approval, on the most friendly terms with the Princess Dowager and her Court in Leicester Fields. From this time dates his growing intimacy with Lord Bute, the handsome young Scottish peer, who was already the favourite and chief political guide of the Princess and her son. In 1753 he was able to do some service to this Court, as well as to the Ministry. A charge of Jacobitism against the Prince's instructors, implicating Stone, Newcastle's former secretary, and Murray, Pitt's rival, created a great stir in the country. It was investigated by the Privy Council and found to be baseless, but Bedford revived it in the House of Lords in Cumberland's interest. Pitt thereupon wrote to his friend Richard Grenville, who had then become Lord Temple, and whose suspicious and intriguing disposition would make him listen greedily to such scandals, imploring him : 'if you should entertain any thought of supporting or going with the question . . . to lay it aside, as I am deeply persuaded that nothing could be so fatal to me and to all our views, so nothing imaginable could give me a concern equal to seeing your Lordship take such a step.'

Pitt said of Pelham on his death in March 1754, 'I am sensibly touched with his loss, as of a man, upon the whole, of a most amiable composition. His loss as a minister is utterly irreparable, in such circumstances as constitute the present dangerous conjuncture for this country, both at home and abroad'; and the sincerity of this judgment is borne out by Pitt's conduct, in spite of personal disappointment, during his administration. That he may have been occasionally tempted, as Dodington unkindly expressed it, to make a disturbance and regain his popularity, is most probable with an impetuous nature like Pitt's nursing a just grievance. But if so, though he had plenty of opportunities during the Pelhams' frequent quarrels, he never yielded to it. He was too patriotic and too well satisfied with Pelham's able finance and administration, and his skill in conciliating parties, always a great aim of his own, seriously to think of creating difficulties for him. But for a weaker and less capable successor who should continue to disregard his own right to a responsible office, such forbearance was not to be expected.

CHAPTER VII

PITT'S PRIVATE LIFE AND FRIENDSHIPS

τέκνον ἐμὸν, καρτὸς μὲν ’Αθηναίη τε καὶ ῞Ηρη
δώσουσ’, αἴ κ’ ἐθέλωσι, σὺ δὲ μεγαλήτορα θυμὸν
ἴσχειν ἐν στήθεσσι.
HOMER, *Iliad*, ix. 254.[1]

THE fallow years of Pelham's administration were useful to Pitt for other things besides giving him a better insight into State affairs. Under the genial influence of wealth and leisure his character ripened and expanded. An income of close upon £5,000 allowed him to indulge some of his extravagant tastes. He was still unmarried, and had few family interests to absorb his energy in private life: he thus had time for the increased social intercourse, as well as for the studies which were to fit him for the last strenuous period of a life almost wholly devoted to the public welfare.

Pitt's chief extravagance throughout life was building and the laying out of grounds. Landscape gardening was then the mode, and all who could afford it vied with one another in conveying an illusion of vast spaces, distant prospects, and grandiose scenery within the smallest compass. It was an age of vistas, of rivulets aping the appearance of mighty rivers, of embankments fashioned into the semblance of beetling brows or rugged mountain-sides, and of antique temples bearing witness to the designer's classical lore. 'Whether to plant a walk in undulating curves and to place a bench in every turn where there is an object to catch the view; to make water run where it will be heard, or to stagnate where it will be seen;

[1] 'My son, the gods may give thee power, if they will, but look thou to keep a brave spirit within thee.'

to leave intervals where the eye will be pleased, and to thicken the plantation where there is something to be hidden, demands any great powers of mind?'—Dr. Johnson forbore to inquire. 'Perhaps a sullen and surly speculator,' he adds, 'may think such performances rather the sport than the business of human reason. But it must at least be confessed that to embellish the form of Nature is an innocent amusement; and some praise must be allowed by the most supercilious observer to him who does best what such multitudes are contending to do well.'

Pitt entered with zest into the innocent amusement. Before he had house or grounds of his own his friends allowed him to give his fancy rein on theirs, for none was thought to excel him in 'pointing his prospects, diversifying his surface, entangling his walks, and winding his waters'; and Warburton no mean judge, gave him the palm before so expert a professional as Capability Brown, the gardener of Stowe and Hampton Court. He was consulted freely by Lyttelton on the rebuilding of Hagley, and devoted 'very mature consideration' to the proper setting for a rotunda in the park. He designed a walk at West Wickham for Gilbert West, the Grenvilles' pious cousin, laid out another friend's grounds 'to resemble Milton's Bower of Bliss,'[1] and helped to plan for George Grenville the enchanting two miles of water scenery still to be seen at Wotton in Buckinghamshire. Both Cobham and Temple successively took counsel of him for the additions they were constantly making to the adornment of Stowe, the most famous and characteristic example of the taste of the period. Here were Elysian fields, a stalactite grotto by the lake—where the Princess Amelia and Horace Walpole once took cold—Doric arches, sacred groves, hallowed fountains, and temples dedicated to Venus, to Ancient and Modern Virtue, and to Friendship, containing busts of those who had earned Cobham's or Temple's esteem: in one of these Pitt himself had his niche.

Pitt also advised humbler friends. Near Hagley was The Leasowes, famous as the seat of the poet Shenstone, who piqued himself on rivalling his grand neighbour, Lyttelton.

[1] *Chatham MSS.* 34: E. Wyndham to Hester Grenville, November, 1746.

Here in tiny compass were to be seen all the paraphernalia of vistas, temples, seats, and inscriptions, to embellish a scene naturally beautiful. When staying at Hagley Pitt would often ride over to confer with Shenstone on his summer-houses and walks. 'Nature,' he once ventured to tell him, 'has done everything for you, Mr. Shenstone'; to which the bard replied with becoming spirit, 'But I hope I have done something for Nature too by displaying her beauties to the best advantage.'[1] Shenstone's biographer, Graves, also relates that

Mr. William Pitt, though a younger brother and his fortune then not large,—with a noble contempt for money any further than as a means of doing good or conferring favours—as he saw several possible improvements, which Mr. Shenstone could not afford to execute, gave him a hint . . . that with his permission Mr. Pitt would please himself by laying out £200 at the Leasowes. This, however, Mr. Shenstone considered as a species of dalliance with his *mistress*, to which he could not submit.

But Shenstone was grateful, and recorded in verse that,

> Ev'n Pitt, whose fervent periods roll
> Resistless thro' the kindling soul
>   Of Senates, Councils, Kings;
> Tho' form'd for Courts, vouchsafed to move
> Inglorious thro' the shepherd's grove
>   And ope his bashful springs.

With his new wealth Pitt could afford the luxury of a house and grounds of his own. As Paymaster he had an official residence in Whitehall overlooking the park. In 1747 he bought from Lady Charlotte Edwin, an old acquaintance at the Prince of Wales's Court, the lease of South Lodge in Enfield Chace, with the sixty-five acres attached, which was originally one of the three Baileys or Lodges appertaining to the Royal Forest.[2] He immediately set to work adding to the house and laying out the grounds. In 1748 his carpenter's bill came to £1,358 for work, which included making a new drawing-

---

[1] Shenstone's complacent reply to Pitt finds an echo in Whistler's to the lady who had found a scene in Nature resembling one of his etchings: 'Nature is creeping up, Madam.'

[2] See *Chatham MSS.* 31; and Lysons, *Environs of London.*

room, dressing-room, library, and kitchen, a billiard table, as well as ' building a temple ' and providing a bridge, ' a porticoe and hexigon,' and a ' pyramid for the garden.'[1] Whateley, in his ' Observations on Modern Gardening,' is enthusiastic over the situation of the temple, which was dedicated to Pan, and describes it as

of the usual oblong form, encompassed by a colonnade; in dimensions and in style it is equal to a most extensive landskip; yet by the antique and rustic air of its Doric columns without bases; by the chastity of its little ornament, a crook, a pipe and a scrip, and those only over the doors; and by the simplicity of the whole both within and without, it is adapted with so much propriety to the thickets that conceal it from the view that no one can wish it to be brought forward, who is sensible to the charms of the Arcadian scene which this building alone has created.

Pitt's own friends were also loud in admiration of the Arcadian scene. Mrs. Montagu pronounced the Temple of Pan worthy of arousing poetic enthusiasm; Gilbert West waxed rhapsodical over ' every sequestered nook, dingle and bosky bower from side to side in that little paradise opened in the wild '; and his sister Molly, who seems to have had a tender feeling for the great man, had such implicit faith in Mr. Pitt's taste and judgment, that she often stole out by herself and, in defiance of wind or rain, walked many times over the enchanting round.[2] Other friends found greater delight in the sport and intellectual pleasures offered them by Pitt in this sylvan retreat. South Lodge was ' an accession to the common stock and Republick of sportsmen ' for the woodcock and snipe it provided, wrote Legge, who also looked forward to the winter parties at Enfield, ' those *noctes cœnœque Deorum* at which we will discuss politics, poetry, or that greatest of all the *Nepenthes*, nonsense *pro re nata*, as our genius shall prompt.'

Pitt was never satisfied with any house for long, and South Lodge was no exception. He loved the work there, but was too restless to enjoy the full fruits of it. Five years after he had bought the house he told Mrs. Montagu, with

---

[1] *Chatham MSS.* 71.   [2] Climenson, *Mrs. Montagu*, ii, 8, 10.

some slight exaggeration perhaps, that he had never lived there for an entire week ; and in 1753 sold it to a Mr. Sharpe with all the contents except his silver and books and the Duchess of Marlborough's portrait.[1] Little is now left of Pitt's work in the grounds of South Lodge. The Temple of Pan and the pyramid have vanished, the sequestered nooks, the dingles and bosky bowers are overgrown and unrecognisable ; the two lakes still remain, one with a wooded island which may have been planted by Pitt, the other still haunted by wild-duck and snipe ; but the rustic bridge is gone. The house, however, still stands with its solid well-proportioned rooms, its fine wood-carving in the dining-room, and its spacious views over Chace and valleys, much as it was when Pitt, with the Grenvilles, Lytteltons and Wests held *noctes cœnœque Deorum* ; nor would he have been displeased that it has become a school for the education of young Englishmen.

Pitt was no pedantic follower of the prevailing mode for sophisticated beauties. He put down his own skill in gardening to ' the prophetic eye of taste,' and knew when to hold his hand. ' The ground rolls and tumbles finely here,' he declared of a wonderful meeting-place of the hills and the waters at Ilam in Derbyshire,[2] and was content to admire. Until the end of his life he took delight in riding about the country or driving in a four-horse chaise, always at a great pace, yet always with a keen eye for the features in a landscape ; ' on passing a place where he had been ten years before,' his granddaughter told Meryon, ' he would observe that there used to be a tree, or a stone, or a something that was gone, and on inquiry it always proved to be so.' After a five days' solitary jaunt in Sussex in 1753 he jerked out his impressions in disjointed phrases :

Battel Abbey is very fine, as to situation and lying of ground, together with a great command of water on one side, within an airing.

---

[1] *Chatham MSS.* 71. In *Chatham MSS.* 74 are three rough sketches, apparently by Pitt, of designs for laying out grounds.

[2] Ilam belonged to a friend of the Pitts, Mr. de la Porte. A good description of it is given in Pinkerton, *Voyages and Travels*, ii, 483. Congreve also was fond of the place.

ENCOMBE AND JOHN PITT

Ashburnham Park, most beautiful; Hurstmonceux very fine, curious and dismally ugly . . . Crowhurst, Colonel Pelham's, the sweetest thing in the world; more taste than anywhere, land and sea views exquisite. Beach of four or five miles to Hastings, enchanting Hastings unique; Fairly Farm, Sir Whistler Webster's, just above it; perfect in its kind, *cum multis aliis.*

Encombe, near Corfe Castle in Dorsetshire, was one of Pitt's favourite haunts. It is ensconced in a vale that opens to the English Channel and contains in the grounds a piece of water so happily managed as to have the appearance of forming an inlet of the sea. Here, too, were white cliffs, where Pitt loved ' to kick his heels and look like a shepherd in Theocritus.' The estate belonged to his cousin John Pitt of the Strathfieldsaye branch, who inherited large estates in Dorsetshire and later became known as ' the Great Commoner of the West ' after his greater cousin. Pitt had a great affection for him and in writing to him drops the stilted style which was growing on him, rallies him on his love affairs, and sends a thousand kisses to his little son. When he is bored with his own society at Bath he bids John Pitt come over, for ' you cannot do so great a charity as to come and hunt prospects with me and keep me from hanging myself ' ; and of course he takes charge of the embellishment of his cousin's property. When he could not superintend in person he wrote directions : ' Throw about your verdant hills some thousands of trees . . . group away, my dear Pitt ; nay, if you indulge me in this request I believe I shall give up my miserable constitution to you to practise upon.' He sends his ' benedictions, to the hills, rocks, pines, shores, seas, &c. of Encombe :

> Benigni habbiate, et il sole, e la luna,
> E delle ninphe il choro ; '

and in 1757, from his office in London, wistfully regrets that he cannot set ' business for an instant aside to go to my country recluse and follow his walks through the solitudes of verdant Dorsetshire, through warm leases, heavy ewes and bounding lambs, rocks, sea beach, foaming billows and what not ! '[1]

[1] See Lady Chatterton's *Memorials of Admiral Gambier,* i, 8 *sqq.*

Radway under Edgehill was another house where the Paymaster was pleased to unbend. Its owner, Sanderson Miller, was a kindly soul, popular as a host in the Midlands. His weakness was a taste for debased Gothic architecture, which he persuaded his friends, including Lyttelton and Lord Chancellor Hardwicke, to adopt at his bidding. For himself he built a mediæval tower still standing on the summit of Edgehill, which his friends were expected to visit, to enjoy a cold collation and a glorious view over the battlefield. Besides the tower he had a noted garden containing

> A Laurel walk and Strawberry Bank
> For which the Paymaster I thank,
> The Paymaster well-skilled in planting,
> Pleased to assist when cash was wanting.
> He bid my Laurels grow, they grew
> Fast as his Laurels always do.

Pitt often visited Radway and, like most of Miller's friends, treated him in a tone of airy banter, at which, it must be confessed, he was somewhat ungainly :

A thousand thanks [he writes when returning a horse] to my dear Miller, for the use of his Horse, who, I hope will arrive safe. My own are now in condition, and will wait in readiness at seven, Saturday morning, to bear you to the Fairest of the Fair, the great Beautiful, as you sublime Platonists term it. May you every hour become more and more like a Seraph ! not forgetting the sublunary amusement of a little mortal packing-up.

Again, in wishing his friend success at a picnic, he gambols heavily :

May the grand Landskip Painter, the sun, spread his highest colouring o'er the sweet scene, and the fairest Naiad of the Lake frisk all her frolick Fancy at the Cascade, and be, what you must ever think a pretty Girl, most charming in her Fall.

Pitt's most memorable visit to Radway was in 1748 when he forgathered with Fielding and Lyttelton. Fielding had just finished ' Tom Jones,' and, in the long summer afternoons after dinner, read it out to Miller and the two statesmen, as they sat under the trees over their walnuts and wine.[1]

Unfortunately Pitt's pleasures had to be snatched in the brief intervals when he was not seeking relief from his persistent gout. Astrop Wells at Kings Sutton in Northamptonshire, Sunning Hill in Berkshire, Tunbridge Wells and Bath, the most recommended watering-places, were all tried in turn with indifferent success. Pitt complained of the 'incessant, trifling, unavoidable occupations' of such places, as well he might under the despotic sway of Beau Nash and such solemn triflers, but contrived to get some enjoyment out of them, notwithstanding. Astrop Wells, that he talks of as a dungeon, was at any rate near Stowe and Radway. Bath and Tunbridge Wells were fashionable enough resorts to attract at the proper season of the year most of the men and women with any pretensions to social or intellectual gifts, whether they were ailing or not. At Tunbridge Wells in 1748 a contemporary print shows Pitt in company with Dr. Johnson, Colley Cibber, Garrick, Richardson, Whiston (the translator of Josephus), Speaker Onslow, Lyttelton, and, to enliven these serious gentlemen, the 'virgin' Chudleigh displaying her buxom charms. All these were personages of fame in their day and most of them were well known to Pitt. With the lady he once at least exchanged some appropriate badinage. Garrick he had known since 1741, when he and Lyttelton went to see him play one of his earliest parts in 'The Orphan.' Pitt was so delighted with the performance that he sent for Garrick and told him he was the best actor the English stage had ever

[1] In one of his visits to Radway, Pitt planted a couple of Scotch firs and a mountain ash, still commemorated by an urn placed under them by his nephew. In 1908 a paper with the following record was discovered in the urn: 'In the year 1754 The R. Hon. William Pitt Esq. planted three trees, two Scotch Firrs and one Mountain Ash, being then on a visit to Radway with Sanderson Miller Esq. In the month of July 1778 Thoms Pitt Esq. of Boconnok in Cornwall being at Radway, thought it would be proper to place this Urn under these trees and sent it from Bath and it was set up April 21, 1779, by Sanderson Miller Esq. Sanderson Miller, Mrs. Miller, Miss Miller, Miss Anne Miller, Fiennes S. Miller, Charles Sanderson Miller, Miss Maria Ruding, Mr. Edward Welchman, Mrs. Trotman, Master Hirons Mason, and George Ransford were present when this Urn was put up April ye 21, 1779. George Regnante, C. Miller 17 years old.' (See *Sanderson Miller*, *passim*, and Godden, *Fielding*, pp. 178–9.)

produced. This verdict of the great orator had some influence on Garrick's career, for he quoted it as an argument to his brother against leaving the stage. Two years later Pitt interrupted his attacks on Carteret to attend the rehearsals of Thomson's 'Tancred and Sigismunda,' which Garrick was producing, and made suggestions 'which were heard by the players with great respect.'[1] The friendship then begun continued to the end of Pitt's life.

In 1753 Pitt was again at Tunbridge Wells. He went in May to cure a bad attack of insomnia and nervous depression. So ill was he then, that West, who went with him, expressed the gravest anxiety at 'the extreme dejection which appears to-day in Mr. Pitt from a night passed entirely without sleep. . . . While he continues under this oppression, I am afraid it will be impossible for me to leave him, as he fancies me of the greatest use to him as a friend and a comforter.' But the waters, an open-air life, a glorious summer, and pleasant company had in time a healing effect. He, with Mr. and Mrs. West and Miss Molly West, took Stone House on Mount Ephraim, and their friend Mrs. Montagu, the famous blue-stocking, came with two young ladies to settle at a neighbouring house. Mrs. Montagu went over to dine at Stone House whenever she felt inclined for company; Pitt and the Wests sometimes spent the evening at Mrs. Montagu's and applauded the young ladies' efforts to practise the minuet, before they appeared in the public rooms. The two households went to the assembly room balls together and combined for expeditions in the country, 'wandering about like a company of gipsies, visiting all the fine parks in the neighbourhood,' a form of amusement 'good for the mind and the body,' said Pitt, 'since an occasional day without drinking the waters gives them a greater effect.' On these expeditions he often acted as host, which he loved to do *en grand seigneur*. One afternoon, writes Mrs. Montagu, 'Mr. Pitt provided us a good dinner at New Vauxhall; the view from it is romantic; we stayed there till the cool of the evening and then returned home.' Another summer day 'we drank tea . . . in the most beautiful rural scene that

---

[1] Davies, *Garrick*, i, 78; Knight, *Garrick*, 35.

can be imagined, which Mr. Pitt discovered in his morning's ride about half a mile from hence ; he ordered a tent to be pitched, tea to be prepared, and his French horn to breathe music like the unseen genius of the wood.' This life gradually restored Pitt to his old self. When the Lytteltons came to visit him in July George reported that ' he has recovered his flesh, rides fifteen miles a day, eats like a horse and has as much wit as ever he had in his life. I hope another month's use of the Tunbridge waters will quite remove all his complaints, real or imaginary.' He himself admitted he had ' appetite enough for a Dorsetshire shepherd, while I imagine the air as appetizing (to use the Scotch word) as the breezes of Mount Ephraim,' and in August was able to attend lectures on philosophy from a Mr. King. Pitt must have been a formidable student, for, ' being desirous of attaining knowledge in this way,' he made Mr. King ' explain things very precisely.' When he left Tunbridge in September for a round of visits to Dr. Ayscough's, Stowe, and Hagley, West and Mrs. Montagu were in despair. West took to reading Demosthenes ; but, imagines Mrs. Montagu, ' You would rather have passed this evening with the British than the Grecian Demosthenes, whom in talents perhaps he equals and, in grace of manners and the sweet civilities of life, I daresay he excels.'[1]

The Bath waters were thought even more necessary for Pitt's health than Tunbridge Wells. After 1744 he passed few years without a visit to the city of which he had been made a freeman in 1738 ;[2] and in 1754, at a cost of £1,200, built himself a house in the Circus, a fashionable part of Bath, where Clive, Gainsborough, and the Duke of Bedford also had houses.[3] His chief friend there was Ralph Allen, the Maecenas of Bath, who had gotten wealth for himself and had also profited the public by his enterprise as a postal contractor and by exploiting his quarries of Bath stone. This wealth he spent munificently. He

[1] See Climenson, Lady Chatterton, Sanderson Miller.
[2] See above, p. 70.
[3] Mrs. Montagu says the house was finished in 1754 (see Climenson ii, 51), and in that year Lady Hester Grenville says that her brother Henry admired it. In 1755, however, he speaks in a letter to his wife of building still going on there. The house was No. 7 and is now divided into two houses,

was a public-spirited citizen, an upholder of municipal purity, and a great benefactor to local charities. Many also enjoyed his private generosity, especially literary men, of whom the most notable was Fielding. The novelist lived for some time at Widcomb Lodge, a house belonging to Allen, and immortalised his benefactor as Squire Allworthy in 'Tom Jones.' Allen's country house, Prior Park, was beautifully situated on a wooded hill outside the city. Here he entertained the distinguished company who came up to admire the view of Bath from his classical portico and enjoy his warm hospitality. Frederick, Prince of Wales, and his children visited him there; and the great Mr. Pope and his commentator Warburton, who married Allen's niece and heiress. With Pitt Allen soon contracted a warm friendship; both were men of broad, tolerant views on religion and domestic politics, shared the same exalted idea of England's position in the world, and had literary sympathies in common. This friendship stood Pitt in good stead later on, when he was in need of a seat in Parliament unhampered by oligarchical connections.

Pitt's personal appearance at this time is recorded in a portrait painted by Hoare. He looks a somewhat self-satisfied young man, elegantly dressed and without much indication of power in his countenance. Pitt himself liked the picture, which is no doubt true to the character he sometimes assumed of a courtly squire of dames, providing the music of a French horn in the woods near Tunbridge Wells, or attending them to a philosophy lecture by Mr. King. He had not yet gained that full self-control which responsibility brings; but even Hoare cannot quite tone down the strength shown in the long, aquiline nose, in the sensitive lips, and the hawk-like eyes. He was tall and had a small head and thin face, in his person he stood erect, and was famed for his courtly manners, while the grace of his figure and gesture, well indicated on the canvas, was one of the orator's abiding possessions.[1] To the lightning of his eye all witnesses agree. 'An eye that

---

[1] His tall figure is noted by the younger Beckford and other contemporaries. In this respect the wax figure in Westminster, though otherwise a remarkable likeness, gives a wrong impression.

would cut a diamond,' says Shelburne. 'His eyes were gray,' says his granddaughter, ' and yet by candle-light, from the expression that was in them, one would have thought them black. When he was angry or speaking very much in earnest, nobody could look him in the face.'

Pitt, had now overcome the shyness and aloofness which embarrassed him at Eton. His friends were many, chiefly among politicians, but also in the literary world. Fielding, Garrick, Mrs. Montagu all loved him ; Glover, the fashionable author of 'Leonidas,' was glad to claim his friendship ; and Home, another minor poet, sent him his ' Agis ' for his opinion. Small wonder that he attracted admiration and affection. In an age, of which the dominating notes were caution, lack of enthusiasm, and sterility of ideas, Pitt stood out singular for his zest in life, his audacity of conception, and his contagious enthusiasm for any object, great or small, that he undertook. About this enthusiasm of his a story is told. He had promised to lay out the grounds of some friend, when late one evening an urgent summons called him back to London on State business. Rather than break his word, he called at once for men with lanterns, and, while his coach was being made ready, sallied forth into the grounds and staked out his plan for their improvement. At table he was abstemious, temperate, and regular ; yet even Wilkes, though, as we should expect, he preferred to spend his nights with Rigby and his jovial friends, would willingly have spent all his days with Pitt, who ' by the most manly sense, and the fine sallies of a warm and sportive imagination, can charm the whole day, and, as the Greek said, his entertainments please even the day after they are given.'

His chief friends were still the Lytteltons and Grenvilles, bound to him, says Glover, by his ' private good qualities, friendship beyond professions, industry and ability to oblige.' He watched over Lyttelton tenderly when he lost his beloved first wife, and, at the request of Lyttelton's father, helped the youngest son to find his feet in the world. His affection for the Grenvilles was even closer. Unattractive the men of this family were, rapacious, dull, and self-satisfied ; yet with all their faults they were public-spirited and had a genuine love of liberty. Here may be found one bond of union between them and Pitt. Another was gratitude. Temple, though he presumed on his superior wealth to the extent of looking on Pitt almost as a dependent, was not ungenerous to him; and the brothers' political constancy to Pitt was of incalculable value to the career of this otherwise isolated man. At any rate Pitt was grateful, even before a closer tie united him to them; and he already looked on himself as one of the family. James, the third brother, was his especial favourite, and remained faithful to him through all the family dissensions. When Thomas, the sailor brother, was killed in Anson's action off Finisterre, Pitt felt that for him 'public joy is quite sunk in private concern. The high esteem and love I had for poor Grenville and what I feel for his most afflicted brothers, reduces me to the hard (and, I hope, pardonable) condition of being a mourner in the midst of public rejoicing.' Five years later he was still busying himself with the monument erected to Thomas's memory at Bath. In 1749, when his old patron Viscount Cobham died, he helped the eldest brother, Richard, to obtain the coveted earldom of Temple for the family; two years earlier he had defended them vigorously in the House of Commons. Their tyranny in Buckinghamshire, where they formed a clan rivalling the old Scottish clans in power and self-assertiveness,[1] had made them extremely unpopular: their numerous enemies were consequently delighted at a proposal to reduce the importance of Buckingham, a town entirely dependent upon them, by removing the assizes to Aylesbury. In the debate some hard things were said about the Grenvilles, but Pitt came to their rescue, repaying with interest the taunts and invectives of their opponents, and declaring in his haughtiest strain that the 'violent torrent of abuse on a whole family is founded on no reason in the world, but because that family is distinguished by the just rewards of their services to their king and country.'[2]

February 19, 1748.

[1] See *Egmont MSS.* 212.
[2] For Horace Walpole's part in this debate, see his *Short Notes on My Life.*

Pitt had need of good friends, for his relations with his own family had become extremely unhappy. He and his favourite sister, Ann, had never apparently renewed their old intimacy after the objections he had made to her visit to France. When Pitt removed to the Pay Office he did not take her with him, though they had previously shared a house together. Their estrangement may possibly have been caused by her friendship with the Bolingbrokes, with whom he had long been at variance : once a diversity of interest had revealed itself, two such people, both equally domineering, '*qui se ressemblaient,*' says Walpole, '*comme deux gouttes de feu,*' could hardly have lived together in peace. Pitt felt deeply the disturbance of that 'harmony between sister and brother, unexampled almost all that time,' as he once wrote to her, ' the loss of which has embitter'd much of my life and will always be an affliction to me.' Though unwilling to live with her, he took care she should not suffer thereby. The loss of her post as maid of honour after Queen Caroline's death had straitened her means : as soon as his own allowed him he gave her £200 a year. In 1751 he made an attempt at reconciliation, but it was not cordially received. Ann accused him of demanding ' absolute deference and blind obedience to his will,' and, on a report that he had spoken to others of the allowance he made her, angrily proposed to repay it. In his answer Pitt displays to her a tenderness and humility of spirit revealed to few :

I have infirmities of temper, blemishes and faults, if you please, of nature without end ; but the Eye that can't be deceived must judge between us, whether that friendship, which was my very existence for so many years, could ever have received the least flaw, but from umbrages and causes which the quick sensibility and tenderest jealousy of friendship alone at first suggested. . . . Indeed, sister, I still find something within that firmly assures me I am not that thing which your interpretations of my life (if I can ever be brought to think them all your own) would represent me to be. . . . I have often, too often reproached you, and from warmth of temper in strong and plain terms . . . [but] I was never so drunk with presumption as to expect *absolute* deference and *blind obedience to my will.* . . I also declare as solemnly before God and man, that no consideration could ever have extorted from my lips the least mention of the trifling assistance you accepted from me, but the cruel reports, industriously propagated, and circulating from various quarters [1] round me, of the state you was left to live in. As to the repayment of this wretched money, allow me, dear Sister, to entreat you to think no more of it. The bare thought of it may surely suffice for your own dignity and for my humiliation without taxing your present income, merely to mortify me : the demonstration of a blow is, in honour, a blow, and let me conjure you to rest it here.

But Ann was deaf to this appeal and to Pitt's further attempt in this year at a reconciliation. Two years later, however, when her unaccommodating temper had lost her the post of Privy Purse to the Princess Dowager, offered her in 1751, and she was living a retired life in France, she at last yielded to Pitt's renewed entreaties.

I am unable to express [he writes] the load you have taken off my heart by your affectionate and generous answer to my last letter. I will not give you the trouble to read any more; but must repeat in the fulness of my heart, the warmest and tenderest acknowledgements of your goodness to, my dear sister, your most affectionate brother, W. PITT.

Although Pitt on his side was evidently sincere in his belief that he and Ann had become reconciled, the old intimacy was never renewed. The two lived apart, Ann for several years in France, where her mordant tongue and pen were not sparing of her brother. Pitt's own letters to her insensibly grew more stilted and less familiar, as it was borne in upon him that the old days would never return. But he always retained his respect for her, and helped her when it was in his power. When his youngest sister, Mary, came up to London he wrote to her regretting that Ann was not there to give 'her Countenance and her Advice and Instructions, superior to any you can otherwise receive,' and urged Mary to 'imitate her worth, and thereby endeavour to deserve her esteem, as you wish to obtain that of the best Part of the World.' On his engagement Ann was among the first to whom his thoughts turned for sympathy, and he tried, with but moderate success, to encourage

[1] E.g. Horace Walpole, who talks of Pitt having 'shaken her off in an unbecoming manner.'

sisterly relations between her and Lady Hester. In 1758 he was full of anxiety on her account. She was still in France, the country against which he was then directing hostilities, and could not bring herself to return to England. Physical illness had brought on symptoms of a disordered mind, whereby she became almost unable to form any decision. Pitt, very like her in nature, may well have taken this as a warning to himself of that family tendency, inherited from the Governor, whereof nine years later he also showed signs. In her melancholy state he redoubled his tender solicitude. With some difficulty he obtained leave from the French minister, Bernis, to send a friend over to her, and chose him with special care. This friend, regarded with much suspicion by the French ministers and local commandants, and resisted by Ann, found it no easy task to bring her away from Valence to England.[1] On arriving at Dover she was met by a warm letter of welcome from Pitt, who invited her to come to his house. Ann was touched and softened by his kindness. He

continued as he began, [she wrote to her friend, Lady Suffolk] as soon as the King had put him in the place he is in, by giving the strongest and tenderest proof of his affection . . . I was so sunk and my mind so overcome with all I have suffered . . . that I do not believe anything in the world could have made it possible for me to get out of this country, but my brother's sending a friend to my assistance and choosing so proper a person. . . . My brother has always seemed to guess and understand all I felt of every kind and has carried his delicacy so far as never once to put me in mind of what I felt more strongly than any other part of my misfortune, which was how very disagreeable and embarrassing it must be to him to have me in France.[2]

After her return to England Ann continued for some time to cause Pitt trouble by her vagaries, and on her recovery

[1] *Aff. Etr. Angl. Corr. Pol.* 441 contains a long correspondence on this affair. Bernis and other ministers wrote for reports from local officials, who were told to watch Pitt's friend very carefully, lest he should abuse his opportunity by spying; and almost daily notes of his and Ann Pitt's movements were sent to Paris. The friend is reported to have said, ' qu'on ne lui avait dite malade que de corps et qu'elle l'est prodigieusement d'esprit.' He found her staying at the Croix d'Or at Valence.
[2] *Suffolk Corr.* ii, 23.

exasperated him by moving heaven and earth to obtain a pension. First she applied to him, but was told that 'having never been a Sollicitor for favours, upon any occasion, how can I become so now without contradicting the whole tenour of my Life.' Next she turned to the rising star, Bute, and through his influence obtained a pension charged on the Irish revenues. Pitt had always protested against the scandal of imposing English pensioners on the Irish list, nor was he best pleased at the source of the favour, and expressed his anger warmly :

On your account, [he wrote] I rejoice at an addition to your income so agreeable to your turn of life, whatever repugnancy I find at the same time, to see my name placed on the Pensions of Ireland. Unmixt as I am in this whole transaction I will not doubt that you will take care to have it thoroughly understood. Long may you live in health to enjoy the comforts and happiness which you tell me you owe to the King, singly through the intercession of Lord Bute, and to feel the pleasing sentiments of such an obligation.

Ann's reply showed unwonted humility, and concluded with the hope that ' an advantage so very essential to the ease and comfort of the remainder of a Life, which has not hitherto been very happy, shou'd not be a cause of uneasiness to You.' [1] Poor woman ! With much of her brother's capacity and all his fire, she suffered from never finding a sufficient outlet for her vigour, either in action or in a happy marriage. The rest of her long life she spent amassing more pensions and enjoying herself with the brilliant society she collected at her house near Kensington Gravel Pits.

Pitt had four other sisters. Harriet, who married Sir William Corbet of Stoke, and Catherine, who became Mrs. Needham, entered very little into his life. Mary, the youngest, who was born nearly twenty years after him, he treated like a daughter in his own house both before and after his marriage. She seems to have been almost the only colourless member of her fiery family, and little more is known of her than can

[1] Ann's humility was not of long duration. When in the following year, 1761, Pitt himself was given a pension, she was only deterred by her friends from sending him congratulations couched in the same ironical strain as his letter to her.

be gathered from a letter of Mrs. Montagu, written in 1754 : ' Miss Mary Pitt, youngest sister of Mr. Pitt, is come to stay a few days with me ; she is a very sensible, modest, pretty sort of young woman, and as Mr. Pitt seemed to take every civility shown her as a favour, I thought this mark of respect to her one manner of returning my obligations to him.' [1]

Elizabeth, the sister next in age to Ann, showed clearly the strain of madness in the Pitts. She was the beauty of the family, but so scandalous in her behaviour that in an age not noted for squeamishness she became a social outcast. For a time she was allowed by her elder brother to live at Down House, the old family mansion at Blandford ; later, when Thomas's means became straitened, William provided her with Grately Lodge, ' the habitation,' she writes to him, ' which your goodness has bestowed upon me.' Driven from this place by the notoriety of her relations with her married neighbour, Lord Talbot, she was given an allowance of £200 a year by Pitt—£100 under bond that she conducted herself properly, and £100 without condition. She went to live in France, and there met a young diplomatist, Dutens, to whom, on his departure for England, she gave a letter of introduction to her brother. But on discovering afterwards that her companion's beauty had greater charms for him than her own, she wrote accusing him of boasting that ' he was well with me,' and begged Pitt ' to order one of your footmen to give him the treatment he merits,' [2] a request with which he complied. In 1754 she had left France for Florence, where she came under the observation of that diligent trifler Horace Mann, who wrote a full account of her irregularities to Bubb Dodington.[3] They were ' of such a nature as forms the most dangerous character imaginable, and so much the more as she is still handsome, has wit and great art.' In addition to making herself ridiculous by her pursuit of various men, she openly embraced the Roman Catholic religion and then demanded protection from Count

---

[1] Climenson, ii, 53.
[2] See *Chatham MSS.* 52, supplemented by Dutens's own account in *Mémoires d'un voyageur qui se repose.*
[3] *Hist. MSS., Various Collections,* vi, 25, 26.

Richecourt, the Emperor's envoy, on the ground that her conversion ' would be disapproved by her *nation*, and that *it* would become her enemy.' Two years later she was back in England disputing about her allowance with Dr. Ayscough, the trustee appointed by Pitt. Ayscough's experience of her convinced him that she was ' the worst, the wickedest and the most wrong-headed woman in the world.'[1] Walpole said she handed Pitt's private letters to the editor of an opposition journal as proof that he had cheated her of £100 a year : all they proved, added Walpole, was that ' he once allowed her two, and after all her wickedness still allows her one.'[2] Pitt continued her allowance, but the two ceased to correspond until, in 1761, she announced her engagement to J. Hannan, a man considerably younger and richer than herself. After that nothing more is heard of her until her death in 1770.[3]

The elder brother, Thomas, did little more credit to the Pitt family. Though he had inherited most of the Governor's property, his extravagant expenditure at Cornish elections and on himself reduced him to desperate straits for money. In 1749 he was trying to save himself from ruin by selling the nomination to Old Sarum to the Prince of Wales, and raising loans from the trustees of the family estates and from his younger brother. After the death of the Prince of Wales, two years later, he was still worse off, for he lost his employment as Warden of the Stannaries, worth £1,500 a year, and was compensated by a pension of only £1,000. For this he never forgave his brother William, who was deputed by Pelham to tell him he had been deprived of his office, and who afterwards refused to make him minister to the Swiss Cantons, a post for which he was obviously unfitted. In 1755, being unable to raise any more money in

---

[1] *Chatham MSS.* 17.
[2] *Walpole Corr.* (January 7, 1757).
[3] One of her least objectionable manias was to change her name. In a portrait painted of her in 1758, commemorating her as the ' author of the scheme for erecting Publick Magazines for corn to relieve the necessities of the poor and sister to the Right Hon. Wm. Pitt,' she appears as Clara Villiers Pitt. She also signed herself Elizabeth Villiers Pitt. This habit gave some work to the lawyers, who on her marriage professed to doubt whether she was the plain Elizabeth Pitt entitled to a marriage portion under the Governor's will.

England, he retired with his daughter to the Continent, where Shelburne once met him at Utrecht, and spent the whole night listening to his abuse of William, whom he denounced with a great flow of language and a quantity of anecdotes as a hypocrite, a scoundrel, and an impostor. He is stated to have been remarkable for grace of bearing and the signs of power in his countenance, and to have had considerable accomplishments. But inordinate pride and an ungovernable temper warped his nature. He was hated in Cornwall, and towards the end of his life seems to have lost all sense of right and wrong. In 1761 he died on the Continent, leaving hardly a friend to lament him.[1]

His son, Thomas, was the object of Pitt's especial care. The father, pleading poverty, would not send him to school, so to make amends Pitt took charge of his nephew's education. He first made suggestions to his pedagogue, Mr. Leech, the parson of Boconnoc, and in 1751 began the famous series of letters to the boy himself, then aged fourteen. He also gave material help. When the father was for withdrawing young Thomas from Cambridge in 1755, Pitt gave him the means of continuing his terms there.[2] When he was ill from overwork Pitt, newly married, invited him to stay at Sunning Hill, promising that 'the muses shall not be quite forgot: we will ride, read, walk and philosophise, extremely at our ease and you may return to Cambridge with new ardour, or at least with strength repaired.'

The 'happy delightful task' Pitt set himself in the letters to his nephew was to qualify him for the part in society

to which your birth and estate call you. You are to be a gentleman of such learning and qualifications as may distinguish you in the service of your country hereafter; not a pedant who reads only to be called learned, instead of considering learning as an instrument only for action, . . . manly, honourable and virtuous action upon the stage of the world, both in private and public life, as a gentle-

---

[1] See *Dropmore MSS.* (Hist. MSS. Commission), i, 133–5; *Add. MSS.* 32737, ff. 187, 302; *Chatham MSS.* 52; *Egmont MSS.* 277 (April 5, 1751). Bussy, writing to Choiseul on July 21, 1761, says Pitt had heard of his brother's death that morning and therefore put off his interview. (*Aff. Etr.* (*Angl. Corr. Pol.* 444, f. 32.)

[2] *Chatham MSS,* 52; *Chatham Corr.* i, 123, 142–3.

man, and as a member of the commonwealth, who is to answer for all he does to the laws of his country, to his own breast and conscience, and at the tribunal of honour and good fame.

In this task Pitt persisted until his nephew left Cambridge in 1758, allowing neither gout, political anxiety, nor even the conduct of a great war to stop the correspondence. Letters of counsel to the young were then a favourite exercise of their elders. Even Bubb Dodington practised it and Chesterfield is famous for it. These cascades of advice sometimes made prigs of those on whom they fell, and young Thomas shows signs of the failing in some of his answers to his uncle. But there are worse faults for a young man of spirit; hypocrisy for one, such as the spectacle of a Dodington uttering moral sentiments must have evoked,[1] or the premature cynicism which Chesterfield deliberately inculcated. Every letter of Pitt to his nephew, stilted as some are, is pervaded by a tone of magnanimity and sincerity in striking contrast to that of the more approved letter-writers of his day. He and Chesterfield happened to write about the same time on politeness, and a comparison of their definitions brings out the wide difference between the two. Chesterfield's letter to young Stanhope on *les bienséances*, his characteristic name for politeness, is full of useful hints on deportment. 'To women,' he says, ' you should always address yourself with great outward respect and attention, whatever you feel inwardly... There is a *bienséance* also with regard to people of the lowest degree: a gentleman observes it with his footman, even with the beggar in the street ... he corrects the one coolly and refuses the other with humanity.' Chesterfield

---

[1] Dodington's real sentiments on civic virtue were given to the world in a little poem, which he called *Shorten Sail*:

> Love thy country, wish it well
> Not with too intense a care;
> 'Tis enough that when it fell
> Thou its ruin didst not share.
>
> . . . . .
>
> Void of strong desire and fear
> Life's wide ocean trust no more:
> Strive thy little bark to steer
> With the tide, but near the shore.

recommends *les bienséances* for their practical value to the young man anxious to succeed, while Pitt, a very noble gentleman, enjoins politeness because it is right, forbids rudeness because it is wrong :

> I would venture to call politeness *benevolence in trifles*, or the preference of others to ourselves in little daily, hourly occurrences in the commerce of life. A better place, a more commodious seat, priority in being helped at table, etc. what is it but sacrificing ourselves in such trifles to the conveniences and pleasure of others ? And this constitutes true politeness. It is a perpetual attention (by habit it grows easy and natural to us) to the little wants of those we are with, by which we either prevent them or remove them. Bowing, ceremonious, formal compliments, stiff civilities will never be politeness : that must be easy, natural, unstudied, manly, noble. And what will give this, but a mind benevolent and perpetually attentive to exert that amiable disposition in trifles towards all you converse and live with. Benevolence in greater matters takes a higher name, and is the queen of virtues. . . . Towards servants never accustom yourself to rough and passionate language. When they are good, we should consider them as *humiles amici*, as fellow-Christians, *ut conservi* ; and, when they are bad, pity, admonish, and part with them if incorrigible. On all occasions beware, my dear child, of anger, that demon, that destroyer of our peace :
>
> > Ira furor brevis est, animum rege, qui, nisi paret,
> > Imperat : hunc frenis, hunc tu compesce catena.

Pitt knew well the temptations to anger, but learned to practise what he preached. ' When I first saw him,' says the nephew to whom this was written, ' he was intemperate towards his servants, full as much as my own father, but it is to his honour that when he owed a better example to his children he got the better of that habit.'

Thomas's career did some credit to his uncle's care. Soon after leaving Cambridge he cut off his own entail in order to pay his father's debts and find portions for his sisters ; and in politics, without distinguishing himself, he showed ability and a high sense of honour. But he felt small gratitude to the uncle who had watched over his youth, and treated him with rancour in the memoir he wrote for his son's benefit. The cause of the quarrel is unknown, but as likely as not it was Pitt's fault, for he was not good at retaining his friends. He quarrelled with nearly all his relations, and sooner or later with all those, save possibly James Grenville, with whom he had once been intimate. Chesterfield accounted for this by his bitter saying that Pitt had neither love nor hatred in his nature; an explanation which his tenderness to Ann, and later to his wife and children, entirely disproves. But there is a grain of truth in Chesterfield's addition that 'those who are worst with Pitt to-day are likely to be well with him to-morrow.' With his impetuous and deeply sensitive nature he craved for friendship, gave much to those he cared for, and was inordinately grateful for kindness shown him. But his haughtiness could ill brook contradiction even from the closest friends, and so led to sudden estrangements. With him, too, private friendship was always subordinated to public interests, and disagreement on politics became a fatal bar to friendly intercourse. It is so with nearly all the greatest statesmen, who command the sympathy and attention of masses and think more of great principles and causes than of the idiosyncracies of those who help them for the time to serve those causes.

So, until he married, Pitt, in spite of all his friends, was a lonely man. But he had resources within himself. He read much, and at South Lodge began collecting a library of the books most useful for the life he had planned: books on America, travels, treatises on diplomacy and the law of nations, the classics, and above all a good collection of historical works.[1]

---

[1] In *Chatham MSS.* 74 are several booksellers' bills and notes in Pitt's handwriting which indicate some of the contents of his library. Among these books were the following: *The State of North America*; Colden's *Indian Nations of Canada*; Labat's *Voyage en Amérique*; *Histoire des Antilles*; Norden's *Travels in Egypt and Nubia*; Breval's *Travels through Europe*; Chishal's *Travels in Turkey*; Voltaire's *Histoire d'Allemagne*; Ludlow's *Memoirs*; Hume; May; Birch's *Memoirs of Queen Elizabeth*; Forbes's *Transactions*; Lediard's *Naval History*; Blair's *Chronological Tables*; Addison's *History of Revolutions in Turkey and Morocco*; Camden; Stow's *Survey*; Picart's *Ceremonies and Religious Customs*; Grotius; Comte d'Avaux's *Négociations* and various treaties; Racine; D'Alembert; *Don Quixote* in English; Guillim's *Heraldry*; Wood's *Athenæ Oxonienses*; Marvell's *Satires*; Harrington's *Oceana*; Jortin's *Life of Erasmus*; Evelyn *On Medals*; Dr. Johnson's and Savary's *Dictionaries*; besides many other miscellaneous works on natural history, the classics, and books of more ephemeral interest.

At Bath he subscribed regularly to Bull's Library, and when he was ill used to have the attendant of the library to read aloud to him, principally from Josephus's 'History of the Jews.'[1] He used his learning so little for display that he was sometimes accused of being superficial, and his sister Ann once said absurdly that the only thing he knew thoroughly was Spenser's 'Faerie Queene.' But his speeches show that he read to some purpose. He can quote the customs of the Romans on the question of a nightly watch for Bristol, or Shakespeare, Locke, and Thucydides on America with as much ease as he uses the homely instance of his crutch to convict his countrymen of folly, or hums a line of doggerel to confound George Grenville. He flattered the vanity of Mrs. Macaulay, the Whig historian, by citing her with approval in the House, and caused Hume the greatest vexation he ever experienced by strictures on the Tory bias of his work. He found an apt parallel to the aristocracy of his own day in Robertson's description of the grandees of Spain, and owned to Fox that Cardinal Ximenes was his favourite character in history. He read Bailey's Dictionary through twice to improve his vocabulary, and for style studied Barrow's sermons,[2] besides the great orators, Cicero 'for copiousness and beauty of diction, nobleness and magnificence of ideas,' Demosthenes for the 'irresistible torrent of his vehement argumentation, his close and forcible reasoning, and his depth and fortitude of mind.' Well might an admirer say of him, 'We have got a man of learning and parts, who has read the antients and avails himself of his reading.'[3] He had that keen love of good literature for its own sake which has been one of the best traditions of our statesmen. Homer and Virgil he recommended to his nephew as not only the two greatest poets but as containing 'the finest lessons for your age to imbibe.' Shakespeare, especially 'Henry IV' and 'Henry V,' he loved, and was fond in later life of reading aloud, though, when he came to the passages of buffoonery,

---

[1] So the younger Pitt was told when he subscribed to the same library in 1802 (Rose, *Diary*, i, 509).

[2] Pitt was also fond of Abernethy's sermons and of those of Mr. Zachariah Mudge of Plymouth, the friend of Sir Joshua Reynolds.

[3] *Plain Reasons &c.*, by O. M. Haberdasher, London, January 1759.

he would hand over the book to some other member of the family.[1] There is also a tradition that in his last year he learned Spanish in order to enjoy 'Don Quixote' in the original. Plutarch's 'Lives' was a favourite with him, especially for the account of Pericles. A scholar named Smith, who published a translation of Thucydides, relates that, finding a speech of Pericles 'that bore hard upon the translator,' he took his first 'faint and imperfect attempts' to Pitt, 'the greatest genius of the age, . . . who, as he thinks and speaks like Pericles, could not endure that any of his words should be depreciated,' and thereupon undertook the task himself.[2] But, as the choice of his books and his letters to his nephew show, English history was the study that had the greatest fascination for him. 'Well acquainted with all modern history, but a real scholar in English history,' one of the French agents justly calls him. Writing to Thomas he urges that histories should be carefully chosen for their bearing 'on the true principles of our happy constitution': Father Orleans for his remarks on the revolutions of the Houses of Lancaster and York, but no further, 'for the father contains nothing more than a system of slavery, body and soul, supported by the sincerity and veracity of a Jesuit'; Habingdon and Hollinshed for Edward IV and Richard III; Bacon's Henry VII, Lord Herbert of Cherbury on Henry VIII, Camden on Elizabeth, and, for the 'times of trouble,' Clarendon, with caution, and Ludlow. 'But you cannot peruse,' he adds, 'and consider too much all the great state-pieces of that period' in Whitlocke, Rushworth, and the collections of letters—'I mean

---

[1] Dodington, on the other hand, chose only those scenes of Shakespeare to read aloud in which buffoonery was the subject (Cumberland, *Memoirs*).

[2] Charles Butler recorded on the authority of the second William Pitt that his father had translated 'the speech of Pericles in Smith's translation of Thucydides.' One would naturally expect '*the* speech' to refer to the Funeral Oration in the second book, but the versions of both that and the first speech in Smith are extremely wooden. Only on turning to the last great speech, in which Pericles defended himself against attack, is the spirit of the great English orator apparent, and Pitt's handiwork is made certain by the note, quoted above, which Smith appends to it. A specimen of Pitt's translation will be found at the head of chapter xviii. Smith's translation in two vols. was published in 1753 and dedicated to the Prince of Wales.

[3] *Aff. Etr. Angl. Corr. Pol.* 454, f. 44.

such letters between the great actors as relate to critical and important points; these are very few, and all the rest are waste paper and loss of time'—a sentiment with which Carlyle would have heartily agreed. For later times he suggests Ralph, the Continuation of Rapin, and Burnet.[1] He also strongly recommended Sir John Davies's 'Discourse' on Ireland, and Nathaniel Bacon's 'Discovery of the Laws of England,' much of which was inspired by Selden, and which contains such excellent Whig sentiments as that

The King oweth Allegiance both to the Law and the People; different from that of the people's in this, that the King's Allegiance is due to the Law that is originally the People's Election; but the People's to the King under a Law of their own framings.

The best honour of the King's work is to be *Nobilis Servitus* ... or, in plain English, Supreme service above all, and to the whole.[2]

If Pitt had few with whom he could take counsel, he had a noble counsellor in his own soul. He was not one of those content, when the awakening of youth has passed, to live on unthinking in the groove then cleft. The constant surprises of his vigorous revivals, the originality of his conceptions, that age could not stale, bear witness to this. Even more direct proof is found in the jottings of his note-books. The entries are undated and there is little clue to the occasions which called them forth. But they are evidently the reflections of many years, the outcome of internal struggles harder than the gout, of which his closest friends had little inkling. In his private communings this proud, self-opinionated and ambitious man, as he appeared to his contemporaries, reveals a singular humility and an earnest desire to overcome his besetting temptation to pride and sudden anger:

[1] Among the subscribers to Burnet's *History of My Own Times* in 1724 appears a Mr. William Pitt. It is possible that this may have been one of Pitt's cousins, but it is tempting to believe, and not inconceivable, that even as an Eton boy he may have wished to possess a volume of the great Whig Bishop.

[2] Pitt's views on a course of historical reading are to be found in the published letters to his nephew. There is also an interesting unpublished draft, summarising his system, in *Chatham MSS.* 6 (to T. Pitt, July 23, 1755). From this some of the phrases in the text are taken. See also below, p. 268.

It is ill-judged, though very common [he reflects] to be less ashamed of a want of temper than of understanding; but what is most dishonourable of all is, for a man at once to discover a great genius and an ungoverned mind; because that strength of reason and understanding he is master of gives him a great advantage for the government of his passions.

Again:

'He that is slow to anger,' said Solomon, 'is better than the mighty.' I know the world calls them heroes who have made the greatest havoc and destruction among their fellow-creatures; who, to gratify their ambition and lust of power, have been the plagues and terrors of their own species, spreading desolation and carnage wherever they went: whereas, in the judgment of true wisdom, he that yokes a stubborn lust, curbs a boisterous passion, and subdues an unruly appetite, yielding to nothing but the dictates of virtue and religion, obtains the greatest victory and deserves the truest honour.

Pitt had a deep religion of his own, but it was a religion far removed from the intolerant and persecuting 'Church spirit' which he attacked in 1753.[1] Among his papers is a fierce denunciation of those 'who converted, with prophane timidity, a reverential awe into a superstitious fear of God, and made the existence of a Supreme Being, who ought to be the Comfort, the Terror of mankind, [and so] ran into one of those extremes; mediating, interceding, atoning beings; or represented God hating, revenging, punishing &c.'[2] To

---

[1] See above, p. 176.
[2] See *Chatham MSS*. 74. A 'Letter on Superstition,' said to have been originally published in *The London Journal* for 1733, has long been attributed to Pitt. Unfortunately the copy of *The London Journal* in the British Museum is defective and does not appear to contain this letter. It was, however, reprinted in Pitt's lifetime and attributed to him. This copy is to be found in a British Museum scrapbook dated 1760. It was reprinted—twice in 1819, in 1820 as a hawker's broadsheet, in 1851, in 1867, and again in 1873 by A. Holyoake as a secularist tract, always with the same attribution. Dr. Von Ruville also prints it as an appendix to his *Life of Chatham*. That Pitt really wrote this in 1733 seemed improbable, for he was then a cornet in the army and hardly likely to have written on such a subject for a newspaper; an entry in the diary of Lord Egmont, father of the better-known eighteenth-century politician, under date September 16, 1733, confirms this doubt. The passage runs: '... now Dr. Tyndal is dead, the head of the Unbelievers is

him the most antipathetic of all creeds was contained in the 'errors of Rome . . . rank idolatry,' he calls it, 'a subversion of all civil as well as religious liberty, and the utter disgrace of reason and of human nature.' Pitt's was a simple faith in God, the 'All-wise and Almighty Father constantly watching over His earthly children, whose life must be a constant struggle through faith and good works to come nearer to Him.' It was a courageous and hopeful belief that human life becomes ennobled and exalted, becomes divine, by the attempt to approach God's perfection: 'Let us not think it beneath us,' he writes, 'to exert ourselves against the least of God's enemies and our own; since it is a progress towards perfection which is required of us; let us think and act as if we thought it our duty to make this progress.' He himself took this maxim as a guide for his life. To the end he was learning, to the end stepping to higher things over his dead past.

Dr. Pellet. . . . One Pit, who writes the *London Journal*, is another of them. He has an office in the Customs.' (*Egmont MSS.* 80.) This 'Pit' was probably 'James Pitt, appointed viewer and examiner of tobacco' in 1731. (*Calendar of Treasury Books and Papers*, 1731–4, p. 68.)

It can hardly be doubted that the 'Letter' in *The London Journal*, subsequently attributed to William Pitt, was written by this James Pitt.

CHAPTER VIII

GLOOM AND SUNSHINE

I

Adversis rerum immersabilis undis.

PELHAM died on March 6, 1754. 'Now I shall have no more peace,' exclaimed the King. Pelham was not a great minister, but he had silenced opposition more successfully than any since the Hanoverian accession, and had been a safe guardian of the country's interests : and never was prudent and conciliatory government more needed. Abroad the outlook was threatening. Since the Peace of Aix-la-Chapelle desultory fighting with France had never ceased in India, in America, or in the West Indies ; while in Europe the Dunkirk dispute still dragged on. Now another great war with her seemed imminent ; and it looked as if we should have to engage in it single-handed. The Empress had been estranged since the peace forced upon her in 1748 ; Frederic of Prussia had fresh grievances against us ; and Newcastle's treaties with electors were as useless as they were expensive. At home the King, then seventy-one, seemed drawing near his end ; when he died, bitter contention was almost certain to break out.

Three distinct interests had to be considered in the choice of Pelham's successor : that of the King, who had all the obstinacy and prejudice of his years, hated change, and was implacable to any man who had insulted his royal dignity ; that of the Princess Dowager, who had already abandoned the attitude of self-effacement, temporarily assumed after her husband's death, and was busy forming plans and a party to serve her in the likely event of her regency ; and that of the Duke of Cumberland, who had his followers pledged to support him as president of a council of regency. Neither of the two last interests could be safely disregarded, for though George II's sympathies were with the Duke of Cumberland, it would have been unwise to alienate the Princess, with her prospect of an early accession to power. The Duke's strength, in addition to his father's favour, rested on his control over the army ; and his chief man in the House of Commons was Henry Fox, the Secretary at War. The Princess had a less clearly defined party : the Pelhams, however, had recently inclined towards her, while Pitt and the Grenvilles had renewed their old ties with Leicester House. In the Cabinet no one had the commanding personality required to reconcile these jarring interests or cope with the foreign dangers. Newcastle was a muddle-pate ; Hardwicke merely a prudent critic ; Anson a first-rate administrator but no statesman ; Granville took little part. Outside the Cabinet was one whose transcendent capacity was already recognised, but want of political influence and the jealous monopoly of power by the governing clique seemed fatal to his chances of advancement.

To Pitt a united Government, loyal to the existing arrangements, seemed as needful then as it was in the last years of Queen Anne ; and his own claims to a leading position in such a government were incontestable. When he threw in his lot with the Pelhams his ambition had been for a post offering scope for his capacity, and he accepted the Paymastership merely as a stepping-stone, on the understanding that the King's objections to his attendance in the Closet would be removed. He had now worked eight years for the Government, but, though the Ministry had been three times rearranged, he had always been put aside on the old plea of the King's aversion. By his loyalty to the Ministry, in contrast with his former violence, and by the comparative obscurity of his office, he had actually lost ground in the estimation of the public. Now at last he thought his reward had come. He had then no wish or expectation, it is clear from his letters, to succeed Pelham as Leader of the House, but he at least expected to change his present office for one of real authority and responsibility. The Duke of Newcastle had always expressed the greatest sympathy with his aim and a desire to serve him. During 1753 he had sent him the most friendly letters on public affairs, and in October had promised, at Pitt's request, to find him another seat for the approaching general election.[1]

Unfortunately Pitt was seriously ill at Bath, and could not look after his own interests on the spot. His long course of treatment at Tunbridge Wells in the previous summer had brought him only a short respite; and since October 1753, except for his appearance in Parliament to speak on the Jewish question, he had been kept a prisoner enduring torture from suppressed gout. Three violent attacks at the end of February and beginning of March left him prostrate in his 'great chair,' miserably depressed in spirits and quite unable to travel.[2] 'I am indeed much out of order,' he laments on the day of Pelham's death, 'and worn down with pain and confinement: this gout which I trusted to relieve me has almost subdued me: I am the horse in the fable, *non equitem dorso, non frœnum depulit ore*'; and during the next week, when he felt that he might have done something by his presence in London, he frets sorely at his infirmity. He writes of his 'unspeakable mortification' at being kept in Bath and of his 'almost intolerable' impatience to be in London. 'I am carried downstairs and packed up like a bale of goods in my chaise to inure me to motion. . . . If no relapse comes I hope a week will go a good way towards enabling me to crawl, if not to walk. As soon as I am capable of that degree of self-motion I will set out,' he writes on March 14. Though unable to travel Pitt could write, and between March 6 and April 8 he sent off twenty-two letters, three sometimes on one day, counselling and exhorting his friends, stimulating or scornfully reproaching those indifferent to him, leaving no stone unturned to make amends for his absence from the scene of action. But his letters were a poor substitute for himself. Whenever he had a

---

[1] *Add. MSS.* 32733, ff. 26, 63.
[2] H. Walpole, with his usual sneer, says Pitt, 'had, or had unluckily acted, very ill health,' at Bath.

definite course of action to prescribe, no one could write more clearly and succinctly; but when he had to feel his ground, especially on a question of office for himself, few great men have shown so much vagueness and obscurity in their correspondence as Pitt. This obscurity was now probably aggravated by his illness, which at times made him almost despair of again taking an active part in politics, also by a very natural uncertainty as to the dispositions of the leading actors in the ensuing drama. Pitt's incapacity at this crisis of his own and the nation's fortunes was indeed the hardest blow fate had yet dealt him.

On March 6 Pitt heard that Pelham was seriously ill, and wrote at once to the Duke of Newcastle condoling with him on the 'adverse and unhappy event which threatens you and yours.' Next day, on news of Pelham's death, he exhorted Newcastle to bear in mind that it was 'a great occasion for all your strength of mind to exert itself. May all good men make it their glory to support your Grace in the generous effort.' To the Grenvilles and Lyttelton he sent a joint letter of advice on the common policy to be followed by their small corps. He is clear enough on 'the present dangerous conjuncture for this country both at home and abroad,' and in defining the public interest, 'the object to be wished for,' as an obligation 'to support the King in quiet as long as he may have to live; and to strengthen the hands of the Princess of Wales, as much as may be, in order to maintain her power in the government, in case of the misfortune of the King's demise,' by continuing Pelham's policy of uniting all parties who had the public interest at heart. But when he comes to consider candidates for office he at once becomes ambiguous. Fox seemed to him without question the candidate with the best claims for Pelham's posts of Chancellor of the Exchequer and Leader of the House, but he was afraid that if the King put all power into his hands the prospects of the Princess's regency would become precarious.[1] This danger might, he said, be averted if Fox's elevation were counterbalanced by

[1] In one of his letters Pitt says that he himself felt unequal to the Exchequer but not to the Secretaryship.

favours shown to their own small party, 'by marks of Royal favour, one of the connection put into the Cabinet, and called to a real participation of councils and business.' But there was to be no hint of faction : reserve might be shown towards those who come ' to fish and sound your dispositions, without authority to make direct propositions'; but even in case of disappointment, 'I don't think quitting of offices at all advisable, for public or private accounts; but as to answering any further purposes in the House of Commons, that must depend on the King's will and pleasure to enable us so to do.' In a third letter of the same day, addressed to Temple, Pitt warns him to preach prudence and reserve to Sir George Lyttelton, who is indiscreet. Fox, he repeats, is the most likely to obtain the Exchequer, Grenville in that case should accept an offer of the Secretaryship at War; 'the Chancellor is the only resource; his wisdom, temper, and authority, joined to the Duke of Newcastle's ability as Secretary of State, are the dependence for Government. The Duke of Newcastle alone is feeble : this not to Sir George.'

From these somewhat involved utterances it is obvious that Pitt at first expected that the chief change in the Ministry would be the promotion of Fox to Pelham's places and that he would have acquiesced in it, provided that the Cabinet were at the same time strengthened by the admission of one of their connection, who would most naturally be himself. But he never said so explicitly. A day or two later, however, he got a letter from Lyttelton, describing an interview with Hardwicke, and letters from Hardwicke and Newcastle, which seem to have dashed any personal hopes he may have held. None of these letters is extant, but it is clear from Pitt's answers that he was asked for his views on the conduct of business in the House of Commons, and that Hardwicke even dropped a hint that, had it been possible to overcome the King's prejudice, he might himself have been offered the Exchequer and the lead in the Commons. Whatever the proposal to him was, it was nothing definite, and in reply Pitt became even more oracular than before, both as to his own wishes and the policy his friends should pursue. He seemed more anxious to await the proposals of others than to state his own, and might have done better for himself could he have brought himself frankly to formulate his demands. But he had little confidence in the discretion of Lyttelton, who, in spite of his warning to Temple, had either constituted himself or been deputed by the others to be their mouthpiece. On March 10 Pitt wrote him two letters, one for his private use, the other to be shown to Hardwicke in response to his overtures. In the private letter he told him that though ' far from meaning to recommend a sullen, dark, much less a double, conduct, . . . and determined not to go into faction . . . I mean not to open myself to whoever pleases to sound my dispositions . . . and by premature declarations, deprive ourselves of the only chance we have of deriving any consideration to ourselves from the mutual fears and animosities of different factions at Court.' In the letter meant for the Chancellor's eye indignation at the King's continued exclusion of him moved him for the first time to more open language about himself. Even if the King were willing, he would never, he hinted, have aspired to Pelham's place, but he was none the less disgusted at being thought unworthy of any promotion :

I am so truly and deeply conscious [he wrote] of so many of my wants in Parliament and out of it to supply in the smallest degree this irreparable loss, that I can say with much truth were my health restored and his Majesty brought from the dearth of subjects to hear of my name for so great a change, I should wish to decline the honour, even though accompany'd with the attribution of all the weight and strength which the good opinion and confidence of the master cannot fail to add to a servant; but under impressions in the Royal mind towards me, the reverse of these, what must be the vanity which would attempt it ? . . . I need not suggest to his Lordship that consideration and weight in the House of Commons arises generally but from one of two causes—the protection and countenance of the Crown, visibly manifested by marks of Royal Favour at Court, or from weight in the country, sometimes arising from opposition to the public measures. This latter sort of consideration it is a great satisfaction to me to reflect I parted with, as soon as I became convinced there might be danger to the family from pursuing opposition any further ; and I need not say I have not had the honour to receive any of the former since I became the King's servant. In this humiliating and not exaggerated view of my situation within the House, of how little weight can I flatter myself to be there ? . . .'

Next day he wrote to the Duke of Newcastle, with whom his personal connection, as he reminded Lyttelton, had a peculiar circumstance of obligation, referring him to Lord Hardwicke for his views, and bidding him 'summon all your fortitude and recover Yourself into action as soon as you can ; the more irreparable the King's and the Publick's loss is, the more there is incumbent upon your Grace's shoulders.' To Temple he dashes off a few breathless sentences :

The essence . . . is to talk modestly, to declare attachment to the *King's* government, and the future plan *under the Princess*, neither to intend nor to intimate the quitting the service, to give no terrors by talking big, to make no declarations of thinking ourselves free by Mr. Pelham's death to look out and fish in troubled waters, and perhaps help trouble them in order to fish the better : but to profess and to resolve *bona fide* to act like public men in a dangerous conjuncture for our country, and support government when they will please to settle it ; to let them see that we shall do this from *principles of public good*, not as *the bubbles* of a few fair words, without effects (all this civilly) . . . and *saying very explicitly*, as I have (but civilly), that we have our eyes open to our situation at Court, and the foul play we have had offered us in the Closet : to wait the working of all these things in offices, the best we can have, but in offices.

Keep the party together, he urges him, and gain new adherents ; 'pardon, my dear Lord, all this freedom, but the conjuncture is made to awaken men and there is room for action.'

After his letters of March 11 he ceased attempting to influence the course of events. On the 12th Grenville wrote deploring his absence ; in his answer of the 14th Pitt lamented his inability to travel for at least a week, in spite of his ' need of seeing the faces of my friends again, after a long absence, and tedious scene of pain and confinement.' On March 20 he had still no news of a ministry and wrote to Lyttelton for information. Meanwhile he had been philosophically trying to kill time by reading Bolingbroke's 'Essay of Human Knowledge,' published on the day of Pelham's death. His verdict on it was not favourable: 'The work contains a vast compass of reading; it is writ with much clearness, great eloquence, as much wit, and still more arrogance; but I find it in some parts, not a few, filled with repetitions, from my Lord's fondness of the matter. The arrogance is so excessive that, great as the performance is, it becomes often even ridiculous.'

Lyttelton's letter announcing the changes in the Ministry did not reach Pitt till the evening of the 23rd, although it had been already settled to the satisfaction of Newcastle and Hardwicke and announced nearly a week before.[1]

Newcastle had been so utterly unmanned by his brother's death that for some days afterwards he shut himself up and gave full vent to his grief. But his interests, left in Hardwicke's capable hands, profited rather than suffered by his absence. Hardwicke found the King, as Pitt had expected, inclined to pitch upon Fox as Pelham's successor. Fox had undoubted claims. He was a first-rate debater, clear, concise, and business-like; he understood the work and temper of the House of Commons, and had all the capacity requisite for managing the national finances. He had not, it is true, a spark of enthusiasm or of ambition that was not sordid and personal, and he was cynical in his judgment of men's motives and of national questions. But these characteristics were merits in the eyes of those whose chief desire in politics was to avoid trouble and excitement. He had a special claim to the King's favour as the trusted adviser of his favourite son, the Duke of Cumberland. But Hardwicke cherished a grudge against him. In the previous year his favourite Clandestine Marriage Bill had been riddled with invective and sarcasm by Fox, whose sympathy with oppressed lovers was heightened by his own romantic elopement with a great-granddaughter of Charles II; Hardwicke had retorted in the House of Lords, describing the Secretary at War as 'a dark

[1] On the 18th Lyttelton wrote to Grenville suggesting that an express should be sent to Pitt. But this was apparently not done.

and insidious genius, the engine of personality and faction.' The alliance, too, with Cumberland, which recommended Fox to the King, rendered him suspect to Newcastle and Hardwicke, who had no desire to alienate the future Regent. But their supreme objection to him was that if, in addition to the power of the sword, which he wielded through the Duke of Cumberland, he also controlled the Treasury and the House of Commons, he would entirely overshadow them.

Fox himself did not let the grass grow under his feet. Hardly were Pelham's eyes closed than he called on Hardwicke and sent three humble messages of apology to him for his former attacks. He also called at Pitt's house on the same morning, not knowing that he was at Bath, and before eight was closeted with the Marquis of Hartington, who acted as his intermediary in the subsequent negotiations; for in those days of delicate personal questions principals hardly ever began negotiations, preferring the advocacy of third parties who could proclaim their merits with more effrontery. With the King he exchanged communications through the channel of his mistress, Lady Yarmouth.

Hardwicke was far too astute to oppose the King's idea about Fox openly. But he threw out hints which undermined the King's prepossessions, and so contrived to have the matter referred to a Cabinet Council. Since the Cabinet consisted almost entirely of Newcastle's puppets, Hardwicke could dictate to them the substance and even the wording of their advice.[1] Their opinion therefore was unanimous that Newcastle should become First Lord of the Treasury, with a Chancellor of the Exchequer in the Commons entirely subordinate to him. Under this arrangement Newcastle would retain in his own hands not only the conduct of elections and the government of patronage but also the ' management ' (a polite term for bribery) of the members of the House. The leadership of the Commons, with powers clipped by such conditions, could then safely be offered to Fox in conjunction with the seals of Secretary of State vacated by Newcastle. Legge,

[1] See Harris, *Hardwicke*, ii, 511: Hardwicke to the Archbishop of Canterbury, March 11, 1754.

an adherent of Pitt, but not thought to have much strength of character, was made Chancellor of the Exchequer.

Hartington conveyed the offer of the seals to Fox with a promise from Newcastle that he should always be informed of the members in receipt of secret service money. But when Fox came to see Newcastle, the Duke repudiated his engagement and told Fox that the 'management' of the House, which he was to lead, must be kept secret from him. Fox remarked that in that case 'he should not know how to talk to members of Parliament, when some might have received *gratifications*, others not'; and on the following day retracted his acceptance. Nothing could have pleased Newcastle and Hardwicke more; they had put themselves in the right with the King by offering the post to Fox, who by refusing it had left himself little ostensible ground of complaint. Without a thought of any other candidate, and with almost indecent haste, Newcastle at once suggested for the post Sir Thomas Robinson, who had been a tiresome ambassador at Vienna, chiefly remarkable for his portentously long dispatches, and was now Master of the Great Wardrobe. He pleased the King by his detailed knowledge of German politics, and the Duke of Newcastle by his nullity and inexperience of the House of Commons: he was therefore proposed and accepted with alacrity. Supported by two such Secretaries of State as Robinson and Holderness, Newcastle could be secure of any rivalry in the Cabinet. How far he had strengthened the Government remained to be seen.

Lyttelton, who had been acting for the Cousinhood, actually answered for Pitt's acquiescence in this ridiculous arrangement. For himself he secured the dignified employment of Cofferer of the Household, and for George Grenville, Legge's lucrative post of Treasurer of the Navy. It is quite intelligible in the circumstances that Lyttelton and Grenville should have been in no hurry to inform Pitt of the result of their negotiations. Even when Lyttelton wrote on the 23rd he apparently said nothing of his own and Grenville's appointments. It is more remarkable that, except for Hardwicke's vague and probably insincere hint, nobody of Newcastle's junto seems to have given a serious thought to Pitt. Fox they were afraid of and successfully out-manœuvred ; Pitt was absent, his friends made no energetic bid for his claims, and his eight years of loyal service to the Pelhams had blotted out the memory of his power when roused to opposition. So little were they conscious of the enormity of their neglect, that it did not occur to Newcastle and Hardwicke even to throw him a word of explanation. But Lyttelton had some qualms as to the way in which he might take the news, and, on the day he wrote himself, implored Hardwicke to send Pitt a conciliatory epistle.

Sick and solitary at Bath, Pitt received Lyttelton's express late on the night of the 23rd. Even his philosophy was not proof against the blow. He might have suffered himself once more to be passed over, if union and strength had been secured, but to be passed over for a Sir Thomas Robinson was more than his pride and his consciousness of supreme capacity could brook. His night was restless and troubled. Next morning indignation spurred him to the only action then possible. All the obscurity of his language was suddenly dispelled by the blast of his wrath. He wrote Newcastle a letter, which could leave him under no further misapprehension of the force he had neglected and by his neglect aroused:

Bath. March 24, 1754.

My Lord Duke,—I have heard with the highest satisfaction by a message from Sir George Lyttelton the effectual proofs of his Majesty's great kindness and firm confidence in your Grace for the conduct of his Government.

You have certainly taken most wisely the Province of the Treasury to yourself, where the powers of Government reside, and which at this particular crisis of a General Election may lay the foundations of the future political system so fast as not to be shaken hereafter. But this will depend upon many concomitant circumstances. For the present the nation may say with consolation, ' uno avulso non deficit alter aureus.' The power of the Purse in the hands of the same family may, I trust, be so used as to fix all other power there along with it. Amidst all the real satisfaction I feel on this great measure so happily taken, it is with infinite reluctance that I am forced to return to the mortifying situation of your Grace's humblest servant. . . . The difficulties grow so fast upon me by the repetition and multiplication of most painfull and too visible humiliations that my small store of prudence suggests no longer to me any means of colouring them to the world; nor of repairing them to my own mind consistently with my unshaken purpose to do nothing on any provocation to disturb the quiet of the King and the ease and stability of present and future Government. Permit, my Lord, a man, whose affectionate attachment to your Grace, I believe, you don't doubt, to expose simply to your view his situation, and then let me intreat your Grace (if you can divest your mind of the great disparity between us), to transport yourself for a moment into my place. From the time I had the honour to come into the King's service, I have never been wanting in my most zealous endeavours in Parliament on the points that laboured the most, those of military discipline and foreign affairs; nor have I differ'd on any whatever but the too small number of seamen one year, which was admitted to be so the next; and on a crying complaint against General Anstruther: for these crimes how am I punish'd? Be the want of subjects ever so great and the force of the conjuncture ever so cogent, be my best friends and protectors ever so much at the head of the Government, an indelible negative is fixed against my name. Since I had the honour to return that answer to the Chancellor which Your Grace and his Lordship were pleas'd not to disapprove, how have mortifications been multiply'd upon me. One Chancellor of the Exchequer over me was at that time destin'd, Mr. Fox: since that time a second, Mr. Legge, is fixt: A Secretary of State is next to be look'd for in the House of Commons. Mr. Fox is again put over me and destin'd to that office: he refuses the seals: Sir Thomas Robinson is immediately put over me and is now in possession of that great office. I sincerely think both these high employments much better fill'd than I cou'd supply either of them in many respects. Mr. Legge I truely and cordially esteem and love. Sir Thos. Robinson, with whom I have not the honour to live in the same intimacy, I sincerely believe to be a gentleman of much worth and ability. Nevertheless I will venture to appeal to your Grace's candour and justice whether upon such feeble pretensions, as twenty years' use of Parliament may have given me, I have not some cause to feel (as I do most deeply) so many repeated and visible humiliations. I have troubled your Grace so long on this painful subject that I may have nothing disagreeable to say when I have the honour to wait on you; as well as that I think it fit your Grace shou'd know the whole heart of a faithfull servant, who is conscious of nothing towards your Grace which he wishes to conceal from you. In my degraded situation in Parliament, an active part there I am sure your Grace is too equitable to desire me to take; for otherwise than as an associate and in equal rank with those charg'd with Government there, I never can take such a part.

I will confess I had flatter'd myself that the interests of your Grace's own power were so concern'd to bring forward an instrument of your own raising in the House of Commons that you cou'd not let pass this decisive occasion without surmounting in the royal mind the unfavourable impressions I have the unhappiness to be under; and that the seals (at least when refus'd by Mr. Fox) might have been destin'd as soon as an opening cou'd be made in the King's mind in my favour instead of being immediately put into other hands. Things standing as they do, whether I can continue in office without losing myself in the opinion of the world is become a matter of very painful doubt to me. . . . I am most sure that my mind carries me more strongly towards retreat than towards courts and business. Indeed, My Lord, the inside of the House must be consider'd in other respects besides merely numbers, or the reins of Government will soon slip or be wrested out of any minister's hands. If I have spoken too freely, I humbly beg your Grace's pardon: and entreat you to impute my freedom to the most sincere and unalterable attachment of a man who never will conceal his heart, and who can complain without alienation of mind and remonstrate without resentment.

Pitt enclosed this letter under flying seal to Lyttelton for the Cousinhood to see before it was sent on to Newcastle. He also wrote to Lyttelton, Temple and Grenville. The effort was almost beyond his strength: at the end of the note to Temple he says, ' I am so tired I cannot hold my head down to write any longer.' Yet even after that he managed to scrawl a few lines to Grenville. In the letter to Lyttelton he writes:

My plan still continues fixed, not to quit employments; merely quitting is annihilation; quitting to disturb Government, and make ourselves be felt, must at this time be faction; and faction for others' benefit, not our own: it must increase the present confusion, and produce a system I never think right for this country. Were this conduct sure to turn to our own benefit in the scramble, I can never bring my mind to engage in faction, in so dangerous a public conjuncture.

To Temple, who had apparently written him an indignant letter of sympathy:

DESPONDENCY

Employment may not to us be the place of dignity, but sure I am it is that of importance. . . . All Achilles as you are, Impiger, Iracundus &c., what would avail us to sail back a few myrmidons to Thessaly! Go over to the Trojans, be revenged, we none of us can bear the thought of. What then remains? The conduct of the much enduring man, who by temper, patience and persevering prudence became *adversis rerum immersabilis undis.*

Immersabilis he proved, and a certain grim belief in himself and in the country pierces through even his bitterest mood. To Grenville he writes 'a letter worthy of a profound politician in these dark times—that is, to say nothing. When the day will dawn (for to my poor eyes it is not even twilight at present) I cannot guess: when it comes may it show us a view men will see with pleasure, and not wish to change!' Then, throwing off political preoccupations, he enters upon another criticism of Bolingbroke, 'that intellectual Sampson of Battersea.'

I endeavour, you see, to keep my mind—as far as I can, abstracted from what you gentlemen at London are pleased to call the great world, and which we philosophers at Bath call the little; and instead of such trifles as the government of millions, fate of kingdoms and system of Europe, to hold our minds fixed on the contemplation of nature's system and intellectual and moral worlds.

It was a brave pose, half sincere too, for a few days later he returns to his correspondence with his nephew, which had been interrupted by his illness, without a hint to him of his political disappointment, and, on April 1, genially congratulates his friend Billy Lyttelton on his appointment as sub-Cofferer to his brother:

I wished to see you put into the stream of promotion, which by its natural current, and the right of succession in the gradation of office (tho' not always held indefeasible) commonly bears men to fortune. . . . You will do such work as there is, while the Cofferer reposes in the shades of Hagley and dispenses his own fat bucks.

Meanwhile Newcastle and Hardwicke had been rudely awakened from their fool's paradise. At first Newcastle, in an interview with Lyttelton, had shown scant consideration for

Pitt's claims; but Pitt's letter recalled him and Hardwicke to a dim apprehension of the sleeping volcano on which they had unwarily trodden. It was all very well to have a submissive Ministry, but if the most terrible critic in the House was not equally submissive—even if, as he threatened, he ostentatiously retired from active politics—their troubles might not yet be over. Lyttelton had already warned Hardwicke to pacify Pitt: they began to see the need of it themselves. After long and anxious consideration and an interchange of one another's drafts,[1] on April 2 they each sent him a propitiatory letter full of vague promises and halting apologies. Of the two, Hardwicke's with its self-satisfied obtuseness and its wearisome Latin tags, is the more nauseous. After recounting his successful efforts to make Newcastle Prime Minister, he hints that he attempted to overcome the King's prejudice against Pitt. 'It might have the appearance of something which I would avoid being suspected of, if I told you all I said of particular persons. I was not wanting to do justice to true merit nor backward to show him how real strength might be acquired.' However, ministers cannot do all they want, and Pitt ought to be satisfied with his friends' promotion; above all let him not retire; there had been no neglects as far as he himself and the Duke of Newcastle were concerned. 'I have that opinion of your wisdom, of your concern for the publick, of your regard and affection for your friends, that I will not suffer myself to doubt but you will take an active part. There never was a fairer field in the House of Commons for such abilities, and I flatter myself that the exertion of them will complete what is now imperfect.' Hardwicke lived to regret the 'active part' he here encourages.

The duke was quite pathetic about his own painful situation, aggravated as it was by his uneasiness at Pitt's disappointment. He draws a harrowing picture of his melancholy and distress at being forced by the commands of the King and the entreaties of his friends to give up the 'employment he loved' in exchange for the chief power in the State. He had done all he could to soften the King towards Pitt without imperilling his own

[1] *Add. MSS.* 32735, ff. 1 and 20; 35414, f. 135.

position. He would not have dreamed of insulting Pitt by offering him the post of Chancellor of the Exchequer where he would have been subordinate to himself, and as for Robinson, the King himself had proposed him of his own motion. Newcastle then offers the reflection of his friends' promotion as a consolation to Pitt ' I feel for you ; but allow me to say (because I think it) that even with regard to yourself the dispositions are not so mortifying as they might have been, and with regard to your friends, more favourable than perhaps was to be expected.' After this cold comfort comes the effusive ending : ' I am afraid I have wrote too freely. My love and affection for you are my only excuses. When once I begin to write to a friend like you, I write all I think upon the subject.'

Such letters were calculated to inflame rather than to soothe Pitt's resentments ;[1] and their tenor together with his own sad reflections for a time damped even his high courage, causing him to consider seriously whether he should not abandon the apparently hopeless struggle in Parliament and seek some office where ambition had no place. His answers were written at once, on April 4, and sent with this commentary to Lyttelton :

The Duke of Newcastle's letter to me, ... is writ with a condescension and in terms so flattering, that it pains me. I am almost tempted to think there is kindness at the bottom of it, *which if left to itself, would before now have shewed itself* in effects. If I have not the fruit, I have the leaves of it in abundance : a beautiful foliage of fine words ; and if lulling one to sleep would satisfy his Grace, I am quite disposed *à m'endormir, à l'ombre de ses lauriers*, not as de Retz says of the Prince of Condé, of my own. The Chancellor's letter is the most condescending, friendly, obliging thing that can be imagined. I have the deepest sense of his goodness for me ; but

---

[1] The sincerity of Newcastle and Hardwicke in these letters may be judged from the comment by the second Lord Hardwicke, noted on the draft of his father's letter of April 2 (*Add. MSS.* 35423, f. 172) :

'The fact is that this letter tho' prudently and skilfully drawn had no effect with Mr. P. His ill-humour broke out the beginning of next session and he never thought the old M——rs. were in earnest to serve him. The Truth is one [Newcastle] had no mind to have an efficient minister in the H. of C. : and the other [Hardwicke] knew that it would be drawing the King's resentment on himself to propose Mr. P. for the only office wh. wd. have satisfied h:m.'

I am really compelled, by every reason fit for a man to listen to, to resist (as to the point of activity in Parliament) farther than I like to do. . . . Resolved not to disturb Government, I desire to be released from the oar of Parliamentary drudgery. I am willing to sit there, and be ready to be called out into action, when the Duke of Newcastle's personal interests might require, or Government should deign to employ me as an instrument. . . . I am not fond of making speeches (though some may think I am). I never cultivated the talent but as an instrument of action in a country like ours.[1]

In answer to Newcastle's letter Pitt wonders how he shall find words to express his sense ' of the great condescension and kindness with which it is writ '; then, taking up one of the duke's own expressions—

it is most obliging to suggest as consolations to me that I might have been much more mortify'd under another management than under the present: but I will freely own I should have felt myself far less personally humiliated, had Mr. Fox been placed by the king's favour at the head of the House of Commons, than I am at present: in that case the necessity would have been apparent: the ability of the subject would in some degree have warranted the thing. I should indeed have been much mortify'd for your Grace and for my Lord Chancellor: very little for my own particular. Could Mr. Murray's situation have allow'd him to be placed at the head of the House of Commons, I should have served under him with the greatest pleasure: I acknowledge as much as the rest of the world do his superiority in every respect. My mortification arises not from silly pride, but from being evidently excluded by a negative personal to me (now and for ever) flowing from a displeasure utterly irremovable. . . . To conclude, my Lord, and to release your Grace from a troublesome correspondent, give me leave to recur to your Grace's equity and candour: when the suffrage of the party in one instance, and a higher nomination, the Royal designation in another, operate to the eternal precluding of a man's name being so much as brought in question, what reasonable wish can remain for a man so circumstanced (under a fixt resolution not to disturb government) but that of a

---

[1] 'It is a kind of epoch,' says Carlyle, ' in your studies of modern English history, when you get to understand of Pitt's speeches, that they are not Parliamentary eloquencies, but things which with his whole soul he means and is intent to *do*.' It is hardly likely that Carlyle had seen this confession of Pitt's, but he divined Pitt's nature and once hoped to write his life. *Utinam!*

decent retreat; a retreat of respect, not resentment: of despair of being ever accepted to equal terms with others, be his poor endeavours ever so zealous. Very few have been the advantages and honours of my life: but among the first of them I shall ever esteem the honour of your Grace's good opinion: to that good opinion and protection I recommend myself: and hope from it that some retreat, neither disagreeable nor dishonourable, may (when practicable) be open'd to me.

To Hardwicke he wrote very much to the same effect. After a solemn expression of gratitude for his efforts in the Closet: 'your Lordship,' he adds with grave sarcasm, 'will not think me unreasonable, if I conclude from the inefficacy of these efforts in such a want of subjects to carry on the King's business in Parliament, and under his Majesty's strong sense of that want, that these impressions are immoveable.' Having set out ten years before with the same vague hopes that time would remove these impressions—

and bearing long a load of obloquy for supporting the King's measures and never obtaining in recompense the smallest remission of that displeasure I vainly endeavoured to soften, all ardour for public business is really extinguished in my mind. . . . The weight of irremoveable royal displeasure is a load too great to move under: it must crush any man; it has sunk and broke me. I succumb; and wish for nothing but a decent and innocent retreat, wherein I may no longer, by continuing in the public stream of promotion, for ever stick fast aground, and afford to the world the ridiculous spectacle of being passed by every boat that navigates the same river.

Pitt's outbursts of scornful despair and his demands for a 'decent and innocent retreat' are not surprising, when it is remembered that this man had already done the lion's share in laying low two great ministers, and was conscious within himself that he could create even better than he could destroy, while the country for which he cared was left at a grave crisis to an incompetent and unrepresentative Ministry. The Duke of Newcastle took care to let Pitt's request be known, and years afterwards it was distorted into a charge that he had abjectly begged for a pension. Pitt had then forgotten the incident: all he could remember was that he had for two years been almost disabled from attending Parliament by illness, and might have preferred retreat to office. 'But produce the letter, if it exists,' he wrote. This neither Newcastle nor anyone else cared to do.[1]

Pitt continued in this mood for the rest of his sojourn at Bath. At the general election he was nominated for Aldborough by Newcastle in fulfilment of last year's promise. But he was too ill to present himself before the electors, and with Newcastle's consent dispensed with the useless formality. When thanking Newcastle, he speaks of himself as a 'very useless person, and who, I fear, fills the place of a better man. I consider my political life as some way or other drawing to a conclusion.' He adds that if he can in any way serve his Grace in private life he would be delighted to do so, and when his election is announced by the Duke, congratulates himself solemnly on 'standing thus publicly marked as your servant,' an hyperbolical compliment which at any rate shows that he had not yet plumbed the depths of Hardwicke and Newcastle's meanness in using the King's obstinacy as a cloak for their own ambitions, and had no thoughts as yet of active opposition. He was somewhat cheered in his loneliness by a visit from Temple and Grenville early in May, but continued to write of retreat as his sole wish, 'since I am never to be suffered to try to serve my country.' With slowly returning health he professed to have no desire to see London, 'a scene that administers no kind of satisfaction,' and to find complete satisfaction living 'the vernal day on verdant hills or sequestered valleys where ... Health gushes from a thousand springs.'

In June he came up to town for a few days and had a conversation with Newcastle. From this date his anger seems to have taken a more definite turn against him and Hardwicke. For the first time he saw the full extent of the trickery that had been practised upon him, and felt that they might well have overcome the King's aversion, had they been so minded. Henceforth nothing more is heard

[1] The draft of Pitt's answer to the charge that he had 'applied for a pension to a Duke' about five years before is in *Chatham MSS.* 74.

of Pitt's anxiety to retire: he never again spoke of himself as 'publicly marked for the Duke's servant': he felt there was something still left to fight for.[1] But even with this animating thought he was more lonely and more at odds with the world than at any other time of his life. His closest kindred were estranged from him: Lyttelton, his friend from Eton days, had failed him; Legge, a mere adherent, had passed him in the race. Of all his political friends the Grenvilles and Beckford alone remained faithful. In August news came of a serious disaster in America to a party of soldiers who were travelling in British territory under one George Washington; and the country seemed ill-prepared for the war which all foreseeing men knew to be at hand. He passed a melancholy summer, planting trees at the worthy Mr. Miller's in Warwickshire, or watching undergraduate frolics from the Angel at Oxford. Even these mild pleasures were cut short. The gout returned and he was obliged to spend another three weeks nursing it in his 'dungeon' at Astrop Wells.

It was at this darkest moment in his life that the ray of light came to him, which illuminated and cheered all the rest of his days.[2]

II

Is it any waste of time to write of love? The trials of life are in it, but in a narrow ring and a fierier. . . . The love that survives . . . lives because it lives to nourish and succour like the heavens.—GEORGE MEREDITH.

By the year 1754 it appeared unlikely that Pitt would ever marry. He was then forty-six, and physically seemed older, owing to the crippling attacks of gout to which he had been subject during the last few years. Moreover, in spite of his craving for domestic affection manifested in his early relations with Ann, and, after her estrangement, in the care he lavished

[1] This may be gathered from indications in Dodington, *Diary*, pp. 303-6.
[2] A tabular list of correspondence is inserted on p. 249.

on his nephew, he was evidently a man not lightly attracted by women. His passing infatuation for the unknown lady at Besancon, 'une de ces flammes passagères, un éclair qui a passé si vîte qu'il n'en reste pas le moindre vestige,'[1] is the only certain instance hitherto of an intrusion of the tender passion into his thoughts. A hint of another passing inclination is supplied by Horace Walpole, who insinuates that Pitt had supplanted the Prince of Wales in Lady Archibald Hamilton's affections; but of this there is no better evidence. He had not lacked opportunities to marry, for his brave spirit, his noble bearing, and a certain mystery about him made him exceedingly attractive to women. Mrs. Montagu, when she was young and less formidable than she afterwards became, seemed to think no one comparable to him. Her sister, Sarah Robinson, just twenty when he was thirty-five, had 'no inclination to dance with any man but Mr. Pitt, and that I have not acquaintance enough with him to expect; I can only cherish my hopes of future good fortune.' Mary West, often thrown into the society of her brother's friend, appears to have lost her heart to him.[2] But he had always held aloof and seemed untouched.

Yet at the age of forty-six Pitt suddenly discovered a passionate love for one whom he had known and frequently seen for at least twenty years. Lady Hester, the Grenvilles' only sister, was then thirty-three. A portrait of her at Chevening, painted by Hudson when she was twenty-nine, represents her as a young woman full of health and vigour. Rich auburn hair crowns a head set straight and proudly upon her shoulders. She looks a great lady, as well as the sweet and frank woman that the loving tradition in the family still recalls her to have been.[3] Most of her life had been spent in the country at Stowe or Wotton. She was a good horsewoman and fond of climbing hills afoot. Practical and with all her family's business capacity, she shared their zeal for politics. Of friends she had plenty among the girls and women of her brothers' set, the

---

[1] See above, p. 45.
[2] She is possibly the 'pretty little M.' referred to by Lyttelton, above, p. 40.
[3] The portrait of Lady Hester at Orwell Park, reproduced opposite p. 248, appears to have been painted in 1747, when she was twenty-six.

chief being Elizabeth Wyndham, a warm-hearted creature, who had married George Grenville in 1749.[1] She also enjoyed to the full the privileges which come to an only sister much beloved by five vigorous brothers. Thomas, the sailor brother, who was killed in action in 1747, was especially devoted to her. 'Remember me to all the jolly folks with you wherever you are, and God bless you,' he writes with a sailor's bluffness in one of his letters; in another, 'I desire my brother Grenville will by virtue of this letter supply you with as much as you want of the money of mine in his hands, and I beg most earnestly of you that you will make no womanish scruples about taking it.'[2] But all loved their sister Hetty in their several ways, Lord Temple with his coarse joviality,[3] George with priggish airs of protection, Jemmy jocose but with the most enduring faithfulness, while Henry, the youngest, seems at this time to have been very dear to her.

She had already had more than one admirer. Ten years before, her brother Jemmy, in reference to one of these, wrote to his 'incomparable Meg of Wotton,' rejoicing 'that there is a prospect of getting you off to Simon Truelove. He really deserves to have you and it is impossible to hope for a more advantageous proposal. My dear Meg you grow old and it is time to think of a decent retirement from business.'[4] When she was twenty-five there was much talk in George Grenville and Elizabeth Wyndham's letters of a certain Captain Geary, who would seem to have touched her affections during a summer they spent together at Tunbridge Wells.[5] Her cousin Richard Berenger, an authority on horsemanship, wherein they had a taste in common, at one time had tender passages with her, and there are dark allusions in a letter from her friend Jane Hamilton to yet another suitor who was rejected, but still proved troublesome.

---

[1] There is a portrait of her at Stowe.   [2] *Chatham MSS.* 38.

[3] George Grenville in his *Narrative* says that Lady Hester complained of Temple's treatment of her; but little weight need be attached to this statement, which was written at a time when Grenville was raking up every grievance he could against his brother, and is not confirmed by the evidence of Temple's conduct.

[4] *Chatham MSS.* 35.   [5] *Ibid.* 34.

A very likely reason for Lady Hester's obduracy was that she had long admired and perhaps unconsciously loved her brothers' eloquent friend. She treasured up some insignificant notes written by him more than a year before he declared himself. Her sister-in-law had for several years divined that information about him would be acceptable to her. Jane Hamilton too, writing soon after her own marriage to Lord Cathcart in 1753, follows up some charming advice—'Je vous recommende un Marriage comme le mien, ma chere Amie, il n'y a rien de pareil pour le bonheur'—with the pointed conclusion: 'How could I be so stupid to omit telling you that I saw Mr. Pitt at Bath Court on Sunday and He looks well and is thought to be so but is a little thin?' The same lady shrewdly observes, when the engagement was announced, 'As you well remember my wishes have long ago given you to him.'[1]

Pitt himself was for long blind to the happiness he might have secured. There is not a hint in his correspondence or in family tradition that he thought of Lady Hester as a wife when she was growing to womanhood. Up to the last her brothers had no suspicion that such a marriage was possible ; the Temples expressing 'great surprise at the blindness that had prevail'd, and which they appear'd very fond of insisting upon.' There is a formal note of regret from him written before 1753 that a party arranged to take Lady Hester to see South Lodge had fallen through, but, though she treasured it, it bears no indication of warm feelings in the writer. In 1753, however, when he was on the eve of departure for Tunbridge Wells, almost broken in health, the two met several times in London, and Lady Hester by words and letters showed a concern for his welfare which touched him deeply.[2] There for over a year the matter rested.

During the early part of 1754 he was very ill at Bath and absorbed in the political situation ; in August, when he again 'began to want a little repairs,' he went for over a month to

---

[1] *Chatham MSS.* 26.

[2] These notes are attributed by Dr. Von Ruville to the period of courtship. Apart from the formal phraseology, the dates prevent such a supposition. Pitt gave up South Lodge in March 1753, and was not at Tunbridge Wells in 1754.

Astrop Wells. So little idea had he then of an early marriage that he planned to go for the last part of September to Legge's at Holte in Hampshire, thence to Bath, and later perhaps on a visit to John Pitt at Encombe.[1] However, he changed his mind, and at the end of September was staying with the Grenvilles at Wotton, then in all the beauty of its 'deep shades of oak, softening lawns and tranquil waters, like a lively smile lighting up a thoughtful countenance.' Here he found Lady Hester.

Little is known of Pitt's courtship save that it must have been sudden and brief. His heart had already, it seems, 'presumed to form wishes': he had been very few days at Wotton before he ventured to give them voice. One late September morning by the lake in the grounds he and Lady Hester opened their hearts to one another and confessed their mutual love. Once Pitt had made up his mind and won her love, he was carried off his feet by the strength of his passion; he was overwhelmed by the sense of her condescension to a man with 'health shattered and declined.' A few days later he wrote to her: 'I have the glory to be yours, and the happy happy permission to call you mine, and am animated by the thought to discharge any part I have to sustain and to aspire to be less unworthy of you.' She likewise was as if dazzled by love and pride for the man, whose greatness of soul and worth to England she was one of the few fully to recognise. With lovers in such mood, marriage could not long be delayed. But first he had to tear himself away from her for another three weeks to complete his cure at Bath. Later generations have cause to be grateful for this separation. The letters they exchanged during their absence from one another reveal a love to rejoice all lovers and to dignify and sweeten even Pitt's high fame.[2]

At the beginning of October Pitt left for London to talk to the Duke of Newcastle about his Chelsea Hospital Bill and the plans for America, then to Stowe to break the news to Temple,

---

[1] Chatterton, i, 72; S. Miller, 239.

[2] 'Stilted, pompous, artificial documents' these letters have been called by a recent writer. Surely it is possible to see, in spite of occasional lapses into the commonplace epithets and phrases current at the time, the wealth of passionate feeling and sincerity in his letters and hers.

and thence once more to Wotton. During this short absence she wrote a note to him, and he the letter in which he glories in his new-found happiness. 'In this painful interval . . . I shall, I do now press your sweet letter to my heart, run over every word, kiss every letter of it with transports of love and gratitude, blessing the noble, pitying heart that dictated and the dear hand that wrote it; ever, ever, devotedly yours.' He started for Bath on October 9 in storms and rain.

She writes to him that night: 'The storms have given me a thousand fears . . . for poor travellers,' and after affectionate compliments from her family sends him 'something infinitely beyond from myself.'

On October 12, from Bath, the poor traveller tells her of his journey, 'for your goodness has made it not impertinent to talk to you of myself,' a new and surprising sensation for this solitary man. He describes having to walk up Lansdown Hill in the tempest; at the top a good omen!—the monument to Sir Bevill Grenville—which 'sheltered me from the storm that drove.' In the next letter he answers hers: 'Who speaks, who looks, who writes, but above all who could have the generosity to feel, as you? . . . let me read for ever that "*something infinitely beyond*" which could make even the conclusion of your letter sweet to my soul above my powers of language to tell you.'

In averting injury from her lover, she replies, Grenville's monument 'has not done less service to our England but much more' than any Grenville could.

No joy can equal mine in having reason to believe your happiness depends upon me, because the highest ambition and the fondest wish I can form is to bestow it upon you, who are worthy of more than I could bestow, had I all that the world could give. The thought that I am in possession of your Heart is a pleasure and flattery beyond every other. How amply you repay me for every mark of Preference and Love that I can give you! My fame, my Pride, my Glory is centred in you, and I every day approve myself for the admiration, Adoration I had rather say, which my mind pays to y^r virtue and perfections. . . . Her whom you have made *yours* [she signs herself], a word I love to repeat because I know you love to read it.

'How often do I read,' says Pitt, 'and kiss the word, you say you love to repeat because I love to read it? In spite of cruel distance, with fondness looking on your Charms with my mind, and folding them with transport in my Heart, how can I talk to any thing but you?'

A letter of his, which was to have been 'the healing blessing of that day,' has been delayed; fond fears she has had in the past revive, and she tells him of them.

'Has then,' he asks, 'that Preference and love, which you so nobly bestow and so tenderly confess already cost you so many uneasy hours? . . . What Guardian angel of mine can have so blinded you, and pour'd into your noble Heart a tender delusion so infinitely flattering to my glory and partial to my Happiness as to draw from you so sweet an excess of everything that can exalt and bless me above the lot of mortals? . . . You speak,' he adds, 'of my letters as a "healing blessing"; the end of yours to me is "a healing blessing" like the evening sun in Milton after clouds *with farewell sweet*, as he calls it, to cheer drooping nature.'

Her fears have fled even before his letters came:

You flatter me that I write expressively what I feel. If you could but know how poorly to myself my words seem to describe my sentiments. . . Ought not you to be angry if I could quit this Topick without telling you what your own letters deserve. Yes and yet I have but one short thing to say—you speak. That is the only way of praising what I would praise to the highest. . . . How many thanks do I pay you for having perswaded me that you receive y^r happiness from me. Adieu.

Pitt rides out with her brother to a farm near Bath where he had once seen her happy: 'The cascade, the river, the wood, all was delightful, for I saw you in them all the morning.' He fears that she cannot always believe him all that she now does: 'the tender delusion cannot last nor that discernment, blind to nothing else, shut its eyes in my favour—thus my fears.'

Never apply the term delusion [she answers] to the dear, and just idea I have formed of your Excellence and tell yourself that while Life continues I will never part with them. . . . I have either so much or so little of the woman in me that it is an opinion I am determined never to recede from.

They write to one another on the time and place of the marriage. 'The less Preparation,' urges Pitt, 'the less Spectacle, the less of everything but your lovely tender self, is surely best.'

On October 28 she arrived in London at her lodging in Argyle Street, which contained an 'Indian room,' of which they both were fond. A day or so later he returned, and thenceforward her letters to him before marriage cease. But though they see one another daily, Pitt's notes to her still continue. They are dashed off on odd slips of paper or on a card to welcome her on waking, or to tell her when he is coming to see her—dashed off in the midst of official business, after tiresome interviews with Newcastle, or in the intervals of the labour of preparing his Bill for the Chelsea Pensioners and introducing it into the House of Commons. He is if possible happier and more assured of her love than ever. He is never tired of telling her what he feels, interspersing, quaintly enough, with his heart's outpourings intimate details of his ailments and remedies: this no doubt in obedience to her commands. 'I am still not quite well,' runs one billet; 'the worst of my little disorder is that I cannot banquet, for such your delicious chicken is, in Argyle Street. Doctor Wilmot thinks the attack bilious . . . has ordered me an emetick.' 'I hope,' he says in another, 'to find voice enough to tell my adored Life, by and by, that every day and hour adds to my tenderness and most happy sentiments. I am as well as rhubarb will let me be, and hope to be better to-morrow for it.'

Sometimes his swift mind suggests Elizabethan conceits to convey the unceasing wonder he feels at his good fortune:

How shall I pass so long a morning without seeing the adored, tender object my eyes saw escape from them into her loved Indian room last night. It was, at that moment, hardly loved by me. I long for a sweet reconcilement with it, with an impatience you alone can mate and I feel. I am better this morning. What shall I be when I see my lovely loved Lady Hester? Hear the sweet language that her tender heart graces her lips with, and snatch the still sweeter and inexpressible bliss that for ever inhabits there? I hope to have measured that immense space from Whitehall to Argyle Buildings by two o'clock.

'This will find you in your Roxana's tent. Had you been there, the master of the world had never left it,' he scrawls another day; and on the day before the wedding:

I fear this note, late as it is for my anxious Impatience, may be too early in my loved Lady Hester's apartment. What joy will it be to hear she has slept well, and that she has waked free from every complaint: if so, may I tell myself that she does not disapprove my complaint that Friday is so long in moving out of the way of the sweet Day that follows it?

Happily there had been no obstacles to the marriage. The engagement had taken place under the approving eyes of George Grenville and his wife, Lady Hester's dear friend. Henry was delighted at 'an alliance which reflects so much honour to us all.' Jemmy, Lady Hester tells Pitt, 'came to Wotton to thank me, as he said, for giving him as a Brother the man that in the whole world he would have chose for his Honour and his pleasure, to call by that name.' To Temple, as the head of the family, Pitt went at once to seek an approval, which was ungrudgingly given, though the short delay before it came was an agony to Pitt. The warmth of Temple's reply is evident from the answer it evoked:

My dearest Lord [Pitt writes], I cannot suffer a day to pass without expressing a few of the thousand things I feel from your kindest, most amiable of letters to Lady Hester Grenville. You sent m from Stowe, the most blessed of men and every hour I live only brings me new and touching instances of the unceasing goodness and most affectionate and endearing partiality towards me, of the kind, noble and generous fraternity to which it is my glory and happiness to be raised. Don't imagine my dearest Lord, that these are the exaggerations of a heart thinking and talking of the brother of her that for ever fills it. . . . Your letter is the kindest that ever glowed from the best pen speaking the best heart. . . . How generous and how delicate it is in you to state me in the too flattering lights of your own partiality to the eyes of Lady Hester, and to help to furnish her with a kind of justification of, I fear, infinitely too great a sacrifice of her establishment.

This letter, with its overwhelming sense of gratitude, is characteristic of Pitt. With all his aloofness from people of whom he thought meanly, with all his noble self-confidence, he was throughout life intensely susceptible to acts of personal kindness. His pride was no doubt the reason they were rarely offered to him, but like many reserved men he hungered for them, and was all the more grateful when they came in his way. In later years, when George II and George III showed him honour, his expressions of gratitude were of almost oriental submissiveness. The seeming exaggeration reflected his profound sense of a distinction to which he was unaccustomed.

Pitt's friends were equally delighted. With Lyttelton he was on cool terms since the negotiations in March, and he did not even write to tell him of his engagement. But Lyttelton heard of it through Billy and showed a generous spirit in his whole-hearted congratulations to his friend: 'Nothing in my life ever gave me more Pleasure than your letter to my Brother. I know Lady Hester so well that I am sure the possession of her Hand and Heart will give you so much Happiness as my Affection can wish you; and no Friend you have can wish you more, not even her brothers.' Nor could anything be more charming than his phrase to Lady Hester: 'As your friend I congratulate you, and as his I love you for the choice that you have made.'

Legge rejoiced at 'the acquisition to the corps of us married men. . . . I think the breed will be a good one, and can't fail to speak as soon as they are born.' Pitt wrote to Ann directly Temple gave him leave to tell anybody outside the Grenville world, and Lady Hester also sent a shy note.[1] Ann responded to them both with warm congratulations. Mrs. Montagu allowed her satisfaction to appear veiled in mythological allusions to the days 'that Cupid set Hercules to the

---

[1] Though this letter is formal and stiff, it should be remembered that Lady Hester was a younger woman than Ann and did not know her. Moreover, the note to Pitt in which she forwarded it shows how anxious she was to make friends with his favourite sister.

PITT'S MARRIAGE, 1754

distaff'; and the witty Lady Townshend made a joke about the espousals of Solomon and Hester, which left even Horace Walpole's fashionable world in good humour at the engagement.

The settlement, a very formal affair in those days, did not delay the marriage long. As soon as Pitt had obtained Lord Temple's consent, he wrote off to his solicitor Nuthall to prepare the deeds, which were hastened in deference to his impatient instructions. He had little to settle on his side except reversionary interests, which never accrued to him. His interests as heir-presumptive to estates of the Duchess of Marlborough and to Spencer's Sunderland property he settled absolutely on Lady Hester; the Marlborough estates were to be unsettled to enable him to pay any debts on the Sunderland property, buy the borough of Old Sarum and build town and country houses.

On Saturday November 16, 1754, two days after the opening of the session, William Pitt and Lady Hester Grenville were married in her lodgings in Argyle Street. Dr. Ayscough, brother-in-law of George Lyttelton, and an old friend of both families, married them under special licence. A few friends only were present at the ceremony, and on the same day Pitt and his wife went to West's house at Wickham, lent them for their brief honeymoon. Although the provisions laid in by Pitt's cook, Mr. Campion, 'to testify in his own way his respects to his new Lady,' together with those left in the hospitable Mrs. West's larder, would have fed a multitude, 'they came down alone,' says West, 'and have continued alone ever since.' But they were undisturbed together for barely ten days. On the 25th Pitt was back in London making one of his greatest speeches, and, until Parliament adjourned in the middle of December, was kept busy at the House. She came with him to the Pay Office, where we hear much of her 'blew dressing-room' overlooking the Park. But even for the Christmas holidays they could not be left at peace together. He was forced to go for a hurried visit to Bath, partly on business, partly for more necessary repairs to his system. But their love was now secure. 'A thousand new circumstances,' he writes to his 'matchless Hetty,' 'endear my Love to me every day I live with Her. . . . Trials of a noble mind . . . have proved her all that the fondest Passion has been able to figure.' She is no less sure of her ' adored and passionately beloved Dr. Husband.' Her love is ' inseparable from My dear, dear Husband,' in whose letters she always finds an ' angel-like eloquence.' [1]

Thus sunnily began Pitt's perfect happiness in marriage, a happiness which lasted unclouded till his dying day. It was a fitting opening to a period of unparalleled glory both for himself and for ' our England ' that dwelt in all the thoughts of the loving pair.

[1] The correspondence between Pitt and Lady Hester in this chapter is taken from *Chatham MSS.* 5 and 7.

Hester Grenville, Countess of Chatham
from a painting in the possession of E. G. Pretyman Esq.

TABULAR LIST OF CORRESPONDENCE RELATING TO THE NEGOTIATIONS AFTER PELHAM'S DEATH.

Date	Writer	Addressed to	Subject	Where to be found *
1754				
March 6	Pitt	G. Grenville	Pelham's illness	Grenville, i, 105.
,, 6	,,	Duke of Newcastle	,,	Add. MSS. 32734, f. 173.
,, 7	,,	,,	Pelham's death	Ibid. f. 180.
,, 7	,,	Grenvilles and Lyttelton	Plans and policy	Grenville, i, 106.
,, 7	,,	Temple	Private, re Lyttelton	Ibid. 110.
,, 10	,,	Lyttelton	Plans; encloses letter to show to Hardwicke	Phillimore, ii, 449.
,, 10	,,	,,	The ostensible letter for Hardwicke to see	Ibid. ii, 453.
,, 11	Hardwicke	Archbishop of Canterbury	Manœuvres to get Newcastle Prime Minister	Harris, Hardwicke, ii, 511.
,, 11	Pitt	Temple	Collect a party	Grenville, i, 112.
,, 11	,,	Duke of Newcastle	Have sent views to Lyttelton	Add. MSS. 32734, f. 212.
,, 14	,,	G. Grenville	Trying to come to you	Grenville, i, 114.
,, 18	Lyttelton	,,	Shall I send word to Pitt?	Ibid. 115.
,, 20	Pitt	Lyttelton	No news; hope to come to London; Bolingbroke	Phillimore, ii, 460.
,, 23	Lyttelton	Hardwicke	Write to Pitt	Harris, Hardwicke, iii, 3.
,, 24	Pitt	Lyttelton	Views on settlement	Phillimore, ii, 461.
,, 24	,,	Duke of Newcastle	Complains of treatment	Rosebery, 329.
,, 24	,,	Temple	Avoid obstruction	Grenville, i, 115.
,, 24	,,	G. Grenville	Let us talk of Bolingbroke and such things	Ibid. 117.
April 1	,,	Wm. Lyttelton	Congratulations on Sub-Cofferer	Phillimore, ii, 465.
,, 2	Hardwicke	Pitt	Soft words	Chat. Corr. i, 89.
,, 2	Duke of Newcastle	,,	Aldborough	Ibid. 95.
,, 2	Pitt	Duke of Newcastle	Answers letter of April 2	Ibid. 85.
,, 4	,,	,,	Comments on Newcastle's letter	Rosebery, 335.
,, 4	,,	Lyttelton	Answers letter of April 2	Phillimore, ii, 466.
,, 6	,,	Hardwicke	Congratulations on Treas. of Navy	Harris, Hardwicke, iii, 8.
,, 8	,,	G. Grenville	Comments on Ministry	Grenville, i, 118.
,, 20	,,	Temple	Aldborough	Ibid. 119.
,, 22	,,	Duke of Newcastle	,,	Add. MSS. 32735, f. 139.
May 20	,,	Lyttelton	Depression. Our policy	Ibid. f. 143. Phillimore, ii, 468.

* The MSS. sources are referred to only when there is no printed book containing a copy of the letter. In several cases the letter is printed in more than one book; in that case the earliest authority is given.

249

CHAPTER IX

THE GREAT COMMONER

ἡμῖν ἀπρόσιτος ἡ δύναμις αὐτῷ τοῦ λόγου · ἐγὼ δὲ ταύτην μὲν δευτέραν ἔταττον ἐν χώρᾳ τιθεὶς ὀργάνου.—LUCIAN, *Demosthenis Encomium*.[1]

I am not fond of making speeches. . . . I never cultivated the talent but as an instrument of action in a country like ours.—WILLIAM PITT.

NEWCASTLE had just formed his Ministry when the news of a slight skirmish in a far-off American forest heralded the great war which was to be immortally linked with Pitt's name. At the end of May 1754, the twenty-two year old Colonel Washington, at the head of some 150 Virginians, overpowered a small French detachment under M. de Jumonville sent to oppose him from Fort Duquesne near the Ohio. A few weeks later Washington, who had retired to his hastily constructed Fort Necessity, surrendered to a superior force that had come to avenge Jumonville's defeat. In August the news reached London, where it evoked loud indignation from the people, and gave Newcastle an occasion to summon all that fortitude which Pitt had told him he would need. Two small skirmishes in the backwoods of America, far removed from any large French or English settlements, seem a trifling cause for the great struggle which ensued. But the American colonists and the two mother-countries were deeply concerned in the principle underlying these affairs of outposts. In South Africa we have seen in our own time the importance attached to territories beyond their borders by sparse settlers

---

[1] 'No words of mine can describe the power of his eloquence. Yet to that I give but a secondary place, as a tool the man used.'

in a country more than sufficient for their immediate needs, and we have witnessed the mother-country's anxiety to support her colonists in their ambition to provide for future generations. So it was with the America of the eighteenth century. Neither the French Canadians nor the English of the thirteen colonies could claim that the watershed of the Ohio, the main subject of contention, was indispensable for immediate expansion. The French aim was to connect Canada with the struggling colony of Louisiana at the mouth of the Mississippi; the English to withstand the attempt to exclude them from the interior and confine them to a seaboard bounded by the Alleghenies; both nations also claimed the right of trading with the Indians west of the Ohio.

In the pursuit of their common object of free access to the interior the French had hitherto been the more successful. Though the Canadians were estimated to number only 50,000, compared to the 2,000,000 English colonists,[1] they had the immense advantage of being united under one governor-general who could dispose of all the resources of the country for one consistent policy. Since the Peace of Aix-la-Chapelle the Court of Versailles had sent out three vigorous governors, La Galissonière, La Jonquière, and Duquesne, with secret instructions to enforce the rights to the interior first claimed by a charter of Louis XIV in 1712. Forts had been built at Presqu'Île and the Rivière des Boeufs, south of Lake Erie; an English detachment was evicted from a post on the Allegheny river, and a fort, named after Governor Duquesne, erected in its place. It was also designed to interrupt the English communications with their Iroquois and other allies of the Six Nations by dislodging them from their stronghold at Oswego, south of Lake Ontario. The French governors did not even confine their attention to this debatable land south of Canada, but secretly fomented disturbances among the French population of Nova Scotia, and built Fort Beauséjour on territory in dispute between that colony and their own province of Acadia. To this act of aggression Pitt

See anonymous memorandum of 1755 in *Chatham MSS.* 95.

had vainly drawn Newcastle's attention so far back as 1750.[1] The English settlers on the other hand were not all of one mind like the French. Each colony was under a separate governor and was intensely jealous of its neighbours and of the Imperial Government. Concerted action was almost impossible. To remedy this, a scheme for a general congress was proposed in 1754, but came to naught. The chief opposition to the French designs on the interior had hitherto come from a private company of the Ohio, formed with capital contributed partly by Virginian and Maryland colonists, partly by London merchants. This company claimed by treaties made with Indians in 1744 and 1752 to have bought for £400 all the districts watered by the Ohio and its affluents, and through its London shareholders could exert influence on the Government. But in spite of dissensions there was good material among the colonists. The New Englanders had already shown, by their capture of Louisburg in the last war, that they could give a good account of themselves; the Virginians had made an effort to repel the French aggression at Fort Duquesne; and the central and northern colonies were animated by racial and religious hatred of the French Canadians, further embittered by the atrocities and depredations of their Indian allies. All the English colonists needed for victory was a man to direct them and call out their best qualities.

Newcastle was not this man. Although he had for many years been in charge of American affairs, he understood little about them and cared less. They said of him that, being advised to fortify Annapolis, he replied, ' Annapolis, Annapolis—certainly we must fortify Annapolis. Where is Annapolis ? ' When news came of the attack on Washington he was much more troubled with the prospect of war on the Continent and could not see the use of wasting money and men on America. Halifax at the Board of Trade, acting on colonial advice, urged that four expeditions should be directed against the French—one to attack Fort Duquesne, a second Fort Beauséjour, and two more against Fort Niagara on Lake Erie and Crown Point, at the foot of Lake Champlain, to protect the Iroquois

[1] See above, pp. 182-3.

FRENCH AND ENGLISH IN AMERICA

and the province of New York. Newcastle eagerly seized upon a division of opinion in the Cabinet as an excuse for delaying action altogether. Granville thought the colonists should be encouraged to raise men in America, while the Duke of Cumberland was for sending out two regiments on the Irish establishment—a course decided upon by the Cabinet and then countermanded by Newcastle. After weeks spent in fruitless discussions Newcastle took the occasion of a visit paid him by Pitt on October 2 to consult him on the two plans. Pitt at first haughtily refused his advice: 'Your Grace, I suppose, knows I have no capacity for those things and therefore I do not desire to be informed about them'; but on being pressed could not resist the temptation of expounding views, which were not at all to the duke's taste. For he advocated both plans. He had already expressed in private his conviction that it would never do to send mere handfuls of men to America 'to be served up to Indians like steaks at a chop-house.'[1] He now told the duke that the scheme of sending the Irish regiments was good as far as it went, but did not go near far enough; the proposals for artillery, for example, were infinitely too short. He would also adopt Granville's idea of raising some thousand men in America. But above all he urged prompt action and the need for countenancing and encouraging the Americans.[2] Pitt's advice had this good effect—that Newcastle at once withdrew his order countermanding the two regiments. Shortly afterwards the matter was taken out of his hands by the Secretary at War, Fox, who appears to have acted in concert with Pitt as well as the Duke of Cumberland. Without consulting Newcastle, he persuaded the King to sign the warrants appointing officers for troops to be raised in America, ordered them off to their posts, and called upon the Admiralty for transports. By the end of October the Cabinet had agreed to sending troops from Ireland as well as raising men in America, as Pitt had suggested.[3] The Duke

---

[1] *Chatham MSS.* 40: Thos. Hervey to Pitt.
[2] See Dodington, 317, and *Add MSS.* 35414, f. 197, and Rosebery, p. 350, who reconciles the two accounts.
[3] See *Add. MSS.* 32737, f. 307.

of Newcastle consoled himself with the reflection that
the whole responsibility might be laid on the Duke of Cumberland [1]

During the session of 1754-5 Pitt made no direct attack
on the Government policy; on the contrary he supported their
main proposals. But he entered into a deliberate plan of
campaign to render ridiculous and impossible Newcastle's
attempt to govern the House of Commons through a pompous
nonentity like Robinson, or a supple advocate like Murray,
neither of whom could speak with authority on the Ministry's
plans. No doubt personal ambition and natural indignation
at his own exclusion were among his motives, but he was also
influenced by the greater principle of the dignity and efficiency
of parliamentary government. He saw in this attempt to
belittle the House of Commons a direct result of Bolingbroke's
testament politique, as he called it, which aimed at substituting
personal government for the constitutional part of the
legislature in the direction of affairs. Newcastle, as he was
probably well aware, was too muddle-headed to have thought
out so vigorous a policy for himself; but all the sinister
suggestions of Jacobitism in Murray, Newcastle's only capable
instrument in the Commons, recurred to him as partially
explaining the situation. In the first few weeks of the session
he found a powerful coadjutor in Fox, with whom he had
struck up an informal alliance. The combination of the two
proved irresistible; for what Pitt lacked in cool insolence was
supplied by Fox, and Fox's want of high purpose, reflected
in his less inspiring oratory, was made good by Pitt's intense
conviction and burning eloquence. In those days little surprise
was felt at two subordinate ministers attacking their colleagues,
for the idea of joint responsibility in ministers was still hardly
recognised, and each minister, in fact as well as in name,
answered only for his own department.[2] Newcastle certainly
had only himself to blame for these attacks, which he affronted

[1] Coxe's *Lord Walpole*, ii, 368.
[2] This the King made brutally plain to the Duke of Newcastle, when he sought to interfere in appointments to the Bedchamber, by telling him he was not sole minister and should confine himself to the Treasury, which he would have enough to do in setting right. (*Add. MSS.* 35414, f. 269.)

PITT ATTACKS NEWCASTLE'S SYSTEM

with his eyes open, for in October he wrote to old Horace Walpole :

> Some great persons in the House of Commons don't think their merit rewarded and therefore endeavour to have it thought that there is a necessity of having a minister, or the minister, in the house of Commons. . . . I am persuaded that the majority of this house of Commons will not enter into any scheme of this kind. . . . I have now told you the whole grievance.

On November 14, 1754, the opening day of the session, Pitt introduced his Chelsea Pensioners Bill,[1] then went away for his brief honeymoon at West Wickham. Before Christmas the House was chiefly occupied with election petitions, but members as a rule took little interest in proceedings which, thanks to Newcastle's well-disciplined majority, were a foregone conclusion in favour of his candidates. On the afternoon of November 25, the case of the Berwick election was down for hearing. The unsuccessful candidate was John Wilkes, an amusing scoundrel, whose sallies could raise a smile even from Mr. Pitt, as they did later from Dr. Johnson. He was petitioning against the return of Newcastle's candidate, John Delaval. The usual listless and half-empty House was preparing itself for the dreary recital of charge and counter-charge from the two candidates, when it was suddenly enlivened by a speech from Delaval. He dealt with the subject of bribery, of which he was accused,[2] in a vein of so much wit and buffoonery that the House was kept in a continual roar of laughter. Pitt meanwhile had come into the gallery and sat listening with growing indignation to this misplaced drollery. Striding into his place, he rose immediately Delaval sat down, and by his first words brought members to such silence that you might have heard a pin drop. Finding the House in an uproar, he

November 25, 1754.

---

[1] See above, p. 157.

[2] In the matter of bribery there was probably little to choose between the two candidates. Wilkes, however, showed ingenuity in his methods. Delaval had chartered a ship to bring some of his voters from London to Berwick. Wilkes, by a larger fee, persuaded the skipper to call at Bergen on the way, a deviation which brought him to Berwick too late for the poll. Wilkes had no idea which way Pitt would speak, and gave an audible gasp of relief when he found Pitt attacking Delaval.

had inquired the cause, and was astonished to hear that bribery was the subject of their mirth. Was then their dignity on so sure a foundation that they might venture themselves to shake it ? Had it not, on the contrary, been attacked from without for years so that it was now almost beyond recovery ? The Speaker, he hoped, would extend a saving hand to raise it, for he only could restore it—yet scarce he, unless he were supported by all good Whigs in defending their attacked and expiring liberty.

All of us [he cried] must assist, unless you will degenerate into a little assembly, serving no other purpose than to register the decrees of *one* too powerful a *subject* . . . otherwise naught can stop the design of making us an appendix to—I know not what—I have no name for it.

This direct attack upon the all-powerful minister came, says Walpole, as a thunderbolt upon the House, for ten years unused to Pitt's style of fiery invective. The scared members gathered together in knots and murmured to one another in confusion ; on the Government benches Robinson looked grave and said nothing; Murray crouched pale, miserable and silent. The Speaker shook Pitt's hand, ready to shake it off ; none but Legge dared to continue the debate, and he only to emphasise his sympathy with Pitt.[1]

Fox came in too late to second Pitt in this first skirmish, but that very day came another opportunity. The same evening Sir Thomas Robinson ill-advisedly hazarded the opinion that the Reading petition would not last long, since Lord Fane, the sitting member, in whom Pitt was interested, had a poor case. Pitt began the attack. He was surprised and scandalised to hear from one of the chief ministers of the Crown so indecent an expression of opinion on an untried cause. Leading ministers might hold that view, but it was for the House to consider what chance was now left for liberty of election, that foundation of the nation's liberty, wherein consists the strength

---

[1] The scene is described by Walpole and by Fox (who came in just as Pitt had finished) in a letter to Harrington ; also by Calcraft (*Chatham MSS.* 86). Pitt's speech should be compared with Potter's against Newcastle and Pitt himself on November 20, 1747 (see above, p. 162).

and security of the State and the happiness of the subject. Never had he thought to see so melancholy a day for the House of Commons. Robinson did not mend matters by a pompous and rambling reply, in which he talked of his great office, for which he had never been ambitious. Pitt explained that he had not aimed at Sir Thomas but at a higher than he; Sir Thomas, he added, was as able as any man who had lately filled the office or was likely to fill it.[1] Fox then took up the baiting: Robinson, the House should remember, had been twenty years abroad; they should not, therefore, be too hard upon him for his irregular and blameable expression, or for the total inexperience he showed in the matters before the House. Fox drily remarked in the account he gave of this performance to Lord Hartington that Robinson did not like it.

Two days later Pitt turned his attention to the Attorney-General. The debate on November 27 was on a motion of Beckford's to reduce the army from 18,800 to 15,000 men. Nugent, a rough, bullying Irishman of no character, in opposing him uttered a fulsome panegyric on the Duke of Newcastle personally and attacked Beckford for calling the ministers Tories. The Jacobites were extinct, he said, and even those who thought they had nursed up Jacobites were as disappointed in the results as the hen, that had hatched duck's eggs, was at seeing her nurslings take to the water. Pitt gently reproved Beckford for wishing to reduce the army at such a conjuncture; then, turning to Nugent, complimented him on his image of the hen: November 27, 1754.

For, Sir, I know of such a hen, I was bred under such an one, and will tell the House what she has been doing for these twenty years;—raising a succession of treason—there never was such a seminary; and we must not be too sure that all she hatched would ever entirely forget what she had taught them.

Only lately he had been on a party of pleasure to Oxford: while they were at the window of the Angel Inn a lady began singing ' God save great George our King,' but could

---

[1] The best account of these speeches is in *Aff. Etr. Angl. Corr. Pol.* 437; see also Walpole, *Memoirs*, and Waldegrave.

VOL. I.   S

not continue for some lads drinking at a college over the way, who interspersed treasonable sentiments into the chorus. Later, in the High, he had been offered a picture of the Pretender with a Latin motto praying for his return. Jacobitism was not dead yet : he wished it were. It was even suspected in high places—(this with a look at Murray, whose brother had been the Pretender's minister). Oxford was paved with Jacobites, and there was no trusting any man who has been bred there in Tory principles—(with another look at Murray)—because *Quo semel est imbuta recens servabit odorem testa diu*.[1] In both speeches, agree Fox and Horace Walpole, every word was Murray, yet so managed that no public notice could be taken of it ; and Fox declares that Murray, who was sitting next to him, suffered for an hour.

During the rest of the session, which lasted till April 1755, Pitt took little part in debate. He supported the Government bill to extend the Mutiny Act to troops raised in America, and quoted Roman precedents in support of a Bristol Nightly Watch Bill, which also suggested to him a panegyric on the wisdom of our well-balanced constitution. He was once more in an attacking vein, when a bill to continue the Scottish judges, called Sheriffs-Depute, in their offices only *durante bene placito* gave him a chance of torturing Murray for his distinctions and refinements and legal quibbles : arbitrary power, he said, was more detestable when dressed in the long robe than in all the panoply of war, and general maxims of liberty were apt to be obscured by too minute analysis : if we must go for precedents, let them not be sought in the diabolic divans of Charles and James. Ministers sneered at Pitt's zeal for liberty, but gave way to his arguments and extended

December 11, 1754.
January 15, 1755.
February 26, 1755.

---

[1] This conclusion is taken from *The Test*, No. 6; the rest of these speeches (for there were two) is summarised from Horace Walpole and Fox's accounts. Pitt was certainly right in accusing Oxford of being a hot-bed of Jacobitism. Only in that year the notorious Dr. King, in his speech at the opening of the Radcliffe Library, introduced the Jacobite catchword 'Redeat' three times into his speech, pausing each time for a considerable space to await the unbounded applause that followed. Recently, too, he had publicly described the Duke of Cumberland as a man *qui timet omnia praeter Deum*. (Shelburne, i, 27.)

to these judges the Revolution principle of office during good behaviour.

Within a fortnight of the opening of the session Pitt had silenced Robinson and Murray, but Newcastle had been able to hold on, because in December he had won over Fox. He had soon been forced to admit the soundness of the King's advice to him in September, that a responsible leader was necessary in the Commons.[1] The choice had lain between two men, Pitt and Fox. For several reasons Newcastle would have preferred Pitt. He was the better man—even Newcastle saw that—and could bring with him the support of Leicester House, whereas Fox was connected with the hated Cumberland. On the other hand Fox could probably be had at a smaller price, and would be agreeable to the King. At first, however, Newcastle tried to obtain Pitt's co-operation for nothing, on hearing from Legge that Pitt would not insist on being Secretary of State against the King's wishes, if he were treated with confidence and consulted.[2] He sent for Pitt and persuaded him, under the seal of secrecy, to open himself freely to him, and at once reported the whole conversation to the King, 'To do you good, to do you good,' he afterwards explained. Pitt was so angry at the breach of confidence that, when Newcastle next approached him with soft proposals, he cut him short : 'Fewer words, my Lord, if you please, for your words have long lost all weight with me.'

Newcastle then turned to Fox and after some days' negotiation struck a bargain for his support in return for his admission into the Cabinet.[3] Fox consulted Pitt throughout this negotiation, even to the turn of his own letters, and Pitt encouraged him to accept the offer made him, consistently with his previous declarations that he would be content to serve under a man of Fox's

[1] *Add. MSS.* 35414, f. 193.
[2] *Ibid.* f. 223.
[3] This suggestion of taking Fox and leaving Pitt reminded Lord Bath of a story of the Gunpowder Plot. 'The Lord Chamberlain was sent to examine the vaults under the Parliament House, and, returning with his report, said he had found five-and-twenty barrels of gunpowder, that he had removed ten of them and hoped the other fifteen would do no harm.'

authority. Fox on his side was less frank. He refused, indeed, Newcastle's treacherous offer to give him Pitt's place,[1] but in his letters to Hartington in November describes himself as on his guard in all his conversations with Pitt; and, according to Walpole, had no sooner been admitted to the Cabinet than he privately forswore all connection with his ally. Pitt only heard of this in the spring of the following year, 1755, when he came to a party at Lord Hillsborough's boiling with indignation at the news. He declared loudly that all connection between himself and Fox was at an end; Fox was one of the Cabinet and had just been put on the council of regency, while he was left exposed. At that moment Fox came up and Pitt repeated to him what he had already said, adding that even if Fox made way for him he would not accept the seals from his hands, for that would be owning an obligation and superiority which he would never acknowledge, for he would owe nothing to any man but to himself. Fox asked what he meant: was he suspected of trying to rise above him? 'No,' said Pitt; 'but we act on different lines, sometimes together, sometimes apart, for I am independent and can act on my own responsibility: you will sometimes act with me, sometimes you are tied down in implicit obedience to the Duke of Cumberland, whose soldier I am not, and whose commands might at the end of a campaign counteract all that had been jointly done.' After this plain speaking Pitt and Fox had two more interviews within the next few days, but though they parted on terms of politeness, Pitt would never afterwards have any serious dealings with Fox.[2]

Before the beginning of the next session Newcastle's difficulties had grown apace. In January 1755 Braddock had

---

[1] Among other authorities for this offer are the reports of the French envoy, who followed these negotiations closely (*Aff. Etr. Angl. Corr. Pol.* 437, ff. 392, 406, 412).

[2] This accounts for Pitt's subsequent comment on his correspondence with Fox at the time of Newcastle's negotiation, that he felt himself betrayed by him (*Chatham Corr.* i, 124 &c.). Riker (i, 217) gives an ingenious and convincing explanation why this correspondence was post-dated. The originals in the Record Office are undated, and really refer to November and December 1754, not to April 1755, as the editors of the *Chatham Correspondence* thought.

sailed with his two regiments filled with 'Justice Fielding's recruits.' In Virginia he had set all the colonists against him by his obstinate stupidity and his barrack-yard ideas of discipline. In his long march to Fort Duquesne, over mountains and through unexplored forests, he made a hard task still more arduous by the enormous train of baggage-wagons with which he encumbered himself. On July 9, on the banks of the Monongahela, not far from his goal, he was attacked by a mixed force of French and Indians, and was himself killed, while most of his force was cut up. This defeat was not compensated in the eyes of the Ministry by the capture in June of Fort Beauséjour by the despised New England militia. In April Admiral Boscawen had been sent to America to intercept French reinforcements. In an engagement off the mouth of the St. Lawrence in June he captured two French ships, the *Alcide* and the *Lys*, the rest escaping in a fog. As Hardwicke said, Boscawen had done either too much or too little : he had not struck a fatal blow, at the same time he had incurred all the odium of attacking in time of peace. For while Braddock and Boscawen were being sent out, and Hawke with the Spithead fleet was receiving instructions to destroy French commerce but not to attack the French fleet—' vexing our neighbours,' as Granville said, ' for a little muck '—negotiations on the American disputes were still going on between the two courts. When news came in July of Boscawen's attack, the French ambassador broke off diplomatic relations, but war was not declared for another year. Even when hostilities had begun in this half-hearted manner, Newcastle had no conception of what we ought to fight for. It was clear to Pitt that the struggle would be in America and also India, where Dupleix and Bussy had raised French prestige to a pitch never reached before ; but Newcastle still thought of nothing but a continental war. The King, too, who, as usual, had gone to Hanover with Holderness in April, cared only about securing his beloved electorate against a French invasion. Even from this point of view their efforts were futile. The Empress-Queen was approached with proposals for an alliance, but she had long been meditating a change

of system, and offered terms so contrary to English and even
Hanoverian interests that the negotiation was dropped.
Frederic of Prussia was sounded, but that astute monarch was
not yet prepared to give up his French alliance; and the
Ministry attached so little importance to gaining him that
they pushed forward a treaty with Russia for the express
purpose of bringing a Russian army against him if he attacked
Hanover. This Russian treaty and an agreement with Hesse
for 6,000 mercenaries were the only results of all the King
and Newcastle's efforts during the summer and autumn to
contrive a great confederation against France, chiefly for the
benefit of Hanover. So unpopular were these treaties that
Newcastle's own Chancellor of the Exchequer, Legge, refused
to issue the Hessian levy money without the authority of
Parliament, while the disaffection in the country was
such that Archbishop Herring told Newcastle the nation
was in a more critical condition than during the Rebellion
of 1745.

Newcastle remembered Carteret's fate, and trembled to
think that the man who had compassed that minister's fall
was still unreconciled. The last session had restored Pitt to
all his old power and reputation. At Leicester House he was,
said Fox, ' quite master . . . acting and being treated as the
minister there as much as Sir R. Walpole in Queen Caroline's
drawing-room ';[1] Cumberland, too, who was opposed to him
and did not know him personally, declared that, if all he heard
was true, ' Pitt is—what is scarce—a man.' Newcastle saw
the advantage such a man's support would bring him, but still
hoped to get him—not as an independent counsellor with a
voice in the Government's policy, but merely to defend his own
schemes. In April he sent old Horace Walpole to sound Pitt as
to the terms on which he would support the ministerial measures.
Pitt was willing to waive the seals for the present, but he must
be treated with confidence and be informed beforehand of the
measures that he was asked to support; and Newcastle must
contrive to make the King look on him with favour. On
hearing how much power Pitt demanded, Newcastle promptly

[1] Torrens, ii, 238.

disowned Walpole and dropped the negotiation.[1] Two months later the difficulty of carrying the Hessian subsidy treaty through the House made him anxious to renew it. He sent the Chancellor's son, Charles Yorke, with professions of friendship and affection to feel the ground once more, but Pitt was less ready to listen this time : he roundly declared that he would not deal with emissaries who could be disavowed, and that the only proposition he would listen to would be a plain offer : ' Sir, here is the plan of the King's affairs, *this* is the station [meaning the Secretary of State] in which you will be enabled to support them, *these* are your friends, who will join and act with you.'

Newcastle then asked Hardwicke to see what he could do. On Hardwicke's reply that the ' confidence and regard ' Pitt asked for meant more than Newcastle was prepared to give, but that if Pitt, like Fox, could be satisfied with a seat in the Cabinet ' it would be a cheap bargain provided our Master can be brought to it,'[2] Newcastle wrote to Hanover that he was becoming the ' Butt ' of everybody, and that the only hope of ' a proper system . . . to obviate all difficulties ' in the House of Commons was ' the engaging Mr. Pitt upon reasonable terms to support His Majesty's measures with clearness, firmness and cordiality.' ' Notwithstanding the just reasons His Majesty has to be offended with Mr. Pitt,' was the gruff reply, ' the King will graciously accept his services and countenance him accordingly ' by admitting him to the Cabinet, if he will promise to behave himself. Newcastle answered that a Cabinet seat would not be worth much if the King was always rude to Pitt, and asked for a definition. of ' countenance ' ; but, since it was not forthcoming, Hardwicke undertook to ' feel the pulse of the great Pitt.'[3]

[1] Riker (i, 208) suggests that Pitt, not Walpole on behalf of Newcastle, made the first overture in this negotiation, basing himself on a phrase of the younger Walpole's *Memoirs*, ii, 37. But that old Walpole began the negotiation is clear from his letter to Newcastle of April 8, 1755 (*Add. MSS*. 32854, f. 72), from Dodington's account and Charles Yorke's (in Harris, *Hardwicke*, iii, 30), and from Newcastle's letter to Hardwicke in 35415, f. 1. The younger Walpole's account is not really inconsistent with Dodington, as it only gives the conclusion of the interview.

[2] Add. *MSS*. 32856, f. 484.   [3] *Ibid*. 32857, ff. 53, 256 ; 35415, f. 6.

On August 9 Pitt broke his journey to Sunning Hill with Lady Hester to answer Hardwicke's summons. Hardwicke, after delicate allusions to Pitt's 'unlucky steps' in the preceding session, said they had tried with some success to overcome the King's aversion to him and hoped to succeed even better in the future. Meanwhile they could offer him the King's countenance and a place in the Cabinet; later the Secretary's seals he so much desired might be forthcoming. 'I have never applied for the seals,' interrupted Pitt; 'in fact, if they were offered me now, the only use I should make of them, while I lie under the King's present dislike, would be to lay them at his Majesty's feet: I shall never accept the seals till the King likes it and his ministers desire it.' He then came to business: if he were asked to take a clear, cordial and active part in support of the King's measures he must know what they were. 'Our policy,' said Hardwicke, 'is to support the maritime and American war and defend the King's German dominions, if attacked on account of the English quarrel.' Pitt took no exception to this statement, and said he was willing to pay regard to Hanover, if attacked on our account: but on strategic grounds he said it would be as reasonable to concentrate the efforts of a campaign on defending Jamaica, or some other outlying dominion of the British crown, as Hanover. Newcastle's policy of subsidies seemed to him useless, unless a continental war for the defence of Hanover was our main object; and besides being very unpopular, it was very expensive. Over six millions a year, he said, would be required for the American and maritime war and for home defence; a further million for subsidies could not be raised without trenching on the sinking fund, which he regarded as sacred. If Hanover, at the worst, became a camping-ground for French or Prussian soldiers the King ought to be indemnified at the peace; but, rather than embark on its defence now, he would give the King five millions as compensation at the end of the war. Hardwicke then told him about the Hessian subsidy and the proposed Russian subsidy. Pitt did not at once reject the idea of them, but said he must consult his friends, and after

PITT SEES HARDWICKE AND NEWCASTLE 265

agreeing to see Newcastle himself, took his departure for Sunning Hill.[1]

Having gone so far, Newcastle felt that he must see Pitt himself, though he confessed he did not feel ' much glee ' at the prospect. He spent a month corresponding with Hardwicke as to what he should say, and whether he should show Pitt a Cabinet minute of July 30—that ' no treaty of subsidy should be made, or any act done, which should prepare for, or be productive of, a scheme for the support of a war upon the Continent.' This tallied exactly with the clear statement Pitt had given Hardwicke of his own policy, but was not consistent with the Russian and Hessian treaties or the attempts to hire troops from Brunswick and Saxony. Hardwicke advised him to offer the seals, ' in case the King should think of a change . . . this will cost little, as the King is so determined against it.' Newcastle also consulted Egmont, the Princess of Wales, Cresset, her private secretary, and Granville. This old campaigner's advice was to give the seals to Fox, who was equally ready to be for or against them, but, if chosen, would be far more accommodating than Pitt, since he would support any policy. Terror inspired by Granville himself finally screwed up Newcastle to the point of making one more bid for Pitt's support of his ministry. ' My Lord President had dined and talked very unguardedly ' at a Cabinet meeting, to the effect that Newcastle alone was responsible for all the treaties and other unpopular acts of the Ministry. ' I was frightened the whole time,' said the poor duke, and ten days later parleyed with ' the engine at the door.'

Newcastle's conversation with Pitt on September 2 lasted two hours and a half, and his account of it takes almost as long to read. Pitt gave his own version to Dodington more briefly. Newcastle began with the same offer as Hardwicke. Pitt's answer was that such offers were not enough. The duke did not know the state of the House of Commons, which, he might say without vanity, he knew better than anybody; as long as he had life and breath to utter he

[1] Hardwicke's account of this interview is in Harris, *Hardwicke*, iii, 30 ; Pitt's version in Dodington, 366. There is no essential difference between them.

would oppose the duke's system of carrying on business there. It was now an assembly of atoms: the great wheels of the machine were stopped, and such an offer as the duke had made could not be thought sufficient to put them in motion. There must be a responsible minister there, a Secretary of State, and with him a Chancellor of Exchequer, who had habitual, frequent, familiar access to the Crown; in other words, the duke must part with some of his sole power. If the present secretaries, Holderness and Robinson, were so esteemed and thought so fit for their business, what was he called there for? He would support measures he had himself advised, but would not, like a lawyer, talk from a brief. As to policy, it must be tested by an English, not a German standard. The absence of the King in Germany during all these critical months 'without one man about him that has one English sentiment' should have been prevented by the people 'even with their bodies.' He might, indeed, have agreed to the Hessian treaty 'out of deep regard for the King's honour,' and on a definite assurance that it should be the last. But when it came to a Russian treaty also, he saw the beginnings of a continental system which nothing would induce him to countenance. If the King's honour was so much involved in these treaties, why should he not, out of the fifteen millions he had saved, give £100,000 to Hesse and £150,000 to the Czarina to be off these bad bargains? Legge, by refusing to issue the levy money, had proved himself 'the child, and deservedly the favourite child, of the Whigs.' As Newcastle mournfully observes, in summing up the interview, 'There was such a firm resolution, so solemnly declared, both as to persons and things, that if complied with must produce a total change of the present system both as to measures and men.'[1] And this was the last thing Newcastle wished.

Hardwicke told Newcastle he was wasting his time, unless he could bring himself to offer Pitt more power than he gave Robinson or Legge; for the pretence that the King's resistance

---

[1] See *Add. MSS.* 32858, *passim*; this interview is recounted in ff. 294 *sqq.*; also Dodington, 363–5, 369–77.

could not be overcome was tacitly admitted between them to be nonsense. But Newcastle was still unwilling to share his power and thought he could do with hired bravos. Though almost more afraid of Fox's intrigues than of Pitt's ambition, he knew Fox would not be cowed by Pitt in the House, and that he had no very sensitive conscience. Robinson, therefore, was sent back to rumble platitudes from the decent recesses of the Great Wardrobe, whence he had come, and Fox at the end of September received the seals of the Southern Department and the lead of the House of Commons. Newcastle also bribed Hume Campbell with the Duchy of Lancaster, raising the salary from £600 to £2,000, as an inducement to leave a lucrative practice at the bar and stand up to Pitt, with whom he had already had encounters.[1] Some of Bedford's men were enticed with places, and Dodington, forswearing his recent vows never to desert Pitt, accepted the well-paid Treasurership of the Navy. On the eve of the session Newcastle complacently counted over his gains and flattered himself with the delusion that Fox, Murray, Hume Campbell, and his other gladiators could easily face Pitt and the Grenvilles; but, as Alderman Baker told him, ' we are not now to be governed by speeches, that is over. All we want is a man to lead us, and depend upon it we will follow.'[2] Leadership Newcastle would not part with; so Baker and his friends had to wait another year for a man to lead them.

Pitt's sentence was now for open war. On the first day of the session, November 13, 1755, he had few supporters save the Grenvilles, but, says Walpole, was too great a general to regard numbers, especially when there was a probability of no great harmony between the commanders ranged against him. He opened his campaign on the Address, which expressed approval of the treaties of subsidy and an assurance of support to Hanover. The battle lasted from two in the afternoon till five the next morning, twenty-nine speakers taking part in the fray, of whom thirteen were for the Government, sixteen for the Opposition, and of these sixteen three—Legge, George Grenville and Pitt—were ministers. Four speakers, Murray

[1] See above, pp. 139, 140.   [2] *Add. MSS.* 32860, f. 13.

and W. G. Hamilton [1] for the Government, and Pitt and Grenville on the other side, are admitted to have surpassed all the others.[2] Hamilton's speech, says Walpole, was perfection:

What, you will ask, could be beyond this ? Nothing but what was beyond what ever was, and that was Pitt. . . . His eloquence, like a torrent long obstructed, burst forth with commanding impetuosity. He and Legge opened their new opposition in the very spirit of their different characters. The one, humble, artful, affecting moderation, gliding to revenge ; the other, haughty, defiant and conscious of injury and supreme abilities.

November 13, 1755. Pitt, contrary to his usual impetuous habit of speaking early in debates, rose past midnight, after the debate had already lasted nearly twelve hours. Murray had spoken earlier in defence of the treaties, drawing a pathetic picture of the King refusing to ensure peace for the evening of his days by a bad accommodation with France at the expense of his successor and the nation. 'Would you then in return,' he had cried, ' refuse protection to Hanover and sow the King's pillows with thorns ? ' Pitt, dismissing contemptuously the ' flashy reasonings ' of other speakers as mere repetitions of the cry ' follow your leader,' fastened on Murray's ' pathetic picture ' :

This growing and most unparliamentary practice of using the King's sacred name in debate fills me with alarm. Our ancestors would never have stooped to such adulation; they would have brought to the bar a man who dared to do so twice. But for some time every art has been practised to lower the dignity of the House ; and I have long observed it to be dwindling, sinking. No man can feel more veneration for the name that has been mentioned than myself, and I particularly feel grateful returns for late condescending goodness and gracious openings. But with all duty to his Majesty I must say that the King owes a supreme service to his people.[3] I too could draw a pathetic commiseration of his Majesty. I have

[1] By this speech and by his subsequent silence in debate Hamilton earned his nickname, ' Single-Speech.'

[2] Both Horace Walpole and West (to the Duke of Newcastle: *Add. MSS.* 32860, f. 471) agree in picking out these four speeches as the best.

[3] Compare with this passage, ' The best honour of the King's work is to be *Nobilis Servitus* . . . or in plain English, Supreme service above all, and to the whole,' in Nathaniel Bacon's *Discovery*—a book which Pitt had recommended to his nephew (see above, p. 215).

THE RHONE AND SAÔNE SPEECH, 1755

figured him far from an honest Council, figured him surrounded all the summer with affrighted Hanoverians and with no advocate for England near him. And to this picture of the King's distress I might oppose an equally pathetic picture of the nation's distress, which within two years I believe will be so great that His Majesty, so far from securing repose for the evening of his days, will not be able to sleep at St. James's for the cries of a bankrupt people. . . .

Why was this present war undertaken if not for the long-injured, long-neglected, long-forgotten people of America ? And can you expect to carry on this war by these incoherent, un-British measures instead of using our proper force ?

It was our Navy that procured the restoration of the Barrier and Flanders in the last war by making us masters of Cape Breton. After that war, with even that indemnification in our hands, we were forced to rejoice at a bad peace ; and, bad as it was, have suffered infractions of it every year, till the ministers would have been stoned as they went along the streets, if they had not at last shown resentment. And yet how soon have they forgotten in what cause they took up arms ! Are these treaties English measures ? Are they preventive measures, as has been said in debate ? Are they not measures of aggression ? Will they not provoke Prussia, and light up a general war ? If a war in Europe ensues from these negotiations, I will always follow up the authors of this measure. They must mean a land-war, and how preposterously do they meditate it. Hanover is the only spot you have left to fight upon. We are told we must assist Hanover out of justice and gratitude. Why ? Justice is ruled out by the Act of Settlement ; and gratitude for what ? Has Hanover done anything in our quarrel to draw upon her the resentments of France ? Such expressions are unparliamentary and unconstitutional, and the very paragraph containing them ought to be taken notice of and punished. But my objection to the choice of Hanover as our battle-ground is not from fear of prejudices but from its locality ; for, alas ! we cannot suspend the laws of nature and make Hanover not an open defenceless country. Grotius declares it is not necessary even *socium defendere si nulla spes boni exitus*. Can you force the Dutch to join you there ? I remember—everybody remembers, a late minister's time when you did force them : all our misfortunes are owing to those daring wicked councils. Subsidies annihilated ten millions in the last war ; and out of those rash measures sprung up a Ministry[1] —what if a Ministry should spring out of this subsidy ? I saw that Ministry : in the morning it flourished ; it was green at noon ; by

---
[1] See above, p. 146.

night it was cut down and forgotten ! But the strangest argument for these treaties is that, if our navies are defeated, we can turn our eyes to these mercenaries as a reserve. What ! must we drain our last vital drop and send it to the North Pole ? If you must go and traffic with the Czarina for succour, why, rather than her troops, did not you hire twenty of her ships ? I will say why—because ships could not be applied to Hanover. . . . Preventive measure you call this ! If this is a preventive measure, it is only preventive of somebody's[1] exit. . . . I do not know what majorities will do, but this I do know, that these treaties will hang like a millstone about the neck of any minister, and sink him along with the nation. We have been told, indeed, that Carthage, that Spain in 1588 were undone, notwithstanding their navies—true ; but not till they betook themselves to land operations—and Carthage had, besides, a Hannibal who could pass the Alps.[2] . . . A gentleman near me [half turning with an air of the greatest contempt towards Lyttelton]—a gentleman near me has talked to us of writers on the Law of Nations—Nature, Sir, is the best writer ; she will teach us to be men and not truckle to power. The noble lord who moved the Address seemed inspired with the idea of power ! I, who am at a distance from that *sanctum sanctorum*, whither the priest goes for inspiration—I, who travel through a desert, and am overwhelmed with mountains of obscurity, cannot so easily catch a gleam to direct me to the beauties of these negotiations. But there are parts of this Address that do not seem to come from the same quarter with the rest—I cannot unravel the mystery—but yes ! [he cries !—clapping his hand suddenly to his forehead]—I too am inspired !—it strikes me now ! I remember at Lyons to have been carried to see the conflux of the Rhone and the Saône : this a gentle, feeble, languid stream, and, though languid, of no depth—the other a boisterous and overbearing torrent—but they meet at last ; and long may they continue united, to the comfort of each other, and to the glory, honour, and happiness of this nation.[3]

After this speech in the early hours of the morning, Fox—

[1] I.e. Newcastle.
[2] A thrust at the Duke of Cumberland.
[3] This sketch of one of Pitt's most famous speeches is based on the accounts in Walpole's *Memoirs* and *Letters*, Walpole's order being occasionally altered to bring the arguments into greater relief. The rough notes of speeches in the *Memoirs* prove very accurate, when they can be tested from other sources, even to individual phrases ; but they hardly pretend to be more than scattered jottings, nor do they profess to clothe the skeleton of Pitt's speeches with the flesh of his wonderful language, or more than indicate his ' variety of action, accents, and irony . . . and his happy images and allusions.' One of Pitt's most marked characteristics as an orator was the ease with which he could

and small wonder—was feeble and ineffective. He was probably more interested in finding out from Pitt who 'the Rhone' was than in defending Newcastle, and hurried up to him afterwards to inquire. Pitt said, ' Is that a fair question ? ' but, on being pressed to tell whether it was Fox or Granville, replied, ' You are Granville.' That ' the Saône ' was Newcastle there could of course be no doubt. The speech had little effect on the voting—which gave the ministers a large majority. A week later Holderness sent letters to Pitt, Grenville and Legge informing them that the King had no further use for their services. On the day of Pitt's dismissal Temple generously pressed Lady Hester to induce her husband to accept £1,000 a year from him to make up for his loss of salary. Pitt, whose account at his bankers had already been overdrawn £1,000 in July,[1] accepted ' with the warmest, quickest, deepest sentiments of love and gratitude. We could have slept,' he says, ' upon the Earl of Holderness's letter ; but our hearts must now wake to gratitude and you, and wish for nothing but the return of day to embrace the best and noblest of brothers.' Nor, to the surprise of men like Rigby, did he and Lady Hester make any scruple of publishing their obligation to the world.[2]

Pitt was not content with one brilliant speech : he knew that nothing could be done to stop the pernicious policy on which the country was embarking without hammering at it in season and out of season. Never before had he worked so hard for the public. During the rest of the session his great spirit kept him constantly on the watch. On every important question he was ready to come to the House, sometimes straight

return over and over again to the same point, varying it to show the new aspect and yet enhancing the cumulative effect. In this his oratory is like Beethoven's music : he, too, never seems to tire of his own melodies, but always harks back to them to bring out one more sweetness, one more humorous touch or yet another solemn note of doom. Mark here how Pitt luxuriates in the ' pathetic image ' suggested to him by Murray, makes it his own, turns it about and plays with it until it has become a perfect picture : mark how he worries Hanover—is in turn contemptuous, pitying and indignant about it : and yet through all as a ground-note comes the reminder to Englishmen why they are fighting and how they should fight on their own element.

[1] See letter of Campbell in *Chatham MSS.* 25.
[2] Hogarth, in his plate, ' The Eaters,' introduces Pitt saying, ' Well, my brother's £1,000 a year will keep me from starving.'

from his bed, swathed in flannel, to lay bare the ministers' weakness, to expound the country's true policy, to arouse the people. And he would spend whole days preparing himself and mastering his facts. Before the debate on the treaties 'Temple and Mr. Pitt,' we are told, ' live in the Parliament office, and Joe Wright . . . had to light a fire for them and shut them up for three or four hours together among all the treaties of the world '—much, no doubt, to Joe Wright's disquiet, unused as he was to be troubled by statesmen taking politics in earnest. Pitt's example inspired others, and he had soon collected a band of comrades full of hope and zeal. George Grenville never shone as he did this session, Legge surpassed himself, and even Lord George Sackville rose to unnatural heights of patriotism. George Townshend worthily upheld the tradition of Whig common-sense inherited from his grandfather, Walpole's colleague, and his brother Charles first revealed those marvellous talents immortalised by Burke, making one speech of which Pitt generously declared that it displayed such abilities as had not appeared since that House was a House. Pitt soon could do with the House what he liked, except obtain votes. One after another of Newcastle's gladiators tried a fall with him, only to retire crushed and beaten. Lyttelton, who had succeeded Legge, was a child before him. Hume Campbell, in the debate on the Russian and Hessian treaties in December, undeterred by the fate of Robinson, and taking no warning from the late-learned caution of Murray and Fox, rushed blindly at the great orator. He attacked him for his ' eternal invectives,' and talked of the just resentment felt at Pitt's want of respect to ' superiors.' Pitt reminded Hume Campbell of the days, not long past, when they had trod the paths of invective together,[1] and when there had been no talk of ' superiors.' For such language one would have to go back to the servile days of James I, when no doubt another great duke had his slaves about him, who called him ' superior,' yet even they durst not bring such language into the House of Commons. Happily we no longer had a king willing to hire

December 10, 1755.

---

[1] In those days Campbell had applied to Walpole the remarkable expression that he was a *tympany of corruption*.

SLAUGHTER OF THE PYGMIES

a lawyer to threaten those who opposed his ministers' pernicious designs against the people : but if we had he would not want the slavish lawyer : ' but I will not dress up an image under a third person. I apply it to him,' nodding at Hume Campbell : ' his is the servile doctrine, he is the slave ; and the shame of this doctrine will stick to him as long as his gown clings to his back.'[1] Hume Campbell after this did little to earn his £2,000 a year; indeed, he was so terrified of Pitt that once, at an angry glance from him, he implored the Speaker's protection. Pitt could do much with a look or a tone. Turning one day on Murray that awful glance of his, ' I must,' said he, ' now address a few words to the Solicitor ; they shall be few but they shall be daggers' ; he paused, but the look continued, and Murray became more and more agitated. ' Judge Festus trembles,' said Pitt: ' he shall hear me some other day.' Another day it was Morton, Chief Justice of Chester, who had said, ' King, Lords, and Commons, or, as that right honourable gentleman would say, Commons, Lords and King.' Pitt sprang up: ' My blood runs cold at such words— I desire they may be taken down by the clerk.' ' Nay,' spluttered Morton, frightened out of his senses, ' I mean nothing ; King, Lords, and Commons : Commons, Lords, and King—it is all one.' ' I don't wish to push the matter further,' said Pitt in a voice little above a whisper : then higher, ' the moment a man acknowledges his error, he ceases to be guilty : but,' he added in a colloquial tone, ' whenever that member *means* nothing, I advise him to *say* nothing.' Once when Pitt had concluded a speech and was walking slowly out of the House, just as the doorkeeper was opening the door for him, his ear caught the words : ' I rise to reply to the right honourable gentleman.' Turning round, he gave the member a look which made him sit down instantly, and began hobbling goutily back to his seat, murmuring as he went :

> At Danaum proceres, Agamemnoniæque phalanges
> Ut videre virum, fulgentiaque arma per umbras
> Ingenti trepidare metu . . .
> . . . inceptus clamor frustratur hiantes.

[1] Sir W. Meredith's account quoted by Lord Rosebery (p. 431) from *Holland House MSS.* should be compared with Walpole's.

Then, lowering himself into his seat, he exclaimed, ' Now let me hear what the honourable gentleman has to say to me.' The member recounting the scene was asked if anybody laughed : ' No, sir, we were all too much awed to laugh.'[1] In his grim way Pitt must have had a glorious time, ' banging ' the House into submission and exulting in his power. Sometimes his humour took a less awful form. He compared the Duke of Newcastle to a child in charge of a go-cart, driving its precious freight of an old king and his family straight for a precipice. ' Surely,' he said, ' I am bound to take the reins out of such hands.'[2] ' Thou wilt not utter what thou dost not know,' he quoted in derision of some minister's fumbling explanations ; and he dismissed old Horace Walpole's timid talk as ' language fit for a boarding-school girl.' Sometimes he and Charles Townshend tossed the ball to one another. ' Are the resolutions of ministers to be more unchanged than those of the King of Persia or Xerxes with his multitudes at his heels ? ' loftily inquired Pitt. A little later Charles Townshend was called to order for describing an attack on him by Fox as unmanly.' ' Order, order ? ' pursued Townshend. ' Unmanly ! is that disorderly ? Upon my word, these are the nicest feelings in Xerxes's troops that I ever knew.'

November 20, 1755.
On the day he was dismissed Pitt promised the House ' that he would give daily and constant attendance to add to England's strength in armies, navies, or money, and do everything in his power against subsidiary treaties . . . and that for the love of his country he would do anything ' : this promise he almost literally fulfilled. He is known to have spoken in twenty-six debates this session and probably spoke oftener. Working at this strain he was naturally not always on the same high level, and towards the end seems to have

January 23, March 3, 1756.
January 28, 1756.
repeated himself needlessly, to have become irritable, and to have wrangled too often with Fox, the only man whose equanimity he could not disturb. He opposed poor Lyttelton's budget for his raids on the sinking fund, and even objected to a grant of £120,000 for the services of American troops in

---

[1] See Charles Butler's *Reminiscences.*
[2] Cp. a similar passage in speech of Dec. 6, 1743 (above, p. 113).

the war, on the ground that the ministers were not to be trusted with so large a sum without appropriation: they might 'sink it in some avaricious corner of the Court,' or bribe the House of Commons and obtain sham receipts from America. He accused Fox of screening the guilty for his own purposes on an extravagant charge brought by his friend Beckford against the Governor of Jamaica. Fox, who, though an adversary, always had an artist's appreciation of Pitt's great speeches, said of him in January 1756: 'The four last times he has spoke he made such violent speeches (not good ones of their kind) upon such trifling matter, which I have been obliged to take such advantage of, that he is lowered and I am raised by it beyond what his enemies or my warmest friends could have wished.'[1] But these extravagances were quite subordinate to the great constructive work of his speeches this session. For he was critical only incidentally; his main object, as in the first speech of the session, was to teach his countrymen how to wage a great war. He implored the ministers not to stint the navy at such a time, for it was 'a willing, giving House of Commons, on whom the King might call for anything for an *English* object.' When the Government proposed an increase of the army, he asked why they had not done so before, and demanded even greater exertions. By alarming the nation he hoped to make the danger reach the ears of His Majesty: he wanted to call the country out of that enervate state, that twenty thousand men from France could shake it. The maxims of our Government were degenerated, not our natives; he wished to see that breed restored, which under our old principles had carried our glory so high. On a proposal to give French prizes to the captors, to encourage recruiting in place of the press-gang, 'which smells so rank of arbitrary power,' he brushed aside Fox's quibbles that war was not officially declared and begged him to think further than 'that little narrow *now*': France had made war in attack-

January 23, 1756.

November 20, 1755.

December 5, 1755.

December 2, 1755.

---

[1] Torrens, ii. 273. Even Speaker Onslow, a warm admirer, said on the same occasion: 'If Pitt did not provide better matter to make his fine speeches upon, he would soon grow as insignificant as any man who ever sat in the House.'

ing Washington, and we should have to fight it out. 'If we do not deliver the territories of all our Indian allies as well as our own in America from every French post and garrison, we may give up our plantations as well as the ships we have taken ... and our King must submit to be a sort of viceroy under His most Christian Majesty.' With such a task before us, what availed the 140,000 troops of the best in Europe, which Murray boasted were ready for the defence of Hanover? 'Who boasts of the numbers prepared for England? —for America? Compare the countries, compare the forces that are destined for the defence of each! Two miserable battalions of Irish, who scarce ever saw one another, have been sent to America, have been sent under Braddock to be sacrificed!' Instead of doing what Athens would have done, putting herself on board her fleet and so recovering her land— because she fought where she could be superior—we were wasting our resources in subsidies for a continental war. And what effect would this Russian treaty have but to throw our most natural ally, Prussia, into the arms of France? Murray had talked of Russia as a newly-rising northern star, which, if properly managed, might preserve the liberties of Europe:

November 20, 1755.

December 15, 1755.

Come, let us consider this northern star that will not shine with any light of its own—Great Britain must be the sun of all this solar system: could Russia, without our assistance, support her own troops? I am glad this star is a fixed star, for I am certain it is not that star which once appeared in the East and which the wise men worshipped; though it is like it in one particular for it makes its worshippers bring gifts.[1] 'Tis a miserable star, that you must rub up to get it to shine. The really wise man

quae
Desperat tractatu nitescere posse, relinquit.

The Russian treaty brought, however, one benefit, since the menace to himself induced Frederic to conclude a treaty with England in January 1756. The situation was then somewhat complicated. The sole object of the Russian treaty had been to bring a Russian army on Frederic's back, if he attacked Hanover. By the alliance with Frederic a few months later

[1] See *Gray's Letters* (December 25, 1755).

England agreed with him to resist these very Russians or any other foreign troops brought into Germany. Newcastle's simple-minded idea seems to have been that by making treaties broadcast, with almost every European Power, quite irrespective of their relations to one another, he could isolate France and prevent a continental war. Indeed his Ministry had so little conception of the use to which Frederic might be put in diverting French resources from America, that two months after the treaty was signed Holderness wrote to Vienna that England would still support the Empress against any attack from Frederic. Pitt had always desired a Prussian alliance,, but not on such terms. When the treaty was discussed he criticised it partly on the ground that we had bought this treaty with Prussia by sacrificing our rights to arrears of a Silesian loan,[1] still more because it was not the time to be thinking of alliances in Germany, when all was at stake in America, in the Mediterranean, and especially at Minorca, where Richelieu and his French army had already landed. 'I pray to God,' said Pitt, 'that the King may not have Minorca, like Calais, written on his heart.' *May 12 and 14, 1756.*

This clear perception of the national objects of the war was accompanied by a superb belief in his countrymen's ability to fight it for themselves. Ever since William III's days Englishmen had been so accustomed by their rulers to believe that no war could be undertaken without a strong force of mercenaries to back them, that they had almost begun to lose confidence in themselves. Pitt's contagious enthusiasm and trust altered this. When it was proposed that a Swiss adventurer, Prevost, should raise four battalions of Swiss mercenaries and also provide foreign officers for the new levies in America, Pitt, while applauding any scheme to increase our forces in America, protested against employing foreign rather than English officers, who had behaved everywhere with lustre and should not thus be superseded. When *February 9–22, 1756.*

---

[1] After Frederic's conquest of Silesia he had taken over a Silesian loan advanced by England, but had refused to pay the instalments due until some grievances for captured ships had been redressed by the Admiralty. By the treaty of 1756 Frederic gained most of what he had been contending for.

March, April, 1756.

the ministers brought over Hessian and Hanoverian troops on the alarm of a French invasion, Pitt came in blisters and flannel from his sick-bed to protest against the indignity. In 1690—nay, even in Charles II's degenerate days—the national forces had been thought sufficient: why could we not depend on ourselves now? No state could be called a sovereign state unless *suis stat viribus, non alieno pendet arbitrio*. The waste on foreign troops would have conquered America or saved Minorca. It had, indeed, come to a sad pass if 'this great country could neither provide for offence nor defence.'

May 11, 1756.

To remove this disgrace from England Pitt had a plan of his own for reviving the old militia spirit in England. The ancient militia force of the realm was then moribund, and the law empowering the lords-lieutenant to call it out in times of emergency a dead letter. Pitt's speech on the motion of his friend George Townshend for a committee on the militia revealed him in the new light of constructive statesmanship. In the plan he unfolded for the reorganization of the militia he showed a grasp of details and an aptitude for business which he had hitherto had no chance of proving. The force was to consist of 50,000 or 60,000 men, who were to be drilled twice a week, and to receive pay for drills and uniform. The officers were to be drawn from the landed gentry of each county in which the units were formed; and the Crown would have the right of marching each contingent outside its own county in case of necessity. The total annual cost he reckoned at £300,000—cheap compared with the millions spent in subsidies—cheap, too, for the gain in national self-respect.

December 8, 1755.

What an inglorious picture for this country [he said] to figure, gentlemen driven by an invasion like a flock of sheep, and forced to send their money abroad to buy courage and defence! If this scheme should prove oppressive provincially or parochially, I am willing to give it up; but how preferable it is to waiting to see if the wind would blow you subsidiary troops!

In the following months Pitt, helped by George Townshend, Sackville and the Speaker, devoted unstinted labour to settling details of the militia bill thereupon introduced; all the ministers, except Lyttelton, washed their hands of it, and often in committee Pitt was left alone with about a dozen other members. Finally, when it had been committed and re-committed, it was passed after a great speech by Pitt on May 10, 1756, in a sitting which lasted till near six in the morning. In the Lords it received short shrift. Hardwicke opposed it chiefly on the grounds that the statute book was becoming too large and that the bill required too many oaths ; by his influence it was rejected by 53 to 29.

Pitt truly said in one of his speeches : ' We have provoked before we can defend, we have neglected after provocation, and in every quarter of the world we are inferior to France' ; and, as early as April, had with a sure instinct picked out Minorca as the immediate point of danger. Our fleets had at first been employed as freebooters on French commerce, leaving the French fleet intact and doing nothing to stop the reinforcement of Canada. In 1756 the panic of a French invasion kept most of our ships in home waters, and although early in February Newcastle was warned[1] that the French were meditating an attack on Minorca, for two months no precautions were taken. As in Walpole's time, the Governor and most of the officers were in England and allowed to remain there, and no fleet was watching the French Mediterranean ports.[2] At last, on April 6, ten ships sailed from Spithead under Byng, who was known not to have the spirit for an urgent and hazardous enterprize. Byng took nearly a month to reach Gibraltar, where he heard that a French army under Richelieu had landed in Minorca a fortnight before. Even then Byng stayed six days at Gibraltar, and allowed the Governor to disobey the orders from home to send reinforcements for the garrison of Port Mahon. On May 19 he sighted La Galissonière's fleet of twelve sail off Minorca and engaged them next day without result. Opinions differ as to Byng's courage and ability in the action, but of his pusillanimity afterwards there can be no doubt. After cruising about for

May 12, 1756.

---

[1] *Add. MSS.* 35415, f. 147.

[2] For the neglect of warnings by the Ministry, when they could well have spared ships to watch Minorca, see Richmond, *Papers relating to the Loss of Minorca.*

four days, he called a council of war, suggested to it that the fleet could no longer help Minorca, and, having obtained the answer he desired, sailed back to Gibraltar. Had he remained off Minorca he would at least have threatened Richelieu's communications, and might even have compelled him to relinquish a siege which, owing to natural difficulties and the courage of old General Blakeney, proved difficult enough without external interference.[1]

'*Quae regio in terris nostri non plena doloris?*' Pitt wrote on the news of Byng's retreat : ' I dread to hear from America. Asia may perhaps furnish its portion of ignominy and calamity.' This feeling of ignominy was shared by the country : to contend with the power of France seemed to many a hopeless task : to hold up against it in their own lifetime the most they could hope with such a Ministry.[2] The loss of Minorca filled up the cup of national indignation. For it meant to that generation what the loss of Gibraltar would to us. Englishmen were proud of it ; they looked on it as an indispensable port of refuge for our merchants, and indeed would more willingly have spared Gibraltar ; and it had been lost disgracefully. Vengeance on Byng, vengeance on the Ministry that sent him out so tardily was the cry from all parts of England. The City demanded it and offered to contribute liberally to the war if a militia were organised, the fleets set free for aggressive action, and proper measures taken to defend America.[3] Instructions were given to members to call ministers to account. Newcastle received reports of ' almost universal uneasiness and discontent ... the lower sort of people outrageous ... even peers loud in their censures and endeavours to enflame the people ... to demand justice against persons however dignified or distinguished,' persons who he fears must be himself, Hardwicke and Anson.[4] Lord Chief Justice Willes bluntly told him that the only thing to do was to shoot Byng, ' no lesser punishment will satisfy the minds of the people.'[5] Newcastle did not

[1] The garrison did not surrender until June 28, 1756, after seventy days' siege.
[2] See *Grafton Memoirs*, pp. 9, 10.
[3] See their Address of August 20, 1756.
[4] *Add. MSS.* 32867, ff. 111 and 175.
[5] *Ibid.* 32867, f. 1.

need to be told this; his first impulse on news of the disaster was to save his own skin by ordering 'the immediate trial and condemnation of Byng.'[1] 'Oh, indeed, he shall be tried immediately,' he is reported to have said to a City deputation; 'he shall be hanged directly.' But whereas Hardwicke regarded the fall of Minorca as a blessing in disguise, since it might incline the King to stop a war which he was convinced was hopeless and ruinous, Newcastle, though equally sure we were no match for France,[2] was anxious for some dashing exploit to show what a spirited Ministry it was: anywhere would do—the Mediterranean, the West Indies, or North America.[3] But fresh disasters came instead of successes. Even what the Ministry did right became a grievance—notably the release by Holderness of a wretched Hanoverian soldier wrongly accused of stealing handkerchiefs at Maidstone—for it revived all the bitterness felt at a foreign garrison on English soil. Great distress from scarcity of corn aggravated the discontent in the country. Then the whole edifice of foreign politics, laboriously built up by Newcastle during the last eight years, collapsed like a pack of cards when the Empress-Queen signed the treaty of Versailles with France on May 1, 1756. This upheaval of the old continental system was a blessing in disguise, but not one that Newcastle had the wit to recognise. Yet another disaster, the capture of Oswego, was reported from America; and, on September 9, Frederic II suddenly invaded Saxony and precipitated the continental war for which Newcastle was wholly unprepared. No foreign disasters, however, finally decided Newcastle that the game was up, but the loss of his only two capable lieutenants. Murray had no love for the House of Commons, where, he admitted to Newcastle, he felt intimidated by Pitt,[4] and on the death of the Lord Chief Justice of the King's Bench demanded the post as of right, together with a peerage. Newcastle implored him to stay; but Murray, though protesting that it 'stabbed daggers to his heart' to desert him,[5] was obdurate, and had

---

[1] *Add. MSS.* 32866, f. 210.   [2] *Ibid.* 32864, f. 478.
[3] *Ibid.* 32866, ff. 210 and 265.   [4] Walpole, *Memoirs George III*, i, 80.
[5] *Add. MSS.* 32865, f. 205.

to be created Chief Justice and Baron Mansfield. Fox also became restive—'disobliged,' Newcastle called it—refused to take any responsibility for Minorca, and complained he was not treated with confidence. On October 14 he took what he described as the 'necessary but innocent' step of resigning; he had no resentment,' but he found his situation impracticable.[1]

Pitt had become inevitable. He had recently done considerable service to his friends at Leicester House by actively supporting the Princess Dowager's favourite, Bute,[2] for the post of Groom of the Stole in the young Prince's establishment, and in return had all their influence in his favour. Newcastle in May had seen that Pitt was 'Fox's master,' and Fox himself had been only too anxious to gain Pitt to the Ministry. Newspapers and pamphlets appeared urging a strong Ministry under Pitt, and caricatures that denounced the Government for making England 'depend on champions not her own' called for Pitt as the champion of integrity :

> Britannia, nodding, signifies her choice
> And hails in his, God's and the people's voice.

Hardwicke, when things had come to this pass, brushed aside in a sentence the old pretence that the obstacle to Pitt lay in the King. 'Are you really for it in your heart ?' he asks Newcastle ; '. . . if you are, surely ways might be found to try it.' 'I am hand and heart for Pitt at present,' answers the duke. 'He will come as a conqueror. I always dreaded it, but I had rather be conquered by an enemy, who can do our business,' than by a traitor like Fox. Lady Yarmouth, who had great influence with the King, and to some extent

---

[1] *Add. MSS.* 32868 f. 247.

[2] The only circumstance which gives any plausibility to the rumours of Bute's undue familiarity with the Princess is Waldegrave's belief in its truth. On the other hand a very strong argument against it is George III's affection for Bute. He could hardly have been ignorant of the rumours, and it would have been very difficult to deceive him had they been true ; nor was he the man to remain on such friendly terms with Bute had he had the slightest belief in their truth. For another view, see Lovat Fraser, *John Stuart, Earl of Bute*, p. 86.

PITT INDISPENSABLE

merited it by her sound political sense, had long seen the necessity of bringing in Pitt. Even the King himself, on being told by Newcastle that he must give way, was content to ease his mind with a grumble—' But Mr. Pitt won't come . . . and he won't do my German business '—and then consented.[1]

Newcastle was willing enough now to give Pitt responsibility, but he still hoped to make him responsible for the old measures. Such an offer might have tempted Pitt two years before, since he knew that with responsibility he could mould the measures himself. Now it was a case of the Sibylline books, as he told Grenville; and he was not disposed to bear the burden of Newcastle's policy on his shoulders, after two years of opposition to it. When on October 19, 1756, Hardwicke made offers to him, he could not be moved from his ' total negative ' either to joining the Duke of Newcastle or to adopting his measures . . . ' he was surprised that it should be thought possible for him to . . . serve with the Duke of Newcastle, under whose administration the things he had so much blamed had happened, and against which the sense of the nation so strongly appeared.'

The only terms on which he would take office were : (1) An inquiry into past measures, in which he himself should take a considerable part ; (2) That last year's Militia Bill should be passed ; (3) That the affair of the Hanoverian soldier should be inquired into ; and (4) That he should have full personal access to the King and be in the ' first concert and concoction of measures.' Fearing that his refusal to act with Newcastle might be interpreted as a refusal to take office at all, and that Hardwicke's report might not represent his views, two days later Pitt for the first time went to Lady Yarmouth to explain himself fully to her. If the King was to hear the truth, it was the only course open to Pitt, since he had no access to the Closet, whereas it was well known that ' the Lady,' as she was familiarly called, was a safe and certain channel to the King's ears. He not only repeated to her what he had told Hardwicke, but handed in a rough sketch of his Ministry: he and Sir

---

[1] *Add. MSS.* 32868, ff. 249, 251, 281.

Thomas Robinson [1] to be Secretaries; Devonshire, First Lord; Temple, Lord Lieutenant; and George and James Grenville with places. The King, like all obstinate people, never liked it to be thought that he was influenced. 'Lady Yarmouth does not meddle,' he said with palpable untruth, 'and shall not meddle;' and professed to be very angry with Pitt. He sent him a curt message that his proposals were not for his or the public service. Pitt bowed ceremoniously and observed that the King did him the greatest honour in condescending to answer him at all.[2]

Nevertheless Pitt's plain statement of his conditions had cleared the ground. Newcastle saw there was nothing for it but his own resignation: the King then spent three weeks in futile negotiations with Fox and others, but nobody would undertake the thankless task of clearing up Newcastle's muddles except Pitt. On November 15, 1756, he was appointed Secretary of State on almost the very terms he had originally laid down. Legge became Chancellor of the Exchequer again, Temple had the Admiralty, Devonshire the Treasury; Pitt himself had desired the Northern Province, but waived it before the King's objections, leaving Holderness there and taking the Southern Province for himself. The King was not pleased. To Pitt himself he delivered the seals courteously enough on December 4, 1756;[3] but the rest of the Ministry he received 'with the least gracious manner possible.'

Pitt had indeed come as a conqueror. Of the old Cabinet the principal members, Newcastle, Hardwicke, Fox and Anson, three of whom had been in office before Pitt made his first speech in Parliament, were entirely put aside. There had been no such clean sweep since the rout of the Tories in 1714.

[1] Pitt was naturally ridiculed for suggesting as his colleague the man he had attacked a year before. But Pitt had attacked him not as Secretary but as Leader of the House, and had always admitted his knowledge of foreign affairs. It was a characteristic of Pitt to attack a man in a position for which he thought him unfitted, and afterwards to use his services where he thought they would be useful to the public.

[2] See *Add. MSS.* 32868 and 35416, *passim.*

[3] This delay was due partly to Pitt's gout, partly to his desire to be present at the opening of Parliament on December 2, as he would have to vacate his seat on appointment.

Such a victory naturally created disgust among the old Whig official families, and Pitt himself was heartily abused for his arrogance and his eloquence in *The Test* [1] and other papers as 'Our Great Orator,' 'the Man-Mountain,' 'the Dictator,' or 'William the Fourth.' They could not understand a Cabinet based on a principle, not on mere bargaining with powerful factions. Pitt's first Cabinet absorbed nearly the whole of his personal following in the House, and so could count on little support there. Its strength lay partly in the belief in the House that nobody but Pitt could bring the country into safety, still more in the confidence he inspired outside the House. Pitt had to wait until he was nearly fifty to overcome the King's dislike, break through official jealousy, and gain control of the country's destinies. These were then entrusted to him, says Glover, because—

The eyes of an afflicted despairing nation were now lifted up to a private gentleman of a slender fortune, wanting the parade of birth or title, of no family alliance but by his marriage with Lord Temple's sister, and even confined to a narrow circle of friends and acquaintances. Under these circumstances Pitt was considered as the only saviour of England.

Pitt knew it to be true. 'I know,' he said, 'that I can save this country, and that no one else can.'

---

[1] Newcastle also was attacked in *The Test*, and asked Hardwicke to discover its authorship. Hardwicke, after diligent inquiry, discovered that a written copy of *The Test* was carried on the morning of publication from the house of Calcraft (a rich army contractor then closely allied with Fox) by Taylor, a silversmith, to his house at the corner of Cecil Street. Thence he sent a clerk with it to Hooper the publisher, who sent a man with it to Parker the printer near Bishopsgate. (*Add. MSS.* 35416, f. 158.) For a specimen of the abuse levelled at Pitt, see note on following page.

Note (see p. 285).

In *Sanderson Miller* (p. 346) a specimen is given of the kind of abuse to which Pitt was subjected at this time. It was apparently a broadsheet inspired by similar ideas to those of the writers of *The Test* :

SEVEN GOOD REASONS FOR THE CHANGES AT COURT
BEING THE EXAMINATION OF CERTAIN GREAT MEN AT THE PRIVY COUNCIL.

We will that you forthwith discharge all your Ministers and Servants and permit Us to fill their Places ; that so we may be able to satisfie (if possible) his thirst for Gold, for otherwise we know we cannot hold him fast. We also Will, that you place our beloved Brother Lord T. at the head of your Navy, that he may show his inborn Talents, by being in a Province he can know nothing of, for your Naval Expeditions having failed under the direction of Knowledge and Experience, we judge that Ignorance and Presumption will set all right. We Will that you give to the Honourable and Ingenious C. T. [Charles Townshend] some place without business so that his Talents may be concealed, which otherwise would eclipse or rather extinguish our aforesaid little Friend, and might be dangerous even to our own Omnipotence. We Will that you give lucrative Employment to all our Unkles, Brothers, Cousins and Namesakes ; and knowing that in the H. of L— there is but our dear Brother upon whom we can at all rely, We Will therefore that you create such numbers of L—ds as may be requisite for our Support, and as a great Majority of the H. of C—ns have not so good an opinion of us as we have of ourselves, We Will that you dissolve this P—t that so we may render your K—ms sub-servient to our Will and Pleasure. Upon these conditions we will allow you to reign and take upon us the Administration of Affairs.

CHAPTER X

THE AWAKENING OF THE PEOPLE

'Ἄνδρες γὰρ πόλις, καὶ οὐ τείχη οὐδὲ νῆες ἀνδρῶν κεναί.—THUCYDIDES, vii, 77.[1]

'I HAVE called you together in a conjuncture which highly requires the deliberation, advice and assistance of Parliament, and I trust that (under the guidance of Divine Providence) union and firmness in my affectionate people will carry me with honour through all difficulties; and finally vindicate the dignity of my crown, and its indubitable rights, against the ancient enemy of these kingdoms.'

So began the King's Speech with which Pitt inaugurated his first Ministry on December 2, 1756. 'I have drawn it captivating the people,' he wrote, enclosing the first draft to Devonshire;[2] 'as it stands it will go over the whole kingdom and spread a satisfaction which a subsequent message cannot do'; and every line of the Speech breathed a spirit of energy and national pride unwonted in the 'insipid annual opiate'[3] read from the Throne at the beginning of the session. The King grumbled at the length of this first draft, and ejaculated 'Stuff and nonsense!' at some of its expressions; but in its final form it 'touched with gravity and weight,' as Pitt said he intended, 'points indispensably necessary to be mentioned as foundations of supply and descriptive of system.' This system, the same as that demanded by the City in its address of August 20,[4] he proclaimed with no uncertain voice :

[1] 'Men make a city, not walls or ships empty of men.'
[2] Torrens, ii, 342.   [3] Speech of November 22, 1770.
[4] See above, p. 280.

> The succour and preservation of America cannot but constitute a main object of my attention and solicitude, and the growing dangers to which our colonies stand exposed from our late losses in those parts, demand resolution of vigour and despatch. . . .
>
> To this end a national militia . . . may, in time, become one good resource in time of general danger. . . .
>
> The body of my electoral troops, which I ordered hither at the desire of my Parliament, I have directed to return to my dominions in Germany; relying with pleasure on the spirit and zeal of my people, in defence of my person and realm. . . .
>
> I rely on your wisdom, that you will prefer more vigorous efforts (though attended with large expense) to a less effectual, and therefore less frugal, plan of war.

He remembered too the material condition of the people to whom he was appealing for fresh exertions:

> I cannot here be unmindful of the sufferings of the poorer sort, from the present high price of corn, and the disturbances which have arisen therefrom; and I recommend to you to consider of proper provisions for preventing the like mischiefs hereafter.

This direct appeal to the people marks a revolution in the conduct of the country's foreign policy. Foreign affairs had always been treated as the peculiar concern of the King and one or two trusted ministers: with one stroke Pitt made them the concern of the public. By this publicity he did away once for all with the old system. Foreign policy had long consisted chiefly in abstruse calculations of checks and alliances to secure a balance of power on the Continent—a matter of profound indifference to the country. 'We pay all and fight all,' said Pelham,[1] echoing the popular view; but not even Newcastle could have given a plausible explanation of all this paying and fighting, of battles in the heart of Germany and expensive treaties to defend an electorate, the very name of which was hateful to English ears. All our efforts were devoted to bolstering up some other power—Hanover, the Empress-Queen, or at best Holland—while the national interests and the national enemy were alike lost sight of. To these Pitt recalled Parliament and the nation. While Carteret and

---

[1] See above, p. 165.

Newcastle were bothering their heads with Pragmatic Sanctions and Kings of the Romans, and other such will-o'-the-wisps, Pitt, mindful perhaps of his old grandfather's prophecy—that 'trade will flourish rather than decay'[1]—had been learning the real needs of the time through his friends Allen of Bath, Beckford and Alderman Sayre, with other leaders of the great commercial community, too long ignored or looked down upon by the Whig magnates. From such representatives of the wealthiest and most vigorous element in the community came very definite views of the real enemy and the real objects of the war. The two great obstacles to our growing trade were the Bourbon Powers. With Spain there was a temporary understanding since the last war; but France was everywhere aggressive. In two recent campaigns she had captured the Low Countries and stopped our easiest access to the Continent; in India, in America, in the West Indies our merchants and settlers were confronted by her at every turn; by the capture of Minorca she seriously threatened our Mediterranean and Levant trade; even our own shores seemed in peril. Pitt, therefore, instead of making the King's Speech turn on Hanover and treaties to defend Hanover, pointed out the one object of the war, the defeat of 'the ancient enemy of these kingdoms,' and that it should be waged chiefly where her aggressions had been most dangerous—in America. He took the nation into his confidence, he put to it a plain issue, and in return he asked it to fight its own battles—an equally revolutionary idea to a generation accustomed to be ruled by ministers who regarded half of them as disaffected, if not rebellious, and were always ready to run for Dutchmen, Hessians and Hanoverians at any whisper of foreign danger. Pitt's first Ministry would have been justified had he done nothing more than clear the decks for action by this plain statement of policy and courageous appeal for national exertion.

After the King's Speech his most immediate need was to gain support in the House of Commons. Newcastle had truly said after his resignation that the flame which had spread through the country 'did not extend to the members

[1] See above, p. 26.

of Parliament ... and that Mr. Pitt, with the Duke of Devonshire at his head, will have difficulty to support himself.'[1] But Pitt, on assuming the Ministry, no longer regarded himself as leader of a party, but as leader of the nation. 'I have no attachment to persons,' he announced, 'but to things'[2]— an early form of his more concise maxim, 'Measures, not men.' In the debate on the Address he silenced opposition by the discreet and conciliatory tone of his speech. He poured cold water on his friend Beckford's premature boasts of the country's strength; admitted that the loss of the Hanoverians would make a dangerous gap in the defences of the country, though he hoped to find means of supplying it; owned that our fleet was not so strong as he hoped to see it; and declared that he was not going to blame the late ministers before the inquiry on their conduct had been held. Newcastle was for the present content not to offer active opposition unless Pitt took vindictive measures against his administration, and Pitt was far too anxious to prepare for the future struggle to rake up the past unnecessarily. But first he must have perfect liberty of action. By accepting office he vacated his seat for Aldborough, and, instead of seeking re-election for a borough where 'he stood publicly marked as the Duke of Newcastle's servant,' he chose to stand for a vacant seat at Okehampton, where he would be under no such obligations. Secure in his independence, he was prepared to discuss matters amicably with the late ministers. Three days after the opening of the session Hardwicke came to him on a fishing inquiry under the guise of a visit of compliment. He arrived in the evening and was ushered upstairs to a room, where Mr. Pitt was lying up with the gout, one leg wrapped in flannel. Expressions of civility, 'overflowing' on Pitt's side, passed between them, and the two soon found common ground in their objection to Fox. Hardwicke, cunningly passing to the main object of his visit, assured Pitt that Newcastle would never join with Fox, unless violence were displayed in pushing inquiries and censures. 'Censures are not what we require,' said Pitt—' as you might

December 2, 1756.

[1] *Add. MSS.* 32869, f. 27.   [2] *Ibid.* 32871, f. 9.

have known from the moderate tone of my speech on the Address ; but I am pledged to some inquiry on past negligence, and should be ruined and discredited if I did not abide by my pledges.' But he reassured the late Chancellor by adding that to his mind this inquiry into the past was a matter of slight importance. He then touched on his hopes of support in the House of Commons, and, much to Hardwicke's surprise, told him that the Tory country gentlemen had given him assurances of their good disposition and had treated him with generosity and candour. To Hardwicke's inquiry as to conditions Pitt answered, ' None at all : their action was quite free and disinterested, with the object of keeping the ship from sinking.' But he admitted to Hardwicke that he still had many difficulties to contend with from intrigues at Court and from the King, who, though gracious in giving him the seals, had said nothing ' of which he could make a boast.' Hardwicke then took leave, much relieved for himself and Newcastle, and Pitt, not to be outdone in courtly ceremoniousness, said ' he wished for the use of his leggs for nothing more than that they might carry him to visit his lordship.' [1]

Hardwicke had smiled indulgently when Pitt told him of his alliance with the country gentlemen, and was sceptical about its duration. But he was wrong. On the following day Barrington confirmed the news : ' The Tories,' he wrote to the Duke of Newcastle, ' will support the new Administration in a body, and I verily believe without having made *any* conditions. Mr. Pitt told me he desired their countenance no longer than they approved his conduct.'[2] While Pitt was awaiting his election at Okehampton he had employed Potter,[3] his former opponent on the Seaford election, now a close ally, to gain the Tory country party, composed of men hitherto excluded from all hope of preferment and more noted for their devotion to country pursuits than for diligent attendance at Westminster. Pitt's programme and his clearly

---

[1] *Add. MSS.* 32869, f. 253.   [2] *Ibid.* f. 266.
[3] See Potter's letters in *Chatham MSS.* 53. Potter mentions the following members as prepared to band together in support of one another and of Pitt : Prowse, Northey, Beckford, Mordaunt, Tynte, Popham, Carteret, Sagott, Ward, Grosvenor, Curzons, Affleck, Banks.

expressed intention of making no party distinctions awoke in them a new zeal for public affairs : 'they deserted their hounds and their horses,' says Glover, 'preferring for once their parliamentary duty, and under their new Whig leader, the gallant George Townshend, displayed their banner for Pitt.'

The commercial members, Beckford and others, were always with him hand and heart ; and this alliance of Tories and business men with Pitt lasted unbroken until his final fall from power. Lord Westmorland, too, 'a veteran patriot, slow but solid,' Lord Talbot, and Lord Stanhope, Pitt's kinsman, came forth from retirement to support the minister who, even if he had not a solid majority in Parliament, had at his back the Prince of Wales and his Court, the City, the clergy, the army, the law, and the populace.[1] The people acclaimed him by what has become his most honourable title to fame, The Great Commoner.[2]

Having gained the goodwill of the people he was bent on making them work. But first they had to be fed. Much of the discontent during Newcastle's last year of office was due to the distress caused by a sudden rise of 12s. in the price of corn. Following Pitt's recommendation in the King's Speech, the House set up an inquiry into the causes of this rise on the first day of the session, and without loss of time proposed various remedies, such as an embargo on corn for export,[3] a temporary removal of the high duty on foreign corn, and permission to sell duty-free corn captured from the enemy. These measures did not immediately bring down the price, which rose to £3 a quarter in 1757. This and the increased war taxes found

---

[1] Glover's *Memoirs*.

[2] The first reference to this title for Pitt is probably that in *The Test*, No. 8, January 1, 1757 : 'If our great Commoner were like other men.' In No. 22, of April 9, 1757, occurs the phrase, 'a certain great commoner (so he was lately called).' Pitt himself is said to have invented the name, when he applied it to Sir John Barnard, the well-known member for the City, for whom of all his opponents Walpole had the greatest respect.

[3] This action no doubt suggested to Lord Chatham a similar policy in 1766, when he ordered an embargo of corn by administrative order at a time when Parliament was not sitting. Sir R. Peel (*Memoirs* ii, 189) notes the action of Parliament in 1756.

necessary by Pitt caused the people to murmur at some of his measures, as they had against his predecessors ; but before the end of the war corn had been brought down below the price at which it had stood in 1755.[1]

He next appealed to the dignity of Englishmen: 'I want to call this country out of that enervate state that 20,000 men from France could shake it,' he had declared in the previous session, and he began by teaching them to rely on themselves alone. On December 11, in fulfilment of his promise in the King's Speech, orders were sent to the Admiralty to prepare transports for returning the German troops to their own country :[2] before the end of the year the Hanoverians had been sent out of England ; the Hessians were kept some months longer to give time for filling 'the dangerous gap' in the defences of the country.[3] Even on this cardinal point of his policy Pitt was made to feel his weakness in Parliament. The House of Lords, with Devonshire's consent and in spite of violent protests from Temple, actually thanked the King for having brought over these foreign troops to defend our shores. Pitt only averted a similar motion in the House of Commons by threatening instant resignation if it were carried.

To supply the place of the Germans fifteen new battalions were raised, old regiments were increased, and additions made to the Royal Artillery and the Marines.[4] Pitt also adopted the bold experiment of raising two Highland regiments, drawn from clans that had recently fought against the dynasty.

					£	s.	d.
[1] In 1755 the average price per quarter was					1	13	10
,, 1756	,,	,,	,,	,,	2	5	3
,, 1757	,,	,,	,,	,,	3	0	0
,, 1761	,,	,,	,,	,,	1	10	3

At that time the ratio of imported corn to home-grown was as 1 : 570, hence the removal of the foreign duty was of infinitely less importance then than it would have been later. (See Adam Smith, I, xi, for table of corn prices.)

[2] Record Office, *S. P. Dom. Admiralty*, 229.

[3] Most of the Hessians disembarked at Stade on their return journey on May 12, 1757. (Waddington, i, 399.)

[4] See Record Office, *S. P. Dom. Military*, 189. Newcastle's Ministry had decided to raise the fifteen new battalions in September, but left it to Pitt to do so. (Fortescue, ii, 299.)

294   THE AWAKENING OF THE PEOPLE

The experiment had been approved in principle by Cumberland and even by Newcastle, but nobody had yet been bold enough to attempt it. When Pitt, in his interview with Hardwicke, told him of his intention, Hardwicke shook his head over the dangers of enlisting men who were rebels ten years before; but Pitt was unmoved. It would 'gain the Scotch,' he said, and would drain the Highlands of some disaffected clansmen, who would fight well in North America and might not return thence.[1] At any rate he wasted no time in carrying out his purpose. Within the first fortnight of 1757 commissions were issued to Montgomery and Fraser, son of the old rebel Lord Lovat, to command the two battalions, and warrants made out for their establishment and equipment.[2] Frasers, Macdonalds, Macleans, Macphersons and others of disaffected clans were rapidly enrolled. Pitt's courage was fully justified. Nothing probably contributed so much to reconciling the Highlands to British rule as this act of confidence in allowing the clansmen to fight for the King in America, in Germany and in India; and the two battalions earned by their conduct Pitt's fine praise of them and of his own experiment: 'I sought for merit wherever it was to be found . . . I found it in the mountains of the north. I called it forth . . . an hardy and intrepid race of men—men who . . . had gone well-nigh to have overturned the State in the war before last. . . . They served with fidelity as they fought with valour, and conquered for you in every part of the world.'[3] To awaken Englishmen south of the Tweed to a consciousness of their privileges and their corresponding duties, he reverted to his militia scheme rejected by the Lords in the previous session. Two days after the beginning of the session it was brought

---

[1] Pitt possibly had in mind that many would remain there as settlers: it is not necessary to adopt Hardwicke's cynical interpretation that most of them would be killed off. In fact, the two regiments (77th and 78th) were disbanded at the peace, and grants of land in America were given to the men.

[2] Record Office. *S. P. Dom. Military*, 189.

[3] Speech of January 14, 1766. Pitt's merit was not in raising Highland regiments, but in raising them from rebel clans. The Black Watch, the first Highland regiment, was raised in 1739, and Highlanders had fought for England at Fontenoy. (See *Engl. Hist. Review* for July 1902, p. 466; Col. E. M. Lloyd's article.)

in again by George Townshend : it was passed in the Commons, and, though vehemently opposed in the Lords, became law in June 1757. The scheme as passed differed little from Pitt's original proposal.[1] Each county of England and Wales had to contribute a fixed quota of militiamen towards the total of 32,000 ;[2] each man's service was determined by lot ; the period of training, under the supervision of the lords-lieutenant, was three years ; and on an emergency the King, with the sanction of Parliament, could embody the militia for service anywhere in England. This force was not merely useful as a precaution against such humiliating panics as those of 1744, 1745 and 1756, but became a means of uniting hitherto discordant religious and political elements in the countryside by a bond of brotherhood and public duty.

Pitt had declared that England should 'put herself on board her fleet,'[3] and he saw to it that the means were forthcoming. He called for a list from the Admiralty of ships 'requisite for the total stagnation and extirpation of the French trade upon the seas and the general protection of that of Great Britain upon the seas,'[4] and found that, whereas the Admiralty required over two hundred men-of-war and frigates, only 134 had been in commission in the preceeding April.

[1] See above, pp. 278–9. The Act is 30 Geo. ii. c. 25.
[2] The Bill proposed 60,000 ; the Lords cut it down to 32,000.
[3] See above, p. 276.
[4] The list returned by the Admiralty is in *Chatham MSS.* 78. Dr. von Ruville is in error in quoting it (ii, 81) as the list of ships on the stations specified in August 1756. This distribution (given below) is interesting as agreeing in the main with what Chatham laid down as the naval requirements of England in his speech of November 22, 1770 : a strong home squadron, a strong western squadron, and a strong fleet based on Gibraltar.

	Line	Frigates	Armed Vessels	Bomb-ketches	Fire-ships
W. Indies and N. America	32	22	26	—	—
E. Indies . . .	8	4	—	—	—
Coast of Gt. Britain and Ireland and for convoys.	25	20	30	—	—
French Coast and Bay .	31	17	30	5	4
Mediterranean . .	29	16	40	4	2
Totals . .	125	79	126	9	6

A vigorous start, therefore, was made with the shipbuilding; a new make of frigate, especially adapted for the swift and vigorous actions suited to Pitt's ideas of warfare, was designed; within four years the navy was brought up to a total of 412 ships of all classes; and in his first year of office the House of Commons was asked to vote the unprecedented number of 55,000 sailors.[1] The Admiralty, with Temple as First Lord, was at this time entirely controlled by Pitt; even a ship with a cargo of pork could not leave Cork without a convoy, save with his express sanction.[2] Under his masterful rule the Admiralty soon learned that in rapidity of preparation and in overcoming difficulties 'nothing is impossible.'

Plans of offensive warfare were not delayed until all these preparations were completed; work on them was begun at once. It was needed. In America, Pitt's chosen theatre of war, the English cause seemed almost desperate. The French had all the advantage of position. From Fort Duquesne they could harass the western borders of Pennsylvania, Maryland and Virginia; Forts Frontenac, Oswego and Niagara gave them command of the western approach to Canada, Crown Point and Ticonderoga of the approach from New York by the Lake Champlain route farther east, Louisburg of the naval approach by the St. Lawrence. Their 7,000 regular troops in Canada and a good colonial militia, if well handled, were ample for offence as well as defence against the English forces as then organized; and in May a small cargo of talent, worth many regiments, had arrived at Quebec—Montcalm with his staff officers, de Lévis, Bourlamaque and young Bougainville. Finally, the victory over Braddock in 1755 and the capture of Oswego in 1756 had filled the French troops with hope and zest for the fight. The English, already disheartened by defeat, had a much longer line to defend with fewer troops, for though the regulars then in America were 8,000 strong, the provincial levies could not be depended upon as the Canadian militia. The Indians were deserting a losing cause and flocking to the French. From the governors of Georgia and South Carolina came doleful tales of Indian outbreaks, of a French raid expected from the

[1] See Clowes, iii, 5-8. [2] Record Office, *Foreign, Various*, 68.

PLANS FOR AMERICA

Mississippi province, and of no more than a few hundred rangers to cope with them. There was no English commander to match Montcalm. After Braddock's death, Shirley, Webb and Abercromby had in turn held his post, which in July had been taken over by Lord Loudoun—another offshoot of Cumberland's school of 'corporals and sergeants.' Newcastle evidently had no conception of the problem involved ; he had sent only two regiments with Loudoun to replace Braddock's, lost on the Monongahela, and had proposed to send but one more in 1757. Yet without overwhelming strength on sea and land it would have been impossible to defeat the French.

On December 16, 1756, a fortnight after he had received the seals, Pitt called a Cabinet, at which it was resolved to send an 'expedition of weight,' not less than 8,000 men and a fleet, to America. On the 22nd he wrote to Loudoun to make preparations on his side for an active campaign. On January 1 orders were sent to the Admiralty to take up and victual transports. Extra supplies of food and bedding were to be put aboard these, in case Loudoun had nothing ready for the troops on landing, also fishing seynes ' to catch fish for the refreshment of the men.' This last requisition Pitt heard the Admiralty had neglected. ' Mr. Pitt depends on orders being sent by this night's post to Portsmouth,' writes his secretary, ' with regard to the fishing seynes, with the proper cordage for them and leads for the fishing lines ; '[1] and special orders about them were also sent to Cork. While keeping a watchful eye on the transports, Pitt was also preparing the seven regiments chosen for this service from the Irish establishment. First he insisted they should be brought up to full strength. Difficulties were raised by Cumberland as to the mode of recruiting. On this Pitt writes to Devonshire on January 80 :

I cannot delay a moment in saying that this method of augmenting the body cannot be in time, as the expedition ought to sail in February. The train also is quite inadequate to the service ; but twelve 24-pounders, and other supplies much too stinted. I am confident I may speak freely to your Grace, because I know you

[1] Record Office, Adm. Sec., *In-Letters*, 4121.

love your country, and are as much convinced as I am that efforts in America alone can save us;

and later, 'my whole heart is so fixed on the efforts of this summer not being frustrated that I am in danger of becoming troublesome and tiresome upon this interesting subject.'[1] Besides the recruiting, he sees himself to the troops being brought to time to the port of embarkation, sending particular directions to Bedford as to the stages of their march to Cork and Kinsale. He sends reminders to the War Office about their ammunition-flints and their tents; on January 28 gives directions about the battering train to accompany them; and a fortnight later writes to the Admiralty to hurry forward its transport. On February 7 he judges preparations forward enough to order the Admiralty to send twelve ships of the line with frigates to await the transports at Cork and escort them to America.

Three days before, he had written his ideas about the campaign to Loudoun and the American governors so that they might know what to be about, and on the 19th has ready his full instructions to Admiral Holburne and General Hopson, commanding the land and sea forces of the expedition. On the arrival of reinforcements, in April as Pitt hoped, Loudoun would have 17,000 regular troops in America. He was at once to attack Louisburg in co-operation with the fleet. Seeing that in the last war it had been captured by only 8,500 provincials, Pitt judged that Loudoun with his 17,000 regulars should make quick work and certainly be master of it in May. In June, when the St. Lawrence was ice-free, a dash should be made for Quebec. The King thinks, he wrote, 'these two places the great objects of offensive operations for the ensuing campaign in America, and judges the taking of Louisburg to be the more practicable enterprise'; but Loudoun was not tied down to any hard and fast rules: if he found it better to attack Quebec first he was left at perfect liberty to do so. In his instructions Pitt also lays great stress on the need for 'good agreement' between the fleet and the army, and bids

[1] Torrens, ii, 347, 353.

Holburne and Loudoun beware of wasting time on councils of war before every trifling operation, and to act promptly on their own responsibility.

With the American colonists Pitt adopted an entirely new tone. The dispatches of Braddock and Loudoun and of most of the governors had hitherto been full of complaints of their unwillingness to fight or to pay for their own defence, and the language of Whitehall had re-echoed these carping criticisms. Pitt changed all that. He treated them as he had the people of England and Scotland—with confidence, and appealed to their patriotism. He refused to entertain a suggestion of Halifax and the Committee of Trade to raise a tax on them by a stamp duty ; on the contrary, inquired how the poorer southern colonies could best be assisted by the mother-country.[1] At the same time that he sent Loudoun his instructions he wrote circular letters to the governors, 'captivating the people' of America by a frank statement of his plans and inviting them to lend their aid :

The King, having nothing more at heart than the preservation of his good subjects and colonies of North America, has come to a Resolution of acting with the greatest vigour in those parts, the ensuing campaign, and all necessary preparations are making for sending a considerable reinforcement of troops together with a strong squadron of ships, for that purpose, and in order to act offensively against the French in Canada. . . . The King doubts not but that the several Provinces, truly sensible of his paternal care in sending so large a force for their security will exert their utmost endeavours to second and strengthen . . . offensive operations against the French . . . and will not clogg the enlistments of the men, or the raising of the money for their pay &c. with such limitations as have been hitherto found to render their service difficult and ineffectual.[2]

---

[1] See letter of January 21, 1757, from Commissioners of Trade and Plantations, in answer to Pitt's of January 3, in Record Office, *C. O.* 5.7. In the following November an elaborate plan for taxing the colonies was proposed to Pitt by Brigadier Waldo with like success (*ibid.* 5.52 : Waldo to Pitt, 10, November, 1757. See also Pitt's speech of January 14, 1766, vol. ii, p. 193.)

[2] Particulars of Pitt's directions for the American campaign may be seen in Kimball's *Correspondence* and in Record Office, Adm. Sec. *In-Letters*, 4121 ; *S. P. Dom. Adm.* 229 ; *S. P. Dom. Military*, 189.

300   THE AWAKENING OF THE PEOPLE

While seeing to the expedition for America, Pitt had his eye on the French elsewhere. On December 21, 1756, the day before he sent his first letter to Loudoun, he received a despairing account from the Secret Committee of the East India Company of the state of affairs in India : Bussy's intrigues and Dupleix's victories had brought most of the chief native power under French control; fresh armaments were expected from France, against which the Company had less than 2,000 English and native soldiers to put into the field and only five ships under Watson to protect their coast; expenses were rising; and Aldercron, the colonel commanding the King's troops in India, was creating endless difficulties. Had they but known they could have added one more tale of horror; but news of the Black Hole of May 20, 1756, did not reach England till June 1757. On Christmas Day Pitt called a Cabinet to consider this letter, and it was resolved to reinforce the Company with four or five more ships. Pitt sent the orders to the Admiralty on January 2, on the 4th wrote to Watson with instructions to co-operate heartily with the Company's officials, three weeks later recalled the impracticable Aldercron, but allowed his regiment to re-enlist for service in India, and, when news came that a company of artillery for India had been lost at sea, sent urgent orders to Gravesend for another company to be embarked forthwith.[1]

Fighting the French in India and America was not enough for Pitt. Wherever they menaced England or could be made to suffer, he was ready to give battle. On January 19 he got a letter from the Governor of Jamaica complaining of the exposed state of the West Indies and asking for the regiment stationed there to be brought up to strength; on the 26th he sent orders to the War Office to comply with the request. On the same day a letter came to him from the Quaker merchant, Cumming, suggesting a plan for turning the French out of their settlements at Fort Louis, Podor, Galam and Goree on the Senegal coast of West Africa. Pitt sent for him, heard all he had to say, and on February 1 wrote him a

[1] Record Office, *Foreign, Various*, 68, *S. P. Dom. Adm.*, 229; *S. P. Dom. Military*, 189; and *Chatham MSS.* 74, for the Cabinet council.

letter accrediting him to the native chief, who had promised help, and announcing that an expedition would be equipped. In a month's time orders for the small squadron, the marines and the engineer asked for by Cumming, were at the Admiralty and the Ordnance Office.[1]

In European waters France had it all her own way when Pitt came to power. Hawke had been unable to do anything against the Toulon fleet after the capture of Minorca, and had returned to England in October; the French had then slipped over to Corsica, which they captured without difficulty and thus got almost entire control of the Mediterranean. From English consuls at the Italian and Spanish ports came constant complaints that our shipping was at the mercy of the French; the consul at Leghorn wrote that the coast was swarming with French privateers; even the Maltese obstructed our trade; and the Barbary corsairs had lost all fear of English vengeance for their acts of piracy. A few English privateers, chief of whom was the once famous Fortunatus Wright, alone reminded the seafaring folk of the South and the Levant that the name of England had once been dreaded in the Mediterranean. Pitt trusted more for relief to bold attacks on the enemy's extremities than to blockading squadrons; but as long as fleets were making ready in French ports he strained every nerve to destroy them as they came out. Before providing for his distant expeditions he made an attempt to regain the superiority in home waters. His first recorded act of administration, on December 9, was to order the largest available squadron to rendezvous at Spithead, to meet the French fleet reported to be preparing in Rochefort. As soon as possible he reinforced Saunders at Gibraltar and Temple West blockading the Biscay ports. But the ships could not be got ready fast enough. Before they came, Saunders had been unable to stop a French squadron sailing from Toulon to Louisburg; from the Biscay ports de Beauffremont, bound

[1] See Record Office, *Col. Cor.*, *Sierra Leone*, 12, and *Chatham Corr.* i, 221. Cumming himself, according to Smollett, declared that his scheme could be accomplished without the effusion of human blood—as in fact proved the case—otherwise, as a Quaker, he would not have proposed it; and at any rate he desired that his brethren should not be chargeable with his own single act.

for the West Indies, de la Motte for Halifax, and d'Aché for the Coromandel coast eluded West's vigilance.

For the protection of the Levant and Mediterranean commerce Pitt also employed diplomacy. Spain, Naples, and Sardinia were the chief naval powers besides France, and to retain their friendly neutrality Pitt spared no pains. Wall, the new prime minister of Spain, had been a friend of his when ambassador at St. James's,[1] and Pitt, on assuming office, hastened to recall their former friendship and to make use of it to enter into confidential relations with him. To confirm Spain in her neutrality Pitt was most accommodating about matters in dispute between the two countries, and showed his confidence in Wall by giving him early information of the American plans. Wall needed no persuasion to remain neutral, and resisted the baits offered him by France and the Empress to attach him to their side. The same open behaviour was equally successful with Naples and Sardinia. The King of Sardinia was too close to French and Austrian territory to declare his satisfaction publicly, but gave concessions to English traders; Don Carlos paid no heed to the intrigues of his French cousin—partly out of weakness, partly from gratitude to Pitt for excluding the Bay of Naples from the enterprises of Fortunatus Wright and his fellows. It was an inestimable benefit to England during the early years of the war that Pitt managed to keep the Mediterranean Powers in good humour. Had it not been so, we might well have entirely lost our Mediterranean and Levant trade during the war, and our consuls would have been driven from the ports whence they constantly sent Pitt timely information of French naval preparations.[2]

In his continental policy Pitt laid himself more open to criticism for a change of attitude. Hitherto he had sweepingly condemned any participation in a continental war except

---

[1] Elizabeth Wyndham tells Lady Hester in 1749 she had seen Pitt with Wall and others driving furiously to Datchet one summer day, to dine there and return the same day (*Chatham MSS.* 34). They had also drunk the waters together at Tunbridge.

[2] For Pitt's dealings with these countries, see Record Office, *Foreign, Various,* 68.

DIPLOMACY; THE CONTINENTAL WAR 303

for the defence of the Low Countries, and had been especially severe on any regard shown to the particular interests of Hanover in our policy. Only in the summer he had told Newcastle and the House of Commons that even from a military standpoint it was absurd to attempt the defence of the flat plains of Hanover: if the electorate suffered in an English quarrel her losses must be made good at the peace. But, whatever he might have done had he been perfectly free, he found, when he came into office, a treaty in existence with Prussia, which committed the country to take some part in the continental war. By the second article of this treaty, signed on January 16, 1756, England and Prussia were bound to resist any attempt by a foreign Power to introduce troops into Germany. 'By that treaty, the honour of the Crown and the honour of the nation were equally engaged,' said Chatham fourteen years later,[1] and he was the last man to repudiate such an obligation. He had to consider how to keep this pledge without diverting attention from England's main object of crushing France as a naval and colonial power. Fortunately he had in Frederic an ally who saw as clearly as himself where the real interests of England lay, and was too wise to ask her to undertake the aimless adventures in Germany favoured by Carteret and Newcastle. Before starting on his march to Dresden Frederic had asked for a Hanoverian and Dutch army to hold the Rhine against France and for an English fleet in the Baltic to overawe Russia. Soon afterwards Newcastle fell, and English politicians were too much occupied with the domestic crisis to pay much attention to Frederic, who lost patience and said England would do better to think of external dangers than of internal intrigues. Forgetting his previous commendations of Pitt,[2] he said, on seeing a list of the new Ministry, that he knew none of them except Holderness, 'un galant homme et un sujet de grande capacité et de mérite,' a judgment less acute than were most of Frederic's. But he sent over three memoirs on English policy,

---
[1] In his speech of November 22, 1770.
[2] See above, p. 148. This forgetfulness of Frederic's is an indication how much Pitt had lost ground during his faithful service with the Pelhams.

which came into Pitt's hands in December, 1756.[1] In these he pointed to the complete success of France in the preceding year and made a forecast of her future plans: to drive the English out of Madras and out of America, to overrun Hanover and Cleves, and to destroy English trade in the Mediterranean. Coming to England's best policy he advised a bold offensive in Canada and in India, descents on the French coast and the capture of Corsica; on the Continent England should send an army of German auxiliaries to hold the Rhine against a French invasion of Hanover, detach Denmark from France, and keep Russia quiet. But Frederic neither asked nor expected England to help him in his own main operations against the Empress-Queen, because he saw that she would be serving his purpose better, as well as her own, by holding his right flank against France.

Pitt accepted Frederic's plan almost unchanged. The vigorous offensive in Canada and India and the descents on the French coast tallied with his own ideas; the plan of an army of observation on the Rhine he adopted, partly as a necessary consequence of the alliance, and very soon from a growing conviction that it was the country's interest to help Frederic in diverting France's energy from the colonial struggle. The only alternative would have been to consent to a neutrality for Hanover, which the King early in 1757 secretly attempted to secure from Vienna. The Austrian Court was prepared to agree to this if a free passage through Hanover were granted to the French troops. But Pitt set his face against this base desertion of Frederic and by his opposition put an end to the negotiation.[2] He already saw that the defence of Hanover was necessary not merely for electoral purposes, but to prevent the French army now gathering on the Rhine from closing the circle on England's only effective ally. At the end of December Holderness informed Frederic that his plan was accepted and that an army of observation would be formed near Wesel, the fortress defending the passage of the Rhine to Hanover. At a Cabinet meeting

---

[1] The memoirs are to be seen in *Chatham MSS.* 89.
[2] Waddington, *Guerre de Sept Ans*, i, 169, *sqq.*; and Corbett, i, 153.

on January 16, 1757,[1] Frederic's suggestion for a treaty of subsidy with Denmark was agreed to, but the Danes were already too deeply committed to France to consent to more than neutrality. On February 17—the first day, it was malevolently noted, he had been able to appear in the House as minister— Pitt came with a message from the King, that seemed inconsistent with all his former professions, asking for power to form an army of observation 'for the just and necessary defence and preservation of . . . the electoral dominions and those of my good ally the King of Prussia . . . against the irruption of foreign armies and for the support of the common cause.'

February 17, 1757.

Next day, on the vote for £200,000 for the King of Prussia, he explained his policy. The army of observation, 60,000 strong, was to be composed of 36,000 Hanoverians and 24,000 Hessians and Prussians. England would be at the expense of the Hessians and Prussians only, for the King had agreed to take the Hanoverians at the charge of the electorate; and, since Russia had not fulfilled her obligations, the £100,000 due to her by treaty would be saved. He appears to have made no apology for his own change of front, but explained the two reasons that made this policy necessary—loyalty to our engagements with Prussia, and the danger of allowing France a free hand in Germany while Frederic was taken up with the Austrians and Russians. He attacked Austria for her ingratitude after the sums lavished on her in the last war, and Russia as a useless ally; and concluded with a glowing panegyric upon Frederic, the sole champion besides England of the liberties of Europe, which were threatened by the sinister alliance between the two Catholic powers, France and Austria.[2] Fox could not forbear reminding Pitt of his simile of the millstone of German measures round the late ministers' necks, and hoped this particular millstone would be an ornament to Pitt's,[3] but no one else ventured to answer

February 18, 1757.

[1] Torrens, ii, 353. Pitt was not present at this council, owing to illness.

[2] Sanderson Miller, p. 353, where there is an account of the speech by Jenkinson. Michel also gives an account to Frederic (*Pol. Corr.* xiv, 344) and the Saxon envoy to Brühl (Record Office, *Confidential*, February 22, 1757).

[3] See above, p. 270. In a later speech Pitt retorted that a millstone of 2lb. might not sink a man while one of 4lb. would; it was not the same thing to be fighting with the King of Prussia as against him.

March 11, 1757.

a speech which Lyttelton thought the finest ever made in the House of Commons. Tory and City merchant vied with one another in cheering Pitt, whose policy seemed to all 'just the happy medium in which we ought to steer.' Inconsistency there was in Pitt's new attitude; but of this nobody in the House cared to make much. Pitt himself thought little of the appearance of inconsistency. Newcastle's men were well pleased to hear Pitt advocating their chief's German measures, without inquiring closely into his reasons; the Tories and City men were converted to measures against which they had always protested, by his clear statement of their changed object. To them still, as Potter told Pitt, 'the bitter part of the pill is Hanover, the sugar Plumb the King of Prussia.'[1] We were no longer to fight in Germany mainly to defend Hanover or the Empress-Queen's rights: the army there was to play an intelligible part in world-wide operations directed against the one enemy, France.

Frederic was no less pleased than the House of Commons by Pitt's speech, with its generous tribute to himself and its loyal appreciation of the alliance, and instructed his envoy to compliment the Secretary in terms as warm and affectionate as he could conceive. During the rest of Pitt's ministry the confidence in each other felt by the two great leaders of their time was never seriously shaken. To Pitt Frederic was the Protestant hero; while Frederic said of Pitt, 'England has long been in labour, but at last she has brought forth a man.'[2] Each respected and understood the other's enlightened patriotism, and had a common object in the destruction of France. Without Pitt's England to distract France, Frederic knew he must be overwhelmed by the three hostile powers encompassing him; without Frederic and the best army in Europe to wear away more than half the French resources, Pitt soon came to see that his dream of empire would be unattainable.

This work of preparing expeditions to Germany, to America,

---

[1] *Chatham MSS.* 53 (Potter to Pitt, undated).

[2] This was said in October 1759 (Bissett, *Mitchell*, i, 171); see also letters of Mitchell and Pitt in *Chatham Corr.* i, 124-7.

CABINET INTRIGUES

to India, and to West Africa, of equipping fleets, of raising new regiments, and all the time reassuring and reanimating the people of England had to be carried on under enormous difficulties.[1] For the first three months of his Ministry Pitt was so ill with gout that he rarely appeared at Court or in the House. He was forced to spend most of this time in bed at Hayes, his lately-bought house in Kent: here he worked, attended by clerks in his office or ministers sent down by the King to consult him.[2] Even Cabinet Councils were held at his bedside. Unfortunately few of his colleagues could be trusted. Old Lord Granville was so effusively polite at Cabinet Councils that even Pitt 'thought the dose a little too strong,' but he told his friends privately that with all his 'great ideas Pitt was impracticable.'[3] None were capable of relieving him of his burden; Halifax had 'not too partial a regard to the body of which he was one';[4] and Holderness betrayed him daily. Newcastle complained to Hardwicke that they had not somebody stronger than Holderness 'behind the curtain':[5] but Holderness proved useful enough for Newcastle's purpose. He retailed with relish the slights put upon Pitt and his friends by the King, revealed Cabinet secrets, carped at the decisions taken there, and even apologised to the duke for his delay in sending him important foreign dispatches, on the ground that he had been 'ordered' to send them forthwith to Devonshire and Pitt. The King, Fox, the Bedfords, the Duke of Cumberland were all working against him; Newcastle was holding his hand only from fear of the inquiry still impending. The opportunity for breaking him came just at a moment when his popularity seemed on the wane.

Byng, for a person of his mean capacity, had a considerable influence on the history of these years. Had he been more

---

[1] See table at end of chapter for a survey of Pitt's activities during this Ministry.
[2] *Political History of England*, vol. ix (Leadam), p. 247, *note*.
[3] *Add. MSS.* 32869, f. 268; 32870, f. 21.
[4] *Historical MSS. Commission, Various*, vol. iv, p. 37.
[5] Hardwicke unctuously responded that 'we must not be ministers behind the curtain,' but seems to have had no scruples about gathering what information he could from such a source. (*Add. MSS.* 32869, ff. 69, 76.)

enterprising, Minorca would probably not have been lost; he was the chief cause of Newcastle's fall; he helped to bring Pitt's first Ministry to an end. The court-martial on the admiral found, on February 14, 1757, that, though not guilty of cowardice or disaffection, he had not 'done his utmost to take or destroy every ship, which it shall be his duty to engage,' or to relieve Port Mahon; and, by their reading of the 12th Article of War, felt they had no option but to sentence him to death. They nevertheless considered the extreme penalty too severe and recommended him to mercy. Pitt took the same view. When the sentence was brought up for discussion in the House on February 17 and 23, he attacked the rigour of the Article, which was as severe on cases of venial negligence as on treason or gross cowardice; 'more benefit,' he said, 'would accrue, more honour redound to King and country from the pardon of the unhappy admiral than from his execution.'[1] But Newcastle's, Hardwicke's and Anson's efforts to stimulate popular fury against Byng had been only too successful:[2] the nation thirsted for his blood, and regarded anybody, even a Pitt, who tried to save him as an enemy of the country. Pitt was told to his face in the House that Byng would be the means of turning him out as well as the late ministers,[3] he was abused in the City, and he received numerous anonymous letters vilifying him for the part he took in trying to mitigate the severity of the sentence. A paper was handed to the King telling him that Pitt 'has lost by this factious job all that he had acquired with the City. If he presumes again, Sir, discard him; your people will stand by you.'[4] But Pitt was unmoved. On the 24th he saw the King and attempted to obtain a pardon. But the King was not to be moved by any consideration Pitt

[1] This sentiment, couched in varying language, is attested by Walpole, Almon and *The Test*.

[2] Hardwicke and Anson, to their shame, assisted, while still ministers, in supplying material for Mallet's pamphlet against Byng. (Torrens, ii, 358; and Richmond, *Papers Relating to the Loss of Minorca*.)

[3] *Weston Underwood MSS.*, March 5, 1757: E. Owen to Weston (*Historical MSS. Commission*).

[4] See also letter from 'A Friend' to Pitt, quoted in Ruville, ii, 101.

could bring forward. Bedford and Temple added their representations in the Closet, also in vain ; Temple, indeed, only made matters worse by insinuating that Byng's conduct at sea was no worse than the King's at Oudenarde. At last, however, came a ray of hope. On Friday, 25th, Keppel, a member of the court-martial, declared in the House that some of them had a material statement to make in Byng's favour but must first be absolved from their oath of secrecy. The execution was fixed for Monday 28th ; unless a motion was made before the Speaker put the Orders of the Day the last chance would be lost. Horace Walpole, zealous for Byng, but at the moment not a member of the House, appealed to Fox's generosity, but he excused himself and left the House. At the last moment Sir Francis Dashwood was found willing to make the motion. Pitt thought members of the court-martial could have stated their doubts to the King without an Act absolving them from the oath of secrecy, but, having regard to their scruples, suggested a Saturday sitting, and promised to ask the King's leave to bring in a Bill. At a Cabinet Council hurriedly called next day, Pitt drafted a message from the King alluding to Keppel's statement in the House and granting a reprieve till the matter could be cleared up. Granville and Robinson protested against the breach of privilege in this allusion to proceedings in the House, but Pitt brushed aside such technicalities [1] and carried his draft into the Closet. The King sanctioned the message, but when told by Pitt that the House of Commons wished the admiral pardoned, George II drily retorted, ' Sir, *you* have taught me to look for the sense of my subjects in another place than in the House of Commons.'

February 25, 1757.

When Pitt brought in the message Fox at once fastened upon the breach of privilege. Pitt replied with indignation that the time had been too pressing to consult precedents : he had not thought the life of a man was to be trifled with while clerks were searching records. In informing the King of the previous day's proceedings he knew he was only following the sense of the House and thought it his duty to do so. What would Fox have done ?—*not* have represented it ? or basely and

February 26, 1757.

[1] *Add. MSS*, 32870, f. 220.

timidly run away and hid his head as if he had murdered somebody under a hedge ? Pitt's action was supported by the general sense of the House, and the Bill absolving the court-martial from their oath of secrecy was introduced and hurried through all its stages in two days ; but it was rejected in the Lords, because it appeared that, after all, the members of the court-martial had nothing material to say. On March 14, 1757, therefore, Byng was shot on board *The Monarch*. Pitt had done his utmost to upset a sentence which he thought unjust, and for a brief space lost some popularity thereby. But, as he said in the debate, answering the King's taunt by implication, ' May I fall when I refuse pity to such a suit as Mr. Keppel's, justifying a man who lies in captivity and in the shadow of death. I thank God I feel something more than popularity : I feel justice.'

Many reasons now induced the King to shake off Pitt. Though deferential in the Closet, ' he makes me long speeches,' grumbled George II, ' which may be very fine but are greatly beyond my comprehension ; and his letters are affected, formal and pedantic. As to Temple, he is so disagreeable a fellow there is no standing him.' The Byng affair had impaired Pitt's credit with the public, and some of his supporters in the City were not yet converted to his change of front about Germany. His allies the country gentlemen complained that they were not enough consulted, and began to grow restive under his haughty dictation. Many of his colleagues were disloyal: even Legge, Pitt's particular nominee to the Exchequer, was preparing to desert the sinking ship. His long illnesses gave the impression that his work was neglected, and he gained little credit for preparations which had, as yet, shown no result. The Prussian envoy reported to his master on April 1 that owing to constant indisposition Pitt had only had six audiences of the King and attended only fifteen sittings of the House as minister; Frederic himself, in a fit of impatience, longed for a Ministry ' more devoted to business and more hard-working than had been those of the Duke of Newcastle and Mr. Pitt : one that would take a serious and comprehensive view of the present condition of affairs in Europe.'[1] Fox thought that 'by his faults and want of judgment' Pitt had put himself in their power,[2] and helped to spread this view by weekly attacks on him in *The Test*. The final blow came from the Duke of Cumberland. At Frederic's request the duke had accepted the command of the army of observation, but made it a condition that Pitt should be dismissed before he went to take it up, for he would not take orders from a secretary of state allied with the Princess Dowager or be dependent on his goodwill for supplies and reinforcements. Throughout March the King had been sounding Newcastle and others for a successor to Pitt, while Fox and Dodington were busy concocting a Ministry on the convenient principle that 'capacity is little necessary for most employments.'[3] Newcastle craftily advised that nothing should be done until Pitt had obtained the supplies for the year; by the end of the month this had been done. On Monday, April 4, Temple was curtly dismissed. The King hoped Pitt would take the hint and resign. But Pitt, who told Devonshire he thought it more respectful to the King to wait to be dismissed, and agreed with Temple that it would also be better policy, went to Court as usual on Tuesday and Wednesday. On the Wednesday afternoon, April 6, 1757, Holderness was sent to demand the seals of him. Three days later Cumberland set sail from Harwich with a light heart.

Pitt had never been more than a minister on sufferance. He had been forced upon the King by the country, but had no majority in the House of Commons. Directly the people seemed less zealous for him, Newcastle's majority counted on returning to its own. But if the King and Cumberland had reckoned on Pitt's waning popularity they were quickly undeceived. The news of his dismissal was the signal for one of the most remarkable revulsions of popular feeling ever known in our history. The stocks fell at once. With hardly an exception the press writers were on his side, describing him in print or in caricature as 'The True Patriot,' the only saviour

---

[1] *Pol. Corr.* xiv, 501, &c.
[2] *Historical MSS. Commission, Various*, vi, 38, 39.
[3] *Ibid.*

of his country. The City's enthusiasm, momentarily quenched by the Byng incident, blazed forth anew, and the freedom of London was voted to him and Legge by the Common Council. This example was followed by most of the chief towns of the three kingdoms. The cathedral towns of Exeter, York, Norwich, Chester, Worcester and Salisbury; Bedford, Berwick, Yarmouth, Tewkesbury and Boston; the royal borough of Windsor; Newcastle, Bristol and Bath; Dublin and Cork in Ireland and Stirling in Scotland all offered him and Legge their freedom. Exeter inclosed her certificates in boxes of hearts of oak; from most of the other towns, in Lady Hervey's words, 'it rained gold boxes.'[1]

This wave of feeling over the country was the real justification of Pitt's short-lived Ministry. Though he had no success in arms to point to, he had achieved what was of far more importance for bringing the war to a successful issue. He had found a people dispirited by failure, distrustful of their Government, suspicious of treachery in their naval commanders, committed to mercenaries for their own defence, yet willing enough to fight if told the object and the means. Pitt had made clear what England was fighting for and how she should set about it. 'The succour and preservation of my dominions in America have been my constant care; and next to the security of my kingdoms they shall continue to be my great and principal object,' said Pitt, when he returned to power, in the King's Speech closing this long session. And, always in subordination to this principal object, operations to weaken 'the ancient enemy of these kingdoms' were to be carried on in Africa, in the East and West Indies, and in Germany. He had pointed out the means no less clearly. In four months of office he had cleared the country of foreign

---

[1] In *Chatham MSS*. 74 is a 'List of Gold Boxes.' Horace Walpole adds a few more towns. He also mentions that a card was published representing Pitt and Legge as Don Quixote and Sancho Panza in a triumphal car with the motto,

Et sibi Consul
Ne placeat, servus curru portatur eodem.

Pitt, aware of Legge's treachery with Newcastle, was not too well pleased to have him associated with himself in these honours.

RESULTS OF PITT'S FIRST MINISTRY

soldiers and taught Englishmen to enrol themselves for their own defence. In the army and the navy he had aroused a new spirit of vigour and determination, and by his example had shown that old-fashioned regulations and dilatory methods must curtsey to great occasions. Where there had been distrust he had implanted confidence; where there had been disunion he had created unity by rallying men of all parties in and out of Parliament to the common object of carrying England victorious through her life and death struggle with France. By a masterly stroke he had turned rebels into staunch fighters for the Crown, and attached Scotland to the Union as she had never been attached before. In the same King's Speech he proclaimed this aim of unity: 'Let it be your constant endeavour to promote harmony and good agreement among my faithful subjects; that by our union at home we may be the better able to repel and frustrate abroad the dangerous designs of the enemies of my Crown.' And all this had been done at no sacrifice of his own convictions. Trusting the people and trusted by them, he was not afraid to tell them when he thought them wrong. Riots at home he suppressed with a stern hand; the American provincials, whom he loved, he never hesitated to remind of duties they were inclined to forget in their quarrels with governors and mutual jealousies; in the Byng affair he had preferred justice to popularity. Since Cromwell England had not seen such a leader as Pitt.[1]

[1] The following table will give some idea of the extent and range of Pitt's work during his first four months' ministry.

TABLE SHOWING MR. PITT'S ACTIVITIES DURING HIS FIRST MINISTRY.

Date	To whom letters sent	Subject of orders, &c.
1756		
Dec. 2		Pitt speaks on Address in House of Commons.
,, 4		Pitt receives the seals of the Southern Department.
,, 5		Pitt's interview with Hardwicke.
,, 9	Admiralty	Collect largest possible squadron at Spithead on news of French preparations.
,, 11	Admiralty	Orders to embark German troops (signed by Holderness).
,, 14	Ambassador in Spain	Special compliments to Wall: wish to keep friendly relations with Spain.
,, 16		Cabinet decides on 'expedition of weight' to America.
,, 18	Lord Lieutenant of Shropshire	Riots in Shropshire.
,, 21	*From* East India Company	Troubles in India.
,, 22	Lord Loudoun	Sending reinforcements to America.
,, 22	Governor Lawrence (Nova Scotia)	Announces preparations for next campaign.
,, 23	Admiralty	Ship may be sent with pork to Nova Scotia without convoy.
,, 27		Cabinet decides to send four or five ships to East Indies.
,, 31	Mayor of Berwick and W. O.	Troops to be sent to Berwick to suppress riots.
1757		
Jan. 1	Admiralty	Take up and victual transports for 7,000 troops.
,, 2	Admiralty	Four ships and frigate to go to India.
,, 3	Lords of Trade	What best help for Southern colonies in America?
,, 4	Admiral Watson	Orders for fleet on Indian station.
,, 4	W. O.	Commissions to Montgomery and staff for new Highland battalion (Holderness).
,, 5	W. O.	Commissions to Fraser and staff for new Highland battalion (Pitt).
,, 11	Ambassador at Naples	English privateers not to operate in Bay of Naples.
,, 11	Ambassador at Constantinople	Excite Turks against French.
,, 14	W. O.	Warrant for arms for new Highland battalions.
,, 19	*From* Lords of Trade	Governor of Jamaica asks for reinforcements.
,, 21	*From* Lords of Trade	Report on Pitt's query of Jan. 3.
,, 25	W. O.	Increase 22nd Foot by 320 men.
,, 26	W. O.	Reinforce 49th Regiment in Jamaica by 320 men as Governor asks.
,, 26	*From* Thomas Cumming	Proposals for West African expedition.
,, 27	Colonel Aldercron	To return from India but to allow his regiment to re-enlist.
,, 28	Duke of Bedford	See to marching of six battalions to Cork and Kinsale for America.

Date	To whom letters sent	Subject of orders, &c.
1757		
Jan. 28	W. O.	Prepare battering train for North America.
,, 30	Duke of Devonshire	To press forward preparations for American expedition.
,, 31	Admiralty	Detailed orders about American transports.
Feb. 1	Admiralty	Send those transports to Cork and take up more for the Hessians.
,, 1	Thomas Cumming	Letter accrediting Cumming to West African native chiefs: sending expedition.
,, 3	Admiralty	All sea-bedding to be landed in America.
,, 4	W. O.	Royal Horse Guards to be augmented.
,, 4	Loudoun	Details of force to be sent to America. Plans for campaign.
,, 4	Governor Lawrence	Ditto. ditto.
,, 4	Governor of Rhode Island	Raise levies in your province.
,, 4	Governors of Southern Provinces	Ditto.
,, 4	Admiralty	Send off American dispatches at once.
,, 5	Admiralty	Stop French privateers' outrages in Mediterranean.
,, 6	Admiralty	Train of engineers to be transported to America: see to victualling.
,, 7	Admiralty	Fleet for Holburne to be sent to Cork: H. to receive orders from me.
,, 8	W. O.	See to tents for America.
,, 9	Thomas Cumming	If African expedition succeeds promises an exclusive charter.
,, 10	Admiralty	Transports with artillery, &c., to join Holburne at once.
,, 11	Admiralty	Fishing seynes to be provided for Holburne.
,, 11	W. O.	Papers about Minorca required by House of Commons.
,, 11	W. O.	Ammunition-flints required by battalions for American service.
,, 11	Ambassador in Spain	Tell King of Spain about our plans.
,, 15	W. O.	Difficulties about raising Highland battalions to be overcome.
,, 17		Pitt brings message to House of Commons about Prussian treaty and army observation.
,, 17		Pitt speaks about Byng affair in House of Commons.
,, 18		Pitt makes speech about grant of £200,000 to Prussia.
,, 18	Ambassador at Turin	Tell King of Sardinia about our plans.
,, 19	Governor in North America	Further details about expedition.
,, 19	Loudoun	Letter about plans and Instructions.
,, 19	General Hopson	Orders for troops to America.
,, 19	Admiral Holburne	Instructions.

Date	To whom letters sent	Subject of orders, &c.
1757		
Feb. 19	W. O.	Have those tents been seen to?
,, 22	Admiralty	Transports for 2,300 men to be taken up for unspecified service.
,, 23		Pitt speaks about Byng affair in House of Commons.
,, 24		Pitt tries to obtain Byng's pardon.
,, 25		Pitt speaks about Byng affair in House of Commons.
,, 25	Ambassador in Spain	Immediate satisfaction will be given to Spain about an outrage on her shipping.
,, 26		Cabinet about Byng affair.
,, 26		Pitt speaks about Byng affair.
,, 26	Admiralty	Byng respited to March 14.
,, 27		Pitt speaks about Byng affair.
,, 28		Ditto.
,, 28	Admiralty	Furnish fishing seynes for Holburne: send them by special messenger to Portsmouth.
Mar. 1		Pitt speaks on Prussian subsidy.
,, 1	Admiralty	Marines to be put in charge of any fort captured in Africa.
,, 1	Ordnance	Send engineer for West African expedition.
,, 8	W. O.	Raise four new Companies of Royal Artillery.
,, 10	Admiralty	Highland battalions to be sent to Charleston and Halifax.
,, 11		Pitt speaks on Legge's budget.
,, 12	Envoy at Algiers	Refuses demands of Barbary corsairs.
,, 15	*From* Hopson	No fishing seynes come yet.
,, 16	Hopson	Am bustling Admiralty about them.
,, 17	Loudoun	Further instructions.
,, 17	W. O.	Marching orders for Highlanders.
,, 17	Colonel Aldercron	Leave your artillery with East India Company
,, 22	Governor of Gibraltar	Make accommodation for naval stores, &c.
,, 25	Ambassador in Spain	Approves his conduct.
,, 27	W. O.	Ammunition for Highlanders.
,, 31	Colonel Fraser	Instructions.
,, 31	Colonel Montgomery	Instructions.
,, 31	Envoy in Berlin	Expresses admiration for Frederic.
April 1	Admiralty	Have given instructions to Gibraltar.
,, 1	W. O.	*re* court-martial on General Shirley.
,, 4		Temple dismissed.
,, 5	W. O.	Replace Company of artillery lost at sea by East India Company.
,, 5	Ambassador in Spain	Approves conduct.
,, 6		Pitt dismissed.

Most of the letters above mentioned are to be found abstracted in Record Office, *Foreign, Various* 68. Others are in Record Office, *S. P. Dom. Admiralty* 229, *Admiralty Sec. In-Letters* 4121; *S. P. Dom. Military* 189; a few are in the *Chatham Corr.* and elsewhere. The list is not exhaustive, but sufficiently indicates the range of Pitt's work during his first four months' ministry.

CHAPTER XI

MR. SECRETARY PITT AT WORK

Salisbury. The French are bravely in their battles set,
And will with all expedience charge upon us.
King Henry. All things are ready, if our minds be so.
. . . . .
You know your places: God be with you all.
                    SHAKESPEARE, *Henry V*, iv, 3.

I

IN his haste to get rid of Pitt and his friends George II had hardly given a thought to their successors. After some difficulty Winchelsea, chief of Carteret's black funereal Finches, consented to take the Admiralty, but 'without joy,' and in the frame of mind in which he would have 'put himself at the head of a company of grenadiers, if ordered to do so by the King.' Others were less complaisant. Even Fox and Dodington excused themselves from kissing hands for the Pay Office and Treasurership of the Navy, the two most lucrative posts in the Ministry. For three months of this critical year the Exchequer and Pitt's department, where most of the business of the war was transacted, were in the hands of caretakers—Chief Justice Mansfield and Holderness, Pitt's fellow-secretary. The affairs of the country were almost at a standstill, since the ministers who remained in office were too solicitous about their own predicament to pay much attention to the nation's. For the second time George II had withdrawn his confidence from ministers in the middle of a serious war without being able to replace them.[1] It

---
[1] For the first occasion, see above; p. 146.

was chiefly due to Pitt that the country's interests did not suffer more on this occasion. During the winter months he had made all plans and issued all orders for the summer campaign, leaving little for the home Government to do but keep the different services up to the mark.

The chief obstacle to the construction of a stable Ministry was that the inquiry into the loss of Minorca was not concluded. If Fox and Dodington felt qualms about accepting office, Newcastle, Hardwicke and Anson were not likely to jump at it till they knew whether they were to be impeached or not. In February the House of Commons had ordered returns to be presented of all intelligence received and preparations made by the Newcastle Ministry,[1] but did not begin reading over the papers till April 19, after Pitt's dismissal. For four days such documents as the office clerks had thought fit to produce [2] were read out at wearisome length to an inattentive House. On the 25th the debate on them began and lasted six days. On the 26th Pitt came down in great state to support the inquiry. Walpole noted his beaver waistcoat laced with gold, his red surtout, the riding stockings over his legs, and his right arm, which, though swathed with fur and in a crape sling, in the warmth of speaking ' he drew out with unlucky activity and brandished as usual.' [3] Walpole would have us believe that Pitt's warmth was merely simulated indignation. The Prussian envoy thought otherwise, reporting that he was most anxious to probe the matter to the bottom. At any rate, after absenting himself from the House during most of the session, he attended the rest of these debates and declared that if the majority attempted to burke discussion he would walk out, leaving the people without doors to draw their own conclusions. In the course of the inquiry, however, he became convinced that Anson, whom in the previous session he had denounced

April 26—May 2, 1757.

---

[1] On February 11, 1757, Pitt instructed his office to prepare these returns according to the order of the House of February 8. Record Office, *Foreign, Various*, 68.

[2] Walpole says Newcastle and Fox had taken care to remove all compromising documents from their offices.

[3] This was not necessarily a proof that Pitt was feigning illness, as Walpole insinuates. In the heat of battle soldiers are oblivious even of wounds.

as unfit to command a cock-boat on the River Thames, was not responsible for the disaster,[1] and on the last day's debate made no serious objection to the whitewashing resolutions proposed by Newcastle's friends. From the first the result was a foregone conclusion; Newcastle had too strong a hold over the majority to be in any danger. Fifteen resolutions were passed on May 2, absolving everybody from blame; Newcastle and Fox, says Walpole, were surprised that they were not actually thanked for losing Minorca.[2]

Although he would allow no glozing over the facts, Pitt evidently was not anxious to press hardly on Newcastle. He had said as much to Hardwicke when he was minister; he was even less inclined to do so now. Since his fall he was becoming convinced that the only chance of carrying out his plans for 'reassuring and reanimating the people' was by the aid of Newcastle's majority. His experience in office had taught him what unsound ground he stood on in Parliament; an incident which occurred after he had left office strengthened the conviction that he could do nothing there by himself. On May 20 a message was brought from the King asking for a vote of credit for £1,000,000 to carry on the war, without any statement of the objects on which the money was to be spent. Pitt protested against voting such a sum when, for aught they knew, it might once more be devoted to the old system of paying subsidies to small German principalities instead of conducting with vigour a British and American war. If any subsidy were to be given to Germany, at least let them be told it was for the King of Prussia, news of whose great victory over the Austrians at Prague had arrived that morning.

May 20, 1757.

He indeed is a king who sees all, does all, knows all, does everything, is everything! If you would deal with such great masses, instead of taking little things in the fond hope that they will make a great one, there might still be hopes; but don't go on subsidising little princes here and there and fancy that all together they will make a King of Prussia. That Prince has never asked a subsidy . . . yet

[1] See speech of November 22, 1770.
[2] For an account of these debates, see Walpole *Memoirs* and *Corr.*; Michel's report, *Pol. Corr.* xv, 83; Torrens, ii, 375; *Add. MSS.* 32871, f. 9.

has raised the spirits of everybody who hopes for a decent end of the war; for offensive operations alone must bring about a peace.

But it was a voice crying in the wilderness. Pitt, without power in the Closet, spoke to deaf ears. The money was voted without any stipulation that it should be used to carry on the war according to the policy he had inaugurated.

Pitt was not easily brought over to union with the Duke of Newcastle. He feared his power in the House of Commons, which made him 'so great that, if he comes in, he would be sole minister'; and he feared his meddlesome intrigues even more than his opposition. When there was some talk of a Fox-Newcastle alliance, Pitt sent Newcastle a message through Lord Granville that, even if such a junction were brought about, he himself would come back before long, and that in any case:

he himself was near fifty years old, broke to pieces with the gout, and it would be of little consequence to him. But if he found the Duke of Newcastle whispered in the Closet or gave any disturbance in Parliament or spread anything about to the disadvantage of the Administration, he might expect all kinds of hostility from Mr. Pitt.[1]

When he had made up his mind that he could not get on without the duke's alliance he made known his conditions to his supporter Glover. He spoke of his difficulties from the prejudices of the Court and the vacillations of public opinion, difficulties which could only be overcome by the support of Newcastle and his cohorts, though he admitted that public misfortunes were more imputable to Newcastle than to any man.

But what is to be done ? Do not imagine that I can be induced to unite with him unless sure of power—I mean power over public measures. The disposition of offices (except the few efficient ones

---

[1] *Add. MSS.* 32870, f. 469. The message is undated, but placed among papers relating to the end of April 1757. It was, however, probably sent before Pitt's dismissal on April 6.

PITT UNITES WITH NEWCASTLE, 1757

of administration), the creating Deans, Bishops, and every placeman besides, is quite out of my plan, and I would willingly relinquish them to the Duke of Newcastle.

Newcastle had long been anxious for union with Pitt, as the only means of checking the Duke of Cumberland, who, having got the command in Germany, seemed to him bent on holding England also *in commendam* through Fox. Stone, the Primate of Ireland, who during the *inter-ministerium* did much mole-work, told the Duke that an administration with Pitt in it ' is what the whole nation calls for,' and the only one that could give the King public tranquillity and domestic happiness.[1] But the duke always preferred crooked to direct methods. Instead of approaching Pitt himself, in April he sounded Legge in a furtive interview at Lord Dupplin's, chosen because it had a back entrance to the park. The only result was that Pitt, who heard of this, became more suspicious of Newcastle. But Newcastle persisted, urged Pitt's claims to the King, and finally, during May, induced Pitt, accompanied by Bute, to have several interviews with himself and Hardwicke. Newcastle's object was to retain all his creatures and his influence in the Ministry, Pitt's to restrict him to a sphere where he could not interfere in business. The negotiations were at first broken off on Pitt's demand to have George Grenville as Chancellor of the Exchequer to look after Newcastle at the Treasury; but Pitt afterwards yielded on this point,[2] and on June 3 the duke proposed to the King a Ministry containing himself, Pitt and Temple. The King then raised obstacles: Winchelsea, he said, must stay at the Admiralty, Temple must be excluded, and Pitt's followers in the Ministry were to be rigidly limited: ' I know,' he wrote, ' that by inclination Pitt will distress my affairs abroad, which are so enough already.'[3]

For the last two months George II had privately been trying to form a Ministry without Pitt. Fox was first pressed

---

[1] *Add. MSS.* 32871, f. 61.
[2] On May 26 (see *Add. MSS.* 32997, f. 177). He also agreed then that Fox might be Paymaster if the King's honour was involved in giving him the post.
[3] *Add. MSS.* 35416, f. 228.

to attempt the task, but gave it up after half-hearted endeavours to persuade some of the second-rate politicians to join his Ministry. Fox, besides being very sensible of his own unpopularity in the City, where they declaimed 'against Mr. Fox and his military administration,' had not the public spirit to lead where there was a risk of failure, and was content to ask for himself the lucrative post of Paymaster. Newcastle was also implored to see what he could do without Pitt. He drew up a sketch of a Ministry with Robinson in Pitt's place, but found it would not pass muster and dropped it hurriedly.[1] On June 8th the King, in desperation, called to the Closet Lord Waldegrave, an honest, sensible nobleman, who had been governor to the Prince of Wales but had no experience of politics and no liking for them, and told him flatly to take the Treasury himself and consult Fox and Devonshire about the rest of the Ministry. Waldegrave consented on Winchelsea's principle, but hated the task, which was hopeless from the outset. Holderness, the sole remaining Secretary, resigned at Newcastle's instigation. Waldegrave had some gloomy meetings with Fox, Winchelsea, Bedford, Granville, Egremont and Gower, and got cold comfort from all but Winchelsea, the Duke of Bedford, who declared that the administration would be the strongest ever known, and the ever cheerful and indomitable Lord Granville. However, he formed a skeleton Ministry. June 11 was the date fixed for Fox to receive the seals of the Exchequer from the King; the other new ministers were in attendance to grace the ceremony. First Mansfield was called into the Closet, formally to deliver the seals which he had been keeping for two months. The Chief Justice's audience was long, and, when he came out, he still had the seals. His timidity was sometimes inspired by common sense; at this interview he told the King that the country would not stand Fox and that such a ministry would end in greater confusion than ever. At last the King gave way and told Hardwicke to bring him the best ministry he could. It was indeed time. Even the House of Commons was becoming restive at the delay in forming a government.

[1] *Add. MSS.* 35416, f. 212.

Once it refused to adjourn on the motion of a minor minister, and on June 10, 'after sitting an hour in silence and suspense,' applauded George Townshend when he expressed a hope that at its next meeting it would 'resume its ancient right (too long disused) of advising the Crown in this dangerous crisis.'[1]

On June 18, after several more meetings with Newcastle, Bute and Pitt, Hardwicke brought the King a list of a ministry on which they were agreed. Some further delay arose about legal appointments which made Pitt very impatient, as well he might be in the critical condition of the country:

I should be very sorry [he writes to Hardwicke on June 26] that any *minutiæ* should retard the execution of a plan which every hour is becoming more necessary for the King and kingdom; but when it is considered what mutilations and changes, in essentials, the paper of arrangements has undergone, I trust your lordship will be of opinion that it is quite necessary for me to see what little remains of the system proposed go into execution at *one* and the *same time*. On *that foot*, I am ready, any day, to begin to take my part whatever forebodings of mind I carry about me.

On that very day everything was settled, and on June 29, 1757, the new ministers kissed hands. Waldegrave, who went 'to entertain himself with the innocent, or perhaps ill-natured amusement of examining the different countenances,' said that Pitt and his friends 'had neither the insolence of men who have gained a victory, nor were they awkward and disconcerted, like those who come to a place where they know they are not wanted.'

Pitt himself on entering his great Ministry once more changed his seat in Parliament. Bath, his second home, and a borough uninfluenced by any patron, had a vacancy. The corporation, with whom then rested the right of election, unanimously asked him to stand; Ralph Allen managed everything for him; and he was not even called upon to be present at the election on July 8. On the following day a member of the corporation wrote to him: 'I believe your election may be easily secured to you as long as you live . . .

[1] *Add. MSS.* 32871, f. 266.

you have not only the *vox corporationis* but also the *vox populi*, which I hope you will ever retain.'[1]

After his part in settling the Ministry Hardwicke declared with pardonable self-satisfaction that it was looked upon as the strongest administration that had been formed for years. 'Then this thing is done, and, my lord, I thank you heartily,' said the King, and seemed a changed man. Pitt's great object had been to retain control of the chief executive offices; and he had succeeded. He returned to his office of Secretary of State for the Southern Department and still had the pliable Holderness as his colleague in the Northern Department. Viscount Barrington, a fair administrator, who then professed to be a follower of Pitt, was kept at the War Office.[2] The Admiralty had been a difficulty. The King would not hear of Temple, or of Legge, who was Pitt's second choice. Hardwicke then suggested his son-in-law Anson, an idea welcomed by the King and Newcastle and readily concurred in by Pitt and Bute.[3] But Pitt insisted that the rest of the Navy Board, so vital to his plans, should consist of his friends.[4] Newcastle returned to the Treasury with Legge as Chancellor of the Exchequer and James Grenville a junior lord as a counterpoise to Newcastle's friends Nugent and Duncannon. George Grenville was again Treasurer of the Navy and Fox became Paymaster—with a warning from the King that if he interfered with the House of Commons he would turn him out.[5] Henley, an Oxford contemporary of

[1] *Chatham MSS.* 38: J. Grist to Pitt. The seat at Bath was vacated by Henley, when he became Lord Keeper. On July 26 Pitt had applied to Newcastle for the Chiltern Hundreds, for, though dismissed, he had not been superseded and was therefore held not to have a new appointment.

[2] Barrington even adopted Pitt's language. In a debate of May 2 it was noted, he professed 'no attachment to persons but to things.'

[3] Calcraft says this appointment of Pitt's was unpopular. (*Chatham MSS.* 86, July 8, 1757.)

[4] Admirals Boscawen and Temple West, Hay, T. O. Hunter, his former agent at the Pay Office, Gilbert Elliot and Admiral John Forbes. When West died in August Anson was anxious to get Sir Edward Hawke in his place. 'Mr. Pitt,' says Lady Anson, 'very civilly and reasonably says ... that as there was nobody on it [the Board] whom Lord Anson had chosen he thought it very proper he should recommend him now.' But Newcastle had a politician for whom he wanted a job. (Anson, *Anson*, p. 149.)

[5] *Add. MSS.* 32871, f. 216.

Pitt, became Lord Keeper of the Great Seal, Temple Lord Privy Seal. Hardwicke had hoped that his son Charles Yorke would succeed Henley as Attorney-General, but Pitt insisted on the appointment of his old Eton comrade, Pratt, the most liberal-minded lawyer of the day. Lord Granville stayed on as Lord President, Devonshire was consoled for the loss of the Treasury with the Chamberlain's staff, and Bedford was made Lord-Lieutenant of Ireland. It was a Ministry, unlike Pitt's first Ministry, formed on the broadest basis and therefore more in conformity with his considered theory of administration. The Newcastle faction, the Bedfords, Cumberland, Leicester House, Pitt's own following, and even the Tories, all had their representatives in the Ministry. With Newcastle's obedient majority in the House of Commons to support him, and the City men and Tories constantly faithful to him, Pitt was himself in the position of a dictator. His experience from 1754 to 1757 had taught him that a majority so obtained was not a wholesome condition for Parliament; but this was not the time to consider constitutional reforms. In the middle of a great war he felt that he must govern by the best means to hand, but above all he must govern.[1]

II

In Pitt's day the two Secretaries of State were responsible for every act of administration not immediately concerned with finance. Between them, in fact, they shared the duties of the modern Home Secretary, Foreign Secretary, and Colonial Secretary, and to some extent of the First Lord of the Admiralty and the Secretary at War. In an emergency one Secretary could perform the work of both offices, but nominally there was a rough division between them. The principal Secretary of State for the Southern Department had charge of all British

[1] For the negotiations which resulted in Pitt's great Ministry, besides the books of memoirs, see *Add. MSS.* 32870, 32871 *passim.* There are also some details in Calcraft's correspondence. (*Chatham MSS.* 86.)

dependencies and of diplomatic relations with France, Spain, Portugal, Italy, Turkey, the Barbary States, and Switzerland.[1] All other foreign countries and Scotland came within the province of the Northern Department. Both Secretaries sent orders to the War Office, the Admiralty, and the Lord-Lieutenant of Ireland. Both dealt with criminals[2] and patents for companies, ordered troops to suppress riots and appointed commissions to investigate them, directed the times of sailing for mail packets, and generally were responsible for the internal administration of England. A more inconvenient division of labour could hardly be conceived. In foreign affairs, for example, Pitt negotiated with Turkey, but solely, as it happened, on questions arising out of our connection with Prussia, for which Holderness was nominally responsible. Even more absurd was the system whereby the two Secretaries might be sending independent orders to the military and naval departments during the progress of a great war. Fortunately the practice was not as absurd as the theory, inasmuch as one Secretary generally overshadowed the other and dictated the common policy. Thus Townshend had left Newcastle

---

[1] The headings in Record Office, *Foreign, Various*, 68–71, the précis books of Pitt's department, show the variety of the Southern Secretary's functions. These are :—

Spain	N America (general operns.)	Indian Affairs (America)
Spanish Consuls		Jamaica
Portugal	Governors of :—	Barbados
Naples	Nova Scotia	Leeward Islands
Venice	New Hampshire	Bahamas
Florence	Massachusetts	Bermuda
Turin	Connecticut	Ireland
Leghorn Consul	Rhode Island	Board of Trade
Malta Consul	New York	Criminal
Switzerland	New Jersey	Treasury and Customs
Turkey	Pennsylvania	Post Office
Barbary Consuls	Maryland	Council Office
Gibraltar	Virginia	Petitions
East Indies	North Carolina	Admiralty
West Africa	South Carolina	War Office
	Georgia	Ordnance
	Newfoundland	Foreign Ministers

[2] For example, Calcraft in a letter to Lord Frederic Cavendish says he has been told by Wood that Pitt had 'a particular delicacy' in interfering in a criminal case arising out of Minden, and that it would be better to apply to Holderness instead of Pitt for a pardon in the case in question. (*Chatham MSS.* 86, July 29, 1760.)

little to do; Newcastle had been equally master of all his subsequent colleagues except Carteret; during Pitt's ministry Holderness was hardly more than his clerk. Originally Pitt had desired the Northern Department, in order to direct German policy, but he soon found he could do so equally well in the Southern Department. In the conduct of the war, especially the American operations, which naturally fell within his province, nobody ventured to interfere with him.[1]

For the multifarious work of his office in Cleveland Row Pitt had a very small staff, consisting of two under-secretaries, James Rivers and Robert Wood, and nine clerks; he also shared with Holderness a staff for duties common to both offices.[2] Wood, his principal under-secretary, was a man of some fame in his day as a scholar and author, and was thereby brought to Pitt's notice: he was a good official and probably none the worse in his chief's eyes for having no original ideas on business. For Pitt was the opposite of Newcastle, of whom it was said that he did his secretary Stone's work while Stone did his. He allowed nobody in the office but himself to take responsibility. Even on a question of transferring a packet boat from the Corunna to the New York station Rivers dare not give a decision without taking Mr. Pitt's pleasure.[3] In externals he maintained great state and exacted the utmost deference from his subordinates: he never appeared at his office save in full dress and tie-wig, and, if Shelburne is to be trusted, would never suffer his under-secretaries to sit in his presence. He expected

[1] Almon's story that Pitt insisted in his second Ministry that Anson's Admiralty Board should sign all orders he sent them without reading them is obviously untrue. Anson and Boscawen were not men to agree to such a humiliating expedient. Moreover, it was unnecessary for Pitt's purposes. As Secretary of State he issued all orders to the Admiralty for the preparation and destination of expeditions and gave instructions to the admirals commanding. The Admiralty merely had to issue detailed orders for the equipment demanded by Pitt. See Knox, *Extra-Official Papers*, i, 14, 'Neither the Admiralty, Treasury, Ordnance, Navy, or Victualling Boards can move a step without the King's commands signified by a Secretary of State.'

[2] This staff included a bishop—Willes of Bath and Wells, in whose family the post of Decypherer of Dispatches seems to have been hereditary. The Secretary of State's salary was £5,680; after paying office expenses it came to about £3,000. (*Chatham MSS.* 71.)

[3] Record Office, *C. O.* 5.52. (March 1761).

hard work and good work from them, and punished any act of carelessness in the severest possible way by taking the blame on himself. One day Wood's servant lost an important dispatch, and Pitt writes to Wood that it is 'a most overwhelming misfortune and disgrace to myself, and on all accounts the most distressful event that has yet happened to me in the course of my life.'[1] Intelligence and industry were the best passports to his favour. When young Francis came as a clerk to the office, old Dr. Francis asked Wood the best way to get his son noticed by Pitt, and was told he had better write a full account of all he had seen and heard in his recent visit to Lisbon. When this memoir had been shown him, Pitt singled out Francis, made him his amanuensis, and, when anybody was in doubt about the gender of some Latin word, would turn to him, saying, 'Ask the St. Paul's boy.' Unless Pitt's office had been methodical and well-ordered the furious energy which enabled him to work miracles of organisation would have been largely wasted; but he took care that it should be. He had abstracts prepared for himself of all negotiations and business on hand with every foreign court in Europe when he came into the Ministry,[2] and for his own department instituted an exhaustive and apparently new system of recording under headings every order he issued and every letter he received, so that the state of any question during his administration could be and can still be seen at a glance.[3] On all he impressed the serious nature of the work they were called upon to do for the country. 'In the present most dangerous and critical situation of Europe,' he writes to one of his ambassadors, 'not only the general ways of thinking concerning the public system of the world, but the ebbs and flows of the more particular dispositions and interior

---

[1] *Chatham MSS.* 68. Wood deprecates Pitt's 'anguish of mind' and takes the blame on himself. Fortunately the dispatch was picked up and restored unopened.

[2] *Chatham MSS.* 84.

[3] Record Office, *Foreign, Various*, 68–71. The précis unfortunately ends abruptly in the middle of 1760. The next volume, 72, contains a précis of Bute's departmental business during 1761, but is merely a letter-book, whereas Pitt's books are arranged under headings (see above, p. 326, *note*). The later books of Pitt's department may have been lost.

passions of every considerable court in Europe are to be watched with the greatest vigilance and improved with the utmost dexterity of management and ability of conduct.'[1]

Much as he asked from his subordinates, Pitt gave more himself. He had trained himself for directing campaigns by his military studies, for diplomacy by his industry in acquiring a knowledge of French history and standard works on treaties and negotiations.[2] He took endless trouble with his dispatches, correcting and re-correcting them until they expressed his exact meaning and nothing else. During his administration, says Sir James Porter, the English ambassador in Turkey, 'there was such a correct knowledge and such an active spirit to be seen in all the . . . concerns of government, and such a striking alteration in the manner as well as the matter of the official communications that these circumstances alone would have perfectly convinced me of Mr. Pitt's appointment or resignation.' Where his own knowledge was deficient he was always ready to learn from those better informed; and welcomed the information and plans of campaign showered upon him by sea-captains, army officers, West India planters, agents for the colonies, provincials, clergymen, journalists, or City merchants. Sometimes, in spite of his readiness to see people, his presence proved too awe-inspiring for their ease: one poor clergyman rushed off to talk to him about Rochefort without waiting 'to dress with decency,' and was so overcome ' by the unaccountable power over the minds of men of a person of his rank and character that though he endeavoured to recollect his mind and fortify it, it was all in vain.'[3] But the general experience was different.

---

[1] Record Office, *Foreign, Naples and Sicily*, 15 : Pitt to Gray, September 16, 1757.

[2] Among other exercises in diplomacy Pitt employed himself in copying out and translating long passages from the memoirs of Comte d'Avaux, a noted diplomatist employed by Mazarin (see *Chatham MSS.* 6).

[3] *Chatham MSS.* 24: Rev. Jos. Brooksbank. A few of Pitt's informants during his administration, noted in the *Chatham MSS.*, are Alderman Sayre, Cumming, Captain Thos. Cole, W. Bollan and Denys de Berdt (successively agents for Massachusetts), Governor Pownall, Abercromby, Lieutenant Clark, Captain Barrett, Ephraim Biggs of Philadelphia, Major Caldwell, all of whose information Pitt used.

'The first time I come to Mr. Pitt upon any matter I find him extremely ignorant,' says the Quaker Cumming; 'the second time I come to him I find him completely informed upon it.' A Carolina merchant complains to Pitt that his servant had been kept waiting five hours for an answer to his letter asking for an interview: Pitt replies at once that, had he known, there would have been no such delay and appoints the interview for the next day. 'The easiness of our access to you,' write the aggrieved owners of the Anti-Gallican galley, 'and your generous protection in our rights and polite treatment in your office, filled every heart with a joy rather to be conceived than expressed, as well knowing that your undertaking this affair was more than an omen of success.'[1]

His regular system of intelligence from foreign countries was admirably organised. His spies, according to his granddaughter, were 'hardy sailors who would get at any risk into a port to see how many ships there were and how many effective men, or a pedlar to enter the camp, and the like'; and she describes her meeting with a woman on the front at Southsea who recognised her by her likeness to her grandfather, and told her she used to dress up as a sailor and send Pitt valuable information in code language from America. But Pitt probably made no great improvement on Newcastle's intelligence system, which was excellent: his wonderful insight into foreign politics lay in his resemblance to Oliver Cromwell, whom he described 'astonishing mankind by his intelligence: he did not derive it from spies in the Cabinet of every prince in Europe; he drew it from the cabinet of his own sagacious mind.'[2]

All these advantages—a well-ordered office, his own industry and knowledge, good intelligence—were subservient to the dæmonic energy with which he executed his plans. His maxim was that nothing was impossible. When an admiral came to him with a tale that his task was impossible: 'Sir, I walk on impossibilities,' replied Pitt, showing his two

---

[1] Letter quoted in the pamphlet *For Our Country, An Ode . . . to R. Hon. Wm. Pitt* (London 1757).

[2] Speech of November 22, 1770.

gouty crutches, and bade him be off to the impossible task. The men he liked for his work were those of the stamp of Boscawen, to whom he said : ' When I apply to other officers respecting any expedition, they always raise difficulties : you always find expedients.' He himself left nothing to chance. He made separate victualling contracts to supplement the Treasury's, on the principle that an excess of provisions was preferable to a chance of his armies starving. When a service was urgent he broke through all official rules and went to the man most likely to see it through. Many are the stories told of his energy. Impatient at a delay in procuring transports for some horses, he wrote to Elliot, a Junior Lord of the Admiralty, ' to use the most uncommon diligence in the matter. . . . Let me entreat my dear Elliot to animate this very urgent service with some of his ardour for the public.' On another occasion the Admiralty were making difficulties about transports for artillery which was needed urgently at Portsmouth ; Pitt, ill in bed with gout, said it should go by land, a method never before used, and told the officer in charge to send him an express at every stage and see that those guns reached Portsmouth next day. They started at seven o'clock that night, and by seven o'clock the following morning were at Portsmouth. General Harvey had come to take leave of Pitt before returning to the army in Germany. ' Well, have all your needs been supplied ? ' Pitt asked him. ' No,' he answered, and mentioned several things wanting. Pitt called in his under-secretary, made him write out orders in the names of the several heads of department : next day, when Harvey started, everything was ready for him. And he was as secret as he was swift, for no one ever understood better than Pitt the art of bewildering an enemy by preparations here, there and everywhere. ' Can you keep a secret, Sir ? ' he once asked a Lord Mayor who inquired of him the destination of a secret expedition. ' Yes, Sir, on my honour,' replied the inquisitive magistrate. ' And so can I,' said Mr. Pitt, with one of his low sweeping bows.

When selecting men for his work he offered them no higher reward than that of his own approbation and their consciences.

With dispensing political favours he would have nothing to do. The making of deans, bishops and other placemen he contemptuously resigned to Newcastle. Electoral corruption he thought beneath him: when Lord Falmouth, brother of his favourite admiral, threatened that his five members should vote against the Government unless he got the garter, 'As long,' said Pitt, 'as I remain in the Cabinet your lordship shall not receive that distinction'; adding to the bystanders, '*optat ephippia bos.*' He as steadily refused to meddle with the regular promotions in the army and navy. He insisted, indeed, as soon as he could, on choosing the commanders for his expeditions, men whom he could trust for the tasks he set them; but their staff he left to their own choice, and all other appointments to the ordinary rules of the service. 'I have declared in the most explicit manner on my legs in the House of Commons,' he wrote to an influential supporter asking for a colonel's commission, 'my opinion concerning promotion of favour ... and I have, as it were, publicly pledged myself to that meritorious class [of lieutenant-colonels] that I would never contribute from any considerations of family or parliamentary interest to their depression.' Once when he had made an exception in favour of two promising lads, for whom he secured commissions, Wood writes to their father, Keith, 'Whatever partiality Mr. Pitt may have towards you, he would not have interfered did he not know your sons deserved attention.'[1] Such a spirit in the Secretary and such care for the best interests of the service awakened a response in the breasts of those whom he most cared to gain. Rodney volunteered for an irksome duty, 'to contribute something to make his Administration what I sincerely wish it to be'; Wolfe thought nothing of his miserable condition of health, if he might serve under him; Clive recognised in him a master spirit. 'No man,' said Barré in his funeral oration, 'ever entered the Earl's Closet who did not feel himself, if possible, braver at his return than when he went in.'

Pitt's Cabinet on the whole worked well with him, for the members rarely ventured to oppose him. Newcastle was cowed

[1] Keith, *Memoirs and Correspondence.*

and could always be brought to reason by a threat of resignation from Pitt; Holderness was too devoid of convictions to give much trouble; the Lord Keeper Henley had not found his feet; Temple was devoted to his brother-in-law and not yet jealous; Anson and Ligonier were really no more than chiefs of the navy and army staffs; Legge was timid; Halifax, of the Board of Trade, was only admitted on sufferance; Devonshire and Bedford took little part; Hardwicke was kept in order by Granville, who had generally dined and pleased himself with unpalatable truths about his colleagues; and Mansfield, if he ever had an opinion to express, was reduced to silence by Pitt's withering ' the Chief Justice of England has no opinion to give on this matter.'[1] Pitt was certainly not accommodating. At a conference held at his house in St. James's Square, when he was in acute pain from gout, high debate arose between him and two of his colleagues on a measure of which he disapproved. Francis, who was present taking notes, relates that ' Pitt, on being asked his reasons, replied passionately : " My lords, the reasons why I consider the measure injudicious are so obvious that I wonder you should be required to be told them. I will venture to assert they will occur to that youth. Speak, Francis: have you heard the question ? " " Yes, Sir." " Then tell their Lordships why I object to their proposals." It was an awful moment,' says Francis, ' but I gave an instant reason, on which Pitt, pleased, said, " I told you how it would be : you cannot answer a boy." '

But, though he sometimes looked in vain to have his meaning taken, he was always careful to explain all his actions to the Cabinet. In the winter months, when plans were being settled, councils were frequently called by Pitt, and Newcastle remarked that he always sent draughts betimes to Hardwicke and himself. Pitt's chief trouble was to persuade them to attend enough to business, and his impatience at their indolence was sometimes expressed in warm terms. ' I am fortunately

---

[1] All these ministers are found attending full Cabinet meetings; but many decisions were taken by an inner committee—sometimes attended only by Pitt, Holderness and Newcastle.

come home from my learned brethren,' he writes to Lady Hester, 'most of whom I have beheld actually sleeping over the literary correspondences of all Europe : the only thing that waked us was an American wasps' nest, almost as great a curiosity as any birds' nest I remember at Eaton School.' [1] To the sluggards themselves he was scarcely less frank. Newcastle had excused his absence from a Cabinet at Christmas time, on the plea that he was entertaining a bishop. Pitt replies that he had hoped for the duke's counsel

concerning so important and extensive a scene as the campaign in America, where England and Europe are to be fought for, and where all the data on which we are to ground any plan are so loose and precarious that I confess I do not see my way as clearly as I wish to do in matters where I make myself responsible. I cannot, however, after the desire your Grace has expressed not to break the agreeable engagements at Claremont, press any further.[2]

Pitt once spent upwards of five hours at night, weighing every word of an important dispatch that Holderness was to send to Prussia, ' weighing words more than matter,' grumbles Holderness at three o'clock in the morning ; ' *tout ceci est bel et bon pour une fois,* but I would not pass such another evening for the King's revenue, or for what is perhaps still more valuable, Mr. Pitt's abilities . . . for I neither can nor will be detained for hours upon the introduction of a monosillable.' [3] Even during his illnesses Pitt infected his colleagues with some of his own contagious energy. One day he asked Newcastle to come to his house to discuss plans. The duke found him ill in bed in a very cold room. Pitt had much to say, and the duke found the cold unbearable ; at last, spying another bed in the room, he crept into it, and the two statesmen were found talking and gesticulating at one another from under the bed-clothes. Every week, too, Pitt insisted on a meeting at the Treasury to hear from the duke and West, the Secretary, the exact state of the army contracts. In after years the duke used to joke at Pitt's despotic manner at these meetings ; but it was no sub-

---

[1] *Chatham MSS.* 5.   [2] *Add. MSS.* 32876, ff. 453–61.
[3] *Ibid.* 32878, f. 30.

ject of merriment at the time, for Pitt used to threaten that if any want of provisions or money were found he would impeach the duke in the ensuing session : and the duke believed him.

The King's feelings towards Pitt became insensibly modified as he grew to appreciate his minister's capacity. It is true there were still difficulties. While Pitt's mind was running on America, George II was troubled about his electorate : ' *Your* America,' he said, ' *your* lakes, *your* Mr. Amherst might ruin *you*, or make *you* rich, but in all events I shall be undone ' ; and occasionally George II indulged in outbursts of violent invective against the man who had become his master. But he was a good judge of a man and showed the right Pitt spirit when he growled out to the courtier, who told him Wolfe was mad : ' I wish then he would bite some of my other generals.' Fortunately, too, Pitt now had a staunch ally in Lady Yarmouth. He is said to have publicly praised her in the House, and wrote ' for how many right things done, and fatal ones prevented, ought we to be grateful to her.' [1]

Had everything been smooth for Pitt at home, his task in directing operations over most of the habitable globe would have been difficult enough. The slowness of communication was one serious hindrance to his undertaking. ' Seas roll and months pass,' said Burke magniloquently,[2] ' between the order and the execution ; and the want of a speedy explanation of a single point is enough to defeat a whole system.' Letters took any time between six months and a year to reach India, and, though military operations were left to the Company's servants, Pitt had to decide on the dispatch of reinforcements of men and ships on information which might be entirely useless by the time he received it. His orders to America were rarely received in less than six weeks in the New England ports ; if they had to be sent to generals or governors up-country there might be a further delay of months before they reached their destination.[3] So great was

---

[1] *Add. MSS.* 32876, f. 461.
[2] Speech on American Conciliation.
[3] In 1758 Amherst, travelling by forced marches along a comparatively good road from Albany to the military base at Lake George took three weeks to cover the 260 miles. Forbes, travelling in Virginia in the same year,

this difficulty of communication that previous ministers had generally been content to send out the men and leave them to work out their plans on the spot ; but Pitt, knowing nothing of America except what he had learned by books and hearsay, and trusting to the cabinet of his own sagacious mind, every year laid down the broad outlines of the campaign for his commanders. How to carry out his plans with the men at his disposal was a harder problem. No governor or general had yet been able to overcome the jealousies and suspicions of the provincials. No colonial levy could be reckoned upon for more than a year ; supplies of money and provisions were uncertain ; billeting soldiers from England was a grievance ; backward colonies hindered the zeal of those more forward. Maryland and the Quakers of Pennsylvania, though attacked on their own borders, would hardly contribute anything to the common cause. The Indians, too, invaluable for skirmishing and scouting work, partly through tactless management, partly owing to the impression made by the first French victories, were everywhere out of hand. Cherokees, Choctaws, Chickasaws and Creeks in the South were a constant terror to the lonely border settlers ; even the Six Nations, the traditional friends of the English, occupying the territory between New England and the lakes, had been half won over by Montcalm. The men Pitt found in high commands in the American army were not fitted to help him out of his difficulties. Webb, Abercromby, and Loudoun, like Braddock, were all of the type which the British army seems to evolve in the fat years of peace, before it has warmed to its work : conscientious plodding men with the best intentions, but dull, unenterprising and tactless, breeders of discontent, inspiring more terror in their own side than in the enemy's. Some of these difficulties Pitt overcame ; many remained to the end as a touchstone of his motto, ' Nothing is impossible.'

---

complained that his letters took three months to reach him from the coast. Some of the correspondence with the southern governors was six months on the way.

III

Pitt's own phrase, 'a gloomy scene for this distressed, disgraced country,' well describes the state of affairs when he resumed control in June 1757 after three months' absence. In the records of the Southern Department there is an almost complete blank for those three months, yet there was great need of action. The expedition planned for Senegal and Goree had been dropped. Holburne, who was to have reached Louisburg in May and, after capturing it, to attempt Quebec in June, had not started before Pitt was dismissed, and only reached Halifax on July 9, ten days after he resumed office. From India the terrible tidings of Calcutta and the Black Hole had arrived in June. Spain was being goaded out of her attitude of neutrality by the English privateers' attacks on her shipping. In the West Indies and America the French were superior at sea. In Germany Frederic's victories over the Austrians at Reichenberg and Prague had been succeeded on June 18 by his crushing defeat at Kolin, where he lost 20,000 men. News of this disaster reached England on the day Pitt's new Ministry kissed hands, and created such profound depression that, had it arrived a day sooner, Pitt might, it was said, have failed to form his Cabinet. In consequence of it Frederic had been obliged hurriedly to abandon the siege of Prague and retire into Saxony. With victorious Austrians to the south, with Russians and Swedes concentrating on Pomerania to the north and east, and with a French and imperial army under Soubise advancing through Westphalia to the west, it seemed as if he could not hold out long. On May 1 a second Treaty of Versailles had been signed, whereby France engaged herself to provide greatly increased succours in men and money to the Empress. This treaty, which plunged France still deeper into the morass of German campaigns, as useless to her as Carteret's had been to us, proved of the greatest advantage to England before the war was over. But its immediate effect was greatly to increase Frederic's difficulties, and, in conjunction with Kolin, considerably to raise the tone of the Viennese Court. The Imperial Ambassador abruptly left London, and the Empress handed over to the French troops the Flemish ports of Ostend, Nieuport and Bruges; communication with Cumberland's army was thus almost entirely cut off. Cumberland himself had been hopelessly out-matched and out-manœuvred by d'Estrées at the head of another French army of 100,000 men. d'Estrées had seized Wesel and the passage of the Rhine in April, while Cumberland was slowly gathering his troops at Bielefeld, 100 miles farther east. In June Cumberland, who never had more than 40,000 men under him, had to abandon Bielefeld and expose Hesse-Cassel and the flat plains of Hanover to the French invaders: Emden, the landing-place for his supplies, also fell into d'Estrées's hands; Stade was the only port left him.

Pitt's first thought was for America. From the Admiralty report in his office he saw the strength of the French fleets there, and on July 1, two days after his return, sent a reinforcement of four ships to Holburne. On the same day, and on July 18, he sent him orders to carry out the operations already planned, then to follow the French fleet home, and generally ' to act with the greatest vigour against the enemy . . . in this critical and urgent conjuncture. . . . and effectually answer the great views of His Majesty and the general expectations of the nation.' He also drafted reinforcements of Highlanders and artillery to Loudoun. Since there were no more fleets to blockade in the French ports, he recalled Boscawen from Brest, to have a fleet in readiness to waylay the French fleet that he hoped Holburne would be soon chasing from America.

On July 14 and 26 he summoned cabinet councils to discuss the measures to be taken in consequence of Kolin and of Cumberland's retreat.[1] With all the ports of landing in French hands it was useless to consider sending reinforcements to Cumberland, even if they could be spared, but he offered a subsidy to Frederic, and again attempted without success to persuade Denmark to send ships against Russia in the Baltic.

[1] Torrens, ii, 402, and *Add. MSS.* 32997, f. 233.

OFFER OF GIBRALTAR, 1757

Frederic proudly waived the subsidy : if his plans against his enemies failed, he told the English envoy Mitchell, he would be so discomfited that the King of England's money would be wasted on him ; if he succeeded he might then reconsider it. But he pressed all the more for an English fleet in the Baltic. Pitt had no intention of wasting English ships, required in America, in the Mediterranean and off the coast of France, in the vain attempt to blockade Russia. His policy was to help Frederic as well as ourselves by creating diversions against France. He thought of forming a close alliance with Sardinia and Naples as well as Spain against France and the Empress, and offered inducements to the two Italian Powers to combine against the Austrian domination in North Italy.[1]

But his boldest bid was for a Spanish alliance. In addition to concessions about disputed captures and a contested right of logwood-cutting in Honduras, he offered as a supreme inducement to hand over Gibraltar to Spain in exchange for Minorca, which was to be recovered with Spanish aid. Gibraltar was then considered less valuable for our Mediterranean trade than Minorca ; the Governor, Lord Tyrawley, had reported unfavourably of its defences, adding that it was ' a matter of great indifference to our neighbours, by sea and land, whether we are at Gibraltar or settled upon the Eddystone, in respect of the use this place is of to us.' To the Spaniards there was every reason to think that the bait would prove irresistible. Ever since its capture by Sir George Rooke in 1704, the sight of their ancient enemies on this noble fragment of Spanish soil had been deeply wounding to their pride. ' Lord of Gibraltar ' was still retained in the Spanish king's long list of high-sounding titles ; thrice in fifty years attempts had been made to recover it by force ; and Philip V used to declare there could be no peace with England while she retained it. But that Pitt and the Cabinet which

---

[1] See Record Office, *Foreign, Sardinia and Savoy*, 67, and *Naples and Sicily*, 15, 16, 17. The inducement offered by Pitt to Naples was security to Don Carlos for retaining the throne of Naples in his family when he succeeded to Spain on Ferdinand's death, and to Turin an accession of territory on the same event.

met on August 18, 1757,[1] should have decided to exchange it, even for Minorca, shows the straits to which they thought England reduced. Once before Walpole had made the offer of Gibraltar, and, on its becoming known, had needed all his skill to avert impeachment by an indignant nation. Pitt in his dispatch of August 23 to Keene, the ambassador at Madrid, enjoined the utmost secrecy and took elaborate precautions against misunderstanding.[2] He dictated the precise language in which Keene was to make the proposal, and said that it was not to be regarded as a 'revival and renewal of any former pretended engagement' or as one to be left open if not accepted immediately. Fortunately the Spanish Ministry was not to be induced, even by this offer, to undertake a war with France. Nevertheless Pitt succeeded in abating Spanish ill-humour by his vigorous repression of the English privateers' licentiousness and in preserving Spanish neutrality for the critical years of the struggle.

Another stroke against France, more congenial to his temper, Pitt already had in preparation, the first of those sudden raids on the French coast suggested by Frederic in the previous December, which became one of the features of Pitt's strategy. Even the abortive expedition to L'Orient in 1746 had, according to information in his possession, drawn off men from Saxe's victorious army in the Low Countries :[3] he hoped by better planned attempts to achieve even more. On July 7 Pitt ordered the Admiralty to take up transports for ten battalions of infantry, 160 horses, ordnance and hospital equipment, victual them for two months and bring them round to the Isle of Wight. On the 20th he sent instructions for a fleet of sixteen ships of the line to assemble at Spithead under Hawke. Anson told him he could not find the ships : 'I shall impeach you, if you do not,' said Pitt; and Anson found them. In the early part of August several meetings of the Cabinet and of a committee composed of Pitt, Anson, Holder-

---

[1] *Chatham MSS.* 92, and *Add. MSS.* 32997, f. 245.

[2] In the office précis-book the dispatch is noted as 'on a subject not to be abstracted.' (Record Office, *Foreign, Various,* 68.)

[3] See above, p. 164. In *Chatham MSS.* 74 is a paper showing the effect on Saxe's army.

ness and Ligonier were held to consider a scheme proposed by Pitt for a raid on Rochefort. The naval and military commanders chosen for the expedition attended ; Lieutenant Clark, who had recently visited the fort, and Thierry, a French pilot, were closely examined on the best mode of attack ; and a statement on the distribution of the French army in July was produced, showing that the coastline from St. Valéry to Bordeaux was guarded by only 10,000 men.[1] As a result of these deliberations Pitt instructed the commanders of the expedition to attack Rochefort and destroy its shipping and arsenals, and afterwards attempt other descents and keep the French coast in a state of panic.

But the expedition was doomed to failure from the outset. Had it depended on the King, the troops collected for the secret expedition would have been sent over to Cumberland, who was clamouring for reinforcements. But Pitt stood firm to his own scheme. 'He would defend it with his head,' he told Newcastle, 'and whoever stopped it should answer for it.'[2] Other obstacles were not so easily overcome. During the weeks of waiting at Portsmouth the expedition was talked down as Mr. Pitt's mad enterprise. At the last moment Hardwicke, behind Pitt's back, obtained an order from the King that it should return within a month.[3] The escorting squadron had good officers, with Hawke to command it, and Howe, Keppel and Rodney among the captains. But it was otherwise with the land force. Pitt had asked for Colonel Conway, Horace Walpole's friend, to command the troops ; but the King said he was too young, and appointed over him Mordaunt, an older man, who had lost his nerve. James

---

[1] *The Court Martial on Mordaunt*, a pamphlet in the British Museum, reports Pitt's evidence on December 14, 1757, in which he gives details of these meetings. He mentions incidentally that at the committees Holderness 'held the pen and not he,' that Clark's proposal was the subject of two nights' conversation, and that Thierry underwent examination 'with a readiness and presence of mind that few men in higher life are equal to.' The full Cabinet's formal approval of the scheme was given on August 4. (*Add. MSS.* 32997, f. 241.) Thierry's examination and the memoir on the distribution of French troops are to be found in *Chatham MSS.* 85.

[2] *Add. MSS.* 32997, f. 256.

[3] Pitt afterwards got this order countermanded.

Wolfe, a colonel of thirty, who went as quartermaster, was the only senior officer of spirit and capacity.

On September 8, after many delays, Hawke weighed anchor. He did not reach Basque Roads till September 19, when Mordaunt and Conway wanted to turn back, to comply with Hardwicke's order. But Hawke refused to listen to such pusillanimous counsels. On the 23rd Howe, with the *Magnanime* and *Barfleur*, silenced the fort on the Ile d'Aix, guarding the approach to Rochefort, and Wolfe set foot ashore to reconnoitre the mainland. He reported favourably on an attempt against the town; Hawke was ready to supply boats and to shell it from his ships; but Wolfe's superiors had little stomach for the venture. Five days were spent in reconnoitring excursions and in vain debates about the best method of attack, when at any moment a bold assault on the undermanned fort would almost certainly have succeeded.[1] At last Hawke washed his hands of the whole affair, and told the generals that unless they could decide on prompt action he should return. Another council was held and the generals decided to abandon the enterprise. On October 3 the squadron and transports were back in Portsmouth, with nothing to show for all the imposing preparations but a few useless fortifications razed on the Ile d'Aix: as Walpole said, it seemed like breaking windows with guineas.

Popular opinion against Mordaunt rose almost as high as it had against Byng, and his trial was demanded. Pitt was loud in his indignation: he attributed Mordaunt's hesitations no less than Loudoun's in America to the influence of the King and Cumberland who looked with disfavour on military activity outside Germany, complained that the officers of the expedition were screened by the King, who allowed them 'to stand round his chair at the opera,'[2] and declared that either he himself or Mordaunt should stand his trial. Mordaunt's court-martial, held in December, brought out

---

[1] In *Chatham MSS.* 85 is a letter written from France in 1758 saying that at the time of the expedition there were under 4,000 men in the place and that an assault would easily have carried it.

[2] *Add. MSS.* 32997, f. 289.

ROCHEFORT EXPEDITION FAILS, 1757

no definite charge against him, even from Pitt, who admitted that Clark and Thierry had not promised more than the capture of the Ile d'Aix; and Mordaunt was honourably acquitted. Excessive caution and want of spirit can indeed rarely be brought home to a man; but Pitt was confirmed in his determination to employ for the future vigorous young men with a dash of his own spirit instead of superannuated and carping veterans, and was unshaken in his policy of raids. The failure of the attempt on Rochefort was chiefly deplorable because it confirmed the orthodox military critics in their objections to Pitt's new strategy, and made it more difficult for him to repeat the experiment. In its main purpose of confusing the enemy it had served its purpose well. Before the expedition set off Soubise and Richelieu had feared that it might have Emden or the Flemish ports for an objective, and had modified their plans accordingly. Pitt had evidence, which he produced at the court-martial, that on the first news of Hawke's approach no less than seven battalions of French guards and ten line regiments had been ordered from Paris to the west coast.[1] On the coast towns, one of his correspondents told him, merchants were burying their treasure, and even inland the harvest was being entirely carried by women owing to the arming of every able-bodied man.[2] The panic had even spread to the Mediterranean: Leghorn feared a *coup de main*, and the Empress sent 5,000 troops to Trieste to secure that far-off Adriatic port from Hawke.[3]

Pitt had good cause to grasp any possible weapon of offence against France, since one of those on which he counted had broken in his hand. On September 8, the very day Hawke set sail, Cumberland by the Convention of Closterseven had signed away the army of observation, which was to protect Frederic's flank and save Hanover. Throughout July

[1] For the evidence given at Mordaunt's court-martial. see the pamphlet referred to on p. 341, *note*. Corbett (i, 227-8, *note*) quotes the official return of the movements of French troops in consequence of the Rochefort expedition. See also report of August 29, that the French had brought 30,000 men to the coast, in *Add. MSS.* 32997, f. 243; and intelligence in *Chatham MSS.* 85.

[2] *Chatham MSS.* 74 : Captain Barrats to Pitt, August 30, 1757.

[3] Record Office, *Foreign, Various*, 68: Gray to Pitt, September 23, 1757; see also *ibid., Admiralty* heading (August 27, 1757).

d'Estrées had been gradually pushing Cumberland eastwards and had beaten him at Hastenbeck on the 26th. Richelieu, fresh from the glories of Minorca, then superseded d'Estrées and began pillaging the electorate more ruthlessly than his predecessor. Cumberland had taken no advantage of Richelieu's bewilderment at the preparations for the secret expedition, which caused him to disperse his forces unnecessarily, but remained cooped up round Stade, his port on the estuary of the Elbe. On August 11, George II, seriously perturbed for his electorate, without telling his English Ministry, empowered his son to treat with Richelieu.[1] Cumberland promptly acted on this permission. By the convention of September 8 he agreed to send home his Hessian and Brunswick troops and to remain quiet with the Hanoverians at Stade; the Duchy of Verden was given up to Richelieu, who could now deal with the rest of Hanover as he pleased.

The news of this convention came on the English ministers as a thunderclap. On August 9 they had decided to give George II a subsidy of £100,000 as long as the French were drawing on the resources of Hanover; on September 5 they ordered a squadron to cruise at the mouth of the Elbe and supplies to be sent to Cumberland.[2] Only on September 10 Pitt heard of the King's letter empowering Cumberland to treat. He instantly declared it a breach of faith to Frederic, of which for their own honour English ministers should disculpate themselves,[3] and, in the hope that it had not been acted upon, caused orders to be sent to Cumberland to move towards Magdeburg, to relieve the pressure of Soubise's Westphalian army on Frederic. At that moment the position of Frederic, encompassed by enemies, was critical. Immediately after the convention Richelieu sent a detachment to reinforce Soubise. Pitt knew that if Soubise was once able to overwhelm Frederic the French would overrun the Low Countries and be free to devote yet more of their attention to India and America. When Cumberland's dispatch arrived, on September 17, even

---

[1] Waddington, i, 490, 502.
[2] *Add. MSS.* 32997, ff. 243, 252.
[3] Torrens, ii. 414–5; see also Waddington, i, 495.

the King was furious. He could not deny he had given his son full powers, but, finding to his disgust that the humiliation of the surrender was not counterbalanced by any promise to respect the neutrality of Hanover, called his son a coward and disclaimed all responsibility for his actions.

The Cabinet took prompt measures. They sent a memorandum to Frederic drawing a sharp distinction between the English and Hanoverian Governments, and declaring that the former had not sanctioned the convention and would not be influenced thereby.[1] Pitt was for refusing to ratify it, but was saved the trouble of taking the first step by the French, who, contrary to stipulation, disarmed the Hessian troops on their way home. On October 7 the Cabinet, at Pitt's instigation, decided that while the convention remained in force England would not spend a penny on the army in Germany, but from the moment it took the field against France in concert with the King of Prussia, England would take the Hanoverians into her pay.[2] 'If only we show spirit now,' he told his colleagues, 'it is in our power to prevent the French wintering in Germany.'[3] 'The present moment is *decisive* ; and *that moment so seldom seized, is rarely offered twice*,' he wrote to Newcastle, underlining the words in his agony of impatience.[4] The King was delighted at the prospect of breaking the convention and of having his Hanoverians paid by England. On October 10 Holderness wrote to Frederic that the convention would be repudiated and offered the command of Cumberland's army to Prince Ferdinand of Brunswick, one of the ablest of Frederic's lieutenants.

Strongly as he felt about the convention, Pitt behaved with chivalry to Cumberland when he returned in disgrace to his father's Court. He had no cause to love the man, to whose representations he owed his dismissal in April, but he was too great to lose his sense of justice or triumph over a

[1] *Add. MSS.* 32997, f. 273; 32874, f. 129. This declaration to Frederic had been decided upon on September 14, before the convention was known, but was sent afterwards.

[2] Hardwicke says the Cabinet minute was 'written by Mr. Pitt' (*Add. MSS.* 35870, f. 284).

[3] Torrens, ii. 420.   [4] *Add. MSS.* 32875, f. 40.

fallen foe. 'I gave him no orders to conclude this treaty,' said the King. 'But full powers, Sir, very full powers,' answered Pitt; and to the Cabinet, after seeing all the papers, 'I must,' he said, 'as a man of honour and a gentleman, allow everywhere that H.R.H. had full powers to do what he has done.' He was one of the first to pay his duty at the duke's levée, and Cumberland owned himself obliged to him for his very honourable behaviour. But, though courteous to him privately, he was not sorry on public grounds to lose a commander-in-chief in whom he had so little confidence. He made no effort to stop the duke from resigning all his military appointments, and suggested in his place the valiant and still vigorous veteran Ligonier, his fellow-member in the representation of Bath. The King was at first inclined to retain the chief command of the army himself, but yielded to the united representations of Pitt, Newcastle and Hardwicke in favour of Ligonier.[1] The new commander-in-chief's military knowledge proved useful to the Secretary of State, and, unlike Cumberland, he had no inclination to oppose Pitt's plans from personal or political motives.

The news from America filled up the cup of Pitt's disappointments during his first year of office. Loudoun, called by Franklin 'a St. George on the signposts, always on horseback but never advancing,' spent the first five months of the year in squabbles with the colonists about their levies, the billeting of the troops, and trivial matters of account, and in reporting the squabbles at inordinate length in his dispatches. By the end of May he had collected at New York all the troops that could be spared from the defence of the Carolinas and Virginia and the northern frontier, and prepared to transfer them to Halifax. He showed soldierly instinct in taking the risk of meeting Beauffremont's superior squadron, then off the coast, and reached Halifax by June 30. Here his activity ended. For three weeks after Holburne's arrival with the fleet and reinforcements on July 9 he kept his 12,000 men

---

[1] Pitt expressed great gratitude to Newcastle for the tact with which he overcame the King's objections. Pitt also insisted that Ligonier should get the Guards as a mark of royal confidence. (*Add. MSS.* 32997, f. 289.)

'making sham forts and planting cabbages,' to the openly expressed disgust of his second-in-command, Lord Charles Hay.[1] Holburne meanwhile had looked into Louisburg Harbour, where he found the united squadrons of de la Motte, Beauffremont, and de Revest, numbering seventeen ships to his own sixteen. This slight superiority and reports of impregnable fortifications at Louisburg decided a council of war to do nothing further that year. Loudoun justified himself to Pitt for following the advice of this council on the plea that he had 'returned to the method follow'd ever since he commanded in America to advise with all he could get benefit from,' and prophesied that even if the English fleet arrived earlier next year, and proved superior to the French fleet, Louisburg could not be taken.

On August 30 Pitt heard that his plans for taking Louisburg and possibly Quebec were dropped. On September 18 he had news of a disaster. On the northern frontier of Albany Loudoun had posted Monro with a garrison of 2,600 men to hold Fort William Henry at the head of Lake George, and General Webb with 1,600 at Fort Edward, six hours' march to the south. Montcalm, instead of waiting to be attacked, while Loudoun planted cabbages, brought his whole available strength, to the number of 8,000, to Ticonderoga,[2] some miles to the north of Lake George. Transporting boats, guns, provisions and equipment through dense forests to the lake, he reached Fort William Henry on August 4. Monro sent to Fort Edward for reinforcements, but, receiving none, surrendered five days later with the honours of war to Montcalm's overwhelming force. Montcalm's victory was unhappily sullied by his Indian allies, who massacred some of the defenceless English soldiers retiring on Fort Edward, an act of barbarity which excited widespread horror and indignation in England and America, and was not forgotten when the French were suing for terms four years later. Montcalm was satisfied

[1] It is characteristic of Loudoun that of the three dispatches he sent home on August 6, two were occupied solely with complaints of Lord Charles Hay and justifications for putting him under arrest. (See *Chatham MSS.* 78, and *Foreign, Various*, 68–71.)

[2] Also called Fort Carillon.

with this victory and retired without attempting Fort Edward. Had he done so, he would have found it an easy prey. Webb had not only refused help to Monro but was panic-stricken for himself. He quietly appropriated the militia reinforcements promptly sent up by Governor Pownall of Massachusetts, and was content to congratulate himself on not having lost Fort Edward.

This ended the campaign for 1757. Loudoun returned to his favourite occupation of dispatch-writing.[1] He told Pitt he had no plans for the next year, but deprecated plans formed in England, which might not prove practical in America, and made the officers there go about ' with a halter on their necks.'[2] Holburne, whose fleet had been raised to twenty ships by the reinforcement sent by Pitt in July, cruised about the coast of Nova Scotia and Cape Breton in the hope of catching de la Motte's squadron on its return to France; but on September 24 he was caught by a terrible gale which dismasted six of his ships and disabled the rest from keeping up the blockade. de la Motte, though he had suffered also inside Louisburg Harbour, seized the occasion to escape in safety to France.

I long to come instead of writing [was Pitt's message to his wife when he heard of the disaster]; but alas! most calamitous news demands me this night, and many. Holburne's fleet is ruined by a hurricane off Cape Breton . . . this matter must yet be unspoken of. I fear we do not stand in the smile of Heaven. May a degenerate people profit in the school of misfortune.[3]

Small wonder that Pitt felt despondent. In Germany, on the coast of France, in America, disaster seemed to dog his steps. The desperate news from America and Rochefort, he told Sackville, ' have sunk me into little less than despair of the country . . . the state of the nation is indeed a perilous one

[1] Franklin, passing through New York, found Loudoun hard at work writing dispatches with his own hand. They were so long that some of them were never finished, which accounts for Pitt's complaint that he got no information from Loudoun.

[2] See *Foreign, Various*, 68–71 : Loudoun to Pitt, August 16 to October 17, 1757 ; and dispatches in Kimball.

[3] *Chatham MSS.* 5.

ATTEMPTS TO RETRIEVE DISASTER 349

and fitter for meditation than discourse . . . and demands all the ability the age can furnish.'[1] This ability he looked for vainly in the senior ranks of the army and navy, and he told the House plainly in the following session where he thought the fault lay. He abused, says Calcraft,[2] both land and sea officers exceedingly. Loudoun he mentioned by name, taxing him with his inactivity in spite of his superior force to the French, and wondering what he had been doing from July 9 to August 5, for he had received from him only one short letter and no plans for the next campaign. He even despaired of the future as long as American affairs remained in such hands. In humiliating contrast to the mismanagement—' treachery,' Pitt called it to his wife—of the regular officers came the glorious news from India of Clive's recovery of Calcutta, a testimony to what one man of vigour could do unhampered by barrack-yard traditions. Even at home the Militia Act, on which Pitt had counted to arouse the people, was causing riots and disturbances in many counties.[3] But though he was despondent he did not despair. To keep himself in health he ' drew the village air of his country house at Hayes by snatches ' during the almost unceasing labour of councils, departmental work, and deep meditations for the country's good, which, he told Grenville, *pernoctant nobiscum, peregrinantur, rusticantur*.[4] A few days before he wrote these lines he had sent out Hawke and Boscawen to intercept the French fleet returning from Louisburg, and was ready for the turn of the tide when at last it came.

December 14, 1757.

On November 9 England was awakened to almost delirious joy by the news of Rossbach, fought on November 5, 1757 Frederic had long been preparing for this stroke. He had shaken off the Russians and Swedes in September and then marched against Soubise, who was at the head of the French and imperial armies in Westphalia. Soubise was inclined to despise the Prussians, and walked unsuspectingly into the trap laid for him by Frederic, who gave him the

[1] *Historical MSS. Commission*, IX, iii, 10.
[2] *Chatham MSS.* 86 : Calcraft to Loudoun.
[3] For events in India, see Vol. ii., chap. xiv. For the militia see below, chap. xiii.
[4] *Grenville Papers*, i, 228.

soundest beating the French had suffered since Marlborough's days. After two years of almost unbroken success the French had not only been beaten but humiliated in the sight of Europe, and that by a kingdom of mushroom growth. In England this victory was felt to be something more than a military triumph. Religion did not count for much with the ruling classes, who made most of the wars; but deep down in the English character it still held firm root. This victory of the Protestant hero over the two great Catholic powers of the Continent aroused an enthusiasm which even its great material advantage could not have stimulated. The clergy, echoing the views of their congregations, preached of it as a triumph of faith over the powers of darkness; the saintly Mr. Whitefield gave solemn thanks at the Tabernacle for Frederic as the champion of Protestantism. The next anniversary of Frederic's birth was celebrated with illuminations and fireworks more gorgeous than if he had been a member of the English reigning family. Frederic was, perhaps, a curious champion of any religious belief, but at any rate he had a hatred of that superstitious Romanism which still prompted the Courts of Vienna and Versailles to acts of religious oppression whenever they had the opportunity.[1]

Pitt, more than any statesman of his time, tinged his politics with a deep religious emotion. He hated Rome and all her works, and had a passion for liberty in religion as well as in the State.[2] He admired Frederic not only as England's best ally, 'who stands,' he wrote to Mitchell, ' the unshaken bulwark of Europe against the most powerful and malignant confederacy that ever yet has threatened the independence of mankind,' but also as the author of ' the late signal success in Germany that has given,' he said in the King's Speech, ' a happy turn to affairs for the great object which I have at heart, the preservation of the Protestant religion and the liberties of Europe.' He was thus well prepared to interpret and turn to the best

[1] The Emperor's oppression of the Protestants of Thorn was still recent, and the Calas case illustrates the cruel bigotry of the French system at that time.

[2] See above, pp. 176, 216.

advantage his countrymen's enthusiasm at this victory. Casting aside as inadequate the plans already made for the ensuing campaign, he postponed the meeting of Parliament from November 15 to December 1, 1757. In the interval he entirely altered his proposals, taking Rossbach as a starting-point for the happier and more glorious campaign he now foresaw.

CHAPTER XII

THE TIDE OF VICTORY SETS IN

Καὶ γῆν φανεῖσαν ναυτίλοις παρ' ἐλπίδα,
κάλλιστον ἦμαρ εἰσιδεῖν ἐκ χείματος.
ÆSCHYLUS, *Agam.* 899.[1]

I

PITT's system of administration was simple and regular. At the beginning of each session he took the people into his confidence with the broad statement of his policy in the King's Speech. This was in November or December. During the winter months he worked away at the detailed plans for carrying this policy into effect, and flashed out the orders day by day to the Admiralty, War Office and other departments; he then left matters to his generals and admirals, giving them full discretion to act as circumstances occurred. But winter, spring, summer and autumn he was always on the watch, ready to repair a defeat by fresh exertions or clinch a victory by one more shattering blow. In the winter of Rossbach, when Parliament met on December 1, he made the King's Speech turn principally on Germany and the new hope sprung from thence:

I have the firmest confidence [it ran] that the spirit and bravery of this nation, so renowned in all time, and which have formerly surmounted so many difficulties, are not to be abated by some disappointments. These, I trust, by the blessing of God and your

---

[1] 'The day of victory cometh at last as the sight of land to storm-tossed mariners.'

zeal and ardour for my honour and the welfare of your country, may be retrieved. It is my first resolution to apply my utmost efforts for the security of my kingdoms, and for the recovery and protection of the possessions and rights of my crown and subjects in America and elsewhere. . . . Another great object which I have at heart is the preservation of the Protestant religion and the liberties of Europe. . . . In this critical conjuncture the eyes of all Europe are upon you. In particular I must recommend it to you that my good brother and ally, the King of Prussia, may be supported in such a manner as his magnanimity and active zeal for the common cause deserve. . . . Nothing [it concluded] can be so conducive to the defence of all that is dear to us, as well as for reducing our enemies to reason, as union and harmony amongst ourselves.

In this speech, which by the touch of sympathy in the use of the pronouns seemed for the first time to identify the King with the efforts, aspirations and weaknesses of his people, the most expressive word was thought to be 'elsewhere.' Everyone saw that Hanover was intended thereby, and yet it passed, says Walpole, ' as a phrase of course like the town of Berwick-upon-Tweed.' In the House not a whisper of opposition was heard. Pitt himself, speaking on the army estimates, encouraged this confidence by his description of a united Ministry that nothing could separate, all animated by the same spirit and aiming at the same goal, and by his panegyric on the King—' burning with zeal for the country's happiness.' A month later, on the vote of £100,000 for the Hanoverian and allied army, he roused the House to enthusiasm by his eulogy of Frederic's achievements in the common cause and by his eloquent pleading for the army of observation under Prince Ferdinand, as the best means of supporting a king whose interests were so closely bound up with England's.[1] A Polish prince who heard this speech said of it disdainfully that it was not the speech of a Secretary of State but of a tribune of the people : to Pitt no higher compliment could have been paid.

December 14, 1757.

January 18, 1758.

[1] Schaefer (7 jähriger Krieg, i, 665, and ii¹, 530) gives accounts from Prince Czartoriski and the Prussian envoy of these speeches. The account of the first speech corresponds very closely with Walpole's. Walpole has no mention of the second.

Pitt had forestalled the sanction of Parliament. In November he was urging on Newcastle that the allied army should 'begin in time and go to work roundly, clearing the electorate and putting an end to the insolence and rapine of the French army in that suffering country.'[1] Immediately after Rossbach he secured Frederic's consent to the appointment of Prince Ferdinand of Brunswick, whose first action on taking up his command was formally to disown the convention. In him Pitt found a leader of a different mettle from the Duke of Cumberland. Trained in the best school of arms in Europe, he had some of Frederic's fire and much of his ability to hold his own against heavy odds. He was too good a soldier, when he had Englishmen under him, to give occasion for complaints of favouritism to his own countrymen; and he knew how to get the best work from all. 'How extraordinarily civil the Prince is to-day,' remarked an English grenadier. 'Yes,' grumbled a veteran in the same company, 'I observed it too, and be damned to him! You'll find he is always so before we are to be damnably peppered.' Within a month of assuming the command at Stade he had driven Richelieu's army back almost to the Weser, and by April 1758 had sent Clermont, Richelieu's successor, flying across the Rhine with more haste than d'Estrées had crossed it into Hanover the previous year. Moreover, by taking the Hanoverians as well as the Hessians and Brunswickers into English pay, Pitt made certain that the army would fight for English objects and was able to insist that it should act only on instructions from an English Secretary of State.[2] Thus all fear of another convention of Closterseven was for the future averted, and Pitt had succeeded, where all his predecessors had failed, in reversing the old relations and making Hanover a province dependent on England.[3]

Frederic had followed up his victory of Rossbach by turning south with lightning speed on the Austrians, whom he defeated at Lissa on December 5, 1757, thereby earning a period of comparative rest till the following April. During these early months of 1758 there was a certain coolness between Pitt and

---

[1] *Add. MSS.* 32997, f. 341. [2] *Ibid.* 32876, f. 152.
[3] So thought Joseph Yorke at The Hague (*Pol. Corr.* xvi, 364).

Frederic. Each had grievances against the other. Pitt, possibly remembering Frederic's frequent changes of front in the last war, wanted to bind him irrevocably to England by a closer treaty and a subsidy. Frederic, still uneasy lest Hanover should attempt another treaty of neutrality, kept harping on his old string of an English squadron in the Baltic to overawe Russia, and demanded besides that English troops should be sent over to reinforce Ferdinand. He made it a condition of signing the new treaty or even accepting the proffered subsidy that these terms should be granted. Pitt's answer was that he could not spare the ships or the men from home defence and his other expeditions. He had the additional reason for refusing the men, that public opinion was not yet ripe for this further development of German policy. Early in the session he had told the House that he would not send 'a drop of our blood to the Elbe, to be lost in that ocean of gore,' and in response to his Tory supporters, who were becoming uneasy at Prussia's demands, was several times called upon to repeat this assurance.[1] Pitt's weapon against Frederic was the menace of withdrawing Ferdinand's army from his flank : Frederic's against England that he would make peace with France. The chief sufferers from the growing irritation of the two great men were their respective envoys. Michel, the Prussian minister, was sharply rebuked by Frederic for paying too much deference to Pitt, ' as if that minister's thoughts were to decide the fate of Europe,' and reminded that he was not Mr. Pitt's secretary but the King of Prussia's envoy.[2] Mitchell in Berlin was as strongly suspected by Pitt of having abetted Frederic in his demands for English troops :

December 14, 1757.

Andrew Mitchell [he writes to Newcastle] is not a fool and therefore he must be something not fit to be the instrument of the present system of administration . . . in a word, if your Grace is not able to eradicate this lurking diffusive poison a little more out of the mass of Government, especially from the vitals, I think it better for us to have done. I do not intend for one that Andrew Mitchell shall carry me where I have resolved not to go.[3]

[1] *Chatham MSS.* 86 : Calcraft to Lord Home, February 26, 1758.
[2] *Pol. Corr.* xvi, 253.   [3] *Add. MSS.* 32877, f. 256.

At a Cabinet held in Pitt's house on February 28, 1758,[1] an ultimatum was drawn up refusing English troops and English ships except in co-operation with another Baltic Power and demanding an immediate answer from Frederic about the new treaty. The same night Pitt, who was most anxious not to drive Frederic to extremities, took infinite pains correcting Holderness's dispatch, and sent Joseph Yorke with it to supersede Mitchell. On the way Yorke met Frederic's envoy Knyphausen, with full powers to sign the treaty: for Frederic was as little anxious as Pitt for a breach in the alliance. On April 11, 1758, this was renewed and made closer by the second treaty of Westminster. After his experience of Pitt's diplomacy Frederic called him ' un homme bien vif et fort entêté,' but admired him the more. The two men might well call quits in the trial of strength. By this treaty both Kings were bound not to make peace without the other's consent; George II engaged to pay Frederic a subsidy of £670,000, Frederic to augment his forces and use them for objects common to both parties. Prussia received no promise of English troops or ships; on the other hand Pitt promised to send an English garrison to Emden, to make further descents on the French coast, and to bring diplomatic pressure on Sweden and Russia in Frederic's favour; before many months had passed he complied with the demand for an English contingent to reinforce Ferdinand's army.[2]

Pitt's rapid conversion to the need of sending English troops to Germany is characteristic of his sensitiveness to a change of conditions. In December, when he refused to allow a drop of English blood to be 'lost in that ocean of gore,' he was still under the impression of the Convention of Closterseven and of the English Ministry's inability to prevent it. But after four months' experience of Prince Ferdinand's work he felt that the case was entirely altered. The army was beating the French and helping to preserve Frederic, and its commander was in full sympathy with his own belief that ' a

---

[1] *Add. MSS.* 32997, f. 372. Only Pitt, Newcastle, Hardwicke and Holderness were present; see also *ibid.* 341.

[2] For the treaties of 1756 and 1758 and the further conventions of December 1758, of 1759 and 1760, see Almon, iii.

year of vigorous warfare would do less harm to my army and more damage to the enemy than two years of slack defensive warfare.'[1] At the same time Ferdinand, whose force was the only obstacle to a junction between the two French armies of Clermont and Soubise, was dangerously weak, being inferior in numbers to either Clermont or Soubise separately. His defeat would have left Hanover and all Western Germany at the mercy of France, and Frederic hemmed in on every side. By the end of March Pitt had determined to send English troops to Germany. His first step was to send Brudenell's regiment to garrison Emden, which had been hastily abandoned by the French on the appearance of Commodore Holmes with a frigate and cutter.[2] He thus made sure of an important base of supply. His only reason for further delay in sending English reinforcements to Ferdinand's army in the field was a fear that the King would insist on appointing Cumberland to command them.[3] But by two brilliant victories Ferdinand put his right to command beyond question. Following Clermont across the Rhine he drove him out of his camp at Rheinberg on June 13, and on the 23rd beat him again at Crevelt. On the 24th, George II signed the order for 5,000 troops to be sent to Germany.[4] When news came of Crevelt, Pitt increased the draft to 6,000, and a week later to 9,000.

'We are sending twelve squadrons of English cavalry to this glorious school of war and I hope to share a sprig of Germanic laurel very soon,' wrote Pitt with boyish fervour to Grenville; and his disgust at the poor spirit shown by the army at Rochefort may well have been one of his reasons for sending it to Germany. As Bute said, ' Nothing would assist the army more and recover discipline than sending them to some scene of action.'[5] Most of the officers were delighted at the prospect of fighting pitched battles according to rule instead of marching through swamps and forests in America

[1] From Pitt's draft (in French) of the King's letter to Ferdinand. (*Chatham Corr.* i, 309.)

[2] March 29, 1758 (Record Office, *Foreign, Various*, 68–71).

[3] See d'Abreu's account of Pitt's hesitations in March in *Chatham Corr.* i, 294–300; see also *Pol. Corr.* xvii, 22, &c.

[4] Add. *MSS.* 32881, f. 35.   [5] Bute to Pitt (n.d.), *Chatham MSS.* 24

or 'buccaneering,' as Sackville called it, on the French coast; and hardly a murmur was heard from the public—hitherto taught by Pitt to suspect all German adventures. On July 11 the first detachment embarked at Gravesend, and by August 21 the Duke of Marlborough had joined Ferdinand with six regiments of foot and six of horse.[1] Ferdinand had asked for two more battalions to garrison Stade, but Pitt would not agree to sending another man that year. At a Cabinet Council on August 2 he declared that if more could have been spared he would have sent them in the first instance, for he did not believe in doing things by halves. His expeditions to France were already cramped by the dispatch of the 9,000, and home defence had to be thought of. When 50,000 German and 9,000 English troops were in their pay they could not be accused of starving the continental campaign. Rather than send English soldiers to garrison a Hanoverian town he would hire 4,500 Bavarians: 'You see by this,' he said to Newcastle, 'I don't mean to avoid the expense but to give the assistance, if it properly can.'[2]

The English reinforcement enabled Ferdinand to hold his own. Though defeated once by Soubise, he succeeded by rapid marches and counter-marches between the two French armies in driving them out of Hanover and Hesse and retired into winter quarters in a strong position covering both principalities. Frederic's activity was even more marvellous than in 1757. Driven out of Bohemia by Daun in July, he turned on the Russians, who were threatening Berlin, and defeated them at the bloody battle of Zorndorf on August 25 and 26. Beaten again by Daun at Hochkirch in October, he was, nevertheless, at the end of the year still in possession of every inch of the territory he owned in 1757. For Pitt the continental campaign had done more than he could have hoped. Frederic was still safe; the French had been signally defeated at Crevelt; two French commanders, Richelieu and Clermont, had been disgraced; over 100,000 French soldiers and French millions sorely needed for the defence of America and India had been wasted.

[1] One of these was Pitt's old regiment, 1st Dragoon Guards (Bland's).
[2] *Add. MSS.* 32882, f. 199.

FERDINAND & FREDERIC'S CAMPAIGNS, 1758

The disappointment of the Rochefort expedition did not prevent Pitt from projecting like enterprises in 1758. Frederic and Ferdinand both urged them, the Leicester House party encouraged him to ignore 'passion and faction' and proceed in a policy which was pronounced 'safe and easy,' on the ground that the French *garde-côtes* were worse fighters than our own peasants.[1] The French were reported to be making preparations for invasion at Boulogne, Calais, Brest and Rochefort;[2] an attack on their coasts would give them something else to think about. In April Pitt gave his first orders to prepare for a descent 'in order to cause such a division of the forces of the enemy as may influence the grand operations of this campaign without going at too great a distance from this country.'[3] On May 8 he ordered transports for 13,000 troops and set Commodore Howe, who had captured the fort on Ile d'Aix,[4] to get ready an escorting squadron; on May 20 he ordered Anson himself to assume command of a covering fleet to watch the western ports, and the Duke of Marlborough, Master-General of the Ordnance, to take command of the troops. He was determined not to risk another Rochefort for want of good men. Hawke, jealous of Howe's appointment, had struck his flag, but Pitt, who could be severe enough on a bad man, 'received with temper' the account of Hawke's petulance, and, wishing 'some means might be found by which he might be preserved to the service,' welcomed Anson's suggestion that Hawke should return as his second-in-command.[5] On taking leave of the generals he said everything he could to encourage them to risk action, and, in the hurry of their departure, characteristically found time to dash off a line to his wife, urging her to think more of her 'dear, dear health,' and telling her that 'the troops are said to breathe nothing but ardor. Heaven go with them.'[6]

---

[1] *Chatham MSS.* 24, Bute to Pitt, n.d.
[2] See Record Office, *Foreign, Various*, 68–71, March 13 and April 4, 1758. On March 13 a letter reporting preparations at Boulogne and Calais came to Pitt. On the same day he ordered the Admiralty to send boats to look into these ports. On the 23rd he had their report.
[3] *Chatham MSS.* 85.   [4] See above, p. 342.
[5] Anson, *Anson*, p. 153.   [6] *Chatham MSS.* 5.

On June 1 Howe sailed with his imposing convoy, and came to anchor in Cancale Bay on the 4th. No time was wasted in preliminaries: on the 5th two brigades were landed, and on the 7th all the shipping and stores in the harbour, to the value of £500,000, were burned. But on news of French troops approaching under the Governor of Brittany the commanders deemed it prudent to abandon the attack on St. Malo and hurriedly re-embarked the troops.[1] The remainder of June was spent in useless demonstrations against Havre, Caen, Honfleur and Cherbourg.

On the return of the expedition Granville, who had 'no great expectations' from such adventures, wished to put an end to them, and Beckford, a good barometer of public feeling in the City, reported that 'the St. Maloes expedition was considered an idle scheme, which is as much ridiculed in France and other places as our late expedition to Rochefort.' But Pitt would not hear of drawing back: keeping France in alarms upon the coast was the most effectual way to distress her, he said, and he even asserted that L'Orient, Rochefort and St. Malo would all be in our possession had not the generals made a present of them to the French.[2] At the moment he was busy sending off the English contingent to Germany; without interrupting this business he rained orders on the Admiralty to supply Howe with cables, anchors, provisions, beer, forage and water, so that a fresh start might be made forthwith; he would hardly allow Howe to land his men until he heard they had become 'sick, ragged and lousy' from long confinement on shipboard. But he had to change his generals. Sackville, who had been second-in-command to Marlborough, wrote 'representing the disagreeable situation he found himself in' and threatening to resign from the army if he were not appointed to a German command. Next day Pitt saw him and the Duke of Marlborough and consented

[1] So hurried was the embarkation that the Duke of Marlborough left his spoons behind. These the Duc d'Aiguillon considerately sent after him in a cartel ship.

[2] For an account of this Cabinet discussion, see Dodington, 409. After Pitt had spoken, Ligonier, turning to Granville, began: 'You must admit——' 'My Lord,' interrupted Granville, 'I will admit nothing. Your Lordship is apt to admit, but I will admit nothing.'

to let them go to Germany; Bligh, who had originally been intended for that command, had, much to his disgust, to take their place. But Pitt made up for this loss of prestige for his expedition by obtaining permission for Prince Edward, George II's second grandson, to embark in Howe's ship. On August 1 Howe sailed again with instructions from Pitt to 'add life and strength to the common cause.' On the 8th Cherbourg was captured and its forts and shipping destroyed, a fine was levied on the inhabitants, hostages taken, and twenty-four brass guns and the town bells carried off as trophies. But again, as at St. Malo, the approach of French troops caused a precipitate retreat to the ships, before Pitt had time to signify his intention of holding Cherbourg until the end of the war. On August 19 Howe was back in Portland harbour refreshing his crews.

The next point of attack was ill chosen. In Brest Howe would have found the French departments of war and marine disputing about the control of the port-batteries instead of preparing for defence; in most of the coast towns the militia were starving, in rags and deserting by hundreds: but St. Malo, warned by the attack three months earlier, was prepared. At St. Lunaire, west of this town, Howe and Bligh decided to land for another attempt on September 3. The landing was rough and the guns and stores could not follow the troops. Howe took his ships for shelter to the Bay of St. Cast, farther west, leaving Bligh, who soon gave up any idea of attacking St. Malo, to wander across the peninsula back to the ships. d'Aiguillon, the Governor of Brittany, acting on a precept which Pitt himself would have endorsed—'to make straight for the enemy when his position is discovered, to make the best dispositions possible and then trust to Providence'—came with 10,000 men and thirteen guns by forced marches within a few miles of Bligh on the evening of the 10th. Bligh struck his camp at night amidst loud drum-beating, and next morning allowed his men to straggle away to the coast. Here the boats were ready to take the men off, but before this operation had well begun d'Aiguillon was attacking. For a time the guns of the fleet kept down d'Aiguillon's artillery, and the difficulty of the ground afforded some protection to the English troops embarking; but the Guards, left to the last, suffered cruelly. A great many were cut down on the beach, some threw themselves into the sea and were drowned, and several boatloads of them were overturned and sunk. The English loss was reckoned at between 1,000 and 8,000 in this 'ill-combined and worse executed' expedition, so young Philip Francis, who was present as Bligh's secretary, called it.[1]

The ridicule excited in England by the failure of this last attempt to singe the King of France's beard was so great that Pitt had to abandon this method of warfare for over a year. The ill-humour or incompetence of all the military commanders entrusted with these descents makes it surprising that they were not more disastrous. But, in spite of tactical failures, the effort had not been entirely wasted. The harbours of St. Malo and Cherbourg, nests of the French privateers that preyed on English commerce, had been destroyed. Anson's blockade of the coast, an integral part of Pitt's scheme, had been so close that no ships had dared leave Brest either to attack Howe or to sail to America. Prince Ferdinand thought Howe's raids so useful in diverting attention from himself that he begged Pitt to continue them as long as possible. In September, according to the Duke of Marlborough, eighteen battalions and four cavalry regiments were taken away from Contades for coast defence. In Brittany alone d'Aiguillon had some 10,000 regulars besides militia, and the whole seaboard from Dunkirk to Bordeaux had to be protected. Pitt, therefore, was not far wrong when he boasted that by his excursions and alarms he had occupied at least 30,000 troops that might have been fighting in Germany or America.

In the beginning of the year, in the midst of preparations for the American campaign, Pitt had given renewed orders for the West African expedition suggested by Cumming.[2] A small squadron under Captains Marsh and Mason arrived at the Senegal River on April 23, 1758, and on May 1 received the

---

[1] Waddington, iii, 348 *sqq.*, has some interesting details about the St. Cast disaster. Dr. Holland Rose publishes in the *English Hist. Rev.* for Oct., 1913, one of the less favourable French reports on these raids from *Chatham MSS.* 85.   [2] See above, pp. 300–1, 337.

surrender of Fort Louis and of all property belonging to the French company. On June 13 Pitt had news of this his first success; on the same day he sent out reinforcements to the garrison at Fort Louis, and at the end of August, on the advice of his friend, Alderman Sayre,[1] prepared to send a larger force to reduce Goree, a French island to the south of Senegal. In October Keppel should have sailed with five ships of the line and some frigates carrying a battalion from Cork, but was delayed by violent storms till November. On December 28 he appeared off Goree, and, after a feebly resisted attack, captured it. Such was the zeal Pitt had inspired in the troops that they complained they had no opportunity of proving their mettle, owing to the 'French not doing their duty.' The grievance was one that appealed to Pitt:

Though the ill behaviour of the enemy [he replied] did not afford the land forces under your command any opportunity to distinguish themselves on that occasion, yet the King does not doubt from the readiness and ardour they showed they would have performed their duty in such manner as would have supported the honour of His Majesty's arms.

All the French factories in West Africa fell into English hands by these easy conquests, as well as the French trade with the interior in gum, gold, ivory, corn and cattle. But the loss of the slave trade was the worst blow to the enemy, and as a result of the English victory the London, Bristol, Liverpool, Plymouth and Guernsey merchants, who annually sent some forty ships and carried some 4,000 slaves from West Africa to the plantations, were set free from all danger of molestation. It was not a great undertaking, but Pitt's management of it illustrates his clean-cut methods. He sent out the right number of men and no more, chose young and vigorous commanders, and showed the same driving force in starting Keppel's little squadron as he applied to greater enterprises.[2]

[1] *Chatham MSS.* 55.
[2] Keppel, for example, lost an ordnance ship in the storm, and Pitt told him not to delay his departure ' one moment ' for it but to let it follow him. Many other such touches are to be found in the correspondence (see *Chatham MSS.* 100, and Record Office, *Sierra Leone*, 12).

After the victories he was mindful of those who had done good work: Cumming, the original projector, obtained a pension; the French pilot, who guided Keppel at Goree, was also recommended for a pension;[1] and Keppel himself was marked out for future service of a hazardous nature.

II

All these schemes for Germany, the coast of France, and West Africa were subordinated to the main business of the war, 'the succour and preservation of America.' The American campaign of 1758 was the first for which Pitt was entirely responsible. He had come into office too late in 1756 to do more than forward to the best of his ability Loudoun's vague projects for the capture of either Louisburg or Quebec. In the interval he had been collecting numerous suggestions from men who knew the country well. One of his most useful correspondents was James Abercromby,[2] agent for Virginia and North Carolina, who gave good advice about his fellow-provincials and the way to avoid the mistakes of the past in dealings with them; from his knowledge of the country he could point out the weak spots in the defences of Canada. Then Bollan, the agent for Massachusetts,[3] supplied information about the French forces in Canada and the strength of Quebec, and suggested remedies for the grievances under which his province was suffering; Pownall, the energetic governor of the same province, sent voluminous reports on the French fortresses dotted about America and on the attitude of the Indians, and suggestions for a plan of campaign; Denys de Berdt,[4] a merchant interested in the American trade, urged him to abandon the policy of attempting to capture French fortresses piecemeal, and to concentrate

---

[1] Record Office, *Dom. Entry Book*, 21. The man's name was Julien du Chêne.

[2] Not to be confounded with the general of the same name. This man's letters, written from Craven Street, Strand, are in *Chatham MSS.* 17, 95, and 97; see also Beer, *British Colonial Policy*, p. 55, *note*.

[3] *Chatham MSS.* 20. *Ibid.* 19; Beer, *ibid.* pp. 175–6.

for a grand attack on Quebec; Bradstreet,[1] who had first seen service as colonel of a Maine militia regiment in the Louisburg expedition of 1745, and had distinguished himself in the present war, proposed that three simultaneous attacks should be delivered on Quebec on lines which Pitt ultimately adopted; and, lastly, Brigadier Waldo, who had also been in the last Louisburg campaign, sent him plans of the fortress and a well-considered scheme for its capture.[2]

By December 30, 1757, Pitt had matured the plans, which he expounded in eight masterly dispatches to the governors and the general in America.[3] By the exordium to most of these he signified the spirit in which he expected them to act: 'His Majesty having nothing more at heart than to repair the losses and disappointments of the last inactive and unhappy campaign and by the most vigorous and extensive efforts to avert, by the blessing of God on his arms, the dangers impending on N. America.' In the previous year he had allowed Loudoun and Holburne to decide whether they should attempt Louisburg or Quebec first. This year Pitt left no doubt. He was convinced that Quebec was the key of Canada and the chief goal of the campaign, but Louisburg, standing as a sentinel at the entrance of the St. Lawrence, was no less the key of Quebec. Its magnificent harbour also made it a danger as a refuge for French fleets and the privateers that preyed on the New England trade and fisheries. Louisburg, therefore, was to be the first object of the next campaign. But, in expectation of its early fall, Pitt also made every provision for the capture of Quebec itself in the same year. The naval and military force destined against the Cape Breton fortress was after its capture to proceed up the St. Lawrence to the ancient capital of Canada; in co-operation with the fleet a land force was to be advancing down Lake George, where Montcalm had beaten Monro the year before, capture the French forts Ticonderoga and Crown Point at the head of Lake Champlain, and approach Quebec

[1] *Chatham MSS.* 95.
[2] Waldo's letters, dated November, 1757, are in Record Office, C.O. 5.52. His scheme was substantially that adopted by Amherst and Boscawen.
[3] These are all given in Kimball, i.

by the Richelieu river and the St. Lawrence. He also provided for a separate force to protect the southern colonies, and, later in the season, for an attack by the fleet on the French settlements in Mississippi.

To carry out this bold and all-embracing scheme, Pitt's first need was for better men to take command. Holburne was put aside and Admiral Boscawen—'wry-necked Dick' the sailors called him—taken from the Admiralty to command the fleet. Loudoun was recalled from his cabbages and his dispatches, and in his place Abercromby, one of his brigadiers, promoted to the chief command. It was not a good appointment, for he was old and had shown no sign of great capacity: but Pitt had little choice, for the King would not appoint young officers to high command, and the best seniors preferred fighting in Europe. At any rate, though Pitt thought well of Abercromby at first,[1] he took care to have a young man whom he could trust at his elbow, and dispatched Lord Howe, elder brother of the commodore, as a brigadier on his staff. 'The best officer in the British army,' Wolfe called Howe; and indeed he ran Wolfe close. With less genius than Wolfe, he had all his love for the profession of arms and more personal charm. A favourite in London society, he was beloved by his men and by all the provincials who met him.[2] On campaign he lived as sparingly and simply as the humblest soldier, taught his men to use their wits, and cared for their comfort; in the rough warfare of America he made them cast to the winds the regulation stocks, gaiters and periwigs which hampered their movements. The colonists he won by treating them as equals and humbly seeking to learn in their school of border fighting.[3] With such a man beside him Pitt hoped that Abercromby would be able to raise the colonial levies without friction, and to direct the secondary Crown Point expedition entrusted to him. The main operations against Louisburg

[1] According to Newcastle (Torrens, ii, 473).
[2] Wolfe, on the other hand, shared the usual contempt in the army for the provincial militia.
[3] There is an account of him on the day before his death lying on a bearskin by the sunlit shores of Lake George plying Stark, the great colonial ranger, with questions as to the best way of approaching Ticonderoga.

Pitt took entirely out of his hands. For this task he chose Colonel Jeffrey Amherst, then commissary of the Hessian troops, a contemporary of his own, they both having taken their first commissions in 1731. The King made great difficulties about promoting so junior an officer, and yielded only to the entreaties of Lady Yarmouth, backed by Pitt's threat that he would abandon the Louisburg expedition if he did not have his way.[1] Amherst was a cautious man of no brilliance and of few words, whose merit, says Walpole, it required penetration to admire. But his caution was not that of the Loudouns and Mordaunts who feared danger; it was more akin to that of a Fabius Cunctator. His very slowness inspired confidence in his men, helped by the belief he showed in them. 'My service to the gentlemen under you,' he wrote to one of his brigadiers. 'Our trade is a fickle one, but proper measures and perseverance in executing them will in the end prevail with the bravery of the British troops, though every day of battle cannot be a day of victory.'[2] By the happiest of combinations Pitt added the fire of a Wolfe to Amherst's caution. He had marked the young colonel as the only military officer who showed any dash at Rochefort, and accordingly named him quartermaster to the Louisburg contingent. For the southern command he chose Forbes, just such another as Amherst, dogged and tenacious to the death. Then, remembering Webb's incapacity at Fort Edward, he even selected the man to take charge of the lines of communication from Albany to Lake George—a Colonel Stanwix, who had already distinguished himself in the South. Thus Abercromby, the old-fashioned general, became the sedentary commander, as Chesterfield called him; Amherst, Howe and Wolfe, young, vigorous and burning with zeal, were to be the acting officers. With such men and with his friend Boscawen to command the fleet, Pitt could feel some confidence that his plans would be understood and followed; especially if both services combined in the spirit of the recommendation, which he invariably inserted in his instructions:

[1] *Add. MSS.* 32876, f. 461, and 32997, f. 310.
[2] *Chatham MSS.* 96.

Whereas the success of this expedition will very much depend upon an entire good understanding between our sea and land officers, we do hereby strictly enjoin and require you on your part to maintain and cultivate such a good understanding and agreement, and to order the sailors and marines under your command to assist our land forces, and to man the batteries when there shall be occasion for them and when they can be spared from the sea service; as we have instructed our General . . . to order that the soldiers under his command shall man the ships when there shall be occasion for them, and when they can be spared from the land service.

The fleet put under Boscawen consisted of twenty-three ships of the line, besides frigates and smaller craft. Amherst's army, some 13,000 strong, was also entirely provided by the mother-country, with the exception of 500 colonial rangers. Pitt possibly felt that since the colonials had captured Louisburg in the last war the regulars should have a chance of showing what they could do there. Abercromby's army was to be composed partly of regulars but chiefly of local levies, and Forbes, to whom only a battalion and a half of English troops were allotted, had to make up his complement with colonials. Pitt was prepared to give of the best that England could afford for his great enterprise, but he expected the Americans to help themselves and the mother-country more generously than in the past. To attain this object he did not gird at them. He assumed that the King's 'faithful and brave subjects in America will cheerfully co-operate with, and second to the utmost, the large expense and extraordinary succours supplied by this kingdom for their preservation and defence,' and, in calling for 20,000 men from the northern provinces, averted disputes about each quota by urging all to raise the utmost possible number, 'his Majesty not judging it expedient to limit the zeal and ardour of any of his provinces by making a repartition of the force to be raised by each respectively.' It was not asking over much, since arms, equipment and rations were found by the King, and a grant in aid of pay and clothing was promised to the provinces that showed zeal.[1] He also removed a grievance which was a serious obstacle to willing service by the Americans. Since 1754 a royal warrant

[1] Nevertheless it was a great saving in expense to employ colonial levies in place of regulars, whose transport to America was very costly.

had been in force, subordinating all colonial rank to the lowest rank in the regular army; according to this even a colonial staff-officer might be called upon to take his orders from some callow English ensign or cornet, a cause of intense and just irritation to provincials, who had some reason for thinking they understood the local conditions of warfare better than the martinets bred in Braddock's school. Pitt cut away this injustice. With his dispatches of December 30 he sent a warrant ordering that for the future American officers were to take rank with the regulars, according to the date of their commissions. He showed his confidence in the colonial troops further by especially ordering one of their officers, Colonel Bradstreet of Maine, to be given an important command These concessions, putting the colonials on a par with their English brethren, had more effect in raising men in America than all Loudoun's bullying or even the New Englanders' hatred of the French. In some cases the effect was instantaneous. When the dispatch announcing the new royal warrant arrived, Pownall was in difficulties with his assembly, who were haggling over a levy of 2,000 men that he had asked of them: next morning, when the dispatch had been read out, the assembly voted that Massachusetts should provide the whole 7,000 originally asked from all the northern provinces. For 1758 the northern provinces voted 17,500 men and the southern 5,800—as much as could be expected of their sparse populations, and more than double what they had ever voted before;[1] and for the rest of the war they continued voting about the same numbers. Every encouragement, too, was offered to regain the Indians, Abercromby being told to be especially careful that all presents voted for the tribes should reach their destination and be equitably distributed.

When the broad principles of the campaign were laid down, Pitt turned to the details. Transports fully victualled to carry troops from New York to Halifax were sent to America; orders were given for a preliminary reconnaissance of Louisburg,

---

[1] In 1756, for example, Parkman says that the New England colonies and New York together raised only 5,000 men (*Montcalm and Wolfe*, i, 397). For the numbers of men raised by the various colonies in each year of the war, see Beer, *loc. cit.* pp. 55–71.

for laying down careening wharves at Halifax, and for the building of special flat-bottomed boats suitable for the navigation of Lake George, Lake Champlain and the St. Lawrence, under the eye of Captain Loring, an experienced officer suggested by Waldo ; and steps were taken to collect a gang of eighty artificers for the siege. Pitt also took care to clear the way for his expedition, by preventing the French from concentrating a superior fleet at Louisburg, as they had done in 1757. Sir Charles Hardy with a small squadron was sent ahead of Boscawen to watch the St. Lawrence, and English fleets were posted in European waters to intercept any attempt of the enemy to steal another march across the Atlantic.

Duquesne and de la Clue were known to be making preparations in the Mediterranean ports : all through the winter Osborn and Saunders, with ten sail, were on the look-out for them at Gibraltar. Osborn had constant information from the English consuls in Italy and Spain and was ready for de la Clue when he sailed from Hyères in November with six ships. The French admiral, not daring to pass him, put into Cartagena to wait for Duquesne. But at Toulon the preparations for Duquesne's fleet had been much hampered by difficulties about money, artificers and even sailors. At length, by dint of engaging men from foreign ports, Duquesne was able to send two ships to join de la Clue early in February, and at the end of that month put to sea himself with three more. Before he could join de la Clue he fell in with Osborn and Saunders, who immediately gave chase. The two largest of Duquesne's three ships, the *Foudroyant* and the *Orphée*, were captured after gallant fights ; the third was driven ashore. After this disaster de la Clue gave up the attempt to sail out and returned to Toulon, leaving Osborn master of the Mediterranean. Hawke had been sent out to watch the Biscay ports. Here the French had been working under cruel difficulties, for half Brest was down with the putrid fever brought back by de la Motte in his foul ships from America. They managed, however, to equip a military convoy for Louisburg in March, but Hawke, sent out in the nick of time, turned them back and drove them aground in Rochefort roads early in April.

Long ere this Boscawen had started, for Pitt had none of his old difficulty with dilatory departments, now they had all tasted his temper. In 1757 Anson had professed to be unable to find ships for some of Pitt's expeditions : in January 1758 he produced Boscawen's twenty-three ships the day after he received Pitt's order, and, when one of them was lost, on the very same day found for him the *Dublin*, another ship of the same rating. On February 19 Boscawen announced to Pitt that he had weighed anchor in this laconic note:

Namure at St. Hellens,
at 2 o'clock in the morning, February 19, 1758.

SIR,—I am now under sail with his Majesty's ships named in the Margen little wind at last and by South, I am,
S^r, your most obedient
and most humble servant,
E. BOSCAWEN.

But in spite of this early start he did not reach Halifax till May 12. ·' From Christopher Columbus' time to our day there perhaps has never been a more extraordinary voyage,' said Wolfe, who suffered torture from sea-sickness in the almost unceasing storms. Amherst himself in the *Dublin* (Captain Rodney) did not arrive until the 28th. Without setting foot on land he joined Boscawen and with him left Halifax at the head of 23 ships of the line, 18 frigates, and 116 transports carrying the 13,000 troops assembled for the siege.[1]

Louisburg lies on a spit of land between the Bay of Gabarus on the west, exposed to the long Atlantic rollers, and a land-locked harbour on the east. Its fortifications, so far from being impregnable, as Loudoun had been ready to believe, were somewhat neglected, and Drucour, the Governor, had only 3,500 men in garrison ; a fleet of thirteen sail lay in the harbour under des Gouttes, an incompetent officer. The strength of the fortress lay in its inaccessibility except by the harbour, which could be blocked by sinking a couple of ships in the entrance, and by the storm-beaten coast of Gabarus Bay. On June 2,

---

[1] Record Office, *America and West Indies*, i, 79 gives a list of ' Troops destined for the siege of Louisburg, May 24, 1758,' amounting to 12,659 regulars and 538 rangers.

when the English armament hove in sight of Louisburg, Boscawen looked into the harbour and Amherst took his two brigadiers, Lawrence and Wolfe, to pitch upon landing-places in Gabarus Bay. Many of the sailors thought a landing too risky and urged Boscawen to call a council of war to consider it; but he preferred the advice of an old sea captain, who told him to have nothing to do with councils and shoulder the responsibility himself, and he declared he would not leave Gabarus Bay without landing the troops. On June 8, the first possible day, Wolfe was told off to make a landing at Freshwater Cove while the fleet and other boat parties distracted the enemy elsewhere. The breakers were formidable and even Wolfe was within an ace of turning back, but one of his boat-loads took the matter into their own hands and made a landing. Then the rest of his party, following Wolfe, drove their boats ashore, overcame the French outpost at the cove, and secured a landing for the whole army. After this the fall of Louisburg was merely a question of time; but Amherst took no risks and approached methodically with parallels and entrenchments. Boscawen meanwhile was dealing with des Gouttes. He captured two out of three frigates that tried to escape, set fire with his shells to three ships as they lay in the harbour, and on July 25 sent in some boat-loads of sailors, who burned one of the remaining ships to the water's edge and towed away another as a capture. Next day Drucour, who had made a brave fight, surrendered his garrison as prisoners of war and ceded the fortress of Louisburg, with the islands of Cape Breton and St. Jean, to England. Amherst had been slow, but he and Boscawen had destroyed a French squadron, that could ill be spared, had 4,000 prisoners and 220 pieces of cannon as trophies, and had taken the main outwork of Canada. One of the most encouraging circumstances of the joint operation was the hearty co-operation and good fellowship between the two services. Instead of the bickering and jealousies which had been the rule since Vernon's expedition to Cartagena,[1] 'the admiral and the general,' writes Wolfe, 'have carried on the public service with great harmony,

---

[1] See above, p. 81.

industry and union. Mr. Boscawen has given all and even more than we could ask of him. He has furnished arms and ammunition, pioneers, sappers, miners, gunners, carpenters, boats, and is, I must confess, no bad *fantassin* himself, and an excellent back hand at a siege.'[1]

Unfortunately this success was counterbalanced by a disaster to the army, which was to co-operate in the attack on Quebec. The ' sedentary ' general did not belie his reputation. At the beginning of July, thanks chiefly to Pitt's elaborate provisions, Abercromby was ready to embark his 9,000 provincials and 6,000 regulars on the 1,000 boats prepared for the crossing of Lake George. The flotilla drifted past the enchanting scenery of the lake in all the pride of war, with bands playing and flags flying. ' I never saw a sight more fair,' said one who sailed in this procession ; and all were full of hope, for was not Howe with them ? But on the morning of the 6th Howe was struck down by a stray bullet in the maze of trees between Lake George and Ticonderoga at the head of Lake Champlain. ' In Lord Howe,' says Mante, the historian of the campaign, ' the soul of General Abercromby's army seemed to expire. From the unhappy moment . . . a strange kind of infatuation usurped the place of resolution.' Montcalm had arrived at Ticonderoga on June 30, when he had a garrison of only 4,000 men to set against Abercromby's 15,000. But he had a well-founded contempt for the British general, ' Mrs. Nabbycromby,' as the colonials called him, and within a week had formed outside his ramparts a huge breastwork of forest trees, rough-hewn and spiked. His only weak spot was Rattlesnake Mountain, which dominated the fort : for want of men to hold it he had to trust to Abercromby's overlooking it. On July 8, two days after Howe's death, Abercromby sent his army towards Ticonderoga by an easier and shorter track than that previously chosen. He himself remained in his camp at the foot of Lake George and kept with him his guns which would have been decisive on Rattlesnake Mountain. The assault on the fort, which lasted the long summer day, was nothing but a senseless carnage. Time after

[1] *Historical MSS. Commission*, Stopford Sackville, ii, 264.

time Pitt's Highlanders and the other brave battalions dashed themselves against the impenetrable obstacle, only to be spitted on the protruding spikes or shot down at point-blank range.[1] In the evening Abercromby drew off his exhausted troops, and though he still had more than three times as many men as Montcalm, hastily re-embarked them and paddled back to the head of Lake George, where he remained idly in camp for the rest of the season.

After the capture of Louisburg Amherst had been anxious to continue the voyage to Quebec, but Boscawen thought the season too far advanced, and when Abercromby's panic-stricken dispatches arrived at Louisburg, Amherst agreed that it was no longer to be thought of. He took prompt measures to relieve Abercromby's anxieties: he sent pilots to take soundings of the St. Lawrence and detachments to reconnoitre Gaspé and destroy French fisheries, to encourage the French in the belief that he was still coming to Quebec and induce them to withdraw troops from Lake Champlain to Quebec. Then with the six battalions he had taken across to Boston by sea, he made a forced march to Abercromby's camp. Abercromby, on the ground that it was too late for further operations, sent him back next day.

Abercromby was the only man found wanting of all those chosen by Pitt for his campaigns in America. Bradstreet, against the commander-in-chief's wish, persisted in an expedition to Forts Oswego and Frontenac on Lake Ontario, and, even when his men were falling off from desertion and sickness, wrote, ' Should the numbers be reduced so low, as that we cannot make out above one thousand men fit to proceed to Lake Ontario, with them I will do my best.' His pluck and determination were rewarded by the capture of the forts, important links in the chain of communication between Canada and the Ohio, and a vantage-ground from which to overawe the Six Nations, the Indian allies of England.

Forbes, too, nobly justified Pitt's choice of him for the

[1] Sir A. Quiller Couch's *Fort Amity* gives a vivid picture of this day's fighting, and indeed of Abercromby's whole campaign.

hard task of defending the frontiers of the Southern States and surmounted all his difficulties by indomitable courage. His idea of defence was to attack the enemy's post at Fort Duquesne, which had already been the cause of two battles. The preliminary mustering of troops was heart-breaking work, for excepting a battalion of Highlanders and a detachment of the Royal Americans he had entirely to depend on provincial levies. Virginia raised her 2,000 without difficulty, but Maryland and Pennsylvania proved more obdurate. Negotiations with the Indians also took time, and disputes as to the route between colonies anxious to profit by the supplying of provisions to the column. Finally, at the beginning of July, he started from Philadelphia with 1,500 regulars and 4,500 Americans, choosing the Pennsylvania route as shorter and less open to attack. He was ill when he started, and during most of the march had to be borne in a litter. Through an almost unknown country his men had to climb ranges of mountains and hew a path through dense forests, carrying along with them large supplies for the posts established at intervals to guard the communications.[1] Almost at the goal a party that he had sent forward to reconnoitre was cut up by the French, but when he and the main body arrived at Fort Duquesne on November 26 the garrison had fled. Forbes left behind a small detachment to hold the fort till the summer and was carried back in agony to die in Philadelphia. His report to Pitt is dated from Pittsburg, a name for which he thus accounts:

I have used the freedom of giving your name to Fort Duquesne, as I hope it was in some measure the being actuated by your spirits that now makes us masters of the place. . . . I hope the Name Fathers will take them [Pittsburg and Forts Ligonier and Bedford] under their protection, in which case these dreary deserts will soon

---

[1] Forbes, writing to Pitt on October 20, 1758, told him that he derived the idea of these posts 'from *Turpin's Essay sur la Guerre*. Last Chaptre 4th Book. Intitled *Principe sur lequel on peut etabler un projet de Campagne*, if you take the trouble of looking into his book, you will see the generall principles upon which I have proceeded'—a detail of information which Pitt would appreciate. It is worth noting that the Pennsylvania Railway follows the general alignment of Forbes's route to Pittsburg (see Hurlbut, *Historic Highways*, v, 204).

be the richest and most fertile of any possesst by the British in North America.[1]

The recovery of this fort, the establishment of which by the French was the reason for Washington's mission and the ostensible cause of the war, finally disposed of the French claim to exclude the English from the Ohio ; and Forbes's great march wiped out Braddock's disgrace. Pitt was quick to recognise the achievement of this fine old soldier, whom the Indians dubbed ' Head of Iron.' He offers his own ' particular congratulations and sincere wishes for the recovery of your health ' in the dispatch announcing the King's approbation of ' the indefatigable zeal you have shewed . . . your constant and unwearied application and perseverance . . . at a time while you laboured under such an unhappy state of health as your distinguished duty alone to the King and uncommon ardor for the honor of His Majesty's arms could have enabled you to struggle with.' These words were written in January 1759 : Forbes died in March. If fate was kind and the winds propitious, the brave man's dying moments may have been gladdened by this tribute from the man whose approval he had been seeking to deserve in the uphill fight against all his difficulties.

III

The loss of Minorca, Byng's hesitations, Braddock and Monro's defeats, the Black Hole of Calcutta, Closterseven, and the failures at Rochefort and Louisburg in 1757 had almost brought Englishmen to feel that the glories of Elizabeth's, of Cromwell's, and of the Great Deliverer's days had gone never to return. The revulsion of feeling was all the greater in England and America as news of victory came pouring in : first Senegal, then Crevelt, the destruction of the nest of

---

[1] Miss Pitt-Taylor, a descendant of Chatham, attended the commemoration of Pittsburg by invitation of the town, and presented it with part of a dessert service that had belonged to her ancestor and was stamped with his arms.

privateers at St. Malo, the sack of Cherbourg, Osborn and Hawke's victories at sea, Frederic the Great's victory at Zorndorf, and, last, the crowning glory of Louisburg. In America Governor Lawrence celebrated the capture of the 'Gibraltar of the West' by fêtes attended by the heroes of the siege, and it is said that 60,000 gallons of rum were drunk in honour of the occasion; Boston had a stately bonfire, and her preachers held services of thanksgiving; New York and Philadelphia were not behindhand, and the New England chaplains in Abercromby's defeated army gave praise for the blow to the servants of the Scarlet Woman.[1] In England the populace celebrated the victories with candles, fireworks and bonfires, with beer-drinking and noisy rejoicings. Pitt and the King of Prussia were the heroes of the hour. Even Horace Walpole was fain to tear himself from his medals and pictures, hobnob with bargemen on the all-absorbing topic, and give them wherewithal to drink the King of Prussia's health. At Plymouth a great ball was given, attended by Prince Edward, who kissed all the ladies to enhance their joy. At Bath Miss Ann Pitt lit a great bonfire in front of her brother's house in the Circus—' to be sure, no such bonfire ever was for beauty,' she said with becoming pride—procured all the music she could to help the company sing ' God bless great George our King,' and distributed ten hogsheads of strong beer.

Pitt himself, on news of Louisburg, which came on August 18, sent off a mounted messenger to his wife at Hayes and had by return her note of triumph on the event so ' happy and glorious for my loved England, happy and glorious for my most loved and admired Husband. I feel all your joy, my Life, the joy of the dear brothers, the joy of my friend Mrs. Boscawen, and the joy of the people of England '; and Temple wrote an effusive letter to his ' dear brother Louisburg.' Pitt also took order for the stately celebration of the victories. To commemorate Louisburg he had a medal struck, especially emphasizing the hearty co-operation of fleet and army; he ordered the guns of the Tower and the Park to tell the victory to

[1] See Wood, *Logs of the Conquest of Canada*, p. 79.

the clouds, the Lord Steward to light the usual bonfires near the royal palace, the Dean and Chapter of St. Paul's to hold a solemn service of praise, and the Archbishop of Canterbury to issue a special form of prayer and thanksgiving to be used in all churches and chapels within the bills of mortality on August 20, and in all others on the following Sunday.[1] Later the twenty-four guns and the captured bells of Cherbourg [2] were dragged from Portsmouth to the Park to be inspected by the King, and the colours taken at Louisburg were paraded before him at St. James's Palace and then deposited in St. Paul's Cathedral. In the following session, on Pitt's motion, the thanks of the House were awarded to Boscawen, Amherst and Osborn. Boscawen as a member received his on the spot and answered in a few modest words. Amherst's were sent to him in America. Osborn, the old sea dog who, during his faithful watch through the winter months to prevent reinforcements for America passing Gibraltar, had become paralysed and lost an eye, answered in a letter worthy of the great service to which he belonged : 'As the House of Commons is so gloriously watchful to encourage the greatest merit, by rewarding the least, England can never want good officers.' [3]

December 6, 1758.

Pitt was justified in making the most of victories, for he never concealed or under-rated defeats. Two days after the news of Louisburg came the dispatch announcing Abercromby's defeat and the death of Lord Howe, and he sent it at once to the *Gazette*. The loss of his friend affected him, he wrote to Grenville, ' more than a public sorrow. He was by the universal voice of army and people a character of ancient times : a complete model of military virtue in all its branches. I have

---

[1] On this occasion Pitt seems to have contented himself with the Archbishop's form of prayer. In the following year, on the occasion of another victory, he made a correction in the draft submitted to him by his Grace.

[2] These bells gave occasion for a good deal of official red tape. They were brought over by Lieut.-Colonel Desaguiliers and ordered to be lodged in the Tower. Before this could be done the Secretary of the Customs exacted duty on them. Six months later Colonel Desaguiliers, who regarded them as his private property, claimed their value ; in November 1759 Pitt ordered them to be restored to him.

[3] *Chatham MSS.* 79.

the sad task of imparting this cruel event to a brother [1] who loves him most tenderly,' a task, Grenville replies, which ' no man living could do with so much gentleness and affection, with so much honour and credit both to the dead and to the living.' The reverse to our arms also affected him—Bute thought too strongly, and sought to console him by a declaration from the young Prince of Wales that when he ascended the throne he would ' by restoring virtue and religion make this country great and happy.'

Pitt did not wait for that event; success and disappointment alike spurred him to redoubled energy. On the very next day, though engaged on refitting Howe's squadron for his third venture on the coast of France, he ordered drafts of 2,150 men to assemble at Plymouth and Portsmouth to replace Abercromby's losses. Newcastle, indeed, alarmed at the cost of the war, was already beginning to think that we ought to be satisfied with the capture of Louisburg and make peace at once by exchanging it for Minorca. But Pitt had no intention of repeating the fiasco of Aix-la-Chapelle; he aimed at expelling the French once for all from North America, and was already on the look-out for other conquests as a set-off to Minorca. ' The only way to have peace,' he reminded Newcastle, ' is to prepare for war.' [2] For this policy he could count on the support of his City friends. Beckford wrote to him a week after the news of Louisburg, imploring him to retain it as a valuable fishing centre, and both Beckford and Sir Theodore Jansen urged that compensation for Minorca should be sought among the French West Indian Islands, recommending Martinique as the island most worth conquering and presenting no great difficulties, if the commanders of the expedition were young and bold.[3] Pitt also found an unexpected ally against Newcastle in the King, who had suddenly become as eager for conquests in America as he had previously been indifferent: ' We must keep Cape Breton, take Canada, drive the French out of

[1] Commodore Howe, who by his brother's death became Viscount Howe.
[2] *Add. MSS.* 32884, f. 436.
[3] *Chatham MSS.* 19 and 98; and *Chatham Corr.* i, 352.

America, and have two armies in Germany consisting together of 80,000 men,' he said to Newcastle; and to Pitt he added, 'we must conquer Martinique as a set-off to Minorca.'[1] On September 4 Newcastle had an inkling of a scheme being concerted by Pitt with Cleveland, the Secretary of the Admiralty, for an attempt on Martinique,[2] and was much disturbed when he discovered the lengths to which his restless colleague had already gone. On August 28 Pitt had given instructions to the Admiralty to take up transports for foreign service, and a fortnight later he ordered a squadron to be made ready at Spithead. When Howe returned from his last unfortunate raid to St. Cast, some of his ships were at once transferred to the new armament, and on October 16 the secret instructions for an attack on Martinique were sent to Captain Hughes, the naval commander, and General Hopson, in command of the land forces of the expedition.[3] By November 20 Hughes was writing to Pitt that he was beating down Channel on his way to join Commodore Moore on the West Indian station.

In the Speech from the throne, which two days before the meeting of Parliament he had read over to the Speaker and an appreciative audience of supporters,[4] Pitt could point to achievements justifying the confidence he had always expressed in himself and the nation. After an enumeration of the year's successes—Louisburg, Cape Breton, the Island of St. John, Frontenac, Senegal, and the destruction of the Cherbourg forts—he justified in one terse phrase the continental war, which 'found full employment for the armies of France and her confederates; from which our operations both by sea and in America have derived the most evident advantage,'

---

[1] *Add. MSS.* 32883, f. 114; 32884, f. 436.

[2] *Ibid.* 32883, f. 273; see also 32884, ff. 27 and 79.

[3] Halifax, the First Commissioner of Trade, in a letter of November 5, suggested to Pitt that, after Martinique, St. Lucia and other islands should be attacked, since we might have to give up Martinique at the peace 'if the balance of war should unfortunately be against us in other parts of the world' (*Egerton MSS.* 929, f. 176). Pitt had already empowered Hughes and Hopson to do so, if they thought fit.

[4] *Add. MSS.* 32998, f. 185.

gloried in the struggle as one for 'liberty and independency,' and rejoiced in the unparalleled security of commerce owing to the fleet's vigilant protection. In place of appeals for union as in 1756 and 1757, 'His Majesty,' the Speech said, 'takes so much satisfaction in that good harmony which subsists amongst his faithful subjects that it is more proper for him now to thank you for it, than to repeat his exhortations to it.' The Address was moved and seconded in a strain of almost hyperbolical eulogy of Pitt. He was compared to a blazing star; one speaker said he would lend all he was worth to support the war; another, not to be outdone, said he would give all he was worth; and, adds Lord Bath, Pitt said he would take all they were both worth. Beckford declared that the late events had put him in such good humour that though he preferred fighting in America he would give £2,000,000 even to the German war. Pitt fairly warned the House that the war would yet cost many millions, which his friend Legge would have to find. It was not a time to look too closely at expense: the ship was at sea; she had winds and waves to meet; and all obstructions must be removed before another campaign, which might prove the last. November 23, 1758.

So much for England's duty to herself. But in the hour of triumph Pitt thought even more of England's debts of honour. Now that she was again mistress of the ocean it behoved her, he said, to show self-restraint and not set all the neutral Powers against her by the excesses of her privateers. England's obligations to her great ally also preoccupied him. Bernis, the French minister, had already made overtures of peace through Denmark. They were rejected on the ground that Frederic had not been included in the offer, but Pitt had a foreboding that he might not always be able to hold his countrymen to their duty to Frederic. Already Dodington had published an anonymous pamphlet against the German war, and it was known that many sympathized with him. Pitt therefore once more defended our support of Frederic, and, looking full at Dodington, he drew himself up, and called out in his loudest tone, 'Is there an Austrian among you? Let him stand forth and reveal himself.'[1] Again, on December 6, he dwelt upon our duty to our ally. Beckford had expressed a hope that no British minister would be bold enough to propose the restitution of Louisburg and Cape Breton. Time enough, said Pitt, to decide on that when the war was concluded and the successes of England and her allies were known. If he were called on as minister to decide on the terms of peace, his principle would be that no ally of England should become a victim of his attachment to us or lose one iota of territory for British considerations, for till all our allies were satisfied it touched England's glory and dignity that no regard should be paid to actual or future conquests in America.[2]

December 6, 1758.

---

[1] Torrens, ii, 400, quotes West's account in *Newcastle MSS.*; see also Schaefer, ii¹, 560, Climenson, ii, 153, and Walpole.

[2] *Pol. Corr.* xvii, 436.

CHAPTER XIII

PITT AND CHOISEUL

> No thought of flight,
> None of retreat, no unbecoming deed
> That argued fear; each on himself relied
> As only in his arm the moment lay
> Of victory.
>
> MILTON, *Paradise Lost*, vi, 236.

IN France no leader worthy of Pitt's steel had hitherto appeared. Louis XV, Madame de Pompadour and the Abbé de Bernis were contemptible enemies. Endowed by nature with ability and political sagacity, Louis XV allowed his talents to rust in sloth and luxury, relieved only by rare flashes of insight never followed up. Tenacious of the personal and irresponsible power bequeathed to him by his great-grandfather, he had not the resolution to use that power for a consistent national policy, but frittered it away in secret intrigues against his own ministers and the projects which he had himself sanctioned. No flattery was too gross for his inordinate vanity, no pleasure of the sense too scandalous for his jaded appetite. Wearied of every sensation but that of his own existence, to which he clung with a pusillanimous terror of the hereafter, he showed during his long life no trace of a single virtue, or of one amiable characteristic. Faithless to man and woman, he would dismiss with a curt word of displeasure and without thought of faithful service to himself or the nation the minister who would not pander to his whims, or the mistress who had ceased to satisfy his passing lust or seemed to be endangering his prospect of heaven. In religion he was a bigot and believed that, as the anointed of the Lord, God would not permit him to be damned as long as he protected and supported the Catholic faith. Nothing indeed reconciled him so much to the Austrian alliance as the conviction that it would enable him to crush the Protestant power of Prussia. Of this vilest of the Bourbons Pope Benedict XIV had said some years earlier: 'No better proof of the existence of a Providence is needed than the sight of France's prosperity under Louis XV.'

As the master, so the crew that surrounded him. Madame de Pompadour, the mistress *en titre*, was all-powerful. By flattery and yet more odious methods she held the King in leash, appointed and dismissed ministers and generals, made and unmade treaties, and had the wealth, the wit and the art of France at her command. There was no secret about it. When the two nations were at peace Newcastle paid his court to France by sending pineapples from Claremont to Madame de Pompadour; when Kaunitz thought of negotiating an alliance with Louis XV he first secured the goodwill of Madame de Pompadour; French generals in Germany, even those who were princes of the blood, found it necessary to address their letters containing sorely-needed self-justifications in terms of flattery to Madame de Pompadour. This power was not lightly gained or held. With an industry truly amazing she gave daily interviews to ministers, was always at the King's beck and call, wrote long letters of advice to her favourite generals in the field, and kept a watchful eye on every branch of government. But of statesmanship she showed no trace. To secure her own influence by saving the King trouble and keeping every agent of government dependent on her will was the whole extent of her statecraft, and therein she was supremely successful. Lately it is true, after Damiens's attempt on his life, Louis XV, in passing terror of future retribution, had excluded her from his presence. But he quickly recovered, forgot his pious apprehensions, recalled the favourite and at her instigation dismissed the ministers of war and finance to whom he had confided his scruples and who had dared to show some independence of her influence.

Bernis had risen to notice by his services to Madame de

Pompadour in negotiating the treaty of Versailles behind the back of the foreign minister, Rouillé, and on its conclusion he had been promoted to that minister's place. He was a man of some capacity and patriotism, but had spent so much of his life in the trivialities of an idle society that he was quite unequal to the strenuous work of administration. Unduly elated by the treaty which he had helped to make and by the early successes of the war, he was as easily cast down by recent difficulties and disasters. Even early in 1758 he had hinted at peace to Vienna and had asked for some remission of the subsidies due from France, owing to the vast expenses of the war. Indeed, the financial burden was becoming almost intolerable. France had been committed by Bernis and his predecessors not only to Vienna but also to Bavaria, the Palatinate and Cologne, to the princes of Liège and Anhalt-Zerbst, to Wurtemberg, Zweibrücken and Mecklenburg, to the Margraves of Anspach and Bayreuth, and to the Republic of Genoa for annual payments amounting altogether to some £2,000,000. Subsidies to Denmark and Sweden were also under consideration. During the course of 1758 Bernis changed his tone almost daily with the fortunes of the war, and by his vacillations imperilled the Empress's confidence in the French alliance. To Madame de Pompadour he complained that his ideas were always hazy and his head in a whirl, and by September had become so conscious of his own incapacity that he was begging for a successor, as the only means of saving his life. A few weeks after making this request he received a cardinal's hat, the chief object of his ambition, and a letter from the King authorizing him to resign his office.

The successor appointed at Bernis's express desire was his friend the Duc de Choiseul, then ambassador at Vienna. Etienne François, Comte de Stainville and Duc de Choiseul, was born in 1719, and was thus the junior by eleven years of the great English minister with whom he was to cross swords. Like Pitt he began life as a soldier, but was more fortunate in being granted the chance of distinguishing himself at Dettingen and in other campaigns of the last war. At Court, in spite of an unpleasing countenance and a poor figure, his wit, his self-confidence and his audacity brought more than one of his amorous campaigns to a successful issue and gained him many friends and enemies. Among the latter was Madame de Pompadour, whose favour, however, he found means of gaining by an act of complaisance characteristic of his society.[1] Thenceforward his fortune was made. Named ambassador at Rome and Vienna successively, in both capitals he revived the arrogant traditions of Louis XIV's diplomacy without sacrifice of the national interests, and by his tact and agreeable manners ingratiated himself with Pope and Empress, and with Kaunitz, the 'coachman of Europe.'

When Choiseul took over affairs in December 1758 France outwardly still seemed the greatest Power in Europe, certainly more than a match for the little island kingdom. In extent of territory she exceeded the limits even of Louis XIV's glorious age. Lorraine as well as Alsace was French, and the fleur-de-lys waved over Minorca and Corsica; in America, Canada and Louisiana and the richest West Indian islands still belonged to her, and the islands of Bourbon and Mauritius guarded the ocean highway to her prosperous factories in India : if England's oversea possessions rivalled hers in extent, they were less closely knit and less materially profitable to the mother-country. While England had a population of barely eight millions to draw upon, France had nearly twenty million inhabitants.[2] France could keep armies of 100,000 men in the field in Germany and have 70,000 more for an invasion of England, besides the troops guarding her own coasts and frontiers and the detachments overseas; England, by putting forth her utmost strength, could raise only 90,000 regulars for all parts of the world, and some 26,000 militia for home defence.[3] Even the navy of France was not markedly inferior in the

---

[1] A cousin of his had excited the King's passion, and had hopes of supplanting Madame de Pompadour. This affair had gone so far that the King had sent her a declaration of his desires. She consulted Choiseul on the matter, whereupon he showed the King's letter to the Pompadour, who exiled her rival from the Court and always remained grateful to Choiseul.

[2] Mirabeau, quoted by Young, *Travels in France*, ch. v, states that the population of France in 1755 was 18,107,000. For the population of Great Britain, see below, vol. ii, p. 50 *note*.

[3] This was in 1761: see *Chatham MSS.* 76.

number of ships on the active list to that of the rival sea-power. According to Pitt's intelligence, in March 1758 France had ninety-two ships at sea or ready to start,[1] three of which had since been lost by Duquesne, while England had some 106 in commission.[2] But for all her imposing aspect France was like the image with feet of clay. She had a grave weakness in her fleet : owing to the neglect of Fleury and his successors the ships were ill-found, the officers were discontented and often incompetent, and it was almost impossible to make up the crews to their full complements. The state of the French finances was even more serious. In 1759, owing to the wasteful and unequal system of taxation, France, with a population nearly two and a half times as great as England's, could barely raise twelve millions sterling, while England, thanks to the enterprise of her merchants and to the ability of Walpole and Pelham in the past, had no difficulty in raising eight and a half millions.[3]

But France's greatest need was for a man to direct her. For years she had been guided by a succession of weak foreign ministers—Puysieulx, Rouillé, and Bernis—and served by a set of incompetent generals—Richelieu, Clermont and Soubise—who had lowered her credit throughout Europe. Choiseul soon breathed a new spirit into French diplomacy and adopted a tone more suited to his country's ancient glories.

I am determined [he wrote a few days after his promotion to his friend Bernstorff, the Danish minister] to drop all negotiations for peace. Undeterred by the fear of misfortunes and confident in the strength and resources of my country, I believe that by patience and firmness alone we shall bring our enemies to a reasonable attitude ; and I should think the same, even if we had lost Normandy and Brittany.

To Kaunitz he wrote a few weeks later :

Three months ago we believed all was lost. Nothing was lost

---

[1] *Chatham MSS.* 87 (Advices from France). La Cour-Gayet, *La Marine . . . sous Louis XV*, 261, reckons the strength of the English and French navies in seaworthy ships and frigates at 110 and 85 respectively in 1755.

[2] On February 20, 1760, according to a statement drawn up for Pitt (*Chatham MSS.* 79).

[3] For the French finances. see Waddington, iii, 456 *sqq.* For English, see vol. ii, p. 48.

but the heads of some of us. . . . The King will not make peace without his allies, . . . and we shall fight until our enemies are destroyed.

He was sure that France could fight and no less sure of whom she would have to fight. ' In our hearts and in all our actions we are the enemies of England,' he said, ' enemies now more than ever, and we neither see nor wish to see the end of this enmity.' In fact his feeling about England was a counterpart of Pitt's about France.

I have so great an idea of the power of this country [he wrote again], that under the direction of a strong man, who has courage and patience, I believe she can always recover from her losses. The King, therefore, is determined to fight against England up to his last crown and his last man.[1]

These brave words were a prelude to vigorous action. His first care was to consolidate the alliances of France and form a vast confederacy against England. Vienna, much disquieted by Bernis's suggestions of peace, was restored to good humour by a new treaty, in which Choiseul re-asserted the determination of France to co-operate in the German war and laid down the minimum conditions of peace : in return the Austrians were persuaded to abate their demands for subsidies. Most of the small German princes were already in the pay of France, but the more important northern Powers had been strangely neglected. Choiseul made approaches to Russia, hitherto held at arm's length by Louis XV, chiefly from motives of personal pique. He succeeded in drawing closer together Sweden and Denmark, whose friendship with France had been neutralized by mutual jealousies, and in March 1759 induced those two Powers and Russia to form a league against England with the object of excluding foreign men-of-war from the Baltic and safeguarding the interests of neutrals. He encouraged the Republican and anti-English party in Holland and secretly urged the Dutch to make the most of their complaints against English privateers. But he pinned his

[1] See *Correspondance entre Bernstorff et Choiseul* (Copenhagen, 1871), and Waddington, ii, 484.

CHOISEUL IN POWER, 1758   389

faith chiefly to the hope of gaining over Spain. Though willing to make the most of the Austrian alliance which he found existing, he had no illusions as to its value in a maritime war with England. The only nations able to influence the balance of power, he explained to the French ambassador in Madrid,[1] were those possessing colonies, commerce and naval strength : thus even Austria, Russia and Prussia were, he said, secondary Powers compared with England, France, Holland and Spain. Of these Holland had become subordinate to England, and France was being crushed by her; unless, therefore, Spain came to France's assistance, England would have no rival on the sea and would impose her will on the continent of Europe. Before he had been in office many days Choiseul was prophesying the imminent fall of Canada unless he could obtain help from Spain, and warning that country of her own danger unless that fall was averted. 'Urge them,' he wrote to the French ambassador on December 21, 1758, 'to make common cause with us. . . . Moments are precious and there is not one to lose. . . . Only the concerted navies of the two crowns can impose respect on our common enemies.'[2] As long as the feeble King Ferdinand lived, Choiseul had little chance of stirring Spain to action, but, by his careful and tactful diplomacy before Ferdinand's death in August 1759, he planted the seeds of a policy which in due course was to bear fruit.

His activity was not confined to foreign affairs. The discipline and administration of the army and navy engaged his attention even when he was only foreign minister; in 1761 on Belleisle's death he took over the ministry of war and, later, that of marine, and in both departments cut down wasteful expenditure and aroused a better spirit of service. Within a year, too, of assuming office he relieved the country's finances by reducing to a half the foreign subsidies of 52,000,000 livres. Thus, to his country's great advantage, he soon acquired such control over all branches of administration as no minister had held since Fleury's death. Though hampered by Louis XV,

[1] A. Bourguet, *Choiseul et l'Alliance Espagnole*, p. 159.
[2] *Ibid.* p. 5.

who occasionally undermined his foreign policy, he had the skill to render Madame de Pompadour innocuous, while allowing her to believe that she was still all-powerful. In his days of power he contemptuously eschewed all support from Court intrigues, showed no rancour to political opponents, and had something of Pitt's ability to make use of any instrument likely to be of service to the country. He was especially free, no doubt owing to his own want of convictions, from the religious bigotry of his Court. When a complaint was made to him that the Spanish minister, Wall, whom he was anxious to gain for political reasons, was a dangerous Jansenist, 'however that may be,' he replied, 'the amount of confidence we have in his sentiments and intentions will depend not on his behaviour as a Christian but on his thoughts and actions as a minister.'[1] Above all, in days of national despondency he always kept a brave heart. When told of a crushing defeat his ready retort was, 'Misfortunes cannot discourage us : they only spur us on to redoubled efforts.'[2]

But, though far superior to any of Louis XV's recent ministers, Choiseul was no match for Pitt. This was partly due to the circumstances with which he had to contend. At the end of 1758 England had gained too great a start for the ground to be recovered in one war. The entanglement of the Austrian alliance was a serious hindrance, and with such a monarch as Louis XV the confusion in French foreign and domestic administration was too great for one man to set right in a few years. In spite, too, of abundant activity and a high conception of his country's honour, Choiseul's own qualities were not those of which the greatest statesmen are made. His better judgment was apt to be carried away by the impulse of the moment : thus he was more moved by Frederic's stinging gibes at Louis XV and France in 1759 than by all Frederic's previous victories.[3] Ingenuity rather than profound thought mark his attempts to retrieve disaster : he wasted much energy in negotiations bound to be fruitless with Denmark, Sweden and Holland ; when the French fleets might have been

---

[1] A. Bourguet, *Choiseul et l'Alliance Espagnole*, p. 194.
[2] *Bernstorff et Choiseul*, p. 50.   [3] See Waddington, iii, 455.

CHOISEUL COMPARED WITH PITT

usefully employed in carrying relief to Canada and India he frittered them away in abortive attempts to invade England; and even his great stroke of an alliance with Spain came too late to avoid disaster to either country. His industry was more fitful than Pitt's, his brilliant improvisations less effective from the want of that stability, which was the outcome of Pitt's intense convictions. As a diplomatist Choiseul won many passing triumphs by his wit and cleverness, but made little impression on the actions of the two greatest ministers of his time, Kaunitz and Pitt. Nevertheless he was the best that France could then produce and better than the France of Louis XV deserved. Both he and Pitt paid one another notable compliments. Choiseul said of Pitt: 'Glory is his passion: though intoxicated by success he is capable of forming the most extensive designs. But though he knows he will have to quit office the moment his master has no further need of him, which will be the moment peace is signed, he looks on that day with haughty indifference.'[1] Of Choiseul after his fall Pitt said with pardonable exaggeration that, 'since the days of Cardinal Richelieu, France has had no minister so great as the Duc de Choiseul.'[2] The French minister's fellow-countryman, Bésenval, was perhaps nearer the mark in saying that under Louis XIV Choiseul would have seemed fashioned on a small scale, but that under Louis XV, when the proportions of everything, including the Crown, had dwindled, he fitted well into the place of a great minister.

Pitt soon learned that he had a more vigorous enemy to deal with at Versailles. In the early days of his ministry Choiseul formed a bold conception for the campaign of 1759— no less than to turn the tables on Pitt by imitating his raids on a larger scale. His first idea was that French fleets from Toulon and Brest should meet in the Channel and escort Soubise with an army of 50,000 men to invade the south of England. In combination with them a joint expedition of 12,000 more French troops under the Duc d'Aiguillon, 12,000 Russians and

[1] Quoted by A. Bourguet, *Études sur la Politique Étrangère du duc de Choiseul*, p. 152.
[2] *Correspondance de Madame du Deffand*, i, 340; and Walpole, *Memoirs o George III* (January 25, 1771).

12,000 Swedes were to sail under escort of a Swedish fleet to Scotland. To secure the co-operation of Russians and Swedes he carried on active negotiations at St. Petersburg and Stockholm, and had proclamations prepared for distribution broadcast in Scotland, inviting the submission of the inhabitants and offering to grant peace on British soil.[1] In December 1758 Pitt had hints of the danger and talked over schemes of defence with Newcastle,[2] but he did not allow an enemy to dictate to him a plan of campaign, nor was he lightly to be diverted from a considered policy of aggression by a menace nearer home. Before attending seriously to Choiseul, therefore, he completed his arrangements for foreign expeditions.

That to the West Indies was already well in train. Hughes's squadron, destined for Martinique, had sailed in November 1758.[3] Owing to storms and other delays it did not reach the meeting-place at Barbados until January 1759. Here Moore, the commodore on the West India station, took over command of the joint squadron, and Hopson supplemented his six regiments from England with troops inured to the climate, whom Pitt had ordered the West Indian governors to have in readiness. As in his first two American campaigns, Pitt had to make the best of a senior general unsuited to his methods, for Hopson, like Abercromby, was too old. He took care, however, that a capable second-in-command should go with him. This was the Secretary at War's brother, Brigadier Barrington, whose appointment out of his turn caused murmurs against Pitt but was justified by his conduct.[4] The attempt on Martinique failed, although the guns of the fleet had silenced the batteries of Port Royal, owing to Hopson's refusal to attack some strong entrenchments of the French. After this check Moore and Hopson decided to make an attempt on Guadeloupe, as Pitt had authorized them in his secret instructions of October 16, and on January 24 they landed without opposition at Basseterre, the French retiring to the mountainous

---

[1] These are to be seen in *Aff. Etr. Angl. Corr. Pol.* 442.
[2] *Add. MSS.* 32888, f. 431.
[3] See above, p. 380.
[4] Lord Barrington himself had shown rare public spirit in refusing to urge his brother's claims for the appointment.

districts of the interior. On March 6 Pitt received their dispatch, and immediately answered that if, as he hoped, Guadeloupe was already in their hands, they should reduce St. Lucia, useful for its excellent harbour of refuge during the hurricane months.[1]

The plans for the American campaign of 1759 were in hand almost as soon as those for the West Indian expedition. On September 18, 1758, a month after the news of Ticonderoga, Pitt recalled Abercromby and appointed Amherst to the supreme command. During October and November he was considering the instructions to be given for the capture of Quebec, the crucial enterprise of the American war.[2] Quebec could be approached either entirely on shipboard by sea from Louisburg and up the river St. Lawrence, or by a land army starting from the military base at Albany. For the land army there was also a choice of routes—one due north by the two long narrow lakes George and Champlain and the river Richelieu, striking the St. Lawrence midway between Quebec and Montreal—the other westward by the Mohawk river, across a carrying-place to Lake Oneida, then by Lake Ontario to the place where it falls into the St. Lawrence some way above Montreal. Abercromby's plan had been to take the first of these mainland routes, but he was stopped at the outset by his failure to capture Ticonderoga ; Bradstreet, by his capture of Fort Frontenac, where Lake Ontario joins the St. Lawrence, had opened the second. Both required a large fleet of canoes and flat-bottomed boats to carry troops over lake and river ; but these had already been prepared for Abercromby. Beckford strongly urged Pitt to confine himself to the sea and river approach from Louisburg, and Wolfe, on his return in November with Boscawen, also recommended this plan ; Pitt, however, decided that attacks should be delivered both by sea and by the mainland.

[1] The secret instructions are summarised in Record Office—*Foreign, Various,* 68–71 ; Pitt's dispatch, dated March 9, 1759, is in Kimball, ii, 56.

[2] In a plan submitted to Pitt in 1756 it is said : ' When the spring is diverted or cut off the river must dry up. Such is the position of Quebec that it is absolutely the key of North America, and our possession of it would for ever lock out every Frenchman.' (*Chatham MSS.* 95.)

On December 9, 1758, he sent out his first batch of dispatches, calling on the provincials to redouble their efforts for the next campaign and ordering Amherst to build forts on Lake George and at the carrying-place to Lake Oneida, and to collect his boats for an early advance. On December 29, a week after his conversation with Newcastle on Choiseul's plans of invasion, he sent his final orders, clear and detailed as usual. The main attack was to be by sea and river from Louisburg, as Wolfe had recommended. Commodore Durell, with the ten ships already in American waters, was at once to blockade the mouth of the St. Lawrence and prevent all communication with France. Transports were ordered from England to New York, where Amherst was to embark 12,000 men to be conveyed to Louisburg. Here a second fleet of fourteen sail, also from England, was to arrive in time for the whole force to start up the St. Lawrence not later than May 7. Simultaneously another army was to advance from Albany for the subsidiary attack by land, river and lake, either to Montreal or Quebec itself. Lastly, Forbes's work of the previous campaign was to be completed by posting English garrisons in Forts Duquesne and Oswego and expelling the French from their remaining forts at Niagara and on Lake Erie, thus entirely cutting them off from the Ohio and from communication with the south.

Exactly the same care as before is shown by Pitt for details affecting the comfort and efficiency of the troops—such as a provision of spruce beer and rum against scurvy, of whale-boats for navigating the St. Lawrence, of a battering train and carpenters for the siege ; the same sense of proportion in subordinating minor matters to the paramount consideration of rapid and vigorous action, as exemplified in orders to ' forbear making dispositions of arms &c. in Europe that would cause the least delay to the sailing either of the ordnance ships or of the transports to New York,' [1] or in orders to hire additional ships for sending on belated equipments ; the same wise confidence in allowing Amherst to choose his own route to Montreal or Quebec by lakes George and Champlain, or by the more westerly way of Lake Ontario, ' according as you shall from

[1] To Saunders, January 20, 1759 (Kimball, ii, 11).

PLAN FOR QUEBEC EXPEDITION

your knowledge of the countries, through which the war is to be carried, and from emergent circumstances, not to be known here, judge all or any of the said attempts to be practicable.'[1]

In this campaign Pitt had nothing left to fear from his generals and admirals. From Amherst as commander-in-chief and leader of the land attack, if he could not expect dashing adventures, he was certain of courage and persistence. For the combined naval and military expedition by the St. Lawrence he gave independent commands: Admiral Saunders replaced Boscawen, who had been promoted to the Mediterranean fleet when Osborn was invalided home. Saunders was one of that brilliant band who had sailed round the world with Anson in 1740; since then he had done good service with Hawke in the late war, and more recently as second in command to Osborn at Gibraltar and to Anson in the Bay of Biscay; he had also learned something of the seas to which he was now destined, as commander on the Newfoundland station. Anson and Pitt had found in him the power of swift decision and the courage essential for the adventure they entrusted to him. And a perilous adventure it was. He was responsible for forty-nine men-of-war,[2] and was to escort some scores of transports up the uncharted course of the St. Lawrence, past shoals, reefs and narrows, hitherto thought impassable for a hostile force unused to the channel.

To command the land forces of this main Quebec expedition Pitt chose just such another as himself. James Wolfe had not yet completed his thirty-third year, but had spent more than half his life in the King's service. The son of a soldier, he entered the army at fifteen, had fought at Dettingen and Culloden, and was a lieutenant-colonel at twenty-three. A long, ungainly figure gave little promise of the spirit within, to which his flashing eyes alone bore outward witness;[3] at

---

[1] To Amherst, December 29, 1758 (Kimball, i, 432).

[2] Durell already had ten men-of-war in America, Saunders was to take out fourteen more; the remaining twenty-five were frigates, sloops and bomb-ketches.

[3] Wood, *The Fight for Canada*, 317-8, gives reason for believing that the traditional portrait of Wolfe, with its weak chin, retreating forehead and turned-up nose, is not authentic. He gives a portrait showing a far more pleasing countenance; but of his ugly red hair and his gawky figure there is no doubt.

home and in camp he was always subject to attacks of gravel and rheumatism, and in the long voyages, to which his duty called him, he suffered misery from almost constant sea-sickness. But he loved his profession with a passion that consumed his frail body. Like all great soldiers he studied military science and history deeply.[1] Intrepid in danger, he took no chances except of his own life. 'My maxim is slow and sure,' once said to him an engineer of the dilatory school. 'And mine,' retorted Wolfe, 'is quick and sure—a much better maxim.' The training he gave his regiment (the 20th) endeared him to his fellow-officers and men, and created in it a tradition of good service still abiding ten years after his death. In the present war he was the one officer in high command at Rochefort who had shown determination, and at Louisburg he had been chosen by Amherst to bear the lion's share of the danger. After the conquest of Louisburg he had prepared himself for the next campaign, exploring the mouth of the St. Lawrence, interviewing river pilots, forming his views of the force necessary for the siege of Quebec. In England the reputation of the young soldier had grown so high that a common toast associated 'the eye of a Hawke and the heart of a Wolfe,' and so evident was his fitness for the Quebec command that after his departure three of his fellow-colonels in America wrote to Pitt asking that he should be appointed.[2] This choice had already approved itself to the Secretary of State. Wolfe himself had been eager to fight in Germany, but hearing of Pitt's intentions for him, at once put himself at his disposal.

Writing on December 1, on his way to Bath to nurse his ailments and court Miss Lowther, he said, 'I have this day signified to Mr. Pitt that he may dispose of my slight carcass as he pleases, . . . I am in a very bad condition both with gravel and rheumatism, but I had much rather die than decline any kind of service that offers.' During the month Pitt saw

---

[1] See for example his letter of July 18, 1756, quoted in Beckles Wilson, *Life* (p. 295); and referred to above, p. 42 *n*.

[2] See Beckles Wilson, *Life*, p. 401. Many of the details in this account of Wolfe are taken from that book.

him to discuss plans. He could not spare more than half the men Wolfe asked for, but complied with all his other requests. Finding that Wolfe attached great importance to an early blockade of the St. Lawrence and distrusted Durell's activity, he sent repeated orders to America to hasten Durell's movements. He allowed Wolfe to choose his own staff and chief subordinates, and insisted on his list being accepted without alteration. When the King objected to the young colonels he found there, and especially to Carleton, who had spoken disrespectfully of the Hanoverians, Pitt bade Ligonier

tell his Majesty . . . that in order to render any general completely responsible for his conduct he should be made, as far as possible, inexcusable if he should fail; and that consequently whatever an officer entrusted with a service of confidence requests should be complied with.

Two of Wolfe's brigadiers chosen by himself were Murray and Monckton, the third was Pitt's friend, George Townshend, whose eminence in the political world enhanced the compliment he paid Wolfe in volunteering for service under him. The last time Pitt saw Wolfe was the day before he sailed, at dinner with Temple. The story goes that during dinner Wolfe was most abstemious, but afterwards, much to the astonishment and disgust of his hosts, began walking excitedly round the room, flourishing his sword and talking wildly of what he should do. The story may well be true of Wolfe. Though naturally modest, he had an immense and well-founded belief in his own military capacity, and though calm in action he had an excitable temperament, which had once before allowed him to run riot in a moment of strain. It is less credible that Pitt, as Temple represented, should, even for an instant, have been shaken in his faith in Wolfe. He also had his moments of arrogant self-confidence and could understand them in such another. On February 14, earlier in the year than any previous expedition to America, Admiral Holmes, with the vanguard of Saunders's squadron and sixty-six transports, set sail from St. Helen's.

The preparations in France for the defence of Quebec

had been very different. At the end of 1758 Bougainville, Montcalm's aide-de-camp, had been sent home to represent the colony's desperate situation and to beg for reinforcements. Bougainville saw Madame de Pompadour and all the ministers, but Choiseul, who was already supreme, gave him cold comfort. All the men and ships available were required for his new scheme of invading England; nothing could be spared for Canada except a few cargoes of provisions and stores and plenty of good wishes; and with this Bougainville had to content himself. Choiseul had no great belief in the value of Canada to France, and probably regarded the colony as already past praying for— as indeed it was without more assistance from the mother country. Of the 20,000 combatants Montcalm could still put in the field only 3,500 were regulars from France and 1,500 trained Canadians; the rest were composed of untrained Canadian militia and Indians.[1] The French were thus in a marked inferiority to the English, who could muster nearly 50,000.[2] The want of harmony between the self-sufficient and incompetent governor Vaudreuil and the commander-in-chief Montcalm, and the shameless robberies of the intendant Bigot and his rapacious subordinates, added to the difficulties with which the French had to contend. The soldiers Montcalm, Lévis, Bourlamaque and Bougainville were the only strength of the colony: they, especially their great-hearted leader Montcalm, were worthy representatives of the courageous adventurers and administrators who had made French Canada. With such men to lead, a few more battalions and a few more ships might well have made hopeless the task which even Wolfe and Saunders found all but impossible; and, had they been sent, they would almost certainly have arrived in time. For Wolfe's forebodings about Durell were justified. He had not begun to blockade the St. Lawrence when Saunders arrived

---

[1] *Cp.* Parkman, ii, 178. Waddington (iii, 254) estimates the French numbers at only 10,000, but on p. 266 enumerates over 16,000.

[2] This figure, even if the levies from both northern and southern provinces are included, is rather above the mark. The colonial troops never reached the figure of 20,000 asked for by Pitt. The regulars in America at the highest amounted to under 30,000; in 1760, for example, the total is stated at 29,396. (*Chatham MSS.* 96; see also *ibid.* 76, *Army* 1757–74.)

at Halifax in May, and had allowed Bougainville with his storeships to slip past him into Quebec.

India also called to Pitt during these busy winter months, and not in vain. He sent out Coote with a newly-raised regiment, two men-of-war and a convoy in January 1759, and a few months later promised to obtain a grant of £20,000 to assist the Company in their struggle with France. Nor was Gibraltar neglected: in spite of the drain of men he never allowed the garrison to fall below four regiments.¹ In December 1758 Prince Ferdinand asked for 12,000 more English troops, and George II's Hanoverian ministers presented demands for large increases in the German contingent of the army of observation. With the menace of a French invasion hanging over England, Pitt refused to let another man leave the country save for the capital operations in America and the East and West Indies;² but he agreed to the 12,000 additional Hessians. In his speech proposing the Hessian and Prussian subsidies he appealed for unanimity on behalf of the Protestant cause and the liberties of Europe, a unanimity which, he said, 'on great occasions made the universal *vox populi* the *vox Dei*.' January 26, 1759.

His own business dispatched, Pitt had leisure to think of Choiseul's intentions. From December onwards through the first half of 1759 Pitt and the Cabinet were kept informed of Choiseul's preparations through intercepted letters and spies. In January it was known that Choiseul's proposal to Sweden to reinforce his expedition against Scotland with 8,000 men from the army destined for the invasion of Prussia had been coolly received; but it was also known that the French were preparing to embark 40,000 of their own troops:³ intelligence came in February of the work being carried on at Brest, Rochefort, Toulon and other French ports, and in April of troops

---

¹ In his speech of December 2, 1777, Chatham claimed that he always kept at Gibraltar eight battalions, reckoned at 6,000 men. This was an overestimate, for according to the army lists in *Chatham MSS.* 76 the four regiments at Gibraltar never exceeded an effective strength of 4,354 men, and sometimes fell considerably below this.

² Manners's *Granby*, p. 73, and *Add. MSS.* 32886, ff. 323, 431.

³ *Add. MSS.* 32887, f. 252.

assembling at St. Omer, Dunkirk, Bruges, Ostend and Lille;[1] and in July an escaped English prisoner brought over a full account of all that the French were doing in their ports.[2] All this seemed very terrible to Newcastle, who had lost Minorca in 1756 from his fear of a similar invasion, and now thought the only way to avoid destruction was by giving up Pitt's wild schemes of conquest and obtaining peace at any price. 'To think of being able to extirpate the French from North America,' he moaned, ' or, if we could, that our business was done by so doing, or that such a nation as France would sit down tamely under it, is to me the idlest of all imaginings.'[3] Pitt was less moved by Choiseul's preparations than by his intrigues with the Swedes, Danes and Dutch. He was not anxious to have more enemies on his hands, and was aware that these nations had grievances against the English privateers which would dispose them to listen to Choiseul's overtures. It seemed to him not unlikely that the Danish and Dutch fleets, taking advantage of a moment of unreadiness in England, might seek to avenge their injuries by swooping down on the Channel and attaching themselves to the French fleet.[4] One of his first precautions, therefore, was to remove a grievance which he had always felt to be well founded.

Ever since he had become Secretary of State the English privateers had given Pitt trouble. The French navy being unable to protect its own commerce, this was generally transferred to neutral bottoms, where it was scarcely more respected by the English than if it had been in French ships. Any enterprising ruffian who could afford a few guns for his craft turned privateer, attacked neutrals and enemies indiscriminately, and seized cargoes whether contraband or not. Neutral ports were not always safe from their depredations, even the person of a Spanish ambassador was not respected on a Danish ship, and several instances occurred of prize-ships, released by an English court, being waylaid as they came into the Channel and recaptured by the same or another

[1] *Add. MSS.* 32890, f. 70.
[2] Record Office—*Foreign, Various*, 68–71: Rigby to Wood, July 3, 1759.
[3] *Add. MSS.* 32890, f. 130.   [4] *Ibid.* 32886, f. 431.

privateer. In the first year of the war the Spanish ambassador gave Pitt a list of fifty such complaints, and the list was always growing. Denmark and Holland were hardly less exasperated. In 1759 the Dutch had 110 ships detained in English ports and sent over special commissioners with peremptory instructions to obtain their release. Nor was the grievance confined to European waters: American skippers took to privateering with still less ceremony than their English brethren and found a rich harvest in the Dutch and Spanish ships engaged in the West Indian trade.[1] Pitt had always discountenanced such proceedings: 'England the mistress of the Ocean should not act despotically there,' he told the House of Commons; and he sent stringent instructions to English consuls in European ports and governors in America and the West Indies 'to apprehend and bring to condign punishment the persons concerned in a crime of so atrocious a nature,' telling them that the King had the 'utmost horror and detestation ... of practices which, if not repressed, must involve his Majesty in odious disputes with all the neutral Powers of Europe,' orders which resulted in the hanging of four pirates in Antigua. He also made efforts to hasten the dilatory proceedings of English prize courts, and on rare occasions persuaded captors to release their prizes of their own accord. But, finding that the abuses still continued and that neutrals were growing more clamorous, in May 1759 he introduced a bill giving him greater powers of repression. The bill was extremely unpopular, for every little port in England had its privateer, and the commercial community was interested in a business for which it provided a large part of the capital. In 1758 Bristol alone fitted out fifty-one privateers, armed with 996 guns, and manned them with crews numbering 6,000 altogether.[2] Beckford, generally a warm supporter, opposed the bill in the House, as the representative of the merchants: but Pitt's arguments prevailed:[3]

I have often, [he said] had the happiness of having my ideas of May 4, 1759.

[1] The American traders showed their impartiality in the pursuit of gain by their equal willingness to supply the French with provisions and munitions of war. (See Beer, *British Colonial Policy*, 73-4, 130-1.)

[2] *Chatham MSS.* 78.   [3] The Act is 32 Geo. ii. c. 25.

carrying on the war approved by the majority of my countrymen; but when it is otherwise I must do the best I can. In such a case the government is bound to show firmness till the prejudices and misinformations of the people are dispelled. The misfortunes accruing to this country from the robberies committed by privateers are such that, unless a step is timely made, the country is undone. Were we to suffer the practice longer, the neutral nations would all be offended. Great moderation is consistent with true dignity and it is best to use it before the storm (which might happen in a month) should break over our head. Then concession would be taken for fear.[1]

Pitt's bill did not entirely remove the grievances of neutrals, but it secured better control over the swarm of privateers and reduced their numbers, and, as an earnest of England's pacific inclination, removed any desire in Holland and Denmark to join the French against England.

Pitt did not await the passing of this bill to take more active measures of defence against France. He ordered the thirty-four ships of the line in home waters to be put into commission as soon as possible, and, finding from a return presented to him in February that the crews were short, he contrived that within three months the number of sailors available should be raised from 18,000 to 25,500 men.[2] Having, according to his wont, made all preparations on his own responsibility, on May 8, 1759, he called a full meeting of the King's Servants to settle on the disposition of forces. He was now able to practise what he had preached in 1756. There was no sending for Hanoverians and Hessians. The first line of defence against invasion was to be the home fleet, based on Torbay and keeping watch up and down the Channel; a force of regulars was established in the Isle of Wight ready to be drafted instantly to a point of danger; and as a third line of defence the new militiamen were called out to defend their own homes. Pitt still took the danger of invasion less

---

[1] For this speech cp. *Hist. MSS.* IX, iii, 78 b (Frederick's account to Sackville), and Torrens, ii., 499 (West to Newcastle).

[2] See *Chatham MSS.* 78. On February 19, 1759, there were eighty-seven ships and frigates in home waters with crews amounting to 18,049 men; on May 9 the crews had risen to 25,525 men.

seriously than some of his colleagues, but, as he told them at this meeting, 'we have given the alarm, we must now make people easy by taking proper measures for their security.' He first demanded a vote of credit for £1,000,000, and sent a message to the House calling out the militia. He insisted that this message should be a spirited document about the 'imminent danger of invasion,'[1] and in introducing it expatiated on the different kinds of fear, defining the fear which prompted his motion as due not to pusillanimity but to magnanimity. The address in reply reflected Pitt's spirit and possibly his language. The House declared unanimously that its members would

May 22, 30, 1759.

support the King with their lives and fortunes; his faithful Commons, with hearts warm with affection for His Majesty's sacred person and government, and animated by indignation at the daring designs of an enemy, whose fleet has hitherto shunned, in port, the terror of his navy, will cheerfully exert the utmost efforts to repel all insults, and effectually to enable His Majesty not only to disappoint the attempts of France but, by the blessing of God, to turn them to their own confusion.

The militia service, on which Pitt pinned his faith to take the place of German mercenaries, had not at the outset been welcomed by the people. When the Act was first put into force in July 1757 there was still much distress in the country and suspicion of the Government's intentions. In 1756, in Fox's time, militiamen embodied under previous Acts had been drafted into foreign service regiments against their will,[2] and when the ballot for service under the new Act was instituted in the autumn of 1757, fears of the same breach of faith caused serious riots in many of the counties. Magistrates who attempted to carry out the provisions of

---

[1] *Bedford Corr.* ii, 374; *Add. MSS.* 32891, ff. 77, 233, 267. It is characteristic of Pitt's care for accuracy that he insisted on the phrase 'imminent danger *of* invasion,' but rejected 'imminent danger *from* invasion'; he knew the French had every intention of attempting an invasion, but was convinced there was no danger to be feared *from* such invasion and refused to alarm the people by hinting that there might be, even when he wanted to obtain £1,000,000 for defence. The vote of credit was asked for on May 22, the message about the militia brought down on May 30.

[2] *Chatham Corr.* i, 259.

the Act were mobbed and the ballot lists seized and burned. At Cirencester, Lechlade and Gloucester Pitt had to send five companies of foot to repress the tumults. Lord Robert Sutton, a county magistrate, went in danger of his life at Nottingham; Potter reported serious disturbances in Bedfordshire and Lord Irwin in the East Riding; houses were demolished at York; Woburn House was threatened, the Duke of Dorset attacked at Knole, and the Speaker insulted at Guildford.[1] Though many of the magistrates did their duty, several showed excessive timidity, and others plainly expressed their disapproval of the Act. The worst offender in this respect was Lord Hardwicke, who had always disliked it, and advised his son Lord Royston not to pay attention to the Secretary of State's instructions for raising the militia in his county.[2] Pitt took a thoroughly democratic view of the situation. If he found the opposition to the militia universal, he told Newcastle, he would give it up altogether, but if it was merely local to some counties, he would make severe examples to maintain the law.[3] It proved as he thought, merely local, and by some salutary punishments of ringleaders in the riots and plain language to recalcitrant lords-lieutenant and magistrates Pitt calmed down the excitement.[4]

Within two months of the House of Commons address of May 30, 1759, Pitt had called out the militia of eleven counties, and by the end of the year of thirteen more.[5] Some difficulties still remained. A few more disturbances had to be suppressed, the publicans of Winchester and the mayor of Appleby, who objected to billeting the militia, had to be met

[1] For accounts of these riots, see Manners, *Granby*, p. 45; Record Office—*Foreign, Various*, 68–71; *Add. MSS.* 32997, f. 273.

[2] *Add. MSS.* 35352, ff. 74–9.

[3] *Ibid.* 32997, ff. 252, 273.

[4] Lord Exeter wrote Pitt an insolent letter accusing him of some breach of faith about the Rutland militia. In answer Pitt informed him that 'the matter of your Lordship's letter surprises me as much as the style and manner of it. I never deceive, nor suffer any man to tell me I have deceived him. . . . I desire, therefore, to know what you Lordship means by presuming to use the expression of being deceived by me. . . . I delay going out of town till I hear from your Lordship.' (*Chatham Corr.* i, 293.)

[5] Record Office—*W.O.* i, 678-9, In-Letters. For the numbers called out in 1761, see *Chatham MSS.* 76.

MILITIA CALLED OUT, 1759

partly by persuasion, partly by peremptory orders. But these were the last flickers of opposition. In November 1759 Pitt told Bedford, ' 14,000 men were in actual service, headed by gentlemen of the best families and properties in the kingdom, . . . many of them from before haymaking and harvest . . . and serving without a murmur.' Within two years thirty-nine counties had their militia embodied, and the number of men mustered had been doubled. Most of the militiamen were collected in three camps, at Chatham, Winchester and Plymouth, which Pitt himself went to inspect.[1] The principal use he made of these citizen soldiers was to man fortresses and garrison towns and to guard French prisoners of war, of whom there were already hundreds at Winchester and other towns, thereby setting free a corresponding number of regulars for more active service. In expatiating to Parliament on the unselfishness of the militia, he declared that it would enable him to land a fresh body of troops in Germany in the following spring.[2] But the chief value of this embodiment of the militia was its moral effect on the people. Men thought the more of their country for being called upon to fight for her instead of trusting to foreign hirelings ; and Pitt's militia welded together discordant classes and parties in a way nothing else had done. Tory country gentlemen, who for the last fifty years had sulked in their villages, were proud to take military rank in the new force : Churchmen and Dissenters learned to sympathize with each other in a common interest. Lord Shaftesbury, relating to Pitt his experience of the Dorset militia, notices

the remarkable zeal testified for His Majesty, His Royal Family, and government amongst all ranks and degrees, Churchmen and Dissenters (many of whom as well officers as privates are in the battalion) joining most cordially to promote the public service.[3]

Lord Poulett writes of the Somersetshire contingent that

the establishment of the militia has already given people in this

---

[1] See speech of December 11, 1777.
[2] *Historical MSS. Commission*, Weston Underwood, p. 319 (November 23, 1759)
Chatham MSS. 56.

part of the country such a military turn as to make it become the
fashion even for those who are not of the elect to learn the manual
exercise and many of the better sort of people, the modern yeomen
of these days, have formed themselves into separate companies and
learnt to do the Prussian exercise very well under the name of
Prussian Volunteers. Another very great advantage has arisen
from having planned this militia in such a proper manner as has
in a great measure destroyed all distinction of parties in this county,
for none who voluntarily enlists in his Majesty's service and take up
arms in his defence can go any longer under any denomination than
friends to the Government. Gentlemen now associate and act
together who were very shy lately and scarce knew one another.[1]

Pitt's steadfastness in carrying his militia policy against
the opposition of all the chief Whigs and in nursing it through
its early stages earned its reward. 'The people of England,'
said Beckford, 'look on you as the patron of the militia, and
every measure that is taken which shall affect this constitutional
body of men will be ascribed to your council and direction.'[2]

In addition to the militia, many towns and individuals
raised special volunteers to meet the emergency. The mayors
of Berwick, Bristol and Liverpool asked for arms and
ammunition to enable the inhabitants to defend themselves
against the invader, requests which Pitt promptly granted.
The Common Council of London resolved on August 14 to
offer bounties to able-bodied men enlisting at the Guildhall
in the land forces; next day Pitt informed the Lord Mayor
of the King's entire satisfaction ' in this signal proof of unshaken
resolution of the City to support a just and necessary war,
undertaken in defence of the rights and honour of the Crown,
and for the security of the colonies, trade and navigation of
Great Britain.' A regiment of Light Dragoons was raised
from the footmen and chairmen of London by Colonel John
Hale, who boasted he would lead them against the King of
France's best household troops. Pitt was delighted with the
spirit of the chairmen and their colonel's boast, and referred
to them with pride in the House of Commons. Eleven new
infantry regiments and six dragoon regiments were raised
in 1759, several at the expense of patriotic individuals. The

[1] *Chatham MSS.* 53.   [2] *Ibid.* 19.

heir to the Throne, following the example of his brother, who sailed with Howe in 1758,[1] petitioned for a military employment.

While Pitt was thus busied during the first half of 1759, Choiseul had been developing his original plan of invasion and pushing forward preparations with all his natural impetuosity. It was a brave effort and the task harder than any Pitt had to face in his worst days. For Choiseul had to deal with a people seething with discontent and hating the war, with soldiers demoralized by the incompetence and rapacity of their chiefs, with a navy spiritless and cowed by English successes and with a Treasury unable to find the money for current wages and pay. His allies, too, were useless. Sweden and Denmark, to whom he had appealed, refused to co-operate with him. With buoyant optimism he nevertheless persisted in his grand project. Canada was starved of men for it, and the resources of the Treasury, the dockyards and the army were strained to the uttermost. Flat-bottomed boats to convey troops across the Channel were hastily constructed at Havre and other northern ports. De la Clue was ordered to bring out his Toulon fleet and once more attempt to run the gauntlet of Gibraltar and work round to Brest. There another fleet was being equipped under Conflans, who was to be reinforced by de la Clue, by Bompart, recalled from the West Indies, and by la Marnière from the Pacific. Choiseul's final scheme was that Conflans's great fleet should engage the attention of the English home fleet and, under cover of this diversion, two expeditions should invade Great Britain. A force of 20,000 men under the Duc d'Aiguillon was to be embarked at Brest on ninety ships and, escorted by nine men-of-war, to sail round Scotland and attack Edinburgh. Another army of 50,000 was to be conveyed in the flat-bottomed boats from Norman and Flemish ports to the Thames. To command this force Soubise was taken from the Westphalian army, with Chevert from the army of the Rhine as his second. Thurot, an enterprising young privateer, was taken into the King's service and entrusted with six ships and 1,200 men for an independent raid from Dunkirk. And, in spite of all these extraordinary

[1] See above, p. 361.

exertions, Choiseul piqued himself on maintaining and even increasing the numbers of his armies in Germany, where it was important to leave Prince Ferdinand no leisure to interfere with the preparations in the Flemish ports. In this he had been successful until July; for Ferdinand had suffered a reverse at Bergen and had lost the important fortresses of Minden and Munster.

By August the two rivals had everything ready for move and countermove. Choiseul, who had staked all on his great plan of invasion, had his fleets at Toulon, Brest and Dunkirk, his regiments in Brittany, Normandy, Picardy and Flanders, and his flat-bottomed boats to receive them. Pitt was ready at home with his militia garrisons, his reserve of regulars, and his flying corps, encamped in the Isle of Wight; and he had strengthened the army in Ireland with two battalions brought from Gibraltar. But these home defences were in his eyes chiefly valuable to give confidence to the people: for safety he trusted entirely to ships. At every possible approach from France he had squadrons posted on the watch. Boscawen and Brodrick were at Gibraltar to stop de la Clue, Hawke in the Bay of Biscay on the look-out for Conflans, Rodney was sent to bombard the flat-bottomed boats in Havre, Boys to keep an eye on Thurot in Dunkirk, while Sir Peircy Brett was stationed in the Downs. And with all this defensive armament Pitt had not allowed one of his distant expeditions to suffer. Not a man had been withdrawn from Germany, and the campaigns in India, the West Indies, and America were allowed to proceed as if England had no reason whatever for fear at home.

END OF VOL. I.

Spottiswoode & Co. Ltd., Printers, Colchester, London and Eton.

For Product Safety Concerns and Information please contact our EU
representative GPSR@taylorandfrancis.com
Taylor & Francis Verlag GmbH, Kaufingerstraße 24, 80331 München, Germany

www.ingramcontent.com/pod-product-compliance
Lightning Source LLC
Chambersburg PA
CBHW071235300426
44116CB00008B/1053